REGINAE SANCTORUM OMNIUM

"AND THEY WERE ALL FILLED WITH THE HOLY GHOST."—
Acts ii. 4.

THE HOLINESS OF THE CHURCH IN THE NINE-TEENTH CENTURY

SAINTLY MEN AND WOMEN OF OUR OWN TIMES

BY

REV. CONSTANTINE KEMPF, S.J.

From the German by
REV. FRANCIS BREYMANN, S.J.

"And I saw a great multitude which no man could number, of all nations and tribes and peoples and tongues, standing before the throne and in sight of the Lamb, clothed with white robes, and palms in their hands."—Apoc. vii. 9.

BENZIGER BROTHERS

NEW YORK, CINCINNATI, CHICAGO
BENZIGER BROTHERS
PRINTERS TO THE | PUBLISHERS OF
HOLY APOSTOLIC SEE | BENZIGER'S MAGAZINE

Imprimi Potest

> A. J. BURROWES, S.J.,
> *Praep. Provincialis,*
> *Prov. Missour.*

AUGUST 15, 1915

Nihil Obstat

> REMIGIUS LAFORT, S.T.D.,
> *Censor Librorum.*

Imprimatur

✠ JOHN CARDINAL FARLEY,
Archbishop of New York.

NEW YORK, SEPTEMBER 25, 1916.

FOREWORD

T HE author puts forward no claim of presenting
new material. He has only bound into a bouquet
the flowers which others have found and gathered.
May the bright hues and the fragrance of them convince the reader that such flowers thrive only in a
garden that is watered by the dews of Heaven.

In 1867, Dr. M. Scheeben anticipated our subject in
a small brochure of 31 pages, entitled "Die Heiligkeit der Kirche im Neunzehnten Jahrhundert."

Even then, it is true, this mark of its divine character was manifest in the Church of the nineteenth
century, but the material available in proof of it was,
of course, far less rich and abundant then than it is
to-day. Hence the present work can hardly be
thought superfluous.

In 1901, the Congregation of Rites published a cata-
logue of all the processes of beatification and canonization in progress that year. (Catalogus ac Status
causarum beatificationis Servorum Dei et Beatorum
canonisationis, quae apud Sacram Rituum Congre-
gationem per viam non-cultus incedunt. Anno
MDCCCCI. Romae 1901. Typis Vaticanis.)*

This publication is the chief source for the names
of those persons in the nineteenth century to whose
holiness the Church has been petitioned to give official
recognition. Since then many new processes have been
introduced. Due notice has been given of these from
time to time in the "Acta Apostolicae Sedis," and
"Analecta Ecclesiastica" and in other periodicals.

In 1907 the Sacred Congregation of Rites published

---

*Consult the interesting article on this subject by Card. Stein-
huber in the "Stimmen aus Maria Laach," LXVIII (1905), 1 sqq.

3

a list setting forth all the processes then in progress before the Congregation, and this list has also been made use of in the preparation of the work.

In submission to the decrees of Urban VIII, the author declares that for the terms "holy," "Blessed," "Venerable," "miracle," "revelation," "supernatural," and the like, no other than human credibility is claimed, in as far as they may not have been authorized by the decision of the Church.

THE AUTHOR.

CONTENTS

CONTENTS

7

PAGE

THE HOLINESS OF THE CHURCH IN THE NINETEENTH CENTURY

THE ancient strife still wages fiercely. More wildly than ever break the waves upon the rock of the Church. Against her very foundations, the bulwarks of her faith, is raised the war-cry. Every form of craft and science serves as an arsenal for the general assault —deceitful promises and undisturbed earthly felicity, indulgence and tolerance of the dreadful power of the lower passions, Art, the Press, Technics, Trade and Industry—all the springs of the clockwork of the world-machine are released against the Church and her faith.

Therefore, duty imperiously demands that we take down our arms from the wall and march forth to the defense of the Bride of Christ. What weapons shall be ours? Surely those of the spirit and of truth. A clear and impartial statement of the Church's origin, of her continuous existence, of her works, and their results—this is our weapon. Whoever of her foes has courage fairly and freely to look her in the face, must find his weapons fallen from his hands and he will kneel and believe. Let any one become truly acquainted with the Church and he can not but love her, can not fail to recognize in her the work of God.

Such was the conviction of the Vatican Council. In the third chapter of the Constitution on Faith, the Council first declares that, partly from miracles and prophecies, partly from the unequivocal words of Holy Writ, we can easily recognize the fact of the divine Revelation and of the foundation of the Church. An unbiased mind can find without difficulty where is the Church that has all the marks which must necessarily belong to the Church of Christ. Then the Council goes

13

on to say: "*Quin etiam Ecclesia per se ipsa ob suam nempe admirabilem propagationem, eximiam sanctitatem, et inexhaustam in omnibus bonis foecunditatem —ob Catholicam unitatem invictamque stabilitatem magnum quoddam et perpetuum est motivum credibilitatis et divinae suae legationis testimonium irrefragabile. Quo fit, ut ipsa veluti signum levatum in nationes et ad se invitet, qui nondum crediderunt, et filios suos certiores faciat, firmissimo niti fundamento fidem, quam profitentur.*"[1]—"Moreover, the Church of herself, by reason of her wonderful propagation, her extraordinary holiness, and inexhaustible fertility in all good works—by reason of her Catholic unity and invincible steadfastness, is a great and perpetual motive of credibility, and an irrefragable witness to her own divine mission. Hence it is, that like *a standard set up unto the nations,* she both invites those who have not yet received the faith to come to her and assures her sons that the faith which they profess is fixed upon the firmest foundation."

In the splendid raiment of the Church are set five radiant gems to which the Council directs our attention. The present sketch will be concerned with only one of them—the extraordinary holiness of the Church, to the end that we may refresh our minds and hearts with its wondrous beauty, and enkindle anew in its flaming rays our devotion and our love for the Bride of Christ.

It is evident that the true Church of Christ must be holy, for Christ founded the Church to guide mankind unto holiness through her. (Eph. v. 26, 27; Titus ii. 14). The Church exists only to smooth the path that leads to heaven. Therefore (1) her doctrine must be holy; (2) she must be able to supply us with the means which will help us to live according to her doctrine;

Note.—All references in figures are to the List of Authorities on page 389.

and, finally, (3) she must produce saints in very deed.

1. The *doctrine* of the Church is holy. Her tribunal has never approved even the smallest sin. How often she has had to see the lives of her dearest children sacrificed, to endure most cruel persecutions, to behold her sanctuaries pillaged and made desolate because she would not permit the doing of evil. Her heart bled grievously when whole nations were torn from her because she inflexibly held fast to the moral law of her Founder. Whether powerful rulers or the popular mob make unholy demands of her, it is one and the same to her; and she ever answers with the words and the firmness of the holy Precursor of her Spouse: *"Non licet tibi,"*—"It is not lawful for thee" (Mark vi. 18). She has the courage to demand from all her children a continual and inexorable warfare against their evil passions. Be the times as effeminate or as morally degenerate as they may, the Church knows no other chastity than that which gave to martyr-heroes their supernatural strength, and she yields not her position, although it has often been her sorrowful experience that it was the very severity of her moral demands which estranged so many from her or deterred them from acceptance of her doctrine.

Yet, not content with waging war against sin to the death, the Church exhorts us to strive after the highest ideal of every virtue. The most unselfish love of the neighbor, that shares in the suffering of others; cheerfully gives up even life itself for the fellowman; and even repays hatred with love, steadfast fidelity, and truthfulness even in the least matters, humble submission to God and to His representatives on earth, virginal continence, boundless confidence in God, a fervor of holy love of God which no ocean of suffering and adversity, no torrent of the world's sensual delight can ever extinguish—such are the sublime virtues with which she would warm our hearts. Yet not for our

own honor nor for the reward that may be ours are
we to aspire to this eminence of holiness, but for a
generous and great-souled love of God. *The Saviour
is the ideal of the Church.* All that she has learned
in listening to His words, all that His conduct in life
has proclaimed to us, she seeks to write deep within
our hearts so that all our thoughts, aspirations, and
actions may be influenced thereby.

2. But Christ has given to the Church a superabundance of *means* by which the sublime end of holiness may be put within reach of the faithful. First
and above all He promised to her the Holy Ghost and
sent Him to remain with her until the end of time.
Not only is the Holy Ghost the supreme teacher and
guide of the Church, He is the vital power itself, the
Church's soul, so to speak, which is active in her every
member. For it is He who creates, conserves, and
increases her supernatural life, whence He is called
the Vivifier, the Sanctifier. He transforms the body
of the just man into a temple in which He dwells and
works and produces the fruits of holiness. When we
resist temptation, foster holy thoughts and desires,
and perform good works, it is He who is the motive
power. Just as a decaying tree can not assimilate
nourishment, can not grow nor thrive nor blossom
nor bear fruit, so the man who is without the indwell-
ing power of the Holy Ghost is unable to perform
supernatural works.

But the Church has still other most particularly efficacious means of increasing holiness in us; namely,
the sacraments. These are visible signs which, instituted by Christ, produce an invisible grace. Every
sacrament infallibly increases the sanctifying grace in
us, i. e., the degree of holiness, and imparts moreover
a special grace in accordance with its nature, for
instance, help to avoid evil more effectually and to
practise virtue more easily—in a word, to become

holier. These graces are, of course, invisible, but their effects are often quite visiblè. Think, for example, of the frequent reception of the sacraments of Penance and the Holy Eucharist. How many have risen by their help out of the mire of sin into a life of virtue? How many young men have found in them the strength to preserve their faith and purity unimpaired through all the struggles of their lives? How many a bosom has been inflamed with inspired desire for heroic sacrifice, for virginity, for martyrdom, at the very moment of their coming into contact with the incarnate fire of divine love? After Holy Communion we should be as St. John Chrysostom says, *"tanquam leones ignem spirantes,"* "as lions breathing forth fire" —animated with lion-like courage in our strife against sin for virtue's sake! And the Fathers of the Church call Holy Communion, *"Vinum germinans virgines,"* "the wine that begets virgins," because that food which is the pure Lamb of God makes us most like to Him. It surpasses all human reckoning to know how many graces the Church imparts to the world through the daily offering by her priests of the unbloody renewal of Christ's death on her numberless altars and through the presence of the Saviour Himself, whom she harbors in her tabernacles where He may live and work for us and without ceasing draw us near to Him. Finally, the prayers in the manifold sacramentals of the Church are always linked with graces which make easy the accomplishment of our salvation.

Our Saviour speaks clearly of two states of life in His Church. He distinguishes between the keeping of the commandments and the following of the counsels, that is, the life of voluntary poverty, chastity, and obedience. The latter is the more perfect (Matt. xix. 21). He recommends it and promises to it a magnificent reward (Matt. xix. 29). Therefore, the Church must be able to aid us in reaching the perfection of the evangelical counsels. No proof is needed to show that she has always given patronage and preference to the religious state of life; though on this account she has had very much to suffer from her enemies. She well knows that if she possessed not a state of life which by virtue of its vows aspires to perfection and aims without reserve at the closest following of Christ, thus offering a sure and easy means for the attainment of holiness, she would be deprived of a jewel of great price.

3. If the doctrine of the Church is holy, if she possesses so many means to holiness, *she must actually produce saints in every age* of her existence or she would fail in the achievement of her chief end. What, then, is a saint? Here we must distinguish between essential holiness, extraordinary holiness, and holiness which is officially recognized by the Church. Essential holiness consists in the possession of sanctifying grace, which is infused into the soul in justification. This grace is called sanctifying because it makes us holy. Those who depart this life adorned with it will enter heaven and will be saints eternally. Extraordinary holiness requires special gifts of grace and the heroic exercise of the principal virtues. Finally, to obtain the Church's official acknowledgment of holiness, miracles, performed at least after death, must be proved. Our Saviour foretold that such extraordinary *charismata* would not be wanting in His Church (Mark xvi. 17; John xvii. 22; 1 Cor. xii). Even in the Old Testament this glory of the reign of Christ had been foretold (Ps. lxxi. 7; Isaias lxii. 3).[2]

That the Church from day to day bestows sanctifying grace upon very many souls needs no proof, and we may confidently hope that the large majority of her children die adorned with this grace and are numbered among the saints. But there are many besides who endeavor unceasingly to resist evil, who, to the best of their knowledge and ability, live according to the precepts of the Gospel and who are ready to accept any sacrifice for the sake of God. The good that is done in the world is for the most part hidden, it is true. Evil obtains more notoriety, makes a great noise, and is impudent in its demands. History tells us far more of human baseness and malice than of good deeds. If a vassal loyally serves his king his story is more briefly told than if he were always planning rebellion, treacherously deceitful, respecting no human rights, and trampling down everything that obstructs his path. Many have been immortalized in the world's history only because they were wicked; while others, who have heroically battled for God from childhood to the tomb, have disappeared from the memory of mankind. The world knows nothing of heroic acts of self-denial, of patient endurance of injustice suffered, of victory over many temptations, of humble submission under the holy disposition of God, of the interior fervor of divine love. Goodness is by nature unassuming; it loves concealment.

But there is much, too, that gains a wide publicity. Even the world often yields admiration and approval to the noble deeds of godly souls. At times a priest or a layman, animated by the spirit of God, exercises great power and charm on those around him. And most clearly is this manifest in those who are truly saints. For when we use the word "saints" we commonly mean those whom the Church acknowledges to be such. She has never been wanting in men and women of extraordinary holiness. What names of clearest luster her history presents to us! Almost endless is the array of martyrs, of confessors, and of virgins who have obtained the crown of victory! How dwarfed we feel when we read of the heroic deeds they have accomplished! It is God's own care to provide the Church with such heroes, and He confirms their works by extraordinary signs to encourage and to quicken the weak and indolent and to give to the world in all ages manifest proof whereby may be found the true Church of Christ.

It is just on this point that the objection is often raised: "In the primitive Church and in the Middle Ages there were saints, of course, but where are they in our days? And how much is really true of what they tell us about some saint of the dim past?" Language of this sort betrays a complete ignorance of the facts. We assert that *the Church of our own times is quite as prolific of saints as she was in the ages that are past.*

To prove this consoling truth is the purpose of the present work. We shall confine ourselves to the *nineteenth century.* It will show for itself that the century which, animated by a fanatical hatred of Rome, has made use of all the power of politics, of art and science, of all the acquisitions of modern culture, as weapons against the Church—a century which has brought about the most dreadful depravity in morals and has spread abroad the grossest infidelity, is nevertheless not inferior to any preceding age in the number and greatness of its saints. We find to-day the same joyful, enthusiastic martyrdom as in the days of Nero, the same burning zeal for souls, the most intimate spirit of prayer, heroic love of the neighbor, faith firm as a rock, angelic chastity, royal magnanimity, cheerful love of the Cross, childlike humility and simplicity, and seraphic love of God as in the saints of days gone by. And there is the power of working miracles and there are supernatural gifts of grace just as in the most glorious ages of faith.

To prove this we need only a brief review of the lives of some of the servants of God whose death occurred in the nineteenth century. We choose to present only those in whose case there is well-founded

probability that they will be raised by the Church to
the honor of her altars. They will be chiefly those,
therefore, whose process of beatification has been
already finished or is in actual progress.

Our sketch, to attain its purpose, need not be
altogether complete. In fact, it can not be such, for it
is impossible at the present time to ascertain how many
there were during the last century who died with the
reputation of holiness. It is a well-known fact that
many years may pass, sometimes even centuries, before
a beatification is begun. God has His own designs as
to the time when He will raise His servants to the
altars. But it is not necessary to give a detailed
account of all the saints of the nineteenth century.
The material at our disposal is quite sufficient to prove
that the declaration of the Vatican on the extraordinary
holiness of the Church can be applied to that century.
Partly because fuller information is wanting and
partly because we would not have this work become
too voluminous, we often limit ourselves to the mere
mention of names.

A brief explanation of the progress of a process of
beatification or of canonization will enable us to understand more easily what is to follow.[3]

If some one dies in the repute of sanctity and this
reputation is confirmed after his death by miracles, it
is the duty of the bishop of the diocese to take the first
step by investigating the matter. A committee of
judges appointed by the bishop must then proceed to
gather sworn testimony on two points. 1. On the
fact of the reputation for sanctity had by the servant
of God in question and of the actual occurrence of the
miraculous events alleged to have taken place (*processus super fama sanctitatis, virtutum, et miraculorum
in genere*). 2. On the non-existence of public worship (*processus super noncultu*). Their findings in
the case are to be sent to the Congregation of Rites at

Rome, whose duty it is to examine minutely into the authenticity and credibility of the testimonies and to decide other preliminary questions. If everything goes on favorably, the proper inception of the Apostolic process may take place ten years later (*introductio causae*). By this act the reputation of the deceased for holiness is acknowledged and approved and under certain restrictions the faithful are permitted to call him "venerable."*

It again becomes the duty of the bishop to institute the minutest inquiry into the virtues and miracles of the servant of God. The Congregation investigates whether the theological virtues have been practised by him in a heroic degree, or, when the question is about a martyr, whether he was put to death particularly and really out of hatred for the Faith. Then follows the scrutiny of the miracles. At least two of the alleged facts must be proved to have been true miracles, as when there is question, for instance, of sudden cures. In this case the work is done with the most scrupulous accuracy and precaution. Competent physicians must prove the impossibility of a natural cure. If a special permission be not granted by the Pope the Congregation is not allowed to continue its inquiries concerning the heroic degree of his virtues and miracles until fifty years have elapsed since the death of the servant of God. Suppose that finally all difficulties have been removed. Then three consultations are had, the last of which, a general Congregation, is to decide in presence of the Pope and under his presidency whether the beatification may take place. The final decision is left to the Pope, who, according to custom, postpones his decision for some time and then publishes it under the form of a decree.

*According to the latest decree, this appellation is permitted only after the official acknowledgment of the heroic degree of virtue. Acta Apost. Sedis, 1913, 436 sq.

If a person who has been beatified is to be canonized it is further required that new miracles shall have occurred through his intercession after the beatification, and also that at least two of these miracles be approved as genuine.

POPE PIUS IX

WHENEVER the Church has had to struggle through difficult times, God has always raised up great men who, by their eminent qualities, by the holiness of their lives and their convincing devotion to the things of God, have encouraged the timid and have given new life to wavering faith and relaxing zeal. The nineteenth century was to the Church an ordeal by fire. That she has come out of it unscathed and purified is due first to the assistance of God and after this to the faithful allegiance of the supreme pastors to whom her destinies were confided. All the Popes of the nineteenth century were an honor to the Church, distinguished by their virtue and learning, powerful beacons who spread wide a heavenly light throughout the darkness of the world.

For the longest time of all Pius IX stood out as the guardian of Sion and it was he who steered the Bark of Peter through stormiest seas. There is scarcely any pontificate that surpassed his in importance and which was obliged to solve such weighty problems. But Pius IX was in every sense the man whom Christ could put in charge of His flock during that critical period. A saint was needed in whom the sharp eye of the enemy could not discover any fault—a man inflamed by the zeal of faith, who would not sacrifice a single jewel of that precious heritage which the spirit of the time sought with determined energy to drag away from the Church. Such a man was Pius IX. Only a few facts from his virtuous and eventful life are needed to convince us of this. The whole life of Pius IX was pervaded and sustained by the spirit of faith, the most precious heritage he received from his parents. He was born at Sinigaglia on May 13, 1792, son of Count Jerome Mastai-Ferretti, and he received

24

in baptism the name of John Mary. Once his pious
mother, kneeling before a picture of the Mother of
Sorrows, lifted up the infant John and said: "O Mary,
adopt him as your son as you adopted his patron,
the beloved disciple. I consecrate him to you and give
him up wholly to you."[4] Thus at his mother's
breast the boy learned to know and to love Mary and
later on he was to bear witness before the whole
world and to all coming generations what a mighty
flame of holy love for the pure Mother of God had
been then enkindled. We shall see how Mary on her
part showed herself the most powerful protectress of
his life. To the Mother of Sorrows he had been dedicated and the sword of sorrow would often pierce his
heart.

Another trait which manifests the true Christian
spirit of the family is too touching to leave unmen-
tioned. It was in those sad days when the French took
Pius VI a captive into France. The mother, who said
prayers in common with her children, was accustomed
to add an Our Father and a Hail Mary for the Holy
Father. One evening she told her children with tears
what a hard trial had come upon the Holy Father and
that therefore they should pray for him with the
greater fervor. John, then only seven years old, knelt
down weeping. When the prayers were ended, he
asked how God could permit His representative to be
so ill-treated. His mother tried to make him understand that the Pope was the Vicar of the Crucified
Saviour and on this account had to suffer very much.
"But then," pursued the little reasoner, "they are
wicked men who treat the Holy Father so cruelly and
we must pray that God may punish them." "My
child," was the reply, "we should never pray God to
punish any one. What did Our Saviour Himself do,
even on the Cross? He prayed for His enemies; and
Pius VI surely does the same at this very moment.

Let us join him then and pray to God, not that He should punish all these wicked men who have laid sacrilegious hands upon the Lord's anointed, but rather that He may enlighten them and turn their wicked hearts toward good." Then all of them knelt down again and said a second "Our Father" for the welfare of the enemies of the Pope. If the boy could have looked into the future and have known what was to come he would have seen that it would be the chief feature of his life to be persecuted as Christ's Vicar by the enemies of the Cross and to implore Heaven's mercy in behalf of those very enemies. Joyful and happy were the days spent in his father's palace. We may be assured that his devout parents were very careful to keep everything evil far from their promising boy and to plant virtue deeply in his young heart. After making his first Holy Communion, John Mastai in his tenth year was sent to the old mountain town of Volterra to apply himself to higher studies in the college of the Piarists. It was not long before he became the favorite of the whole house on account of his angelic modesty and amiability, his piety and docility. His talents enabled him to acquire the knowledge required of him without difficulty and his teachers could never sufficiently praise the purity of his morals.

After six years John had completed his college course and the youth of sixteen found himself confronted with the weighty problem of choosing a state of life. He had hesitated between the career of a soldier and the priesthood. But God had taken the decision into His own hands.

Once during his boyhood John Mastai while playing had fallen into a cold lake and was saved from imminent death only through the presence of mind of a servant. But after that time he became sickly and there gradually developed the dreadful disease of epi-

lepsy. Physicians declared that a cure was impossible.
So the young man with his splendid mental endowments was doomed to a life of inactivity. All his
bright hopes for the future were stricken from him
at one blow which made him incapable of bearing arms
and unfitted him for service at the altar. But difficulties are for the saints only the rounds of a ladder on
which they ascend to the height of their confidence in
God; and young Mastai was not the man to fold his
arms in discouragement. His lively faith knew well
the grand promises held out to persevering prayer.
Therefore, his resolution was quickly made—he decided to dedicate himself to God in Holy Orders and
by unremitting prayer obtain freedom from the malady
that would bar the door of the priesthood against him.
In the spring of 1809 he received the tonsure and then
returned to his home, because, for the time, he could
do nothing more than to take care of his sick body
and to pray.

In the meantime grievous trials had fallen to the lot
of the successor of St. Peter. Pius VII pined in
French captivity. But Providence exacted a terrible
retribution for the crime and in the very same castle
of Fontainebleau where he had kept the Pope a prisoner, the French Emperor was obliged to sign his abdi-
cation. The coming home of Pius VII was like a
march of triumph, so splendid as never had been seen
by a Roman emperor. The way led the Pope through
Sinigaglia and here he was the guest of Count Mastai-
Ferretti. The whole event made a deep impression on
John Mastai, who was at the time twenty-two years
of age. He accompanied the Pope and entered the
Eternal City with the Pontiff on that memorable day,
May 24, 1814, while all Christendom rejoiced. He
resided in the house of his uncle, a canon of St. Peter's,
and attended the lectures at the Roman University.
He undertook besides to assist the director of the

orphan asylum, Tata Giovanni, in the instruction and management of the children. Still his insidious malady did not leave him. He now began to think that it might be better for him to join the noble guard of the Pope. Then one day he suffered an attack in the street more violent than any he had had before. Pius VII himself heard of it and bade the young man to come to him, for the Pope wished to console him. Soon after, John Mastai disappeared from Rome and remained a considerable time at Loretto, making most fervent appeal to the Blessed Virgin. When he left Loretto, all was bright and sunny in his heart, for he did not doubt that Mary had heard him. His sickness speedily diminished and he immediately applied to obtain the necessary dispensation for the reception of Holy Orders. On April 10 the goal was reached at last, and on the day following he celebrated his first Holy Mass in the midst of the orphan boys of Tata Giovanni. What the Blessed Virgin does, she does thoroughly. After the day of his ordination to the priesthood all traces of epilepsy disappeared and until his death, at the venerable age of eighty-six years, Pius IX was never seriously ill. So his sickness was in the designs of Providence only a means to bring him to his true vocation, to compel him to rest his confidence in God alone, and to give him an evident proof of the favor of the Mother of God, to show him the power of her intercession.

For a while the young priest retained the humble position of assistant at the orphan asylum. During this time he drew great spiritual profit from an intimate intercourse with the noble-minded prelate, Prince Charles Odescalchi. Through the latter he became acquainted with the Venerable Vincent Mary Strambi of the Congregation of the Passionists. The choice of such friends shows the tendency of his own mind. The beatification of the Venerable Strambi is not far

distant* Odescalchi also died in the repute of sanctity.
In 1838, Odescalchi, then a cardinal, obtained permission from Gregory XVI to renounce his purple and
finally to realize the vocation to which his heart had
drawn him from his earliest years. He became a member of the Society of Jesus and the former prince and
cardinal took his place with the young novices and
asked to be treated in every respect as the youngest
of them. After living three years in the Society of
Jesus he was called to receive the reward of his blameless life.

In contact with these and similarly minded men of
mature spirituality and holiness, the religious life of
Father Mastai increased in depth and substantial worth
while faith sank its roots ever more firmly into his
susceptible mind. The years that followed were free
from burdensome occupations. It was now his opportunity to seek intimate and loving intercourse with
God and to learn how inestimable to the priest are the
enlightenment and consolations of prayer. Else there
would be danger that, later on, his mind might be swallowed up in merely external affairs because of the
multitude of his distracting occupations and would not
be able to penetrate into the depths of the life of faith.
Now he could gather fuel for the kindling of that fire
of divine love which he was afterward to spread
throughout the whole world.

It was not long before the eminent qualities of the
young priest were recognized. Toward the end of
1823 we find him in distant Chile as Socius of the papal
delegate, Mgr. Muzi. After his return, he became
president of the great Hospice of St. Michael in 1825,
was made archbishop of Spoleto in 1827, transferred
to the see of Imola in 1832, and was created a cardinal
in 1840. These were years of wide activity, very difficult affairs in his dioceses requiring settlement. With

*See page 48 et seq.

consummate skill, however, he always made himself
master of the situation. His paternal mildness and the
purity of intention on which lay the foundation of his
indefatigable zeal gained even the most obstinate
hearts. The high confidence placed in his ability was
evidenced by the fact that he was elected Pope on June
16, 1846, after a conclave of only two days, although
he was one of the youngest cardinals and the electors
knew well what heavy storms the Church was about to
encounter. The Pope-elect quite broke down under
an agony of tears when he saw that the required two-
thirds of the votes really bore his name. Asked if
he would accept the election, he looked up at the image
of the Crucified and said: "Lord, behold Thy unworthy servant, Thy will be done."

In grateful memory of Pius VII he took the name
of Pius. When amidst the acclamations of an immense
multitude he was on the following day driven to the
Quirinal, he said to his companion: "To-day begins
the persecution." It was a prophetic word. The
ninth Pius was to be a martyr of the Papacy.

It would exceed the limits of this work to picture the
heroic combats and unspeakable sorrows of the "Grand
Sufferer," Pius IX, or realistically to sketch in full
effect the grandeur of his character and the blessing
his pontificate bestowed on Christendom. His life dis-
plays traits of likeness to that of Him whose representative he was. What most excites our reverent admiration in Our Lord Jesus Christ is His great submission
to the will of His Heavenly Father, His love for mankind, and the excess of suffering and humiliation
undergone of His own free will. *"Non possumus,"*
"We can not," was the firm expression of Pius IX
when, with their shocking menaces, the foes of the
Church demanded of him anything that was against
the divine law. His kindness of heart and his ineffable
meekness toward all, even toward his enemies, exer-

cised an overpowering charm. Yet soon after his accession to the throne of Peter, in fear for his life, he must flee the Eternal City and hear from afar how the holy places were profaned with the wildest abominations.

In defiance of all international law they despoiled him of the inheritance of St. Peter, and among all the heads of the world's governments not one had the courage to protest against the crime, save only the noble Garcia Moreno, president of Ecuador. Finally, as a prisoner, Pius IX came to the close of his thorn-crowned life.

We shall lay particular stress upon three events which gave a very special significance to his pontificate; namely, the declaration of the dogma of the Immaculate Conception, the proclamation of the Syllabus of 1864, and the definition of papal infallibility in faith and morals.

The modern world hates the supernatural. The doctrine of grace, of sin and redemption, is for it a senseless puzzle. It had no understanding, therefore, of the realm of things above nature, of the nobility of the divine sonship, of the grand meaning and wondrous deep beauty of redemption through Christ. This is why it sinks more and more deeply into all the sins of the flesh and seeks its happiness in sensual delights alone. In direct opposition to this, Pius IX dared to bind the whole world to believe in the Immaculate Conception of the ever Blessed Virgin Mary, a fact of the supernatural order. This mystery demonstrated as none other the high esteem God has for sinlessness. What a glorious ideal Pius IX proposed to the sinful world! The splendid white purity of our heavenly Mother shall fix our attention and charm us to imitation. Through Mary Pius IX hoped to save our age from the horrible curse of impurity. His act met with enthusiastic approval in the hearts of all true Catholics, and contributed mightily to foster love and imitation of the Stainless Virgin.[5]

Infidelity had cloaked itself with the garment of science. By means of false principles it sought to penetrate secretly into the Church and to consume the very marrow of her life. But this treachery did not escape the watchful eye of the supreme pastor. The Syllabus of 1864 pilloried a large number of such false teachings and the fury of the unmasked deceivers was unbounded. They clamored about unheard-of fetters with which the Pope had shackled science. But these fetters were none other than the laws of truth, and he had really secured freedom to true science against the caprice of passion and the uncertain currents of the spirit of the age. If in anything, certainly in this, we must admire the wisdom and courage of the Pope. And succeeding years have shown that he was right. The truth has never yet contradicted the Faith.

The third evil of the times was the spirit of revolt against authority. Here, too, Pius IX dared lay his hand upon the wound. It would have been a bold deed for Gregory VII to proclaim the Pope's infallibility an article of faith; but now, in the revolutionary nineteenth century, which raised the worship of self to apotheosis, was it not to be feared that the faithful would abandon Rome in multitudes? Many, indeed, believed so. But Pius saw further. The Church's enemies themselves had necessitated an authoritative declaration of this dogma by the war they had raised against it. To be silent now would show weakness on the part of the Church. Men prepared their plots against her, the press raged in all countries of the globe, political powers made threats, misguided Catholics showed themselves ready to apostatize, but Pius knew no fear when the performance of his duty for the welfare of the Church was in question——and exceeding must be our gratitude for his constancy. No dogma shows us the divine guidance of the Church in a clearer light than does that of papal infallibility. In the limitless confusion about the most important questions of our existence, it is the greatest consolation for a Catholic to know that the Pope is the organ of the Eternal Truth Itself. The papacy under Pius IX lost its temporal possessions; but it made immense conquests in the spiritual domain. Through the doctrine of papal infallibility it has been interiorly strengthened and possesses the greatest conceivable authority.

To bring all this about Providence chose Pius IX. He was the instrument which possessed all the qualities for the realization of the designs of God in His Church. He was as the *"Stimmen aus Maria Laach"* portrays him, "a character consummate in its perfection, a great man, greater than any other of the generation in which he lived, for no one consecrated so long a life as he to so grand an idea with such energy and wisdom; no one bore so loftily as he the standard of truth and justice on the cruel battle-ground of these evil days."[6]

A man who exhibited a martyr's courage in defense of the principles of faith certainly would give life and expression to this faith in his personality. When Pius IX died on February 17, 1878, even his bitterest enemies bestowed unreserved praise upon his private life. No one dared call in doubt the spotless integrity of his conduct or the sincerity of his piety. Others who are great as scholars, poets, politicians, military leaders, and the like, are often most miserably small if we measure their lives by the standard of Christian morality. The only thing they found to blame in Pius IX was that he was "too Catholic." Those who knew him more intimately considered him a saint. Cardinal Patrizzi once said that if he survived Pius he would immediately inaugurate the process of his canonization.

Pius IX had all that mildness and charming amiability
which is peculiar to the saints.   He was inflexible
against any encroachment on the sacred rights of the
Church, inflexible also against anything in himself
which did not correspond to the highest ideal of Christian perfection.   Therefore, we find him so modest,
so angelically pure, so affable, so childlike in his piety,
so fervent in zeal, and so strong in suffering.   Even
during his lifetime miraculous works were related of
him, and such occurrences so increased year by year
after his death that in the year 1907 Pius X ordered
the first inquiries in the process of his canonization to
be inaugurated.[7].   Let us hope that the Pontiff who
placed the diamond crown upon the brow of heaven's
Queen will himself soon win the victor's crown of
sainthood.

HOLY BISHOPS

THE episcopate of the nineteenth century can point with pride to those of its members who were adorned with the charisma of sanctity. In this chapter we shall commemorate some of its illustrious leaders who have obtained the crown of victory as confessors of the Faith.

John Nepomucene von Tschiderer

1. The little Tyrolese city of Trent, renowned in the history of the Church, beheld upon its episcopal throne at the third centenary of the Council to which it gives its name, a man possessed of that full perfection which the same Council demands of a successor of the apostles—John Nepomucene von Tschiderer.[8] The earlier years of this holy prince-bishop, who was born on April 15, 1777, of an ancient and noble family of Bozen, fell within the sad times of the so-called "Eclaircissement," which misrepresented altogether the true character of the Church and despoiled so many young people of the jewels of innocence and faith. But the watchful solicitude of a pious mother and the wise guidance of an experienced confessor preserved both virtues with untarnished splendor to the young von Tschiderer. After completing the Latin classes conducted by the Franciscans in Bozen, the boy, who had not yet reached his sixteenth year, went, for his philosophy, to Innsbruck, where only "liberal" professors were then tolerated. But the zealous Minorite, Father Herculan Oberrauch, one of the foremost moral theologians of the day, understood in his masterly fashion how to attract the Innsbruck students to himself, to direct them in their many difficulties, and to guide them into the right pathway. His influence against the "liberals" was so great that the director

of the General Seminary was not able to counteract it except by forbidding his students from having intercourse with Father Oberrauch. The means which the latter regularly employed was nothing else than the frequent use of the sacraments. He wrote these impressive words: "Among the thousands of young men whom I directed I do not know of even one whom I saved uncorrupted unless he went to Holy Communion every two weeks; and the numerous others, whom I could not save, nearly all had to ascribe their fall to the neglect of the sacraments. I am quite sure of it." Tschiderer entrusted himself to the direction of this experienced priest, to whom every week he manifested the state of his soul in the sacrament of Penance. With this good priest as his guide, the young man made the choice of his state of life and until the death of Father Oberrauch in 1808 there was between the two a most intimate correspondence. John von Tschiderer stood in the highest repute amongst his fellow-students for the angelic purity of his morals. Many of them used to call him "St. Aloysius." His engaging appearance and friendly nature attracted many to him; but he avoided most carefully every too intimate familiarity. Twice when temptation approached him he fled at once, following that admirable counsel of St. Philip Neri: "In a combat of this sort it is the feet that gain the victory, and one is the better off the faster he runs away." The liberal teachings of his professors and "the frivolous, malicious, and most worldly treatment of Church history," as says his biographer, did not have any influence on his love and enthusiasm for the Church. On the contrary it was just this that aroused him to opposition and grace, that plainly worked in him, led him easily to recognize the perverseness of the whole tendency of the "Liberal Movement."

On July 27, 1800, Tschiderer was raised to the

priesthood. After devoting a short time to the care of souls, he spent a year and a half in Rome making further studies; after which he returned to the duties of assistant priest until, in 1807, he was called to the chair of moral theology in the Lyceum of Trent.[9] In 1810 he was again engaged in the care of souls as parish priest of Sarntheim and in 1819 as parish priest of Meran. In 1826 he received a canonry in Trent; became auxiliary bishop of Vorarlberg, with his see at Feldkirch, in 1832; and was made prince-bishop of Trent in 1834. Two virtues were especially prominent in this servant of God; namely, generosity and humility. Whatever he possessed belonged to the poor. He could not see any misery without relieving it. He did not wait until his help was asked, but of his own accord whenever time permitted he searched for those who might be in distress. Many thought it the greatest miracle of his life that he had always something to give. His own manner of life was as simple as possible, so poor, in fact, that others remonstrated with him on the matter. Charitable persons knew how well he disposed of their gifts and therefore his fountain never ran dry. Even during his lifetime it was said playfully: "When he is canonized he will be called John the Almsgiver." Some of his relatives, not at all pleased with such liberality, would have been glad to have had him placed under guardianship. A couple of works of art were all he left them at his death.

Humility made the holy bishop the servant of all. Considerations of self were foreign to him. Toward all, especially to the common people, he was condescension and friendliness itself. "The lowlier the person, the more friendly and familiar was the dean with him," says a witness of his labors in Sarntheim. When bishop he treated the simplest priest with such politeness and veneration that some found it quite embarrassing. On one occasion, he said to two newly ordained priests: "Behold now you are invested with a great dignity, but do not seek to make it a stepping-stone to offices and honors. For my own part if I were to be born into the world a hundred times, a hundred times I would become a priest; but I would prefer to serve a secluded mountain village and would not seek to be a bishop—indeed not." All the distinctions conferred on him by Rome or by the imperial court he kept carefully secret. Even when the claims made upon him by others were ever so unfair, he invariably yielded to them. "What harm is it?" thought he. "Perhaps I shall gain a soul for God."

Out of this humility arose a great meekness and gentleness in his dealings with others. He was ingenious in finding mild expressions for necessary admonitions and reprimands, fully understanding the saying of St. Paul of the Cross that "admonitions given with mildness will heal the wound they cause, but if they are dealt out with bitterness, the one wound will become ten." But it would be false to conclude from this that he was not unbending in what he had determined upon. When all kindness proved of no avail, he could strike like a thunderbolt. Mild in manner, firm in deed, was his maxim, and it was this that gained him his powerful influence over others. This power was particularly manifest in his administration of the sacrament of Penance. Men wondered wherein lay the mystery of the powerful attraction he exerted upon his people. From near and far all flocked to his confessional. His mild but heartfelt admonitions made so deep an impression that people who had made their confession to him in their youth, even only once, still remembered it in old age. He always sought to enliven the despondent spirit of a penitent with renewed confidence. As the pastor of his clergy he recommended them to imitate the Good Shepherd in their spirit and work as confessors.

He was most particularly solicitous for the well-being of the young. It is not possible to tell in a few words the pains he took to improve the schools. His heart always warmed toward youth. He knew that precisely this period of life, in spite of its apparent gaiety, suffers most from downheartedness and timidity and therefore greatly needs the encouraging words of the priest. Wherever he met the young it was his invariable custom to begin friendly conversations with them, to show interest in their affairs and by his charming manner was always able to bring in some apt religious advice.

For the rest, the exterior life of this servant of God offered little that was extraordinary. He was a man who did his duty in everything as conscientiously as possible. He carefully avoided whatever was extravagant, for, according to St. Vincent de Paul, "every singularity is only a corner for vanity to hide in." When in the society of others he always contributed much to the cheerfulness of the company. Yet every one who, like his parish children and the clergy of his diocese, came in close contact with him, said: "He is a saint." When he died at the venerable age of eighty-three years, December 3, 1860, this had become the universal conviction, for even before his burial he had begun to work miracles. Little though he valued himself during his lifetime, God glorified him after his death. Only two of the many miraculous cures obtained through his intercession will be mentioned here. In 1867, a child, four and a half years old, so utterly blind that the most piercing light did not arouse any sensation, suddenly recovered its sight by means of a relic of Prince-Bishop Tschiderer. In 1871, a young priest, so far advanced in the last stages of consumption that the last sacraments had already been given to him, was likewise restored by a relic of the holy bishop and within three days was freed from all traces of his disease. The process of beatification, it is expected, will soon be brought to its conclusion.

Venerable Franz Joseph Rudigier

2. The neighboring little district of Vorarlberg rivals Tyrol in the hope of seeing a son of its mountains raised to the honor of the altar. To see the Venerable Franz Joseph Rudigier,[10] the devoted, undaunted, and sorely-tried warrior for the liberty of the Church, numbered among the ranks of the blessed would bring joy not only to every native Austrian but to all whose hearts beat warmly for the welfare of the Church. This servant of God came from a poor peasant family of Parthenen, in the valley of Montafon in Vorarlberg. He was born on April 7, 1811, and was the youngest of eight children. When twelve years old he was sent to study the Latin elements under his brother Joseph, who had just been ordained priest and whose duty it then was to say early Mass in Schruns.

Thence he went to the gymnasium and to the University at Innsbruck and then to the theological seminary in Brixen. In all these schools he easily surpassed his fellow-students, but he was chiefly distinguished for his noble character and his earnest endeavor after virtue. Ordained to the priesthood on April 12, 1834, he was engaged for a short time in the care of souls at Vandans and Bürs, but in 1838 he went to the Frintaneum in Vienna to pursue special studies. After a year and a half we find him in the seminary of Brixen a professor of both Church History and Ecclesiastical Law and afterward of Moral Theology. Here he lived in most intimate friendship with two of his colleagues, Vincent Gasser and Joseph Fessler, who had been well known to him during his student days. Both of these likewise became distinguished ornaments of the Austrian episcopate—the first, prince-bishop of Brixen; the second, bishop of St. Poelten. In Vienna the excellent qualities of Rudigier had been long remarked and in 1845 he was appointed court chaplain and spiritual director of the Frintaneum. The disturbances in 1848 gave Rudigier a favorable opportunity of freeing himself from his position at court. He was named Provost of Innichen in Tyrol, but in 1850 he became prebendary and the regent of the seminary of Brixen. His position at last became fixed with his appointment as bishop of Linz in Austria.

The office of an Austrian bishop in the middle of the last century was certainly full of difficulties. The destructive spirit of Josephinism had become incarnate among the officials of the State. To protect the inalienable rights of the Church against them was a gigantic task. A concordat was finally concluded, but the entire liberal and Jewish press made a tremendous outcry and aroused a most venomous agitation against the government and the Church. In consequence of this ceaseless baiting it was impossible to carry out the concordat. Austria's ill success in the war with Prussia was also used against the Church. The emperor consented to the appointment of a liberal ministry, which enacted several laws impeding the necessary freedom of the Church, and in 1870 this ministry, for its part, annulled the concordat. The Catholic press was controlled in the severest manner, whereas the liberals were allowed to profane with impunity everything sacred and to spread broadcast the most infamous calumnies against the Church.

One of the most heroic defenders of the Church in those sad times was the bishop of Linz. His sermons, admonitions to the clergy, pastoral letters, and his speeches in the Austrian Diet always struck fire in the hearts of the right-minded to the great anger of the liberals. Finally, the latter, using as a pretext a pastoral letter on the questions of schools and of marriage, succeeded in having him taken by the police and dragged before the General Court of Justice on July 5, 1869. He was condemned to fourteen days' imprisonment on July 12. But this only steeled his courage. From all parts of the Catholic world addresses of congratulation poured in upon the unyielding confessor of Christ. In later years Bishop Rudigier always considered it a day of special honor on which he was permitted to suffer contumely for the name of Jesus. His firmness impressed even his bitterest opponents. One of them said: "With this bishop every fundamental principle is set as fast as the stones in the walls of his cathedral." Rudigier once wrote to Cardinal Rauscher: "Our dignity and future depend on our loyalty to our principles. If we depart but a needle's breadth from those that are fundamental, we shall find and deserve our destruction."

During his whole life he remained to the Church-baiting press the standing object of its jeers. His influence toward the restoration of religious life was too conspicuous. He did very much for the promotion of pious associations and a good press, for the training of an efficient clergy, and for missions to the people; and he proved himself a great protector of the regular Orders, especially of the Jesuits and the Redemptorists. An eminently notable trait of his character was his zeal for the veneration of the Mother of God. His biographer gives him the title of "Mariophilus." He sought to introduce May devotions and the daily recital of the Rosary in all parts of his diocese. At half-past eight every evening he himself summoned all the members of his household to his private chapel and led in the recitation of the Rosary. On his Confirmation trips he always recited it with his servant even if the hour was late. In his old age he gloried in the fact that he was a member of the Sodality of the Blessed Virgin at Brixen and an honorary member of the Sodality at the Stella Matutina in Feldkirch. He celebrated the proc-

lamation of the dogma of the Immaculate Conception
as solemnly as possible. On this occasion he formed
the noble design of commemorating the high prerogative of his heavenly Mother by the erection of a magnificent cathedral. When the question of undertaking
the building was brought up at the provincial Diet,
he particularly specified that the chief purpose of the
new cathedral was that it should stand as a memorial
of the Eighth of December, 1854, and he never rested
nor shirked any sacrifice until the plan was executed.
He did not, it is true, see the completion of the work
in this world. He died a loyal servant of Mary on
November 29, 1884, on a Saturday, the first day of
the novena in honor of the Immaculate Conception.
His last words were the concluding verses of the
Stabat Mater:

> "Christe, cum sit hinc exire,
> Da per Matrem me venire
> Ad palmam victoriæ.
> Quando corpus morietur,
> Fac, ut animæ donetur
> Paradisi gloria."*

Then his breathing ceased; he did not pronounce the
Amen; it was spoken by the Eternal Judge. Immediately after the death of the bishop the word passed
from mouth to mouth: "The diocese of Linz has one
more intercessor in heaven." Soon followed extraordinary answers to prayers. The apostolic process of
his beatification was begun in 1905 and we are now
permitted to call the servant of God "venerable."

*Lord, through her who brought Thee hither,
Let me, hence departing whither
  Thou the way hast found,
Come, through death's opposing portal
To the victors' palm immortal
  With thy glory crowned.
                    (*Tr. by Fr. Tabb.*)

JOHN NEPOMUCENE NEUMANN

3. John Nepomucene Neumann, bishop of Philadelphia, Pa., was by birth an Austrian.[11] He was born on May 23, 1811, the same year as Bishop Rudigier, and was the son of a municipal official in the little town of Prachatitz in Boehmer Wald. His boyhood foretold the future saint. He served Mass with extraordinary love and devotion. Once, when he saw a poor schoolmate begging, John besought his parents to be permitted to collect alms for the boy. At the age of twelve, having manifested his desire to become a priest, he was sent to the gymnasium of Budweis. Eight years later he began the study of theology in the seminary of Budweis and continued it afterward at Prague. During this time a fellow-student wrote an anonymous letter full of bitter calumnies against him, which brought John a severe public reprimand. He knew who the writer was, but, far from seeking revenge, he endeavored to win his calumniator by showing him greater love and friendship. While a student, John Neumann had read the reports of the Leopold Society on the foreign missions. This enkindled his zeal for souls. He determined to take St. Francis Xavier as his model and to go off to the missions as soon as possible. After completing his studies he resolved to proceed immediately to North America. Before leaving he desired first to be ordained priest for the consolation of his parents; but this petition was not granted. As he left home he consoled his weeping father and mother, saying that he was not born to strive after honor and renown but to seek out the lambs that had gone astray.

On his landing in New York in 1836, Neumann was kindly received by the bishop and sent to help the pastor of the German church of St. Nicholas in preparing the children for first Communion. Shortly after this, the bishop ordained him and appointed him pastor of Williamsville, near Buffalo. All the privations of a missionary there awaited the newly-ordained priest, but the sight of so many forsaken souls and their deplorable ignorance of religion made the sacrifice light for his zealous heart. Restless, he hastened with long and toilsome journeys through pathless wilds seeking the forlorn sheep, while at home he had absolutely no one to serve him or to prepare a lodging to shelter him sufficiently from the severe colds of winter.

For a long time Neumann had been deliberating on joining a Religious Order so that he might labor more efficiently as a missionary. Finally, in the year 1840 he obtained permission to enter the Congregation of the Redemptorists. But the novitiate did not give him much rest from his apostolic labors, for the need of priests was very great. A year after taking his vows Neumann became superior at Pittsburgh. Later on he was chosen to govern the whole province and after this was made rector in Baltimore. While occupying this position he was assailed by calumny and as a consequence deposed from his office. He said nothing in his defense, but it was only a short time before his innocence came clearly to light. His superiors did all they could to make amends for the injustice done him and reinstated him in his former office. Then came the unexpected news to the humble priest that he was nominated bishop of Philadelphia by the Propaganda. He used every effort to avoid this dignity, but Rome was inexorable.

Now that he was bishop, Neumann's zeal could be exercised almost without limit. He was indefatigable in preaching, in hearing confessions, in visiting his far-extended diocese. Philadelphia owes to him its cathedral and its ecclesiastical seminary. He took care to establish Catholic schools everywhere.

At the desire of Pius IX he went to Rome for the proclamation of the dogma of the Immaculate Conception in 1854. He took the opportunity of visiting his home, to the great joy of his father, who was still living. They prepared a splendid reception for him, but it was his modesty and deep piety that made the greatest impression on the entire population. The ever active bishop was only forty-eight years of age. But he had already wasted his strength in the service of the Lord. On January 5, 1860, he was stricken with apoplexy while in the street, and the stroke brought about his death. He still wore his penitential girdle even on his death-bed. The apostolic process of his beatification was begun in 1896.

John Hám

4. The Hungarian episcopate is represented by the servant of God, John Hám, bishop of Szatmár on the Szamos.[12] He was born on January 5, 1781, in the town of Gyöngyös and was the son of a tradesman of moderate means. A Franciscan priest, observing the excellent qualities of his mind and character, assisted him in his studies and remained a prudent and watchful admonitor to him during the years of his development. A few months after his ordination to the priesthood, which took place on March 17, 1804, John Hám was appointed professor of theology in the seminary of his native diocese of Erlau (Eger). He afterward became regent of the seminary and canon of the cathedral. While exercising these offices he unexpectedly received his nomination as bishop of Szatmár in 1827. A striking feature in Bishop Hám was his unaffected, deep humility. He shunned every mark of honor. He made himself the servant of all, not only of his clergy but even of his domestics. It was thus that he won the confidence of all. They knew that he did not seek his own advantage, but only the welfare of his flock. It was said that his mildness was like that of St. Francis of Sales. If a priest, so it was remarked, received a reproof in the forenoon, he was sure to get

an invitation to dinner. In the episcopal residence everything was as simple as possible. It was like the house of a religious community. The same was true of the bishop's own life. The time was accurately distributed between prayer and work, and the whole household had to be present at appointed common prayers in the domestic chapel. "To pray more interiorly and with greater devotion than Bishop John is given to few mortals," says his biographer. He had had for himself satisfactory experience of the blessings of prayer. His demeanor during celebration of the Holy Mass and at liturgical ceremonies made a deep impression on all. They could see how convinced he was of the sacredness of these functions. The servant of God crucified his body by severe practices of penance. On Fridays and Saturdays he ate, as a rule, only bread and fruit, and for his rest at night he rarely used a bed.

The good bishop was indefatigable in the care of the flock entrusted to him. He considered it his first duty to train up a clergy distinguished for knowledge and virtue. As far as his occupations permitted he devoted himself to preaching the word of God. Again and again he exhorted his priests not to neglect the religious instruction of the people, knowing well that the enemies of the Faith could prevail little on a people well instructed in their religion. Therefore, he contributed willingly from his own means to the erection of schools and of new parishes. In the city of Szatmár alone, not to mention other works of less importance, he founded a large institution for the education of girls, which he confided to the Sisters of St. Vincent, a college for boys under the direction of the Jesuits, a convent of Franciscans, and a hospital of the Brothers of Charity of St. John of God. He was, in truth, a good shepherd who had no other interest than to lead his flock into green pastures and to protect it from the attacks of the wolves.

To be sure, the enemy of all good was unceasingly at work to hinder the bishop's activity. He was calumniated at the court in the expectation that he would be deposed. But the Catholic population, knowing the falsity of these groundless misrepresentations, stood firmly with its pastor. For a long time they had looked on him as a saint and at the blessed death of the beloved bishop, on December 30, 1857, the whole of Catholic Hungary overflowed with praise for this true successor of the apostles, whom it hopes to have as its powerful intercessor in heaven.

Venerable Vincent Mary Strambi

5. The Venerable Vincent Mary Strambi, Passionist, bishop of Macerata and Tolentino, had even in his earlier years the reputation of a saint.[13] After his ordination to the priesthood he joined the Congregation of the Passionists in 1768 and enjoyed the most intimate relations with its founder, St. Paul of the Cross. His energy and activity contributed much to the internal unity of the Order. He became successively provincial, consultor, and general definitor. In 1801 Pius VII appointed him bishop of Macerata and Tolentino. But as bishop he still remained the same poor and mortified religious with the motto: *Passio Domini Nostri Jesu Christi* (The Passion of Our Lord Jesus Christ). When in 1808 he refused to take the oath of allegiance to Napoleon, which had been forbidden by the Pope, he was transported to Novara and was not permitted to return to his diocese until 1814. By the holiness of his life he exercised a wholesome influence on all who came into contact with him. When on account of old age he resigned his bishopric in 1823, Leo XII appointed him his consultor. Soon after, the Pope fell dangerously ill.[14] Then Strambi during the sacrifice of the Mass made an offering of his life for that of the Holy Father. After Mass he went to the sick-

bed of the Pope and told him that he would not die
because God had accepted the sacrifice of a life for
that of the Pope. And as the effect proved, the Pope
recovered from that hour, but Strambi, a few days
later, was called to his reward. He died on January
1, 1824, at the age of seventy-nine years.

Venerable Anthony Gianelli

6. The Venerable Anthony Gianelli, bishop of Bobbio on the Trebbia, was held in high repute throughout Upper Italy.[15]. The most prominent feature of his
sanctity was his unwearying zeal for souls. His natural gifts of eloquence served him greatly in this.
While professor of Rhetoric in the seminary of Genoa
he used his spare time in giving missions to the country folk. Later, when archpriest at Chiavari, he
devoted himself entirely to this work and founded a
Society of secular priests, called the Oblates of St.
Alphonsus of Liguori, for the purpose of giving missions and spiritual exercises. After his appointment
as bishop of Bobbio, he verily consumed himself by
his zeal in keeping far from his flock whatever might
bring it harm. His life, says his biographer, recalls
to mind the most amiable and consoling traits found
in hagiography. Widely mourned, this distinguished
bishop died in 1846, in the fifty-seventh year of his
age. A Congregation of Sisters—the Daughters of
Mary del Orto—founded by him when archpriest,
is widely distributed throughout Italy and South
America.

Anthony Mary Claret y Clara

7. Sallent, high in the Pyrenees near the frontier
of France and not far from grace-bestowing Lourdes,
is the birthplace of an archbishop whose holy life may
soon receive the acknowledgment of the Church.[16]
Anthony Mary Claret y Clara, archbishop of Santiago

de Cuba and afterward of Trajanopolis, was born into
this world on December 23, 1807. His parents were
poor weavers, obliged to work hard the whole day long
to provide for their family. But they possessed great
riches in their profoundly religious spirit. The father
insisted on his children's going to Mass every morning.
He recited the Rosary every day with his workmen
and apprentices and was inexorable in dismissing those
whose moral conduct might be dangerous to the others.
He had many a jeer to suffer from his neighbors on
account of his piety.

The little Anthony showed himself worthy of such
a father. Besides hearing Mass devoutly every morning he again visited the church in the evening to worship Our Saviour in the Blessed Sacrament. From his
earliest years the Holy Eucharist and the Mother of
God were the greatest attractions to his pure heart.
The boys of Sallent yielded an involuntary respect to
the authority of Anthony Claret, who always admonished them energetically for any ill-conduct. The
gifted boy had begun to learn Latin, but unfortunately
his teacher soon died, and so nothing was left for him
but to take up the trade of his father. He showed very
great skill in the work, but he made himself still more
useful by his good example and by his beneficial influence upon his fellow-workmen. The father hoped
through his talented son to make the business more
profitable, and, with this end in view, sent the boy with
his brother to Barcelona in 1821, to perfect himself
in the weaver's art.

Claret mastered all the new inventions of the time
with such facility that he was appointed foreman over
the other workmen in the Barcelona factory. He took
lessons, besides, in French and drawing. But his heart
constantly drew him toward the priesthood; and for
this reason he again applied his leisure to the study of
Latin grammar. Once while bathing in the sea he

narrowly escaped drowning. A great wave had surprised him and had carried him far out from the beach.
In his distress he called upon Mary, and against all
hope, as it seemed, one of his companions happily succeeded in saving him from the waves. This accident
made a deep impression on him and he resolved for
once and for all to put into effect his purpose of giving
himself entirely to God. About this time his father
came to Barcelona to consult with his sons about
increasing his business and to inquire into the new
inventions in the sphere of the textile industry.
Anthony surprised his father with his unlooked-for
resolution. But the father was too good a Christian
to resist the pious desire of his son.

In his studies at the seminary of Vich, Anthony
Claret distinguished himself so notably by the steadfastness of his character that the bishop ordained him
on his name-day, June 13, 1835, some time before his
fellow-students. On the feast of St. Aloysius he celebrated his first Mass and began his first labors as assistant to the old pastor of his native town. He soon won
the confidence of his neighbors. No one could resist
the power of his words and in all the surrounding
country he was venerated as a saint. But this field of
activity was too small for the zeal of the young priest
and he longed for the foreign missions. He went to
Rome, made the Spiritual Exercises and applied for
admission into the Society of Jesus. But he had hardly
begun his novitiate when he was attacked by a disease
of the foot, which forced him to leave the Order after
a few months. Following the advice of his former
superiors, he returned to Spain. After a brief employ-
ment in parish work, he devoted himself entirely to
giving missions for the people, principally in Catalonia.
What he accomplished there is almost incredible. He
made his long journeys always on foot, preached three
or four times a day, and was indefatigable in the con-

fessional. His activity brought upon him the hatred and persecutions of the impious, but it won at the same time the repute of a true apostle from the good. To have able co-laborers in his mission work, he founded in 1849 a Congregation called the Sons of the Immaculate Heart of Mary, which developed into a flourishing establishment. In 1900 it numbered sixteen hundred and seventy members distributed among fifty-six residences.[17] By command of the papal Nuncio at Madrid, Anthony Claret accepted, in 1850, his appointment as archbishop of Santiago de Cuba. Accompanied by several priests and religious women he set out for his distant diocese. On the voyage he preached every day and brought the whole crew of the vessel, without an exception, to confession.

Sad, indeed, was the decay of religion in Cuba. But the new bishop did not despair. He went from place to place through his diocese and gave missions everywhere. The results were truly wonderful. At the end of the mission in Santiago, which lasted during the whole of Lent, the distribution of Holy Communion covered six hours. During a mission in another city he brought to their duty about four hundred couples living in concubinage. He did not forget to take precautions that these beginnings might be lasting in effect. He erected schools, provided for religious houses, and opened a seminary for the training of priests. Pius IX, who had heard of this new Spring of spiritual regeneration in Cuba, sent a letter of special approbation to Archbishop Claret, praising him for his apostolic zeal.

The enemy, however, did not lay down his arms. It was especially Claret's successful effort against concubinage that excited the degenerate to make an attempt on the archbishop's life. A secret plot was concocted, and an attack was made upon him which resulted in his being dangerously wounded. Prevented from efficient activity by the constant peril to his life, he asked the Pope to remove him from his archbishopric. The honorable appointment of confessor to Queen Isabella was given to him in 1860. Obedience alone prevailed on him to accept this office, but he remained the same apostle as before, full of zeal for souls. He withdrew as much as possible from life at the court and instead gave missions in the churches of Madrid, soon becoming the most beloved confessor in the city. His influence with the queen, which was very great, he used only for the benefit of the poor. Whenever he was traveling with the court, he preached and taught the catechism wherever they stopped. Seeing the evil caused by bad literature, he wrote and distributed very many good pamphlets, and founded the academic society of St. Michael for the spreading of good books.

In 1869, he went to Rome to participate in the Vatican Council. After its adjournment, he intended to seek rest for a time in the Pyrenees, but he was taken with a serious illness, and on October 8, 1870, received the reward of his tireless labors in the vineyard of the Lord. The process of his beatification was introduced in 1899.

Venerable Justin de Jacobis

8. Another true *vir apostolicus* was the Venerable Justin de Jacobis, Lazarist, bishop of Nicopolis.[18] Justin, born on October 9, 1800, at San Fele, a town near Melfi, in the province of Potenza, Italy, had the fiery temperament of the genuine Southerner. But his pious parents knew how to inspire his lively spirit with the beauty of true ideals alone. At eighteen he joined the Lazarists in Naples, became priest in 1824, then superior in Lecce and finally novice-master. His sermons had great power in attracting souls. They were, indeed, very simple and without rhetorical display, but

they came from the heart and therefore went to the heart. They had that supernatural persuasiveness which is peculiar to the words of the saints and this is why they worked such astonishing conversions. It was a great joy to the servant of God when in 1839 the ardent longing of his youth to preach the Gospel to the pagans was brought to fulfilment. He was sent to Abyssinia as prefect-apostolic. God's blessing rested visibly on his labors; many heretics returned to the Church. When he was appointed bishop of Nicopolis in 1847, he refused for fourteen months to accept this dignity and afterward he sought when possible to conceal the insignia of his rank.

By the contrivance of the schismatical bishop, the prefect-apostolic was put in fetters and imprisoned by the emperor Theodore. Such was his reputation for holiness, however, that the tyrant dared not put him to death, and five months later, still in chains, he was transported across the frontier. But it was not long before the pastor returned to his flock. He took up his abode in a secluded village and journeyed unweariedly to find his scattered sheep. His death was quite like that of his great model, St. Francis Xavier. He died on July 31, 1860, during one of his apostolic journeys, under the shade of a tree in a vast plain, his head resting upon a stone. Even the heretics and the Mohammedans disputed for his body. Remarkable miracles occurred when his remains were brought away in the year 1889. The preliminary process is surpassingly rich in miracles. The apostolic process began in 1905.

ANASTASIUS HARTMANN

9. In the footsteps of Xavier walked the Swiss Capuchin, Anastasius Hartmann.[19] And it was Xavier's spirit, too, that breathed in the soul of this far-sighted, self-denying, and bitterly tried missionary bishop. If the missionary life in itself is beset with

privations, it was doubly so for Bishop Hartmann, since he had not only to contend against the blind specter of heathenism but also with the fanatical passions of a schism that threatened to rend his flock. But the desire to spread God's kingdom was too deep-rooted in the servant of God to permit him to grow disheartened and feeble in this harassing strife or to be moved to unjust concessions.

Anastasius Hartmann was born on February 24, 1803, at Altwis, in the parish of Hitzkirch in the canton of Lucerne, studied at Solothurn and when eighteen years old joined the Capuchins at Baden in Aargau. Though still a young religious he filled with great success the offices of professor, novice-master, and missionary in his own country. His superiors would not gratify his desire for the heathen missions chiefly because the Swiss province of the Capuchins had no mission-field of its own. But in 1841 Father Anastasius presented a petition so eloquent and so inspired with burning zeal that his superiors no longer made objection to this clearly declared vocation.

After two years spent in Rome preparing for mission life Father Hartmann was sent to the vicariate-apostolic of Agra, in British India. He so fully met the expectations of his superiors that before two years had passed he was made titular bishop of Derbe and was appointed the first vicar-apostolic of Patna on the Ganges in West Bengal.

The heathen population of this new mission-district was not less than thirty-seven millions, with about four thousand Christians who had remained loyal. Formerly there had been a flourishing Christian community in Patna, but it gradually fell away. "I began to weep like a child," writes Bishop Hartmann when he beheld upon his arrival the horror of desolation. But he was a man of deeds and did not despair, although, having but four missionaries under him, he was almost without assistance. Exerting all his powers, he organized his extensive diocese, studied the conditions on the spot and obtained money and new auxiliaries from Europe. The unwearying shepherd was almost continuously engaged in pastoral journeys which, being in the Tropics and with poor means of intercommunication, were extremely painful. The bishop had hardly begun to reap the first fruits of his activity when the confidence of the Apostolic See called him to another field of labor. In spite of the papal Bulls, the archbishop of Goa claimed jurisdiction over the whole of India. The schism arising from these pretensions found most of its adherents in the Presidency of Bombay—principally a portion of the clergy who stirred up disobedience to Rome by word and evample. In the year 1850 Bishop Hartmann was given charge of the vicariate of Bombay that he might try to reconcile the schismatics with the Church. But at his arrival, party hatred broke forth with violence. The schismatical priests, for the greater part uneducated men who had been hurriedly ordained in Goa, left no means untried to pervert the people. They succeeded in stirring up even the Irish colonists against the bishop. The press incessantly declaimed against the legitimate pastor. He found it necessary to start a newspaper of his own to defend the cause of the Church—"The Bombay Catholic Examiner," which remains to this day one of the best advocates of the good cause in India. For a while Bishop Hartmann was himself obliged to assume the editorship. Three Goanese priests, who had treacherously deceived the bishop, were the soul of the schismatical movement. Once he was on the point of martyrdom. The schismatics had held him prisoner in a tightly closed church for eight days and nights during a time of extreme heat in order to make him surrender. He was almost dead of hunger and thirst when help arrived from Bombay. But by his tenacious constancy, prudent management, and charitable patience he broke the storm of schism. He had, of course, to pay the price in all the insults and injuries of which the hatred of apostates alone is capable. But the courage of the confessor was on this account all the more admired by the Christian nations of the West.

He had much also to endure from the British-Indian government in the defense of the rights of his flock. Protestant proselytism among Catholics was favored by the government in every way possible, especially by grants of money. So, too, was the schismatical movement much encouraged by the official body. At all times the undaunted confessor paid special attention to the foundation and improvement of schools and educational institutions. For this purpose he called the Jesuits to Bombay in 1851, to begin there an establishment for higher education. Much weakened by incessant suffering and hardship, the bishop in 1856 made a journey to Europe. After protracted negotiations with the Propaganda, an entire transfer of the Bombay mission to the Jesuits was effected. The physicians forbade Bishop Hartmann's return to the Indies, so he resigned his vicariate and assumed charge of the mission college of his Order in Rome. As soon as his health was restored, however, he was obliged again to take up the apostle's staff and for the second time to govern the vicariate of Patna. This had been frightfully devastated during the Sepoy rebellion (1857) and it was believed that the surest remedy for the evils done lay in the well-known efficiency and prudence of Hartmann. The venerable bishop set to work among the ruins of his vicariate with the enthusiastic zeal of a young missionary. For nearly six years, undeterred by any sacrifice or by any labor, he consecrated his remaining strength to the work. His love of immortal souls gave him no time for rest. In the midst of his labors and during a toilsome journey, the dreadful visitor of the Indies, cholera, came and bore him away on April 26, 1866.

A great life had come to an end. In spite of his love for exterior labors, the servant of God did not forget to work for the perfection of his interior life. The inner life of faith was the renewing source of his never failing courage. A heartfelt confidence in God, devout prayer, sincere humility and mortification, and his remarkable mildness were the weapons of his success. All who were well acquainted with him saw in him the type of a perfect missionary.

Bishop Hartmann was also unwearyingly active with his pen in the cause of Christ. Besides publishing many articles in the "Bombay Catholic Examiner" he was the author of a whole series of ascetical, philosophical, and theological treatises, of many translations into the Hindu language and of a grammar of the same.

Other Bishops

10. Other bishops who are expected to receive the honor of beatification are Venerable Vincent Morelli, bishop of Otranto, died 1812; and Venerable Bartholomew Menochio, of the Order of St. Augustine, titular bishop of Porphyrim, papal sacristan, died 1823.

HOLY SECULAR PRIESTS

Blessed John Baptist Vianney

THE Blessed John Baptist Vianney, parish priest of Ars, is certainly one of the noblest figures among the saints of the nineteenth century.[20] If one would know holiness in all its charms, in its ineffable gentleness and amiability, let him read the life of this illustrious ornament of the French clergy. The supernatural power revealed in him is so grand and so clearly manifest that only the ill-disposed can deny it.

John Baptist Vianney, born May 8, 1786, in the village of Dardilly, near Lyons, was the son of simple peasants. Grace attracted him heavenward from the beginning. Reason had hardly dawned in him when it turned toward God. The boy of three or four years was often found praying in some secluded corner of the house. When, at the age of seven, he was sent to tend the cows, he was able to spend almost the entire day in the sweetness of prayer. Even then he gave promise of his future calling. He used to gather the shepherd boys of the neighborhood around him from time to time and give them a little exhortation on the duty of avoiding evil and of persevering in good. He had always before his eyes the best example in his parents, who were models of piety and were most careful to preserve their children from every taint of evil.

Then came the French Revolution, closing the churches and expelling the priests. Blessed John received his first Holy Communion in a barn during the darkness of night. Finally, in 1803 a priest, the zealous Charles Balley, was appointed to Ecully, about three miles from Dardilly. His attention was soon attracted to the virtuous John Vianney. He offered to help John to become a priest. The young man gladly agreed, lodged with relations at Ecully and began to learn Latin. He was then seventeen years old, but had had scarcely any schooling. Study, therefore, proved very difficult for him, for his natural talent appeared to be rather poor. But his tutor, convinced that this upright and innocent youth would serve the Church well by his holiness, if not by his learning, did not lose patience. Vianney sought help from God and vowed a pilgrimage to the tomb of St. John Francis Regis at Lalouvesc. While he advanced steadily but slowly in his studies, it brought him many humiliations. In the little seminary of Verrieres he had to suffer much from his fellow-students and he failed in his examination for entrance into the great seminary of Lyons. It was only through the intercession of his tutor Balley that he was granted a second examination and admission to the seminary. On August 9, 1815, the end was at last attained. Vianney was a priest. His former teacher, Father Balley, asked to have him for an assistant. Ecully rejoiced, for it already knew the profound piety and modesty of the newly-ordained priest. Vianney's good sense in the direction of souls soon showed itself. His zeal was prodigious but not indiscreet or excessive, and he began at once to achieve noble triumphs.

At the beginning of February, 1818, Vianney was appointed parish priest of Ars. The vicar-general said to him: "My friend, you are pastor of Ars. It is a small parish where there is little love for God. Bring it to them." Ars was in bad repute and not without reason. Even among the good attendance at divine service and the reception of the sacraments were limited to what was just necessary. The rest sometimes attended, but only exteriorly. Dissolute pleasure-seeking allowed religion only scant existence.

Still all admired the edifying example of the new pastor in the church and in his humble and modest manner of life. If the sheep did not come to the shepherd the shepherd sought out the sheep. Vianney went from house to house, showed interest in their welfare and their troubles and spoke kinds words of encouragement and consolation. In this way the ice was broken. Sunday after Sunday more came to church, They ventured even to approach the sacraments outside the great feasts. Those who had once experienced in confession what gentleness flowed from the heart of the priest and how refreshing were his words, soon came again. With his heart glowing with love and speaking as only saints can speak he preached on God, death, heaven, hell, and on the Blessed Sacrament so movingly that from eyes which on like occasions had never wept there welled up fountains of tears. In the whole village only one voice was heard: "Our pastor is a saint." In the course of time no one could escape the influence of his personality. It was indeed a long struggle and many years passed before all hearts were conquered, for the love of pleasure made a most stubborn resistance.

The news of this change in Ars and of the holiness of its pastor soon spread throughout the neighboring country round about, penetrating at length to the limits of France and thence abroad. Every day the roads that led to Ars brought greater pilgrimages. Monnin says of them:[21] "These pilgrimages, which went on for more than thirty years with extraordinarily great crowds and under exceptional circumstances, will fill a large page in Christian annals. They give the monograph we now publish a color so living and original, a framing so splendid, that it seems to be poetry as well as history. We find here on a large scale all those wonders with which our ancient hagiographers loved to adorn their narratives. But we have no mythical antiquity before us and no one can find excuse for the belief that our history of this man who is still our contemporary will show any trace of fanciful or exaggerated elaboration. It is a history of our own time which can bring forward witnesses to its truth by thousands and hundreds of thousands, yet we find in it all that we marvel at in the legends of the past—all that in our own day we may regard as extraordinary heroism, perfect mortification, wonderful self-denial, incomparable humility, boundless love of God and our neighbor, and a dominion over souls—a power to draw them from afar, to move them, to convert and to gain them for heaven; and further, as if in proof of this spiritual dominion, a miraculous power over nature, the power to change the ordinary course of things, to heal bodily diseases, to read the depths of conscience as an open book, to foretell the future—in a word, he possessed the miraculous gift of knowledge and of power. This does not constitute, it is true, what is most sublime in the lives of the saints, but it is most convincing with the people—one of them told us: 'Before I came to Ars and saw the good Father [so the pilgrims used to call our saint], I found it hard to believe all that is related in the lives of the saints. Much in them seemed to me impossible. But now I believe it all, for I have seen all those things with my own eyes and even more.' "

In fact, Ars proved to be a constant miracle. Men could not say precisely what it was that attracted these vast crowds from near and far. They saw only a poor little church and a poorly-clad priest. Yet they stood there close-thronged and waited patiently two or three days to confess to him and to listen to his simple catechism, which powerfully stirred their consciences. Many came out of mere curiosity, but on these, too, fell the rays of grace. They could not resist going in and confessing their sins to the holy priest. To these wonders of grace were added the most astonishing cures of the sick, which he effected through the intercession of

St. Philomena, and his wise admonitions, which were certainly inspired by divine enlightenment.

These labors demanded of him the heaviest personal sacrifices. He could hardly allow himself one or two hours of rest at night. A little after midnight he hurried to the confessional, there to remain the whole day except during the times of Mass, of the brief instruction, and of his very scanty meal. One can not understand whence he derived the physical strength for such uninterrupted exertions. Still, not satisfied with all this, he afflicted his body with the severest penances, and it pleased God to send him the most grievous interior trials. His combats with the evil one, which are verified by the best authorities, remind us of what St. Athanasius relates of the hermit Anthony.

All that is related of the gifts of grace and the fulness of virtue possessed by the holy Curé of Ars and of the wonderful cures and conversions wrought by him, is full of consolation. What faith teaches of the power, the beauty, and the grandeur of the soul of the just man was embodied in him. Vianney was to be set against the unbelieving spirit of the age as a visible proof of the truth of Christian teaching.

On July 29, 1859, the Curé, then seventy-three years of age, had been, as usual, for sixteen or seventeen hours in the confessional, and there his strength suddenly gave way. On the morning of the fourth of August his soul took its flight to heaven while Abbé Monnin was reciting the prayer of the dying: *"Veniant illi obviam sancti angeli Dei et perducant eum in civitatem cœlestem Jerusalem;"* "May the holy angels of God meet him and guide him into the city of the heavenly Jerusalem." But his influence was not ended with his death. All Christendom rejoiced when Pius X, on January 8, 1905, numbered this ideal pastor of souls among the beatified.

Venerable Andrew Soulas

2. A contemporary of the Curé of Ars in southern France, the Venerable Andrew Soulas, also won the renown of perfect holiness.[22] He was born at Viols-le-Fort near Montpellier on February 25, 1808. As a boy he was beloved by all for his modesty, and even at this period of his life he is said to have worked miracles. To the consternation of his mother he often donated his shoes, clothing, food, and so on, to the poor. When called to account, he said: "I can wear my older brother's shoes, they do not suit him any more." A life of St. Vincent de Paul, given to him by his pastor, afforded him inexpressible joy and aroused in him the desire of becoming an apostle of the poor. He began his studies at the parish house, but had to interrupt them because his parents were unable to provide for his support. Andrew then betook himself to the Blessed Virgin with tearful prayer. His prayers were heard.

In the seminary he distinguished himself by his notable gift of eloquence. In a sermon on hell he spoke so fervently that the president and students interrupted their meal to listen and were moved to tears. On this account the preparation of the children in the city for first communion was confided to him and his superiors occasionally employed him in giving sermons and religious instructions.

The chief characteristic of the life of this servant of God was magnanimity. Every noble trait he found in the lives of the saints he was bound to imitate. So when he was ordained in 1835, he desired to devote himself to the foreign missions. But his bishop, hoping great profit for his own diocese from the young priest, refused the permission. Soulas at first labored in Salvetat and Montpellier. Then he was sent to give missions to the people in the diocese of Montpellier. The result exceeded all expectations. Later his missionary activity extended over the whole south of France.

This external labor did not hinder his intimate intercourse with God. As a boy, he had delighted in prayer and always visited the church on his way home from school. His companions styled him "the saint." As a priest he spent whole nights before the Tabernacle. At Holy Mass in particular his countenance glowed with devotion. Two priests had gone astray. He did penance for them and by his prayers obtained their conversion. His favorite saints throughout life were St. John Francis Regis and St. Aloysius. A Congregation of Sisters for the service of the sick and orphans owes its foundation to him. When the zealous missionary died, May 4, 1857, all Montpellier was stirred; and both great and small, noble and lowly, made haste to see his body. The streets through which the funeral procession was to pass were crowded for hours. The process of beatification already begun brings to light very numerous and remarkable miracles performed by the Venerable Soulas both during his life and after his death.

VENERABLE LOUIS MARY BAUDOUIN

3. The Venerable Louis Mary Baudouin won for himself the name of an apostle of loyal La Vendée.[23] His early years were quietly and peacefully spent in the bosom of his deeply religious family at Montaigu in La Vendée and in the seminary at Luçon. But he had hardly been ordained priest when the terrible tempest broke forth which demanded of him the martyr's courage. In fact, Baudouin was the first priest imprisoned by the revolutionists in the diocese of Luçon. He had refused the oath of the new constitution and had dared energetically to resist an apostate who pretended to be bishop of Luçon. This was only the beginning of affictions. In 1792, Baudouin, along with several

other priests, was banished to Spain. Their life in exile was very hard. They were often obliged to change their abode, to live on alms, and had no occupation suitable to their calling. The ever dreadful tidings that came from their native land quite robbed them of every joy and consolation and we read that many of these noble and faithful priests became ill from sheer heaviness of heart.

The thought of the misery of so many souls and of the faithful Vendeans, who were deprived of all priestly services, gave Baudouin no rest. Disguised as a laborer he crossed the Pyrenees in July, 1797, and in Bordeaux found good friends who took him aboard a ship and brought him safely to La Vendée. The fugitive found a hiding-place in the house of a rich lady at Les Sables d'Olonne. Here he remained concealed for three years, praying continually that Heaven might have mercy upon his poor country. Only in the darkness of night could he exercise his ministry. Like the Christians in the catacombs, so here the few faithful were often surprised by an unexpected visit during the celebration of the Holy Mysteries. Many a time it seemed a miracle that the priest escaped the bailiffs.

Finally, about the middle of 1800, the First Consul permitted the free exercise of the Christian religion. There was plenty of work for the zealous priest. The people had experienced how empty and disconsolate they could be when the churches were closed or burned down, when the sacraments were no longer administered and the sublime truths of religion no longer preached. The good Vendeans everywhere called for priests, but these were very few. Père Baudouin accomplished superhuman deeds. For eight or nine years there had been no public First Communion, no Church Wedding, no Baptism, no Confession. He tried to restore all. The crimes of the Revolution, moreover, had brutalized many and had opened the way to evil customs. It is not strange, then, that the zeal of God's servant met with resistance. His life was more than once in the greatest peril. But his unselfish charity and patience conquered everything. He went from house to house seeking all who might not be reconciled to the Church. Chavagnes, where he lived as pastor after 1801, venerated him as a saint.

Baudouin saw that it was above all necessary to educate the young in Christian principles. But competent teachers were altogether wanting. So, assisted by a former nun, he founded a congregation of women for the education of girls. He named it the "Ursulines of Jesus," commonly known as the Ursulines of Chavagnes. It grew rapidly and later spread into North America, Africa, and China. The training of a clergy had also to be provided for, because the Revolution had destroyed all institutions for the education of priests. Trusting in Providence, he started, in 1802, a little seminary in his parish. In this enterprise the hand of God was visibly manifest. Unfortunately, in 1812, it was closed for a time by command of the government, which forbade private institutions of the kind. Baudouin, who had proved himself an able educator, was appointed superior of the great Seminary of La Rochelle. When his native diocese of Luçon was afterward re-established, he was sent there to fill the same office. But his activity extended over the whole diocese; he took care of schools, religious establishments, the holding of missions, and many works of importance.

Broken down by his many labors, he retired to his beloved seminary of Chavagnes, which, to his joy, had been re-established. He was always happiest when among these lighthearted boys, whom he so well understood. There, on February 12, 1835, he died a holy death. He was always distinguished by his extraordinary devotion to the Blessed Virgin, especially in the Immaculate Conception. It is touching to read how familiar and intimate were his dealings with Our Blessed Mother. During his active life he founded several pious institutions; in Spain, a society of Mary among the banished priests; at Les Sables d'Alonne, a union for the propagation of devotion to the Immaculate Conception; and later, in Chavagnes, a congregation of secular priests under the title "Society of the Children of Mary," whose purpose was to give instruction in little seminaries and to give missions to the country folk. His biographer narrates many miraculous cures which were wrought even within recent years. May it please God to hasten his beatification.

Venerable Joseph Benedict Cottolengo

4. The example of the Venerable Joseph Benedict Cottolengo,[24] by no means a solitary one, proves how unjust is the man of our day who thinks that there are no longer souls which rise to the loftiest heights of the love of God and their neighbor, and accomplish all things by their immovable confidence in God. Pius IX called the "Little House of Providence," Cottolengo's foundation in Turin, "a house of miracles." But the whole man himself was a continual proof of the power of the supernatural.

The house of Joseph Cottolengo's parents can still be seen in Brá, a little town of Piedmont. The day of his birth was May 3, 1786. It is said that study was at first very difficult for the boy; but he applied with childlike confidence to that light of knowledge, St. Thomas Aquinas, and, to the astonishment of his teachers and classmates, was soon at the head of the class. At seventeen he resolved to become a priest. He made his theological studies in the seminary of Asti, where he was ordained priest on June 8, 1811. After a short but very successful career in Cornegliano,

Cottolengo went to Turin to obtain the degree of Doctor of Theology. After receiving this dignity he joined the *"Corpus Domini,"* a congregation of secular priests, and was made a canon of the church of the Holy Trinity.

In all large cities there is a great amount of misery, both spiritual and corporal, and Cottolengo soon found how plentiful it was in Turin. One day he was called to a sick woman who, with her little children, was in sad destitution. She had been refused admission at all the hospitals. Cottolengo's heart was deeply moved. At once his plan was resolved on. A hospital must be founded where such forlorn creatures could find a refuge. He first asked light and strength in prayer, and then went to work at once. He hired a small house, to which a benevolent lady donated four beds. This was the beginning of the foundation which he called *"La Piccola Casa della Divina Providenza,"* "The Little House of Divine Providence." A physician and a pharmacist voluntarily offered their services. Patients applied in increasing numbers. He had to hire more room. He obtained women to attend the female patients and men for the men. The former he called "Ladies of Christian Charity"; the latter, "Brothers of St. Vincent." The work continually grew in extent, and with it Cottolengo's enterprise and confidence in God increased daily.

But the storm did not fail to come. Among his colleagues he found vehement opponents who considered him rash and extravagant. When the cholera broke out in Turin in 1831, the neighbors, fearing infection, induced the government to close the Piccola Casa. Cottolengo pleasantly remarked: "In my country they say that cabbage thrives better if it be transplanted, so I will transplant my hospital." Before a half year had passed the apostle of charity had secured a little house in a remote quarter of the city, called Valdocco, where he began his work anew.   In fact, the transplanted hospital prospered more than before.   Soon there rose, beside the Piccola Casa, the House of Faith, the House of Hope, the House of Charity, and the House of Bethlehem.   Each of them served a special purpose of charity.   The houses of evil repute in the vicinity soon disappeared and good conduct and fear of the Lord prevailed in that formerly disreputable part of the city. At the entrance of the Piccola Casa gleamed Cottolengo's motto: *"Charitas Christi urget nos"*; "The Charity of Christ presseth us" (2 Cor. v. 14).

But it was yet far from remedying every misery. "Noe's Ark," as Cottolengo called his work, was not yet spacious enough.   Near the department for orphans he erected for boys and girls who had been neglected in spirit and in body, a "Home for good boys" and a "Home for good girls."   He provided for the future of the orphan boys who showed talent and disposition for study or for vocation to the religious state.   He had long before transformed his nursing staff into religious Congregations.   For girls who were too weak for the service of the sick, he founded the "Society of the Good Shepherdesses," who were to attend to the instruction of cretins and orphans.   For elderly sisters he created the "Convent of Intercession" with strict enclosure, for the purpose of helping the souls in purgatory.   Soon after he organized a similar institution, "The Daughters of the Pietà," who were to imitate the women on Calvary and pray for the dying. For those who wished to devote themselves to a severe manner of life, he introduced the rule of the Discalced Carmelites.   Nor did he forget the men.   Besides his Brothers of St. Vincent, he created the "Hermits of the Holy Rosary," who followed the rule of St. Romuald.   When fallen girls were disposed to do penance for their sins he placed them in a new establishment under the patronage of the holy penitent Thais, from whom they were called Thaidines. Five of his Carmelite Sisters were selected to develop this foundation. Finally, he added a congregation of secular priests, whose duty it was to attend to the spiritual welfare of the various foundations.

It would be wrong to think that Cottolengo was led by a blind zeal. All his works were successful. Most of them still exist. His genius for organization was wonderful. There was no disorder in his establishments—he watched over all, provided for all. What is most remarkable is that he founded all these works and kept them up with the help of charitable contributions alone.

Oftentimes his purse was empty; his creditors pressed him hard; but in due time help was ever at hand and often from least expected quarters. If sometimes Providence seemed to be tardy and even to interfere, Cottolengo spent hours upon his knees and struggled with God in prayer, and never in vain. Such was his trust in God that he kept no account of receipts and expenses. In his enterprises he never considered his material resources, but only the needs of his fellowman. Of course, he knew that the fountain whence he drew help would never run dry. It was the treasure of an all-beneficent Providence. If any one wondered at his great success he used to say that it was simply a clear proof that Providence, not Cottolengo, was the founder and director of these works, and that he knew himself to be a bungler.

It would carry us too far were we to do more than mention Cottolengo's heroic spirit of faith, his extraordinary humility and mortification, his ecstasies, his familiar converse with the Queen of Heaven and with the saints, his wonderful knowledge of consciences, and the spiritual and corporal cures he effected. All who dwelt in his institutions had their lives sweetened by the great charity with which they were treated.

When new patients arrived, the founder himself, if possible, cordially welcomed them at the door. He conversed with all like an affectionate father, and their greatest joy was to have him appear among them. It did not need long converse with him to feel that one was dealing with a saint. His fame spread throughout the world. Gregory XVI sent him a Brief full of praise and thanks. King Charles Albert of Savoy was his intimate friend. Even the Marquis Cavour, Syndic of Turin and father of the statesman Camillo Cavour, every year sent him a gift of wine on the feast of St. Vincent de Paul. The French Academy, learning of him from Baron Monyton, once voted him the prize of virtue and solemnly presented him with it through King Charles Albert. Cottolengo replied that he considered it not an honor for himself but a recognition of Divine Providence which accomplished everything in his institutions. The street leading to the Piccola Casa bears to-day the name of Cottolengo.

The strength of the holy man had broken down in the service of charity toward his neighbor and he clearly saw his end approaching. The physicians ordered a sojourn in the country. When leaving, he gave his blessing to all and bade them be cheerful in the Lord and full of trust in Divine Providence. He said to a Sister who anticipated misfortune: "Be at peace. When I am in heaven, where everything is possible, I will help you more than ever. I will hold fast to the cloak of the Mother of God and never turn my eyes away from you." Scarcely had Cottolengo reached his brother's house in Chieri when his condition grew worse. He received the last sacraments with great devotion. No care disquieted him—on the contrary, he was now serenity itself. While they were saying the prayers for the dying, he said softly: "My Mother Mary." Then he raised his voice: *"Lætatus sum in his quæ dicta sunt mihi: in domum Domini ibimus,"* "I rejoiced at the things that were said to me: We shall go into the house of the Lord" (Ps. cxxi. 1). The next moment this father of the poor and the orphan was no more. It was on the evening of April 20, 1842. Cottolengo had not yet completed his fifty-sixth year. King Charles Albert wept at the loss of such a friend and Gregory XVI exclaimed "Turin has lost a saint." God has glorified Cottolengo since his death with so many miracles that we may expect his beatification in a short time.

Venerable Joseph Cafasso

5. At the same time as Cottolengo there lived in Turin another holy priest, the Venerable Joseph Cafasso.[25] In 1835, the Venerable Don Bosco came to take up his theological studies in Turin, and during that time Don Cafasso was his confessor, director, and most trusted friend. If the Church owed nothing else to Joseph Cafasso but the fact that he trained up a Don Bosco for her, she would be obliged to render him the greatest gratitude. But we can not number the persons who were inspired with zeal for Christ and the Church by the word and example of Cafasso. There was at that time in Turin what was practically a seminary for young priests—the Institute of St. Francis of Assisi. In this seminary Cafasso was professor of moral theology, and from 1848 to 1860 director of the Institute. The preparation of the mind and heart of the priest, so that he would be able to meet modern demands in the true spirit of the Church, was the ideal which Cafasso sought to realize. Piedmont can thank him for many eminent priests. His pupil, Don Bosco, writes of him: "All agree that we can call his priestly life rather that of an angel than of a man . . . Some called him a new St. Aloysius on account of his innocence and the purity of his morals; others a St. Francis of Sales on account of his gentleness, patience, and

charity; others a St. Vincent de Paul for his active love of his neighbor; others still a St. Charles Borromeo on account of his mortified life and the severity with which he treated himself; and finally, some saw in him a St. Alphonsus de Liguori on account of his friendliness, condescension, and goodness. For my part, I must say that in the lives of the saints I have found many who excelled in a heroic degree, one by this, another by that virtue, but I believe that rarely can any one be found who actually combined in his person so much wisdom, experience in human affairs, magnanimity, fortitude, temperance, and zeal of God's honor and for the salvation of souls as shone forth from the priest Cafasso."

The activity of Cafasso was by no means confined to his Institute. He had spiritual charge of the prison. Before Don Bosco, he was engaged in caring for children. He had care of the shrine of St. Ignatius of Loyola in Lanzo.

He was much sought for as a confessor, gave many retreats, and all classes of people came to him for advice and help. He died after a short illness on June 23, 1860, at forty-nine years of age. In his notes we find that it was his constant prayer that all memory of him might disappear save remembrance in prayer. But, for our consolation and encouragement, God has not granted this humble petition and the miraculous favors which He grants to the invocation of Cafasso indicate that He will make still more known this example of virtue to the world. Pius X published the decree opening the apostolic processes on May 15, 1906.

Venerable Placidus Bacher

6. Though the blood of Switzerland flowed in the veins of the Venerable Placidus Bacher he probably never saw the mountains of his forefathers.[26] He was born at Naples on April 7, 1781, the son of a Swiss

captain in the service of the king. A pious priest took
special care of the boy's education. Placidus made his
studies at the college of the Dominicans. Frequent
communion and a heartfelt devotion to the Blessed
Virgin, whom he honored every day by saying the
Rosary, kept his youth from going astray.

When Naples was involved in the revolution a heavy
affliction fell upon the Bacher family. They were
imprisoned for their loyalty to the king. Young Placidus was separated from his relatives and thrown among
the worst criminals. Besides this, he had much to suffer from the jailer and the jailer's wife. He himself
tells us that in those days of suffering the Rosary was
his only consolation. It is related in the acts of his
process that the Mother of God appeared to him in
prison, consoled him, and promised him the dignity
of the priesthood. The tribunal of the Revolution was
about to pass sentence of death upon him when, contrary to all expectation, he was acquitted. But he was
hardly set at liberty when a new warrant was issued
against him and it was almost a miracle that he
escaped the police.

After the fever of the revolution had abated Placidus Bacher began the study of theology, and on May
30, 1806, he stood at the altar for the first time as a
priest. He soon distinguished himself by remarkably
successful work as a pastor and was therefore given
charge of the Gesu Vecchio church, in accordance with
the desire of Queen Carolina Annuntiata and the recommendation of the Blessed Francis Xavier Bianchi
of the Barnabites. The church had formerly belonged
to the Society of Jesus, but was in such a state of neglect that it was intended to change it into a theater.
Don Bacher did all he could to restore it to its old
splendor, and especially to make it again a house of
prayer and to fill it with devout worshipers. He accomplished this principally by his impressive sermons. He

moved his hearers deeply when he pictured to them the greatness of God, the malice and punishment of sin, and the sufferings and love of Christ. He had particularly at heart the encouragement of devotion to the Immaculate Conception; and the yearly novena in the Gesu Vecchio before the feast was always like a great mission. He had the picture of the Immaculate Conception over the altar solemnly crowned by Cardinal Ruffo Scilla in 1826 in the presence of the royal family.

To inspire the young with love for the beautiful virtue of purity he always pointed out to them the noble example of St. Aloysius. He set great store by a relic of St. Aloysius which he had. It was a small bottle containing some hard, dried-up blood. It was said to have come from Castiglione, the birthplace of St. Aloysius. It was Don Bacher's private possession and had been given to him in 1837.[27] Every year, from the first vespers of the saint's feast until the second vespers of the octave, the hard crust of blood in the bottle becomes fluid and a fresh red. On this occasion the relic is not touched by any one, but stands on the altar of St. Aloysius and the miracle takes place only after some prayers have been said in his honor. On other extraordinary occasions, also, the hard blood is wont to liquefy. We may imagine how welcome an opportunity such miracles gave Don Bacher to inflame his hearers with a love of virtue; and how fervently he exhorted them to love of God.

He had cared for the Gesu Vecchio for over forty years. His strength was consumed, and on the 19th of October, 1851, he departed this life to possess the life for which alone he labored. His body was placed in the chapel of St. Aloysius. All the people, together with the king and queen and the royal heir of Spain, hastened to see once more the beloved priest. Don Bacher found his last resting-place beneath the altar

of the Immaculate Conception. His cause was introduced on May 12, 1909.

Venerable Vincent Romano

7. The process of beatification is nearly completed
for a priest of the archdiocese of Naples, the Venerable
Vincent Romano,[28] parish priest of Herculaneum.
During thirty-five years Romano labored in his parish,
inspired by an unwearied zeal to gain entirely for
Christ the souls entrusted to him. Fatigued after
working all day, he spent the night in prayer to refresh
his soul and to obtain courage and inspiration for new
labors. But near Naples not only is there turmoil in
the depths of the earth—the spirits of men are also
easily roused to fury and tumult. So Romano was
often in peril of his life because of the wicked, for
whom he had made difficult the gratification of their
passions. But Providence watched over him. He died
in 1831, at the age of 80.

Venerable Ignatius Jennaco

8. The Venerable Ignatius Jennaco was a professor
in the diocesan seminary at Naples.[29] His birthplace
was Torre Annunziata, at the foot of Vesuvius. On
account of his well-known piety, Jennaco was given
free tuition in the boy's seminary of the city. As soon
as he became a deacon he was appointed a professor in
the seminary and he held this office until his death,
December 22, 1828. But his activity was not confined
to the seminary. Throughout the whole city he practised the spiritual and corporal works of mercy.

Ven. John Baptist Guarino—Agnellus Coppola.

9. The Archdiocese of Naples also glories in the
Venerable John Baptist Guarino, parish priest of San
Pietro near Salerno, and in the servant of God,
Agnellus Coppola.

Venerable Dominic Lentini

10. In the south Italian province of Basilicata lies the little town of Lauria in the diocese of Policastro. Here was born, on November 20, 1770, the Venerable Dominic Lentini.[30] On account of the extreme poverty of his parents the boy met with great difficulties in completing his studies. After his ordination Lentini became a professor in the Lyceum of his native town. He strove particularly to enlighten the young as to the false principles of the philosophy of the day by means of many discourses of a philosophico-apologetic kind. In 1779 a liberty tree had been erected in Lauria. When the revolution reached its climax, the cooler heads desired to pull it down, but a crowd of furious revolutionists ranged themselves before it, ready to strike down any one who should dare to touch it. A great uproar ensued. Then the young priest Lentini stepped out before the crowd and resolutely ordered them to pull down the tree and bring it to the nearest hill. They involuntarily obeyed him. Then he made them fashion the wood into a cross and raise it aloft. Beneath it he addressed them with burning eloquence, telling them: "This is the tree of freedom and of salvation. We shall honor no other." Contrite and with hearts redeemed to the ancient Faith, the crowd dispersed. Lentini died on February 26, 1828. Even before his burial he began to work miracles. His grave continually attracts many pilgrims because of the extraordinary things which take place there.

Venerable Pascal Attardi

11. The process of the Venerable Pascal Attardi[31] is one of the most recently inaugurated. He was born at Naples of pious parents, on October 2, 1837, passed his youth in innocence and studied at the Jesuit college in his native city. After ordination, he never filled any high office, serving merely as assistant in the church

of the Most Holy Name of Jesus at Naples. But his
confessional and his sermons exercised a magnetic
influence upon the people. It was the charm of holiness which, in spite of his humility, he was unable to
conceal. His chief occupation was the direction of a
sodality and the spiritual care of a hospital. For a
while he also superintended a private school. He died
on March 25, 1893. At the petition of several cardinals and of many bishops and priests, Pius X published
the decree for the opening of the process of his beatification on April 27, 1910.

ANTHONY PENNACCHI—CASPAR BERTONI

12. Two other Italian priests are candidates for the
honor of beatification, Anthony Pennacchi[32] and Caspar Bertoni.[33] The former lived in Assisi, was a teacher
in a Latin school there, and was popular throughout
the whole city on account of the great amiability he
manifested in all his work for the cause of God. But
he was not spared sufferings from both within and
without. He was sixty-six years of age when he died,
November 9, 1848.

Caspar Bertoni is famed in Verona especially for
his angelic chastity. When a priest he conducted many
retreats for the people, but his principal care was the
souls of the young. An Oratory of secular priests,
named "Of the Holy Wounds," owes its existence to
him. Later he was made director of the Society of the
Daughters of Charity, founded by the Venerable Maddalena of Canossa.* For the last twelve years of his
life he was confined to his bed by a wound in the leg.
On the 12th of June, 1853, he exchanged his bed of
pain for eternal joys.

ANTHONY CHEVRIER

13. Anthony Chevrier gained the repute of sanctity
as a true apostle of the poor.[34] He was born at Lyons

*See pages 197 sqq.

in 1826, the son of a financier, was ordained priest in 1850 and became vicar of St. Andrew's in his native city. Meditation on the mystery of Our Saviour's birth filled him with a wonderful love of poverty and of the poor. He gave up his position as vicar with the view of consecrating himself entirely to the destitute. His compassion was first excited for poor abandoned children who, having no one to care for them, had not made their first communion. He acquired a half-ruined building, called the Prado, in the suburbs, and with the aid of charitable gifts he repaired it for his work of charity. The children remained in this house for six months, were solidly instructed in the truths of religion and then solemnly admitted to holy communion. Those admitted to the Prado were often degenerate. But the prayers, kindness, and charity of Chevrier won the confidence of these unfortunates. Asked the condition for admission to the Prado, the pious director replied: "Three—to have nothing, to know nothing, and to be good for nothing." For the support of his house he depended mainly on alms. Every Friday morning he stood as a beggar for his children at the door of some church.

The work of Chevrier grew more and more extended. Both the civil and the ecclesiastical authorities protected him. Since 1864 he had been selecting good and talented boys and preparing them to enter his Institute for Priests.

The people had long perceived the holiness of Chevrier. He was continually engaged in the parlor, in the confessional, and in the sacristy. The chapel of the Prado was filled not only on Sundays, but every evening for catechism. His question-box was particularly attractive. Any one could hand in written questions to which an answer was desired. On the appointed day Chevrier satisfied as far as possible the wishes of his hearers. He used to say: "The priest

is the glory and riches of God's house; its finest ornament is the priest. A holy priest even in a poor frame
church will attract and convert souls." And in himself
this saying was exemplified. This father of the poor
was called to his reward on October 2, 1879. About
ten thousand persons attended his funeral. Such a
man will surely win the crown of the Blessed and by
his example encourage many to imitate him.

Venerable Andrew Hubert Fournet

14. The Venerable Andrew Hubert Fournet[35] was
likewise distinguished by his great charity. He first
studied law, but afterward became a priest. The French
Revolution offered him an occasion of proving his
strong faith. Refusing the oath of the Constitution
he was obliged to flee into Spain. Later he returned
secretly to his parish of Maille near Montmorillon and,
although a price had been put upon his head, courageously attended to his priestly duties. Assisted by the
Venerable Elizabeth Bichier des Ages, he founded in
1806 a society of women, the Sisters of the Cross of
St. Andrew, for the care of the sick and the instruction of children. God's blessing rested visibly upon the
foundation, which numbered nearly twenty-five hundred Sisters in 1880. The founder died on May 13,
1834, while vicar-general of Poitiers. The process
of his beatification was begun in 1877.

Venerable Louis Edward Cestac

15. The Venerable Louis Edward Cestac[36] was born
at Bayonne on January 6, 1801. After his ordination
to the priesthood he became a canon in the cathedral
of Bayonne. The great dangers which beset young
girls in that city moved him to establish a society
devoted entirely to girls who had fallen or were
exposed to danger. Even during his lifetime it already
numbered one hundred and sixty houses. Cestac had

the happiness of receiving his own mother into the Congregation. He afterward added a department for those girls who desired to do penance for their sins. This branch gave excellent results. After a life full of labor for the love of God and the neighbor, Cestac died on May 27, 1868.

John Mary Robert de Lamennais

16. The beatification of John Mary Robert de Lamennais[37]—brother of the unfortunate Felicité— was introduced in 1911. Nature had bestowed great mental gifts on both. John Robert's youth remained unsullied and he comprehended with all the ardor of his enthusiastic heart the beauty of the Faith. He was born of a distinguished family at St. Malo in Brittany on September 8, 1780. His mother dying early, he went to the house of the bishop of St. Malo and after the expulsion of the latter by the Revolution, to an abbé who took care of his education and his studies until his ordination to the priesthood. The first fruit of his zeal was the conversion of his brother Felicité, who was two years younger than he. Felicité had lost his faith when but twelve years old through the reading of bad books, and with his faith, the power to live a morally pure life. The zealous young priest was indeed happy to redeem his strayed brother from his erring course and to have him make his first communion, though Felicité was already twenty-two years of age.

John Robert had established at St. Malo a school for the poor and an intermediate school for aspirants to the priesthood. But ill-health forced him to give up teaching. In 1807 he retired with his brother to the estate of La Chesnaye, near Dinan, to pray and study. While here the two brothers co-operated in publishing some writings in defense of the rights of the Church against Gallicanism. The elder brother exercised a healthful influence upon the impetuous character of the younger one, knowing how to guard him against extremes, against pride and pusillanimity. If Felicité had always been under the spiritual guidance of his brother he might, perhaps, have been a saint instead of an apostate.

Some time after, the Abbé John Robert took up again his teaching at St. Malo, and later became vicar-general of the bishop of Saint-Brieuc. He saw that it was necessary to educate the young in Christian principles to remedy the evils which unbelief had caused in France. In this respect the country people were the most neglected. So, in 1817, Lamennais established a society of teaching Brothers (*Frères de l'instruction Chretienne*), to give instruction to the country people, since the Brothers of St. John Baptist de la Salle could not accept the direction of parish schools in the country because their rule demanded community life. The abbé's Congregation grew rapidly and spread through all France, into the French Colonies, and even into British territory. In 1903 it numbered about twenty-five hundred and fifty members. In 1904, when a large number was gathered in the mother-house at Ploermel for the Spiritual Exercises they were violently expelled by the police.[38] Their principal residence is now in England.

The activity of John Robert de Lamennais was not confined to the development and direction of this congregation of Brothers. He also founded a congregation of priests for the direction of a clerical seminary at Saint-Méen and for work on the missions. This was later amalgamated with the establishment of his brother at La Chesnaye. In 1822 the servant of God was appointed to the important office of vicar-general of the grand almoner of France. In this position it was his duty to propose the candidates for episcopal sees. After two years' activity, however, he was removed from this office by the minister of public worship, on account of his outspoken zeal for the rights of the Church. After that time he lived for the most part at the novitiate in Ploermel, where he died on December 26, 1860. There the gratitude of Brittany erected a memorial in his honor.

His greatest affliction was the apostasy of his brother Felicité. "To pray and to weep," he wrote to a friend, "is now my only occupation." But he also tried all natural means to bring the erring one to a change of mind. He wrote him letter after letter, each more affectionate than the last. Finally, after eight years, he received an answer. On the news of the dangerous illness of his unhappy brother he set out, although in great suffering himself, to see the dying man. Unfortunately he came too late.

Venerable Anthony Sylvester Receveur

17. The Venerable Anthony Sylvester Receveur (died 1804) was the founder, at Besançon in 1789, of the Fathers of Retreat (*Pères de la Retraite*).

Nicholas John Olivieri

18. The Servant of God, Nicholas John Olivieri, a Genoese priest (died 1864), was a great promoter of the anti-slavery movement. With the assistant of Venerable Mother M. Pelletier* he inaugurated a work for the redemption and education of negro slaves.

Venerable Ignatius Falzon

19. In this place we must mention the cleric, Venerable Ignatius Falzon, son of a lawyer at La Valetta on the island of Malta. He was born on July 1, 1813.[39] When a boy, he daily recited the entire Rosary and, even against the suggestions of his mother, he would never go to bed until he had finished all of the fifteen

*See page 213.

mysteries. To this he afterward added the office of the Blessed Virgin. Ignatius came of a family of lawyers and so at first he studied law. But Providence had reserved him for an entirely different vocation. He gave up profane studies, applied himself to theology and received minor orders. But, because of his humility, he could never be prevailed on to enter the sanctuary of the priesthood itself, notwithstanding the many entreaties of his friends. Nevertheless he considered the apostolate as the labor of his life. His elder brother was a canon in La Valetta, and Ignatius deligently assisted him in his parish work, instructing the children in catechism and preparing them for first communion. But he became in a special way the apostle of the English soldiers. He obtained permission to gather the Catholic soldiers together on certain evenings, gave them an interesting instruction and said the beads with them. These gatherings became very popular, and many Protestants joined them. In this way, not to mention the numbers of Catholic soldiers he rescued from evil ways, he effected the conversion of more than six hundred Protestants and three Jews, as may be seen in the extant register of La Valetta. The Crimean war, during which many troops were quartered at Malta, gave him a particular occasion for the exercise of his zeal. When the soldiers were again moved, he kept in touch with them by means of letters to prevent their fervor from relaxing. He published an English prayer-book: "The Comfort of the Soul," with a special appendix for soldiers, and translated another good book into English. The conversion of England was the constant intention of his prayers.

Falzon also deserved well of the Church in Malta by instructing talented boys who desired to become priests and by obtaining for them material support. Many of his pupils afterward achieved distinction.

Thus the Servant of God spent his life within his family circle, entirely devoted to works of piety. Every one spoke of his great devotion before the Tabernacle and in the reception of the Holy Eucharist, which from his student days had been his daily food. He died after a protracted illness on his birthday, July 1, 1875. The cause of his beatification was introduced in 1904.

THE religious state also gives its testimony to the
Holiness of the Church by its extraordinary
fruitfulness in holy lives during the nineteenth century. We begin with those concerning whom the
Church has already given her decision.

St. Clement Mary Hofbauer

1. The first and, up to the present, the only canonized saint of the last century is the Apostle of Vienna,
St. Clement Mary Hofbauer.[40] We find in him the
genuine type of the saint. He was a man enflamed
with divine love, inspired by the ardent zeal of an
apostle and endowed with an heroic constancy in the
Faith. The source of his strength was his intercourse
with God. All who came into contact with him were
swayed by the power of his personality. But it was
not the influence of natural gifts, it was the grace of
God which he possessed in rich abundance. He had
studied little, yet he spoke with great security and
clearness on the profoundest truths of religion which
in his time were much obscured by the so-called
"Eclaircissement." His sermons were simple, without
rhetorical adornment and in defective German, still
he attracted all and moved their hearts. Providence
had sent him to show the world how Christianity must
become a living fact in us.

The chief features of his eventful and highly interesting life will make clearly manifest to us his providential mission.

Hofbauer was born at Tasswitz, near Znaim, in
Moravia, on December 26, 1751, the son of plain country folk. The family was numerous and of small
means. The father died early and our saint was
obliged to learn a trade, though it was his dearest wish

to become a priest. He served his apprenticeship in a bakery at Znaim and then became a baker in the Premonstratensian chapter-house at Bruck. Here, at the age of twenty, he found some opportunity to learn a little Latin in his leisure moments. But he found the greatest delight in spiritual occupations, so he betook himself at the age of twenty-five to a hermitage near the place of pilgrimage called Mühlfrauen. On account of the unsettled state of the times the hermitage was closed a year afterwards, and Hofbauer found himself thrust back into the midst of the world. In search of work he now turned his steps toward the capital, Vienna, which city was to become the principal scene of his apostolic labors. Here Providence brought him into companionship with a like-minded good young journeyman baker, Peter Kunzmann, a native of Unterfranken. The following year they made a pilgrimage together to the tomb of the Apostles.

After some years of work, they again recrossed the Alps, but with the intention of remaining in the Eternal City for the rest of their lives. On their way they came to the hermitage of Tivoli and resolved to remain there. The bishop of Tivoli, Barnabas Chiaramonti, afterward Pope Pius VII, gave them the habit of the Hermits. But, although Hofbauer felt much delight and consolation in this solitude, the desire to become a priest ever grew stronger. So six months later he returned to Vienna to prepare himself by study for the priesthood. He found friends who helped him.

In the following year he again went to Rome, this time in company with his friend Thaddeus Hübl, to continue his studies. On this occasion both became acquainted with the Redemptorists and applied for entrance into the novitiate. They were the first Germans who entered the Congregation. The saint did not forget his Fatherland. He asked his superiors to be permitted to practise there his apostolic vocation.

His petition was granted. After their ordination in 1786, the two friends returned to Vienna. But here the dominant spirit of Josephinism placed the greatest obstacles in their way. They journeyed, therefore, to the north, seeking a free field for labor. They found a friendly reception in Warsaw and were given the German church of St. Benno. The city soon learned what a treasure it had gained.

The amiable father at St. Benno's drew all hearts to him. His sermons were more eagerly attended day by day, his confessional was besieged. Besides this he went out to preach in the public squares and gathered the young around him for religious instruction. It is particularly noteworthy that the young applied to him for entrance into the Congregation that they might share his labors. A convent of the Redemptorists was established at Warsaw. In 1793, Hofbauer was made vicar-general of the Congregation north of the Alps. His renown spread far beyond the confines of Poland and accessions came even from Germany and France. With Warsaw as center, he undertook the foundation of new establishments of his Congregation in Germany and in Switzerland.

The year 1808 brought the labors of the saint in Warsaw to a sudden end. By command of Napoleon the convent was closed and the Redemptorists taken to the fortress of Küstrin, which was then in possession of the French. After a confinement of four weeks they were individually sent to their native country.

Father Hofbauer bent his footsteps toward Vienna. His residence at Vienna forms the glorious period of his apostolic activity. Although he was seized by the police immediately after his arrival in the city and imprisoned for three days as a suspect and was therefore under almost continual surveillance, against the power of a saint even the police are powerless. The modest room of the former baker's apprentice became the focus of ecclesiastical life in Vienna. Rich and poor, learned men, artists, politicians, nobles, sons of princes, simple tradesmen and citizens, priests both secular and regular, and above all the young, went in and out getting instruction, advice, and consolation and receiving the spirit of genuine Christianity. Through the saint's help innumerable persons found the happiness of faith. Many Protestants and Jews owed their conversion to him. It is enough to name only a few of those who came under his influence— Frederick August von Klinkowström, Zacharias Werner, John Frederic Schlosser, Frederick Schlegel and his wife Dorothea Mendelssohn, Emanuel Veit, Philipp Veit, Adam von Müller, Josepf Othmar Rauscher and others. Frederic Leopold von Stolberg, Clement Brentano and Joseph von Eichendorff also had intercourse with Clement Hofbauer in Vienna.

The saint gained undying merit by the promotion of a good press. In this his friends faithfully seconded him. Whoever really knows the Church must love her. It was therefore the saint's endeavor to spread by means of books and periodicals a true enlightenment among the people, who had been getting only a caricature of the Christian religion from a rationalistic and irreligious literature. Joseph Anthony von Pilat, an editor, made a general confession of his life to Hofbauer and from that time forth his influential paper, "The Austrian Observer" (*Der Osterreichische Beobachter*), was consecrated to the service of the good cause. Especially at the time of the Vienna Congress this paper was a trenchant weapon in defense of the rights of the Church. That the plan of Wessenberg to establish a German national church failed, was chiefly due to Clement Hofbauer.

The saint was a true reformer. He made the world conscious of what it means to act and to think as a Catholic. His admirable life and the example of his heroic virtue was a tangible argument of the divine power of our Faith. He died on March 15, 1820, at midday, while the Angelus bells were ringing. His burial was like a triumphal march such as Vienna had rarely witnessed. By his solemn canonization on May 20, 1909, Pius X gave the great son of St. Alphonsus to the world as an example of how all things are to be renewed in Christ.

BLESSED STEPHEN BELLESINI

2. The Blessed Stephen Bellesini of the Order of Hermits of St. Augustine was also an Austrian by birth.[41] The Bellesini family was established at Trent, but traced its descent to one of the Doges of Venice. The mother of Stephen bore a German name, Mary Ursula Meinchembeck. The Bellesini, we are told, were always distinguished for their loyal devotion to the Church; and for a predilection toward the religious state. In Stephen, who was born November 25, 1774, this pious tendency showed itself at an early age. On account of his precocity and his love of prayer, the parish priest allowed him to receive his first communion at the age of seven. In his parents' house and in the schools of Trent, Stephen was a model of the exemplary and morally good boy. At sixteen, first overcoming some objection on the part of his father, he applied for admission to the Augustinian convent of San Marco in Trent. He made his novitiate at Bologna and his philosophical studies at Rome. While he was studying theology in Bologna, the army of the revolution entered the city and Stephen, an Austrian, was obliged to return to his country. Toward the end of 1797 he was ordained priest. For a while he could live undisturbed in the convent of San Marco at Trent until the sad events of the time brought with them the downfall of the Augustinian monasteries. Many of the monks wept when they bade farewell to one another

and had to take leave of the life to which they had
bound themselves by solemn vows.

Father Bellesini returned into the bosom of his family. His mother was overjoyed to have her son with
her again. But the latter, along with his cousin, who
had also belonged to San Marco, observed at home the
rule of his Order in everything. And he gained
immortal profit for the well-being of his native town
by carrying on a relentless and successful warfare
against the unbelieving spirit of the age. The power
of his word and example encouraged the good and
steadied the wavering. A so-called normal school had
been opened in Trent; that is, a school in which the
young were to hear nothing of God and religion—
to smooth the way to unbelief. Forthwith, and at his
private expense, Bellesini began a school of his own.
His personality exercised a great influence upon the
young and soon attracted a large attendance. The
opposition was disarmed and petitioned the government to close Bellesini's school. The matter was
referred to the magistracy of Trent and they decided
in favor of Bellesini. This meant the extinction of
the normal school and for many years thereafter the
direction of all school affairs in Trent lay in the hands
of our Blessed Stephen.

With a change in State politics the Augustinians
were re-established. Foreseeing that the people of
Trent would be unwilling to let him go, Stephen, in
1817, went secretly to the superior-general of his
Order at Rome. Letter after letter followed from
friends in both lay and ecclesiastical authority urging
his return. But in vain. Then the city council threatened to banish him forever if he did not return at once.
And they did in fact succeed in having the Austrian
government exile him forever from Austria and in
having his birthright and all his honors and offices
declared forfeit. Such was their gratitude for the

wonderful amount of self-sacrificing labor which he had performed in their behalf.

But Bellesini was content to live in his beloved little cloister. His superiors entrusted him with the important office of novice-master. His brethren held him in the highest esteem for his saintly humility. While superior he was the servant of all. He was especially distinguished by his spirit of faith and his love of prayer. To act according to the principles of faith had become habitual in him. When no other duty called him, he devoted hours to prayer. Yet his was by no means a reserved character and he was universally known for his great and cheerful affability.

Since 1826, the novitiate had been at Gennazzano, the famous sanctuary of the Mother of Good Counsel. During the last ten years of his life, Bellesini had charge of the church and the parish which belonged to it. Here, too, he became all things to all and won the noble title of "Father of the Poor." Like the Good Shepherd, he gave his life for his sheep. About the beginning of 1840 there broke out a contagious sickness in Gennazzano. The zealous pastor hastened to every hovel where he could bring help or consolation. Heedless of an open wound he had, he caught the contagion. The announcement of impending death is wont to depress and frighten men and it startles one to read of what heartfelt and open joy the news brought to Bellesini. He predicted the day and hour of his death, the evening of Candlemas day, 1840. If before he had been regarded by the people as a saint, it was now more than ever, for he had fallen a victim of his vocation. Pius X declared him Blessed toward the end of 1904.

Blessed Didacus of Cadiz

3. The death of Blessed Didacus of Cadiz, Capuchin, on March 24, 1801, falls just within the nine-

teenth century.[42] He was born of an illustrious noble
family at Cadiz in 1743, and his full name was
Joseph Francis Lopez Caamagno Texeiro Ulloa de
Balcellar. His parents gave their child a most religious training. The boy Joseph hurried to church early
so as to be the first to serve Mass. At home, too, he
showed his love of prayer. His modesty and angelic
behavior made him beloved by all. But a heavy cross
lay on the brave boy's shoulders—he could make little
progress in his studies. His faith told him where to find
help and consolation. So he went very frequently to
the sacraments. When he applied for admission into
the Capuchin monastery he was refused because of his
deficiency in talent. His grief was unspeakable, but
he was not discouraged and he prayed as fervently
and studied as hard as he could.

At length his perseverance was rewarded. He had
acquired sufficient knowledge and was permitted to
enter the novitiate at Seville. Now, it was his want
of talent that made Father Didacus, for thus our Joseph
was now called, a saint. It impelled him to work constantly with all ardor and to put all his confidence in
God. His recompense was unalterable spiritual joy.
After his ordination he was appointed to preach in the
church of the Order. He declared his unfitness but
submitted his will to that of his superiors. His success surpassed all hope and Father Didacus was sent
to give missions to the people. His sermons were
simple but very stirring. Everyone wondered at the
great oratorical power of a man who had before seemed
so poorly gifted, and it was justly ascribed to his holiness.

By degrees the fame of Father Didacus spread
throughout all Spain. Men spoke of him even at the
Court. The crowds at his sermons were so great that
he was often obliged to preach in the open air, where
the people often listened to him for hours. At the end

he frequently had to be protected by strong men or the people would have torn his habit to shreds for relics. Bad theaters were closed after his missions, forbidden books were burned. He was loaded with honors by Pope Pius VI, by Charles III of Spain, and by many bishops and cities, but he always remained the humble Capuchin, traveled always on foot, wore an old plain habit and observed most strictly the rules of his Order. In the midst of his unwearying activity he was called to his eternal rest at Arunda on March 24, 1801. Before he died he made a touching address to his crucifix. He was beatified in 1904. New miracles taking place since then, the process of his canonization has been begun.

Blessed Leopold von Gaiche

4. At Spoleto on April 2, 1815, there died another great son of St. Francis, the Blessed Leopold von Gaiche, O.F.M.[43] Gaiche was born in the archdiocese of Perugia, where he spent his pious youth. It was a hard sacrifice for his parents when the excellent young man left them at the age of eighteen to lead a life of perfection in the Franciscan Order. In this same year died the great Franciscan missionary, St. Leonard of Port Maurice. The novice Leopold resolved to walk in the footsteps of this man. He kept his resolve.

After his ordination, he had to teach philosophy and theology for some years. This experience was afterward of service to him in his preaching. He traveled as a missionary through the whole of Umbria, his appearance and his eloquence making a very deep impression. In keeping with the subjects of his sermons he often wore a crown of thorns, or bore a cross, or lashed himself with a scourge.

He aroused the greatest enthusiasm by the first communion of the children, which he always placed at the end of the mission.

When the French Revolution drove all Franciscans from their cloisters, Father Leopold, who was then provincial, exhorted all to confidence in God and to perseverance. Because he would not take the oath demanded by the government he was often obliged to flee. But this did not frighten him and he went on with his mission work undismayed. Later he succeeded in gathering his dispersed brethren into a monastery near Spoleto. When death approached, the aged man desired to be placed on the floor, that he might die like his holy father, St. Francis. Leo XIII ranked Leopold von Gaiche among the blessed in 1893.

Blessed Francis Xavier Bianchi

5. Arpino is justly proud of its great son, Cicero. But though he won the applause of the whole world by his oratory, another son of Arpino merits much more the admiration of all by reason of his great holiness. Here was born the Blessed Francis Xavier Bianchi on December 3, 1743, and, as says the process of beatification, "rejoiced as a giant to run the course of perfection," *"perfectionis curriculum ut gigas emensus est in exultatione."*[44] He studied with the Barnabites and chose his vocation under the guidance of St. Alphonsus Liguori. He had to struggle much against the opposition of his parents before obtaining their consent to his entering among the Barnabites. After ordination in 1767, Bianchi was put to teach— first rhetoric and then philosophy. He already enjoyed a great reputation, was much beloved, and his advice was eagerly sought after by the people. Then came a special call of grace to forsake his dealings with the world, to give up science and to devote himself in solitude to prayer and to the meditation of things divine. For fourteen years he prepared himself for the grand apostolate he was afterward to practise at Naples. He had, so to speak, a magnetic power. Crowds ran to

him for help and advice in affairs both spiritual and material. All returned consoled, for heavenly wisdom flowed from his lips and his words gave back peace to the most unhappy. He saw into the future and into the secrets of souls and miraculous events accompanied his labors. Many eye-witnesses assert that in 1805 a lava stream was suddenly stopped by his prayer. Men jokingly said that if they had a Neri (black) at Rome, at Naples they had a Bianchi (white).

During the last years of his life Blessed Francis endured a dreadful affliction. His feet and legs were covered with horrible ulcers. He bore this not merely with patience, but with holy joy and an ardent desire to suffer even more, adding voluntary penance to his pains. During this time he could neither stand nor walk nor move himself, save that, marvelous as it surely was, he had always strength to say the Holy Mass. His apostolate was not interrupted by his sickness. The people came to his bed of pain to get consolation and instruction and they had the happiness of seeing a saint in suffering. On January 31, 1815, Francis Xavier Bianchi went to heaven. His beatification was decreed on January 22, 1893.

BLESSED CASPAR DEL BUFALO

6. The capital of Christendom has the happiness of seeing raised to its altars one of her sons of the nineteenth century, the Blessed Caspar del Bufalo, canon of St. Mark and founder of the Congregation of the Missionaries of the Precious Blood.[45] He was born on January 6, 1786, the son of the head cook of the Altieri Palace in Rome. The child being threatened with total blindness, his mother, strong in faith, brought her affliction to St. Francis Xavier and obtained an almost instant cure. This was the reason that Caspar preserved during his whole life a tender and trustful devotion to the Apostle of the Indies and

Japan, and always kept before his eyes the apostolic zeal of Xavier as an ideal which he strove with all his might to reach. He was one of those chosen souls who at the very dawn of reason consider all things in the light of faith and arrive early at maturity of virtue. His pious mother narrated to her beloved child the life of St. Aloysius in all its detail. It spurred the little boy to imitation. Where other children are fond of play, he sought enjoyment in prayer either at home or in the Gesù nearby. Though but a child, he scourged himself thrice in the week, wore a chain, observed certain days of fasting, and slept on the floor during the night between Thursday and Friday. Enlightened by grace, he was already aware of the necessity and the high reward of penance. After making his first communion at the age of eleven he received the Holy Eucharist three or four times each week and always at the altar of St. Francis Xavier in the Gesù, where he daily served Mass. He preached at home, repeating what he had heard at the church. It was his most heartfelt desire to go among the Turks with the hope of dying for the Faith.

Caspar del Bufalo studied at the Roman College, then conducted by secular priests. At fourteen he received the tonsure and soon obtained permission to instruct children in catechism, and occasionally to preach. All was going on well with him, he had become deacon when suddenly an indescribable anxiety came upon him concerning the dignity of the priesthood and he could not make up his mind what to do. But the Venerable Vincent Strambi banished the uneasiness of his delicate conscience and on July 31, 1808, he was ordained. He became canon at St. Mark's and entered at once into the labors of an apostle.

Meanwhile, Napoleon ordered Pius VII to be led away a captive and demanded from priests the oath on the Constitution which annexed the Papal States to France. Del Bufalo, of course, remained faithful to the head of the Church and was therefore exiled to Piacenza and thence to Bologna.

Two years after, in 1812, he was imprisoned in San Giovanni in Monte for having persevered in refusing the oath. Twice his prison was changed and at last he was listed for transportation to Corsica, when Heaven's chastisement overtook Napoleon. In spite of the many and severe sufferings of those years it always remained a sweet memory to Blessed Caspar that he had endured banishment and prisons for Christ.

On August 7, 1814, Pius VII restored the Society of Jesus. The former members of the Order yet living gathered gladly under the banner of St. Ignatius, overjoyed to have lived until this happy day. Caspar del Bufalo had grown up in the shadow of the Gesú and was most intimate with the old Jesuit fathers. Francis Xavier was his ideal. No wonder then that he soon formed the resolution to enter the Order. He had already been received along with Prince Charles Odescalchi when Pius VII sent for the two good priests and ordered Odescalchi to take up the career of a prelate, while Del Bufalo, who had high repute as a successful preacher, was to devote himself at once to missions among the people. To preach Christ to the world was exactly what the canon of St. Mark's most desired, and now that the Vicar of Christ had chosen him for this office it was to him the will of God. Nor did Pius VII fail in choosing the right man. Del Bufalo's preaching had mighty results. He was a man of no extraordinary oratorical gifts, his language and thought being as plain as possible, and at school he did not rise above mediocrity. But it was the tremendous earnestness, the profound conviction with which he spoke and, at the same time his gentleness, his unction, that laid hold of his hearers. The

Venerable Strambi called his preaching "a spiritual earthquake." A gray old sinner avowed after confession that of the whole sermon he had understood only one word: "Paradise," but that the ardor, gesture, and voice of Del Bufalo thrilled his heart.

His repute for sanctity contributed much to this success. His untiring zeal, his love of prayer, and his ardent devotion during the Holy Mass could not be hidden—much less could he hide the gift of miracles that God had given him. He made extraordinary conversions and foretold future events. His biographer cites witnesses who saw him in different places at the same time.

From the first, Del Bufalo had several priests working with him. There occurred to them spontaneously the idea of forming a Congregation. They took the name of "Missionaries of the Most Precious Blood." They desired by promoting devotion to the Most Precious Blood to excite a greater appreciation of the grace of redemption. The Church owes the Feast of the Precious Blood to the suggestion of Del Bufalo. Pius VII was very favorable to the young society. They soon opened many houses and the great missionary activity of their founder brought them a high reputation. But everything good must have its trials. Leo XII had been misinformed and was little inclined toward the Society. When Del Bufalo had his first audience, however, the condition of affairs changed. "I found him an angel," declared the Pope afterward. Nor did Pius VIII show himself agreeable to the plan of the new Congregation. These were hard days for the Servant of God. It also hindered his external activities. He employed this leisure in perfecting his subjects and in consolidating the spirit of the young society. Only under Gregory XVI did things change permanently for the better.

With the co-operation of Del Bufalo, the Venerable

Maria de Mattias founded a branch of the Congregation for women—"Sisters of the Adoration of the Precious Blood." Both Congregations have proved vigorous and have spread beyond Italy into the United States.

The health of Blessed Caspar had always been feeble. No one was surprised, therefore, when, on December 28, 1837, he succumbed to the hardships of his apostolic life when only fifty-seven years of age. Heaven immediately began to manifest the sanctity of the deceased by miracles. In 1904, Pius X declared him Blessed.

BLESSED GABRIEL OF THE MOTHER OF SORROWS

7. Saintly youths are a great joy to the Church. Prominent among those of the nineteenth century is the Blessed Gabriel of the Mother of Sorrows, a member of the Congregation of the Passion.[46] Leo XIII used to call him "the St. Aloysius of our days." His family name was Francis Posenti. His father was a well-to-do civil official of renowned Assisi in Umbria. Here Francis was born on March 1, 1838, the eleventh of thirteen children. To facilitate the higher education of his children, the father moved to Spoleto in 1842. Unfortunately, however, the mother died soon after. But the father was a deeply religious man. He spent an hour in prayer every morning and then went to Mass, bringing the children with him. Every night he questioned his children to learn where they had been that day and what they had done, then he said prayers in common, always adding some instruction and admonition. What he most insisted on was the avoidance of bad companions.

Francis received his elementary training from the Brothers of St. John Baptist de la Salle, and made his higher studies in the college of the Society of Jesus at Spoleto. From his early years he showed generosity and self-control, he was docile and obedient and had a great liking for spiritual things. But his character had also some dangerous leanings. He was very impulsive and inclined to anger. It was not bad will, however, and whenever his temper carried him away, at once there came repentance and each time he humbly asked his father's forgiveness. Another tendency might have been still more dangerous. He made rapid progress in his studies, was proficient in all branches and won great applause when he appeared in public. Besides, he had agreeable manners and a cheerful temperament, so that he was beloved by all and was known only as "the genial Francis." All this tended to foster his vanity and to end in a desire of pleasing men. Shoes, clothes, cravat, the cut of his hair had all to be of the latest fashion. He eagerly sought after lively and witty society, and delighted in novel-reading, hunting, and theater-going. In the latter he was always accompanied by his father and in all there had been nothing that passed the bounds of innocence. His particular delight was in dancing, and every one knew this. So when he unexpectedly entered the cloister, his professor announced the news to his classmates with the words: "Have you heard what has happened to the young dancer? Who would have thought it: He has left all and has entered the novitiate of the Passionists." In spite of his inclination toward vanities, however, he had avoided bad companions on principle, and if any one dared utter an immodest word in his presence he was sure to get from Francis a sharp reproof. Still there is little doubt that in course of time the siren song of the world would have proved dangerous to him.

Francis had fallen sick and feared that he was going to die. He prayed fervently for health and promised to consecrate his life to God in a Religious Order. His prayer was heard, but it did not occur to his mind that he must fulfil his promise. A second time God cast

him upon the sick-bed and a serious malady of the
throat brought him near to death. In his distress he
called on the martyr Andrew Bobola, S.J., who had
just been beatified, renewing his promise to become a
Religious. Again he was healed, this time consulting
his confessor on the execution of his promise. But
he kept putting the matter off and fell once more into
the vanities of the world, although they now no longer
left him at ease in conscience. Then, while hunting,
he was dangerously wounded. Within a few days
death robbed him of his dearest sister. This seemed
to end his wavering and he made known his promise
to his father. The latter, however, could not believe
that his son was destined for the cloister and tried to
drive the thought out of his head by engaging him in
visits to the theater and in evening parties, and by
expressing his desire that Francis should think of
marrying a girl of respectable family.

At this moment the Blessed Virgin interposed. On
the octave of the Assumption there is carried in solemn
procession through the cathedral of Spoleto an ancient
and much venerated picture of Mary. When it passed
Francis it seemed to him that the Blessed Mother
looked sharply at him while an interior voice spoke
distinctly: "You know that you are not made for the
world. Why, then, do you still remain in it? Enter
soon into some Religious Order." He was conquered
and hid in a corner of the church to conceal his excitement and his tears. His confessor, Charles Bompiani,
S.J., to whom he revealed his secret, approved the genuineness of his vocation and his intention of joining
the Passionists. But Francis said nothing of his interior change to his friends.

At length, on September 10, 1856, he arrived at the
novitiate of Morovalle, near Macerata. What had happened to St. Aloysius now happened to him. As soon
as he crossed the threshold of the cloister he was over-

whelmed with a flood of joy, convinced that he was now in the place where his soul would find rest. On the feast of the Mother of Sorrows, the third Sunday in September, he was given the habit of the Order and the name, Gabriel of the Mother of Sorrows. He now wrote to his friends, taking leave of them and begging pardon for not having given them a better example. His separation from the world was now complete. He would work at his own perfection and the things of the world could no longer have interest for him. In return for this complete surrender God granted him such fulness of consolation and enlightenment that the empty joys of this world became a disgust to him. This great contempt he had conceived for the world excited the wonder of all. To his father, who had expressed some fear for his perseverance, he wrote: "It is impossible to desert so lovable a lord as Jesus Christ and so loving a lady as Mary." It would be a mistake to think, however, that our cheerful young man had suddenly become pessimistic and melancholy. The serenity of his soul had in reality become far more pure and undisturbed. He had found all that his noble mind could long for. The charm of his genial, friendly character had a kindly influence on his brethren and on all who met him. Strangers who had made their retreat in the monastery, frequently would not leave without a talk with the friendly Gabriel. Young people asked for entrance into the religious state on the ground that they had seen a young religious from whose countenance there shone a heavenly gladness. Whenever Gabriel met with boys, he conversed in a friendly way with them and skilfully mingled with his talk some pious exhortation. After a year of noviceship he made his religious vows with a joyous heart.

The young religious made his philosophical and theological studies in Pievetorina and in Isola, near Penne. His religious fervor never relaxed but continually increased. He was not without trials, however. God permitted him to suffer violent temptations against faith and confidence and he experienced a great dryness in prayer. But his firmness remained unshaken during such assaults, his virtue struck only deeper root and soon heavenly consolations came again in manifold ways. "Meditation," says his director, "always so kindled his fervor, that he would have done many things injurious to his health if he had not been so obedient and I had not carefully watched over him. I had no reason to urge him to virtue; on the contrary, I had often to moderate him. During the last days of his life I was obliged to forbid him the usual meditation because he would become so absorbed in the eternal truths that it was an effective hindrance to his health." Love of the Crucified Saviour, of the Sacred Heart of Jesus, and of the Blessed Virgin were his chief virtues.

While Gabriel's years of study were coming to their close, so, too, his earthly pilgrimage was nearing its end. When he was twenty-three years of age he was stricken with consumption. His strength rapidly declined and February 27, 1862, he died a holy death at Isola. His last words were to the Blessed Virgin. Remarkable miracles occurred at his tomb. The deaf, dumb, blind, and lame were cured in so surprising a way that the like is hardly to be found in the records of the saints. The decree of his beatification declares that "the miracles which glorified the beginnings of the Church one could behold renewed at his grave." At the beatification, which took place on May 31, 1908, a brother of the Beatified was present. Since then the miracles at the grave of Blessed Gabriel have not ceased and application for his canonization has already been made. May he be a mighty protector of our youth, whose faith and morals are exposed to gravest dangers!

Blessed Ægidius of St. Joseph

8. A childlike and humble piety adorned Blessed Ægidius of St. Joseph, a lay-brother of the Alcantarines at Naples.[47]   Love of God is not genuine without true love of the neighbor.   Blessed Ægidius did all that his station permitted to relieve the social distress of the lower classes.   He made it his aim to collect large alms for the poor and men gave freely to him because they knew how unselfishly he distributed their gifts. He died on February 7, 1812, and was declared Blessed in 1888.

Henry Thyssen

9. The Servant of God Henry Thyssen, whose process of beatification is in progress, was a member of the Order of St. Francis.[48]   He was a son of the Rhineland and was born in the small town of Gangelt in the district of Geilenkirchen on December 5, 1755. His parents were of the common people, his father being sexton of the parish church.   Henry was marked in his earliest years by his piety, shown particularly in his behavior at church.   Seeing in this a sign that God called him to the priesthood, his parents determined to permit him to study.

Not far from Gangelt is the little Dutch town of Sittard, where a Latin school, conducted by the Dominicans, offered the youth of the country around a convenient opportunity for study.*   Young Thyssen lived with a family who were acquainted with his parents, going home for Sundays.   It is said that he became one of the best in the school both for virtue and piety and for progress in studies.   He was especially distinguished for his mastery of Latin.   Among his schoolmates he was much beloved on account of his cheerful and sociable character.

*The present St. Aloysius College, under the direction of German Jesuits.

After completing his classics in 1775, Thyssen asked admission into the Franciscan Order. He made his novitiate at Erkelenz. This was a period of the greatest happiness to him and the fervor with which he gave himself to prayer and to all kinds of mortification really needed restraint. Experience proved how solid was the foundation of his virtue.

The novitiate lasted a year and then Henry made his philosophical and theological studies at Louvain. While here he conceived a desire for the heathen missions. But Europe was to give him all the privations of heathen lands and to send him souls in plenty to be gained for Christ.

After ordination to the priesthood in 1780, Father Thyssen was at first employed in the monastery of Herenthals. Two years later the confidence of his superiors called him to lecture on theology at Antwerp. He also gave great assistance in the care of souls, for which a particular opportunity was given him in the arrival of German troops when Belgium revolted against the supremacy of Austria.

Soon the French Revolution triumphantly invaded Belgium. The first assault was aimed at the monasteries. In January, 1797, the Franciscans of the monastery at Antwerp were dispersed by the French soldiers. Father Thyssen found a hiding-place in the house of a friendly family. The cellar was turned into a chapel and here many regularly gathered for the reception of the sacraments. The revolutionists made efforts to discover the servant of God, but the angel of God watched over him. Once, while Father Thyssen was bringing the Holy Viaticum in a large milk-can to a dying man he was stopped by the police and asked whether he knew where Father Thyssen was. He replied fearlessly, "Oh yes. I think you can see him at the end of the street," and the servants of the law hurried on full of hope to find their victim.

Two years afterward priests could appear again in public at Antwerp. The house of the Franciscans had been destroyed, but a pious lady placed her house at their disposal and a few of the fathers at least could live here together. They distributed themselves among the various churches of the city to re-establish the kingdom of God. Father Thyssen labored with some of the old members of the suppressed Society of Jesus at the church of St. Charles, which had formerly belonged to the Society. Here he remained till the end of his life. His heart's desire to endure suffering and hardships for Christ was abundantly gratified.

His labors were crowned with the greatest success. His life reads like that of St. Philip Neri. In his preaching and in the confessional he was a masterly director of souls. He went out into the city to find and arouse the negligent and to bring consolation and alms to the poor. He paid particular attention to prisoners and to soldiers and sailors. He might often be seen leading sailors from the docks to St. Charles to hear their confessions. Again he would be surrounded by a crowd of children, whom he instructed in the truths of salvation. The fervor of his love of God showed on every occasion. Whenever God was spoken of his eyes filled with tears. "The father who weeps during the sermon" he was called throughout the city. At Holy Mass his emotion was so great that the sacred vestments were moistened with his tears, and when he arrived at the Canon he was obliged to force himself to proceed. After Mass he had to go out into the open air to cool his heart, and this was the case even in the winter. While meditating on heavenly things he was frequently so absorbed that he did not know what was going on about him. The miracles related of him are very numerous. When he died, on March 31, 1844, people immediately began to invoke him in all their necessities and his compassionate heart gave prompt answer to their prayers.

Louis of Casoria

10. An amiable character that must win all hearts shines forth in the Servant of God, Louis of Casoria, a true son of St. Francis.[49] He was born on March 11, 1814, the son of a vine-dresser. His family name was Palmentieri, but in religion he was called Louis of Casoria, from his birthplace, Casoria, near Naples. To use all his powers in relieving the corporal and spiritual misery of mankind was the guiding motive of his life. Those that place their hopes in God, who bestows His grace according to the measure of our confidence in Him, are made ingenious and enterprising by their love. Louis at once inspired the members of the third Order with efficient love of the neighbor. With their assistance he bought, near Naples, a fine house suited to the sick poor.

Two negro boys were given him to educate. The good results he had with them suggested to him the plan of civilizing Africa through the Africans. In a few years he had gathered together sixty negro boys, who received the benefit of a Christian training. But there were also in Naples very many abandoned children. For these he founded two asylums. In the "Deserto" near Sorrento, he built a hospital for old people, sailors, and fishermen, and also a hospice where penniless strangers might be admitted. Florence is indebted to him for an asylum for poor children and a church of the Sacred Heart, for which he obtained 70,000 lire by begging. In Assisi his ardent zeal obtained means for a home of the deaf, the dumb, and the blind. As long as there was misery on earth there was no rest for him. His confidence in God grew only the greater. Although he had only fifty centimes at the time, he bought an orphanage at Naples in 1872 for 110,000 lire. Finally he bought a ruined palace in Posilipo, near the sea, to serve as a house for sea-folk and as a sanitarium for priests and students. The money for this enterprise and for his other remarkable charities he obtained often in miraculous ways. He also did much for the promotion of knowledge, was a great patron of music, and founded the periodical "La Carita." Besides, he established many religious societies—"The Gray Brothers" (Zigi), the "Elizabethines" ("The Servants of the Heart of Jesus"), who, under the rules of the third Order of St. Francis, devoted themselves to works of charity.[50]

There has been seldom a death so mourned as that of Louis of Casoria. He died on March 30, 1884. In his beautiful last testament he says: "Divine love was my poverty, my obedience, my chastity. The holy vows did not compel me to serve God, but the love of Jesus moved my heart and made my soul, my hands and feet His servants. To enkindle my love I asked God, not for raptures and visions, but for labor, works of charity, and for souls. In my prayers I implored zeal for labor, divine love in labor and distress, in cares and contradictions and I often cried, 'Oh Charity, oh, to die for Charity!' My dear brethren . . . I commend to you the Holy Catholic Church. Strive for her by word and writing and by deeds, and if need be even with your blood. Stand firm, humble, and lowly at the feet of the Holy See. Harken to the Church as you would to the voice of God Himself. Observe her commands, her very thoughts. The Church of Christ is the authority of all authorities. She alone has peace and happiness in her train. All other authority which does not work in union with her and does not listen to her is without life, since it does not labor toward the last end of our creation and for the saving of souls redeemed by Jesus. Live in peace and pray for me. Your poor brother, Louis of Casoria."

Venerable Francis Mangano

11. The various branches of the Franciscan Order can glory in their great number of saintly men in the nineteenth centry. Among these is the Venerable Francis Mangano of the Order of Minorites at Naples.[51] He entered the Order in 1779 at the age of sixteen. Though his talent for study was not great, his untiring diligence enabled him to acquire much solid learning. Two years after his elevation to the priesthood he was appointed novice-master, and later became spiritual director of the Clerics of the Order. He obtained considerable fame in the city as a preacher and confessor. He was of great service to his Order in the restoration of discipline, after the great disturbances at the beginning of the century. He died on December 31, 1841. During the last ten years of his life he was crippled as the result of an apoplectic stroke. He had much to suffer, partly—God permitting it—from his own brethren. This was afterward adduced in praise of his constant and great serenity. The miracles after his death were very numerous.

Venerable Dominic Anthony Galli

12. The Venerable Dominic Anthony Galli belonged to the Capuchins.[52] He was a Roman by birth and died on October 27, 1813. His chief work was the giving of missions, especially in the Campagna and in Latium. The Acts of the process recount many supernatural gifts which he possessed during life.

Venerable Francis of Ghisone

13. The Venerable Francis Mucchielli, commonly called Francis of Ghisone, after his birthplace, was of Corsican ancestry.[53] After the early death of his mother, the boy was sent to his uncle at Rome, where he learned the trade of a joiner. But a desire for the religious state soon awoke in him and his joy was great

when he was received among the Franciscans at Civitella. After taking his vows he was sent by his superiors to study, but when he was to be promoted to the priesthood he asked in his humility to be permitted to remain a lay-brother. Heaven proved the sincerity of his petition, for soon after he was stricken with epilepsy, which never left him till his death, making his life a true martyrdom. In spite of it he carried his zeal for penance so far as to chastise his sick body in almost every possible manner. His humility, patience, and cheerfulness in suffering made him a blessing to his community. His death occurred in 1832. In 1898 the Congregation of Rites published the decree acknowledging the heroic degree of his virtue.

Venerable Marianus of Rocca Casale

14. In the same monastery of Civitella lived and died another holy lay-brother, the Venerable Marianus of Rocca Casale near Sulmone.[54] He first joined the Franciscans of the province of Abruzzi, but at his request was sent to the novitiate of the Roman province at Civitella. Here he was porter for nearly fifty years. He died at the age of eighty-eight on the Feast of the Sacred Heart, May 31, 1886.

Venerable Francis Croese

15. The Venerable Francis Croese of Camporosso, near Genoa,[55] was first a tertiary of the Conventuals, but after two years entered among the Capuchins. With the exception of his novitiate he spent the whole of his religious life in the monastery of the Immaculate Conception at Genoa. The first seven years found him working in the kitchen and in the garden. Then he was appointed alms-gatherer. In this office he found many opportunities for the exercise of his zeal. He exhorted to the reception of the sacraments. Where

he noticed that on account of the poverty of the family the morals of the children were endangered he took care to procure them assistance. He helped poor but talented boys to study. Very frequently he was to be seen at the harbor, exhorting the sailors to a good life. But he did all this with such discretion and amiability that he was gladly welcomed. In all Genoa he was known only as "the Saint." Many, even distinguished and wealthy citizens, came to him for advice. His great love of prayer was long spoken of, and it is said that he spent whole nights in prayer. His greatest delight was to serve many Masses. For twenty-four years the penance-loving brother slept on the bare floor. To be contemned by others he esteemed the greatest grace. He jokingly called himself "only a tethered ass." When the plague broke out in Genoa in 1866, he offered his life to God for the city. He was seized with the sickness and died on October 17, but the plague ceased. The whole city mourned his loss. The newspapers of all shades of opinion gave accounts of his glorious end.

Magin Catalá

16. The Spanish Franciscan, Magin Catalá, had great repute for sanctity in California.[56] He remained continually at work in the mission of Santa Clara from 1794 until his death on November 22, 1830. He was almost constantly afflicted with grievous rheumatic pains, and during the last years of his life could neither stand nor walk without another's help. Nevertheless, he visited the sick and preached while seated at the communion-rail. Nor would he lay aside the practices of penance with which he afflicted his body while he lived. The fame of his miracles and prophecies spread far and wide. He is said to have predicted the great earthquake which wrecked San Francisco on April 18,

1906.[57]   Archbishop J. S. Alemany began the process of the Servant of God in 1894.

Venerable Benvenuto Bambozzi

17. The Venerable Benvenuto Bambozzi was a member of the Conventuals.[58]   He died, aged sixty-six, on March 24, 1875, at his birthplace, Osimo, in the county of Ancona, where he long served his Order as novice-master.   A severe trial for him was the closing of his monastery by the Italian government.

Father Valentin Paquay

18. There lived and worked for fifty years at Hasselt, the chief city of the Belgian province of Limburg, a Franciscan father known far and wide among the people as "the holy father of Hasselt."[59]   A Catholic people sometimes show a remarkable intuition which reverently anticipates the decision of Rome.   So it was in the case of Father Valentin Paquay, O.F.M.   The people had long canonized their beloved "holy father" and the Church with her usual rigorous exactness has approved the life and virtues of this great son of St. Francis, thus ratifying the judgment of the people.

Father Paquay sprang from a pious Flemish family at Tongern, and after completing his classics joined the Franciscans in 1849. Shortly after his ordination in 1854, he was sent to Hasselt, and here remained, except for a single year, until his death, on January 1, 1905.

How great is the attraction of a holy example is clearly shown in this man.   In early youth, Father Paquay had chosen for his patron his countryman, St. John Berchmans, whom he sought to emulate in everything and to whom he always clung with the most tender devotion.   In the confessional and in his conversation he always managed to refer to his "little Berchmans."   Whenever he went to Louvain he hastened to the altar in the Jesuit church where the heart of St. Berchmans was enshrined and spent here a long time in prayer. "Oh," he declared, "I could stay here the whole day." He sanctified himself, as did his model, by the strictest observance of the rules of his Order, doing only what was ordinary but not in an ordinary manner.

Father Paquay achieved his greatest reputation by the prudent direction of souls in the confessional. So, after a few years the citizens of Hasselt depended so much on him, that his superiors, who had stationed him elsewhere, were stormed with petitions by them until their "holy father" was back in their midst. He must have spent the greater part of his life in the confessional. He could hardly find time for his Breviary and for meals. Especially on evenings before Sundays and feast-days, great crowds besieged his confessional. What was the secret of this attraction? They ascribed to the father an extraordinary knowledge of the human heart and the rare gift of setting aright with a few words the unhappy and the discouraged. By reason of this work, he justly belongs, says an Antwerp newspaper ("La Presse," February 9, 1911), among the great social reformers of our time and has done the same service as the ancient saints who by their apostolic zeal won heathen peoples to the Faith.

The most interesting chapter of Father Paquay's life is that which deals with his richly blessed success in the confessional. Besides this, he had to answer numberless requests for advice from high and low. Catholics have a remarkable confidence in the saints.

When the apostle of Belgian Limburg died on January 1, 1905, he was seventy-six years of age. His body was exposed for public honor and for two days a continuous stream of people passed to gaze for the last time on the countenance of the beloved priest and to beg his intercession. A committee was soon formed to erect a monument to the father in the cemetery. The unveiling of this was another grand demonstration for the poor son of St. Francis. The monument fittingly represents him with his hand raised in absolution. He is the beloved of his countrymen and has already obtained renown as a worker of miracles.

Other Franciscans

19. It will be sufficient here merely to mention the names of others of the great family of St. Francis, for whose elevation to the altar steps have already been taken: Venerable Simon Philippovic (d. 1802); Venerable Aloysius a Ssmo Crucifixo (d. 1803); Venerable Modestinus a Jesu et Maria (d. 1854); Paul of Recanati (d. 1842); Francis of Collodio (d. 1863); Michael Angelo Longo (d. 1886); Peter Lopez (d. 1898); Lay-brother Joseph Giraldi (d. 1899); Lay-brother Andrew Philameno Garcia, who died in 1853 at Santiago, Chile. To the Capuchins belong: Venerable Gesualdo di Reggio (d. 1803), a successful preacher and writer;[60] Venerable Francis a Laculibero (d. 1804); Charles of Abbiatecrasso)d. 1859); and the novice Joseph of Palmero (d. 1886).

Venerable John B. Muard

20. A new flower of sanctity in the ancient Benedictine Order is the Venerable John B. Muard.[61] The boyhood of the Servant of God was full of hardships. He was the son of poor parents who could scarcely afford him any education. Luckily his pious grandmother was still living and there was in his birthplace —Vireaux, Diocese of Sens—a zealous pastor who took the boy into his house and gave him his first lessons in Latin. Muard then pursued his studies in Auxerre and in Sens and was ordained priest on May 24, 1834. He displayed the greatest zeal in the salvation of souls. "Souls, O Lord, first many souls, and

then at last, to heaven," was his frequent prayer. This fervent love aroused in him a glowing devotion to the Sacred Heart of Jesus. In the sanctuary, the confessional, in private conversation, and in his letters he urged with irresistible persuasiveness the veneration of the Heart of the Saviour as the best antidote against religious coldness and sloth. "You can hardly believe," he wrote to a friend, "how much I rejoice when I hear of Christians who practise this devotion. What can please me more than meeting souls who love our sweetest Master and Saviour and especially His Sacred Heart." One day, while he was deep in prayer before the tabernacle, it seemed to him that the Saviour stood before him and bade him devote himself to the giving of missions. To make sure that imagination was not deceiving him he asked, as proof of the reality of the vision, the conversion of the six worst sinners of his parish, and that same evening he found all six at the tribunal of penance. After overcoming many obstacles Muard was able to follow the manifest will of God. Later he founded a society of mission priests who followed substantially the rule of St. Benedict and were called *"Benedictins-predicateurs"* (Benedictine Preachers). They were afterward formally incorporated with the Benedictines of Monte Cassino. Muard received the heavenly reward of his holy life in 1854. He was forty-five years of age. His noble motto was: "For the greater glory of God, for the salvation of souls, for my own humiliation."

VENERABLE JOSEPH MARY PIGNATELLI

21. Among the former Jesuits who were so happy as to live until the partial or even until the complete restoration of the Society of Jesus, the Venerable Joseph Mary Pignatelli is pre-eminent.[62] The decree of the Congregation of Rites inaugurating his process says: "He had become like to St. Ignatius, the founder

of the Society of Jesus, had inherited the spirit of St. Ignatius and distinguished himself by so many and so great examples of virtue that it can truly be said Divine Providence gave him to the Society afflicted by many and grievous adversities for its protection and comfort and kept him, in spite of continual ill-health, to gray old age so that in later days he might be to the survivors an example of the original and genuine spirit."

It seems, in fact, the providential mission of Father Pignatelli to have carried over into the new Society, as he had lived in the old, the true and genuine spirit of St. Ignatius. His biographer writes:[63] "Father Joseph M. Pignatelli belonged to the number of those poor and proscribed orphans who even unto death were loyal to their mother, to their spirit and to their virtues and traditions and held fast to the service of God and of His Church. In spite of proscription and exile he persevered for twenty-five years in the practices of his religious life. And when Pius VII issued his call to the sons of St. Ignatius, to raise again the banners of their forefathers and to engage in new combats, Father Pignatelli was one of those who hastened to enlist again before they died, under the standard of the Society of Jesus and to take up again the yoke of religious life which the long years of exile made only the sweeter. In the new generation of the sons of St. Ignatius he resembles those venerable ancestors who had nothing more at heart than to leave their posterity the customs, manners, and practices of their forefathers. Father Pignatelli embraces in his person both the old and the new Society. He is like a precious link in the chain of religious life binding the traditions of the past to the future. With love and reverence the young Jesuits gathered around the venerable old man who bore on his meek countenance the stamp of his long and weary trials and had given to his Order as a simple son of obedience his service and his homage along with the priceless treasure of his experience."

When Pignatelli, a boy of fifteen, entered the novitiate of Tarragona in 1753, the storm of bitter persecution against the Society of Jesus had already broken out. He renounced the prospect of a splendid career in the world and all the advantages and comforts of a distinguished and wealthy noble family. His father was Count Anthony Pignatelli of Fuentos, of the house of the dukes of Monte Leone, one of the first Spanish families of the time. His nearest relatives—his parents were already dead—used every persuasion to keep Joseph from following his religious vocation, but he withstood all their objections. "I consider myself fortunate in following a vocation that gives an opportunity to suffer something for God. I leave the care of my health to Divine Providence. I am ready to shed my blood for the salvation of souls and for the defense of the Holy Catholic Church."

In religion Pignatelli found all he had desired. Study and meditation on the person and life of Our Divine Redeemer filled his heart with unspeakable joy and a solid enthusiasm for his vocation. He showed himself magnanimous in everything. In fact, his superiors found it necessary to moderate his desire for mortification and study. He wrote a moving letter to Father General Lorenzo Ricci, petitioning to be sent to the foreign missions. The Father General gave the prophetic answer that he believed Pignatelli could best serve the Church and his Order in Europe. In the novitiate and the scholasticate the happy religious noticed little of the storms that were raging against his beloved Society. After finishing his studies he was for three years a professor in the College of Saragossa. But in 1767, in consequence of infamous calumnies, there came the banishment of all Jesuits from the Spanish dominions. For Joseph Pignatelli and his brother Nicholas, who had also joined the Order, their relatives obtained an exception from the decree of banishment, but both declared that they would not be separated from their brethren. Six hundred members of the Jesuit province of Aragon were, with unspeakable suffering and privations, transported in thirteen small and crowded vessels to Corsica, which then belonged to the republic of Genoa. The proscribed Religious were assigned to St. Boniface for their residence. There were absolutely no preparations for the reception and stay of so many strangers, and they were without the necessary means of subsistence. The chief support of the provincial during these painful days was Father Joseph Pignatelli, who provided for the lodging, food, and occupation of the poor exiles and did everything to keep them from depression and sadness. In particular he looked after the younger members and managed as far as was possible to enable them to pursue their studies.

They had scarcely begun to put things in a sort of order when a new decree of banishment was issued. Corsica was acquired by France in 1768, and this country had long before ordered the Jesuits from its possessions. In a few days about 2400 Spanish Jesuits were landed in Genoa, but this city refused to receive them. The exiled religious now bent their steps to the Papal States. Ferrara was the journey's end for the members of the Aragonese province. The prudence and kindness of Father Pignatelli won the good will of the citizens of Ferrara for the sorely tried Jesuits, who were at least relieved from the bitterest want. The Pignatelli family frequently tried to persuade the brothers to leave the Order, even offering to use their influence to have the Pope release them from their vows. But neither wavered a moment, and for Joseph it was the greatest happiness when on Feb-

ruary 2, 1771, he was bound most intimately to his
Order by the solemn vows.

But the flood of suffering was not yet full. On July
21, 1773, Pope Clement XIV, yielding to the insistence
and threats of the Bourbon Courts, gave way to force
and signed the decree suppressing the Society of Jesus.
How bitter this cup of sorrow, how heavy this grief
for the stricken fathers is beyond words to tell. Only
one who has been bereaved of the dearest and most
beloved, who finds all the ideals which inflamed his
heart made nought at one blow, can understand. But
as their Master, so died the Society of Jesus—"obedient unto death." Without a word of complaint or dis-
approbation they bowed to the will of the Vicar of
Christ.

Father Pignatelli went back with his brother to
Bologna. As far as possible he maintained the old
manner of life. Prayer and study were at first his
only occupations, since it was not considered expedient
at the time that former Jesuits should engage in the
care of souls. By degrees he acquired a considerable
library. He attended lectures at the University and
thus endeavored to extend and deepen his many-sided
learning. The saints are always apostles. This truth
was manifest in the character of Pignatelli. In private
conversation the influence of his word and example
was the greater since it evidently proceeded from inner
conviction and not from any desire of earthly reward.
He was an angel of charity to his old companions,
many of whom had fallen into extreme want.

One day there came joyful tidings to him. In distant Russia, it was said, there existed a branch of the
Society of Jesus. He at once resolved to journey
thither. But he began to doubt whether the Society
of Jesus in Russia had a right to exist. To settle this
he went to Rome to obtain information from the Pope
himself. Pius VI answered, 'Yes, it exists . . . and

it is not because of me that it does not spread throughout the whole world. I am in complete understanding
with it. Go to Russia. I give you full power without
fear that the habit of the Society will again be taken
away. I have considered the Jesuits in Russia as true
Jesuits and the Society of Jesus which exists in Russia
as existing there by right."

But when Pignatelli was preparing for departure
his health broke down. It was reaction after all the
hardships and sufferings he had borne for long years.
He was obliged to be patient. Meanwhile Duke Ferdinand of Parma asked Catherine II to permit some Jesuits to come to his states. The vice-general, Father Gabriel Lenkiewicz, sent three fathers. They were obliged
to proceed slowly and prudently, lest the old hatred
against the Society, still glowing under the ashes,
should be kindled anew. After the principal arrange-
ments had been completed, Father Pignatelli received
an invitation to join the fathers. Seldom can news
excite such joy in the heart as this offer did in his. He
could scarcely await the hour when he would again
be united with his well beloved Society. On July 6,
1797, he was able at last to renew his vows at Parma.
His spirit and strength were rejuvenated. His activity, rich in blessing, soon gave the young Society great
reputation. When in 1799 it could venture to open a
novitiate at Colorno, Pignatelli was appointed first
novice-master. He, if any man, possessed the necessary prudence and experience in spiritual matters and
the love for his vocation which is required in so important an office. In him was embodied the spirit of the
Institute of St. Ignatius. The novitiate of Colorno soon
resembled the ideal novitiate of San Andrea in Rome.
The Servant of God endeavored to enliven not merely
the novices but all Colorno and the region about it with
spiritual and corporal good works. The Duke of
Parma called him only his "saint." His sublime exam-

ple of virtue, especially hns unbounded confidence in God, which was often rewarded in miraculous ways, justified this mark of veneration.

Pignatelli was appointed provincial in 1803. In the following year he made a journey to Naples. Here he successfully negotiated with King Ferdinand concerning the admission of the Society into that city and the happy result was approved by Pius VII. There was great joy among the people of Naples when the sons of St. Ignatius came back to them. Former Jesuits hastened from all quarters of Italy and asked admission. But some of these were from the dukedom of Parma, for the French were there again, and had expelled them. It was a trying labor for the provincial to organize a new province so speedily in those troubled times. His chief care was to establish from the outset the true religious spirit in every house. The people clung to the fathers with love and enthusiasm. The college at Naples soon numbered over 1200 students. Again it was Pignatelli who by his example excited his subjects to imitation, and won admiration from the people.

But after two years the French came down on Naples also and expelled the Jesuits. Pignatelli went to Rome to find here a refuge for his brethren. In spite of the objections of the diplomatic corps, Pius VII opened the gates of the Eternal City to the refugees and restored to them the Roman College and the professed house at the Gesù. The bishops and the people soon manifested such a desire for the fathers that Pignatelli could not possibly accommodate all. Many cares pressed heavily on the provincial, especially the matter of temporal support for the Order. But Providence never deserted him. He expended large sums on the poor outside. His friends could not explain it except by supposing that money was miraculously multiplied in his hands. Pignatelli's character won for

him the sympathy of both high and low.   Pius VII
wished to raise him to the purple, but the friends of
the father took pains to dissuade the Pope from a step
which would make the humble servant of God altogether unhappy.   It is inspiring to read how, in spite
of his many occupations, he preserved continual intercourse with God and how great were his mortification,
detachment and love of poverty.   He could not bear
to be praised, sincerely considering himself to be the
least and most unworthy of all the sons of St. Ignatius.
Seldom do we meet with a sanctity so evident as is
manifest in his life.   The restored Society of Jesus can
never be sufficiently grateful to him.

During his scholasticate, Pignatelli suffered a hem-
horrhage, and during his whole life had very poor
health.   Severe headaches often tortured him for days.
Add to this the hard trials and strenuous labors in
which he continually showed great heroism and we
must be astonished that his powers were not sooner
consumed.   He showed great joy when, at the beginning of October, 1811, he became aware that his release
was near.   His subjects stormed heaven with prayer
that the life of their beloved provincial might be
spared.   But in vain, for on November 15, Father Pignatelli departed from this earth which had so often
refused him a place of rest.   Belief in the great sanctity
of the Servant of God increased after his death.
Numerous miracles were worked through his intercession.   Among others the well-known writer Bresciani
was thrice miraculously cured by him.   Valiant bearers
of the cross like Pignatelli can not fail to triumph.

Peter Joseph Picot de Clorivière

22. Very similar was the life of the Servant of God,
Peter Joseph Picot de Clorivière, born of a noble
Breton family of St. Malo on June 29, 1735.[64]   Peter
Joseph, with his brother Michel, received his education

in the college of the English Benedictines at Douai. At sixteen he entered the navy, but, having no liking for the service, left it a year after. For two years he remained unoccupied at home, undecided what calling to follow. "With a head filled with a thousand plans," he writes of himself, the youth of nineteen went to Paris to study law. It was his good fortune here that a zealous priest took notice of him. This father warned him of the dangers around him and suggested as the best means of avoiding them the frequent reception of the sacraments. De Clorivière at length conceived so great a desire for holy communion that his confessor was constrained to permit him to receive every day. In this way his vocation soon became clear to him. The thought of being a priest with the duty of daily celebrating Mass gave his soul the greatest comfort and consolation. He writes that his vocation to the Society of Jesus was a direct inspiration from God. He tells of it as follows. One day he communicated in the church of the novitiate of the Jesuits, with whom up to this he had had no acquaintance. When leaving the church he met an unknown person who said to him: "God calls you under the protection of St. Ignatius and St. Francis Xavier. Here is the novitiate, and you must enter." Going back into the church he began to pray interiorly and arose with the fixed conviction that God called him to the Society of Jesus. But lest he might be the victim of a delusion he put the matter before his confessor. The latter after mature consideration decided for the genuineness of the vocation. Objections on the part of his relatives were yet to be overcome, but on the Vigil of the Assumption, 1755, De Clorivière, now twenty-one years of age, entered the novitiate. For only six years had the Servant of God lived in France as a Jesuit when persecution forced him into exile. His superiors assigned him to the English province, which had its house of studies in Belgium. So Father Rivers, as he was called by the English fathers, studied theology in Liège from 1762 to 1766, and then made his third year of probation in Ghent. We find him in England the following year in the care of souls. But when he fell into serious illness there, his superiors gave him an easier office in helping the novice-master at Ghent.

It was especially during the first years of religious life that Father de Clorivière had to endure many trials. His speech was not clear and he stuttered. Hence, he was not able to appear in public and consequently suffered much humiliation. This affliction caused him many an hour of dejection, for he wished most earnestly to preach the word of God and he now felt that nature denied him the power. He feared that he would become only a burden to the Order, yet he clung with great love to the much persecuted Society. But this suffering came from his humility and impelled him to bind himself more closely to God. It is wonderful to read of his heroic determination, his fervor in the performance of his duties. The heavenly favors of which his sickness in England was the occasion, were so great that in his own words one can hardly form any idea of them. Still in spite of this he had afterward many a battle to fight against the lower nature.

In 1777 Father de Clorivière was appointed spiritual director, as far as the constitutions of the Order permitted, of the Benedictine nuns in Brussels. Besides this, of course, he performed many works of zeal for souls. On July 21, 1773, Clement XIV signed the decree suppressing the Society of Jesus; but Father Ricci, the superior-general, learned of it only on August 16, and thus it happened that on August 15, Father de Clorivière had the happiness of making his solemn vows in the Society.

After the suppression, the Servant of God remained at his post in Brussels until in 1775 the government of

Brabant discovered and promulgated a statute of 1752, which declared that no French director of a convent of women would be permitted in the realms of his Imperial Majesty. And a few weeks later we find Father de Clorivière filling the same office for the Benedictine nuns in the abbey of Jarcy near Paris. In 1779, at the request of the bishop of St. Malo, he accepted the parish of Paramé on the Breton coast. His stuttering in the pulpit caused him many unpleasant moments, but his heartfelt prayer obtained for him a sudden cure of this evil. His zeal was rewarded by the greatest success; for in 1786 the confidence of his bishops called him to the direction of the diocesan college at Dinan. Since the Revolution continually became more menacing, he asked John Carroll, the first bishop of the United States, to allow him to go to America. Carroll was himself a former Jesuit and had lived in the same house with De Clorivière in Liège. The day of departure was fixed. But he could not refuse his own bishop, who asked him not to forsake his countrymen in such grievous times. During the worst period of the Revolution De Clorivière lived under a fictitious name at a castle in the neighborhood of Paris. After 1799 he could again appear in public. In 1791 he founded the Society of the Sacred Heart of Jesus, which without community life practically followed the aims of the Society of Jesus. To the same end he founded a society of women—"The Society of the Sacred Heart of Mary," which is still in existence. As soon as freedom was re-established he gave both societies a rule of life. In 1804 Father De Clorivière was arrested by the police. One of his relatives was a participator in the conspiracy of George Cadoudal, and so suspicion was cast on him.* From 1804 to 1808 he was a prisoner in the Temple. His greatest grief

*For an interesting account of this conspiracy, see Historical Records and Studies, Vol. VIII, page 195 et seq.

during this time was that he could not even once offer up the Holy Sacrifice. Yet his friends so managed that he could keep the Holy Eucharist in his cell. The following year brought him some relief, but he was not released until April 11, 1809.

From the Temple Father De Clorivière turned to the vicar-general of the Society of Jesus with a prayer to be received again into the Order. He again received an invitation from Archbishop Carroll to come to America and take up the direction of novices. But in 1814 he received word from Russia that he should rather stay in France and there work for the re-establishment of the Society of Jesus.

This was no light task, for the houses of the Society in France had been closed for more than fifty years and there survived only a few of the former Jesuits. Father de Clorivière himself was seventy-five years old. The first to place themselves at his disposal were members of the Society of the Faith, among them their distinguished superior, Father Varin. A residence and a sort of novitiate were established in Paris. A little later Father de Clorivière was able to obtain the old abbey of St. Acheul, near Amiens, and here to begin a college. Many priests and students sought admission. He was soon in a position to undertake at least a few of the many colleges which were offered him. But his chief care was to school the young religious thoroughly in the ascetic spirit. For this he possessed the ability of a master. God had visited him for many years with interior trials, had given him every sort of experience in the school of suffering, freeing his heart from all earthliness. An old man now, De Clorivière could make use of the rich treasure of his experience and see the result of long years of loyalty in the service of God. After three years the Order in France had five colleges and two residences, with one hundred and forty-five members—a rapid development, indeed.   And the few fathers who had belonged to the old Society thoroughly imbued the younger members with their good spirit.

Father de Clorivière was always distinguished by his devotion to the Most Holy Sacrament of the Altar. Before the tabernacle he was to die.   On the morning of January 9, 1820, the aged man of eighty-four knelt at the communion-rail in the private chapel of the house at Paris, immersed in profound prayer.   Here came the angel of death that he might look face to face upon Him whom he had adored under the sacramental appearance of bread.   This beautiful death increased the repute for sanctity of the Servant of God.

Venerable Aloysius Solari

23. The restored Society of Jesus followed the footsteps of the old.   It has not only experienced the fierce persecution of the enemies of the Church, but has blossomed anew in noble examples of virtue and sanctity. St. Aloysius seemed to exist again in the person of the Venerable Aloysius Solari.[65]   The acts of the process sum up the chief features of his character in these words: "The practice of severe penance, serene and inviolate splendor of innocence until death, obedience to superiors as to God, insatiable, consuming thirst to win souls for God, and zealous promotion of devotion to the Sacred Heart of Jesus to enflame all with love for Him—were the eminent virtues of Aloysius Mary Solari.[66]   He was born on May 13, 1795, of a prominent family at Chiavari in Liguria on the Riviera of the Levant.   In baptism he received the name of August, but afterward called himself Aloysius, to honor the princely youth of Castiglione, in the hope that the saint would make it possible for him to enter the Society of Jesus.

The tendencies of boyhood were at first prominently noticeable in his early years.   He was somewhat wild,

petulant, averse to work, and seemed too much given
to amusement. His father therefore entertained some
anxiety for the future of his only son. But it was all
merely the thoughtless exhibition of the lively temperament of a child that scarcely knew the difference
between good and evil.

When August was sent by his parents to the Lazarists in Savona for his education he soon showed how
seriously he could take the fulfilment of his duties
toward God and man. He attained first rank among
his schoolmates for his good conduct and piety as well
as for his progress in learning. After he had decided
to study for the priesthood and had donned the clerical
dress he used to gather the poor children of the city
at his father's house during vacation days and instruct
them in catechism. He proved also a zealous promoter of the young men's sodality in Chiavari.

The Society of Jesus had but recently arisen from
its grave. The young Solari was inspired by its ideals
and his heart glowed with a great love for it—an
affection he was to preserve through many struggles.
His father had died and his mother would not be
parted from her only son. So the superiors of the
Order advised him to postpone his entrance. Solari
obediently applied himself to his studies and received
the orders of subdeacon and deacon. But his mother
remained inflexible. He would wait no longer and in
the autumn of 1817 fled secretly from his home to the
college of the Jesuits at Genoa. His mother could no
longer refuse the sacrifice demanded of her.

We may imagine what zeal the novice showed for
the vocation he had struggled so hard to preserve.
One thing especially helped him to achieve in a short
time the highest perfection—his devotion to the Sacred Heart of Jesus. He was enraptured by the love,
the nobleness, the rich treasures of the Heart of the
God-man wounded for us. From now on he consid-

ered it his life-work to be an apostle of the Sacred
Heart.

After his novitiate Solari studied rhetoric for a year,
and then taught in the colleges of his Order in Turin
and Naples, after which he completed his theology at
Rome and was ordained. As a young priest he was
sent to Benevento in 1824 to help in the school and in
the ministry. His virtuous example and his zeal soon
attracted the attention of the whole city. His preaching especially was mighty in effect and enkindled in all
his hearers the fire of divine love. Every Friday until
the last before his death he preached on the Sacred
Heart of Jesus. He was the confessor best liked by
the pupils of the college. His zeal, humility, and amiability were a constant incentive to the community.
Since the Order at the time had comparatively few
members he offered himself for the performances of
the meanest services. He chastised his body in such a
way that his superiors were obliged to restrain him.
In the novitiate he had already asked permission to go
to the foreign missions. The newly elected general,
Father Roothaan, was inclined to grant his petition.
But instead of to the Arabs, to whom he had been destined, God called him after an illness of only a few
days to the joys of heaven. He died in his thirty-third
year on August 27, 1829, of scarlet fever. He seems
to have foreknown his death. In his last letter to his
mother he spoke of it with all certainty and to his
brethren he made similar intimations. The whole city
was stirred with emotion by the news of the death of
the saintly father. A guard had to be placed over his
body lest it should be disturbed by persons seeking
relics. On the news of Solari's death the rector of
Naples preached a panegyric to his community on the
virtues of the deceased.

The likeness between him and St. Aloysius is quite
striking. Both had a hard struggle with their families

for their vocation, both preserved angelic purity, had
a holy zeal for penance, a most heartfelt devotion to
the Sacred Heart of Jesus, and both were eager for the
foreign missions.   Aloysius Gonzaga died after six
years of religious life; Aloysius Solari after twice that
time, twelve years, of which he lived half as a scholastic and the other half as a priest.

Venerable Paul Capelloni

24. The renown of the old Jesuit missionaries was
renewed in the Venerable Paul Capelloni.[67]   He was a
Roman by birth and after a youth of innocence was
ordained priest in 1801 at the age of twenty-five.   His
first position was that of tutor in the house of Marquis Vitelleschi, whose sons remained grateful to
Capelloni during his whole lifetime.   They used to call
him "the angelic teacher."   At the same time Capelloni
maintained a considerable activity in the care of souls,
especially in Il Gesù, where he labored in union with
the former Jesuits.   The year 1809 brought him exile,
for he refused the oath commanded by the French.   He
went to Reate, where the Vitelleschi family gave him
refuge.   Reate had reason to rejoice in the coming of
this fugitive.   A heavenly and imperishable gift was
given them in his virtuous example and untiring
zeal.

Paul Capelloni was one of the first to enter the
restored Society of Jesus in 1814.   He was of great
service to the Order in those days and was soon ready
for apostolic work.   The charge of the church of St.
Vitalis was entrusted to him, then for a long time
he labored in Ferrentino and conducted many missions
there.   In 1820 he was stationed at the new Gesù in
Naples, where he remained until his death.   Here he
had his heart's desire—abundance of labor for the
glory of God.   Only prudence and obedience could
induce him to spare his strength.   In a masterly way

he promoted discipline and good order among the soldiers, whose chaplain he was.

He spared no pains to inspire the people with devotion to the Sacred Heart of Jesus and to the Immaculate Conception, and in honor of the former, he solemnly celebrated every First Friday at the new Gesù. His joy in having lived until the day on which the doctrine of the Immaculate Conception was made a dogma of Faith was exceedingly great. At the breaking out of the Revolution in 1848, he was compelled to fly from Naples, finding refuge in the Island of Malta; but this involuntary exile was not a time of rest for him. There were sinners to convert in Malta and men to instruct on the purpose of their existence.

In spite of his ceaseless activity Father Capelloni reached the age of eighty-one. He died at Naples on October 15, 1857; and after his death his body was exposed three days for the veneration of the people, and on the seventh day there was a solemn public funeral. When the tomb was opened fifteen months afterward the body was found incorrupt. He was later entombed in the Chapel of St. Francis Jerome.

PAUL GINHAC

25. How readily God gives His support to a will that strives with consistent fervor and unwearying energy is shown in the example of the servant of God, Paul Ginhac, S.J.[68] Even during his lifetime documents were being gathered that might contribute toward his canonization. The unanimous opinion of his contemporaries was that Father Ginhac deserved to be declared a saint if ever any one did.

Nature, however, had not made it easy for Ginhac to surrender himself fully to the loving guidance of grace. For a long time it seemed as if the desires of the world would take his young heart captive.

Paul Ginhac was born of a very religious family

at the farm of Le Mazel in the parish of Serverette, Department of Lozere, in southern France. At the age of twelve he went to the neighboring town of Mende to attend the academy there; and the example of frivolous schoolmates did not fail to exercise a charm upon him. When he was sixteen his watchful parents sent our student to the boys' seminary at Chirac. But Paul complainted bitterly of this restriction of his liberty, spoke only of servitude and slavery in the institution, was disgusted with everything, and stormed his parents with petitions to let him go back to Mende. They indulged him so far as to permit him to study at Mende, but he was to lodge at the boys' seminary there and not with a private family. This little pleased the liberty-loving student. He became still more ill-humored and he submitted only in as far as external form compelled him. He feigned sickness and so managed to leave the institution for a time at least and was sent home.

The time of his classical training was at length accomplished and Paul rejoiced that he might now enjoy liberty and the pleasures of life. The priesthood was as far from his thoughts as it could be. His family feared the worst for the development of Paul's character, for the more pains they took to correct his levity the more was he confirmed in it. He desired at any cost to go to Paris, but the energetic refusal of his father stood in the way. This difference caused many disagreeable scenes in the family. "Paul, at least save your soul," often repeated his deeply afflicted mother.

All who had intimate dealings with him during this period of his life, however, bear witness that he was never corrupt in heart and that he always kept himself from what was low and wicked. It often happens in those of his age that an unreasonable desire for liberty awakens in their breasts and their inexperienced youth would have the satisfaction of heaven on earth. In all necessary matters Paul fulfilled his religious duties, but beyond this he did not care to go. With the least measure of religious fervor he imagined himself strong enough to withstand the allurements of the great city— a presumption that caused thousands every year to perish miserably by their own fault.

His elder sister, who had consecrated herself to God in the Order of the Visitation, succeeded in persuading the worldly young man to visit a friendly and experienced priest of noble family, who lived near by, and to ask his advice. Meanwhile, in union with her sisters, she implored Heaven for a change of mind in her brother. The priest invited his guest to accompany him in attending a mission which some Jesuits were giving at Mende. Politeness forbade refusal and Paul consoled himself with the thought that the sermons of the Jesuits would afford matter for amusement to his circle of gay companions.

But it turned out quite differently. On the last day a solemn procession was arranged. At a street corner Ginhac met some young people carrying a large crucifix. Paul's attention was at once fixed upon it. It seemed to him that bright rays streamed forth from the image of the crucified Lord and shone into the very depths of his soul. There he read in clear characters what God desired of him. This heavenly light filled him with consolation and gave him a clear insight into the grandeur and beauty of his vocation. All objection was broken down, his whole soul was moved, what God demanded opened to him a rapturous vision of the boundless realms of happiness; and this knowledge was so clear that there could not be the least doubt of its reality.

As on the road to Damascus grace had come so suddenly to his great namesake St. Paul that it permitted no turning back or wavering, so it happened to Ginhac. On the moment he made the saying of the Apostle of

the Gentiles his own: *"Mihi vivere Christus est"*—
"For to me, to live is Christ" (Philipp. i. 21). And
we shall see him working for fifty-two years with all
the strength of his will to reproduce in himself trait
for trait the character of Christ.

The Ginhac family was not a little surprised when
Paul came home so changed and announced that he
was resolved to enter the Society of Jesus. Vincent,
an older brother, already a priest, wrote: "If I had
become an unbeliever, I would have believed again,
so impressed I was to see a young man who was so
haughty and proud that he lorded it over everybody
and would be counseled by no one, resolved upon a
course that must have been so hard for him."

On January 4, 1843, Paul Ginhac entered the novitiate at Avignon. He certainly had still to overcome
many lesser faults, but his was now "the path of heroism" as the general of the Order, Father Martin,
appropriately characterized his life. Before the two
years of his noviceship were completed, he was obliged
to go to Algiers to act as teacher and prefect in the
orphanage of Ben Aknoun. The poverty of the place
and the hot climate limited his life of sacrifice, but
these were days of triumphant joy for Ginhac's magnanimous soul. He became a master in self-control,
and until the end of his life there burned in him an
ardent zeal for the missionary life.

He began his studies in the autumn of 1848 at Vals,
near Le Puy, and received Holy Orders on December
18, 1852. Superiors had him ordained somewhat
sooner than the rest of his fellow-students so that while
completing his studies he might assist the novice-
master in the direction of the novices, for at the time
the novitiate of the Toulouse Province was also in
Vals. After completing his studies Father Ginhac
occupied for a while the chair of a professor of theology. But before the end of 1855 he was entrusted

with the responsible post of master of novices. Except during the interval of the so-called third year of probation he remained in the office until 1869. After 1861 he was also rector in Toulouse, to which place the novitiate had been moved. From 1869 until his death on January 10, 1895, Father Ginhac was instructor of the fathers who were making their third probation.

Thus the servant of God was continually engaged in the spiritual training of the young members of the Society of Jesus. It would be hard to find one better fitted. In the first place, the example of his personal holiness lighted the path for every one. The sharp observations of the novices soon found how truly mortified, humble and immersed in God their superior was and each year corroborated with fresh proofs their exalted opinion of him. Not only the hundreds of Religious who passed through Ginhac's training, but all externs, too, who had anything to do with him, were completely captivated by the overmastering charm of his personality. And yet he was as simple in his manners, as unassuming and unaffected as could be. He was wanting in rhetorical talent, it is said, and possessed no gift of vivid representation, nor was he distinguished by any novelty or originality of thought, but scarcely any one could produce so deep an impression by the Exercises or so easily inspire souls to the closest following of Christ as he. What he taught he had himself practised—it was his own life proceeding from a heart in which the love of God flamed mightily. It was noticeable in every sentence how earnest was his intention, how repeatedly the speaker had proved his truths in himself. It was a genuine and lasting zeal for their vocation that he awakened in his pupils.

The latter reposed the greatest possible confidence in him. In the beginning there undoubtedly lingered in Ginhac's character, as a consequence of his unceasing struggles for self-conquest, somewhat of the disagreeable, harsh, and unkindly. But they did not fail to call his attention to this, and it is most astonishing to note how perfectly he overcame these faults. In fact, it was just his friendly and kindly dealing with others that opened the way to their hearts. "To himself he was a torturer, to others a tender mother," says one who had been under him. He was ingenious in making others feel happy. Nothing escaped his tender solicitude. Yet this goodness of heart did not mean any effeminacy in his manner of training nor was it at the expense of the religious spirit. His pedagogic skill enabled him to inspire others through the law of love with a lifelong zeal for perfection.

He was reputed to be in every respect the ideal of a superior. His edifying example of zeal for duty, his devotion, mortification, humility, and love of vocation did even more than his winning words. He was altogether a spiritual man and only the principles of faith governed his judgments and intentions. Hence he was never short sighted, narrow-minded, or pusillanimous. He allowed his subjects much freedom in their conduct of apostolic work and encouraged their spirit of enterprise. He carried the practice of mortification to a degree that would make the ordinary mortal shudder. We can not but marvel that his body bore it and could endure so much labor. But his loftiest heroism was reached in the constant denial of his own will. His heart rejoiced when he had an opportunity of practising acts of self-abnegation for his suffering Saviour. Once he ended an instruction on mortification with the words: "Rest assured, my fathers, that if a man has once tasted the delight hidden in suffering and mortification, he will desire the cross and voluntary penance with greater longing than that which the sensual man has for his forbidden pleasures." They say that he always began to smile and to speak with greater warmth when he entered upon this topic. A soul so mortified to the world and to sense naturally found its chief delight in intercourse with God. Still, trials of aridity and desolation were not spared to Father Ginhac.

The source from which his fervor ever drew new vitality was, after prayer and the Holy Eucharist, the Spiritual Exercises. His position brought with it the duty of giving the Exercises of thirty days every year. Besides, he was director of the Exercises in many other religious houses. The asceticism of the Book of Exercises of St. Ignatius he had made entirely his own and daily put into practice. "Father Ginhac," writes one of his pupils, "lived the Exercises, and they were embodied in him. Should he one day be declared a saint, in him will the Exercises be canonized in a new and especial manner . . . Just the Exercises, without addition, without missions, preaching or suggestion of high contemplation—in a word, the Exercises a saint so frequently gave and the spirit of which he so perfectly exemplified in his own life."

"Holiness does not consist in the working of miracles, but in a man's doing what he ought and as he ought," was a saying of Father Ginhac. It was literally verified in himself. He worked no miracles during his lifetime, but this norm of duty reproduced in him the magnanimity of the world-redeeming Lover of mankind.

There is no doubt of the extraordinary holiness of this man and, since after his death he has in so many cases proved to be a powerful intercessor, we may hope that the Church will soon present him to our effeminate and characterless world as a splendid example of self-renunciation and steadfastness of character.

VENERABLE FRANCIS MARY PAUL LIBERMANN

26. In the liturgy of Good Friday the Church does

not forget to commend the conversion of the Jewish people to the Heart of the dying Saviour. We may well consider as a proof that this prayer is not in vain the striking conversions of many distinguished persons of the last century—notably those of the brothers Theodore and Alphonse Ratisbonne, Emanuel Veit and Philipp Veit, Hermann Cohen, Francis Libermann, Dorothea Mendelssohn, and others. The honor of being the first Jewish convert with whose canonization the Church is engaged belongs to the Venerable Francis Mary Paul Libermann.[69] But it was a hard road and full of thorns which Providence made him travel to win his part in this rare honor.

He was born at Zabern in Alsace on April 12, 1804, the fifth son of a rabbi. Jacob, as he was called before he was baptized, was the favorite of his father on account of his religious disposition and was therefore destined one day to assume his father's office. So when he was thirteen he was sent to a superior school at Metz for the training of rabbis. Meanwhile the eldest son of the family, Samson, a physician, and with him his wife, became a Catholic. His example was soon followed by two of his brothers. But Jacob remained unconverted, publicly renounced his faith and became a rationalist. Chance placed the Gospels in his hands and the reading of them filled him with a great veneration for the person of Christ. The example and the direct influence of his converted brothers brought his noble soul even nearer to Christianity, although his father strove by every means against it. When Jacob went to Paris to pursue his studies in 1826, the work of his conversion was already quite accomplished. On Christmas day that year he received Baptism. The change gave him undreamed-of consolation and extraordinary enlightenment. From that day he was as profoundly convinced and as Catholic at heart as one brought up in the midst of Catholic surroundings.

After his baptism he vowed to consecrate himself to God in the priesthood. He was received without any difficulty into the seminary of St. Sulpice in Paris. The humble, mortified, and devout convert soon won the affection of every one.

A year afterward a dreadful trial came upon him. He was seized with epilepsy. For nearly ten years this dreadful disease sought to rob him of all powers of body and soul. The confidence in God and the resignation with which he bore this visitation, the glowing ardor for the cross it begot in his soul recall the most moving traits in the lives of the saints. Like so many others Libermann was made a saint by suffering.

Although there seemed little prospect of his ordination the superiors of the seminary were willing to keep Libermann. They well knew that by word and example he was doing much good among the candidates for the priesthood. He was soon obliged to keep up an extensive correspondence to counsel and assist others in their spiritual affairs. In 1837, the Congregation of the Eudists gave him charge of their novitiate at Rennes.

Libermann's attention was directed to the misery of the Negro race by two zealous and congenial seminarists, Frederic le Vavasseur, a native of the island of Bourbon, and Eugene Tisserand, a creole of San Domingo. The three friends—all suffering much in health, planted the foundations of a new missionary society for the conversion of the Negro. Libermann, with his ardent zeal and his fiery activity, was the soul of the enterprise. His letters excited in many clerics a desire for the noble work. But there were not wanting persons even in high positions who derided him as a visionary. At the beginning of 1840 Libermann went to Rome to beg support from the Propaganda. Here he was met with extreme reserve. He fell into the greatest want, but he did not waver in his reliance upon God. He was to win no victory save by suffering. And his patient waiting was rewarded. The Propaganda praised and encouraged his work as highly opportune.

Soon after his return from the Eternal City his health had so much improved that he was able to receive Holy Orders on September 15, 1841, and on the 27th of the same month, at Neuville, near Amiens, he opened the first novitiate of the Society of the Sacred Heart of Mary. The first beginnings labored under the severest privations, but the founder's example and inspiring words, aided by his prudent direction, made these privations only sweet accessories to their beloved vocation. This same year Libermann sent his first missionaries to the Negroes.

In 1843 a heavy blow fell upon him. Of the first seven fathers who had been sent to the Guinea Coast there was only one living after the lapse of a year, and he survived only two years. Father Tisserand, who was shortly after sent to Guinea as prefect-apostolic, suffered shipwreck within sight of the shore and was drowned. But in this case, as ever before, sacrifice only exalted Father Libermann's spirit and increased his own enthusiasm and that of his sons for the mission in that benighted land.

The young Society received new strength in 1848 by consolidation with the Society of the Holy Ghost, which had been in existence since 1705, but which after the Revolution had to struggle with many difficulties. Father Libermann became the first superior-general of the united societies and was commissioned to draw up new constitutions. But his earthly journey was nearing its end. Suffering remained his companion till the end. When he lay dying, the celebrated pulpit-orator, Father de Ravignan, said to a friend: "Come with me and we shall see how the saints die," The same desire led others thither. At midnight of February 2, 1852, while in choir they sang aloud in the death chamber the words of the *Magnificat*, "*Deposuit potentes de sede, et exaltavit humiles*"—"He hath put down the mighty from their seat and hath exalted the humble," Father Libermann gave up his spirit. He had not yet completed his forty-eighth year.

JACQUES DESIDERIUS LAVAL

27. Like Libermann, the Servant of God Jacques Desiderius Laval,[70] the first missionary of the Society founded by him is to share in the honor of the altar. Father Laval, born on September 18, 1803, at Croth in Normandy, had taken up the study of medicine after finishing his classics at the college of St. Stanislaus in Paris. During the time of his studies and also during the first years of his medical practice he was in every way a model in his performance of duty toward God and man. But even the saints are not immune from the allurements of sin. Doctor Laval gradually became indifferent to his religion and at length no longer practised it. In its stead he desired to enjoy life in an orderly way and at the same time taste all its pleasures. Soon, however, he experienced the bitter disillusionment. The void and darkness in his heart grew ever greater. In course of time he recognized this, fortunately before the fetters of vice were fastened too strongly upon him. He suffered a grievous conflict with himself until he found courage to make a penitent confession.

Laval now desired fully to atone for the past and he resolved to become a priest. Though nearly thirty-two years of age, he entered the seminary of St. Sulpice and after three years and a half, on December 2, 1838, he had accomplished his purpose. He went soon after to St. André, near Evreux, where he had practised medicine and there celebrated Holy Mass publicly to repair the scandal he had formerly given. In his two years of labor as pastor of Pinterville, Laval won the reputation of a saint by his love of prayer, his practical love for his neighbor, and his ardent zeal in arousing the faith of the lukewarm.

The desire of apostolic work among the heathen had long taken possession of his heart. So when he heard that Libermann, whom he had known at St. Sulpice, had instituted a society for the conversion of the Negro, he was one of the first to join it. His heart's desire was forthwith come to fulfilment. On June 6, 1841, he set sail for the island of Mauritius in company with Bishop Collier of Port Louis.

At the time of Laval's coming the island numbered 80,000 blacks, who for a few years back had enjoyed civil and political liberty; but at the same time had sunken into the misery of licentious living and ignorance of religion. The recognition of these sad conditions cut deep into the heart of the zealous priest. Still it was for him the desired opportunity to practise the same heroic work of charity as St. Peter Claver, and he did not fail to correspond with this grace. Like his model he sought out the poorest in their misery, interested himself in their welfare and their troubles, helped them as much as he could and consoled them with words of affection. His medical knowledge and experience stood him in good stead with them. He was soon the idol of the formerly shy negroes. They now gladly listened to his discourses on God and the Church. He inaugurated a movement toward Christianity among the infidels. In a short time he had built fifty chapels. New helpers had to be brought from Europe. Yet the tireless priest found time for long hours of prayer on his knees before the tabernacle and in spite of unspeakable hardships and the difficulties of the climate he deemed it necessary to afflict his body with fearful penances. "I must do penance," was his answer to those of his brethren who remonstrated.

Could it have been only chance that he was called to his heavenly reward on the feast of St. Peter Claver, September 9, 1864? His funeral procession was the most magnificent pageant the little island ever beheld. Forty thousand men marched in it to do the last honors to their beloved Father. To this day the grateful islanders celebrate him as their greatest benefactor, their apostle. Fully ten thousand persons, among them even Protestants and heathens, make pilgrimages to his tomb every year seeking help for sufferings of body and soul.

FATHER DAMIEN DE VEUSTER

28. We can here commemorate still another emulator of St. Peter Claver, Father Damien De Veuster,[71] the famous apostle of the lepers of Molokai, toward whose beatification steps have been taken, to the great joy of all his admirers. In Father Damien we have the example of an extraordinary heroism such as is known only in the Catholic Church, and of so sublime a character that even the most degenerate men must admire it. The life of such a hero, who avowed that he drew his strength from religion alone, is a convincing apology for the Catholic Church.

Even the story of Damien's youth shows the fervent love and zeal for the Faith that was hidden in his soul.[72] His parents' home was in Tremeloo, a town near Mechlin in Belgium. The De Veuster family was of modest means. Their most precious possession was a solid and practical faith, and it was their chief care to implant it deeply in the hearts of their children, who fully corresponded with their endeavors. Our Damien, who was born on January 3, 1840, showed himself especially responsive by his great spirit of prayer, his delight in the service of God, and his voluntary practice of penance. He was, moreover, a consistently lively and cheerful boy who loved a boy's games and bodily exercise. One soon became aware of Damien's wideawake spirit. But after his elder brother Pamphile went away to study he had to work at home in the field. Later on his parents sent him to take a course in an industrial school. Here he learned French. "Some Walloons," he writes in one of his first letters, "who ridiculed me for this, I sent home with a ruler."

Damien was now eighteen years old, sound to the core in mind and body. His dexterity and his strong, muscular body made him fit for the heaviest labors, and because of the purity of his life and his upright, kindly piety he was the joy and pride of his parents. At this time he had the happiness of attending a mission. The fruit Damien gathered from it was a resolution to follow that path which would most surely lead him to salvation, and a consoling voice from within told him that for him it would be the religious state. It would be a hard sacrifice for his parents, two of whose daughters had already taken the veil and whose eldest son Pamphile had joined the Congregation of the Sacred Hearts of Jesus and Mary, commonly called the Picpus Society. Damien, together with his father, paid a visit to Pamphile, who was studying theology in the convent at Louvain, and on this occasion Damien asked and implored his father to let him stay there. The acquiescence of his mother made the parting easy, and the surprised father could not withhold his consent.

Since Damien had made no classical studies, he was told that he could become only a lay-brother. He was quite satisfied and rejoiced that he could now belong altogether to God. During recreations his brother Pamphile, just to make the time pass pleasantly, began to teach him a few Latin words and simple sentences.

The result was wonderful. Damien displayed a remarkable memory and a great intelligence. In six months he could read Nepos without preparation. This circumstance induced his superiors to put him at study for the priesthood. After a year and a half of study at Louvain, he made his novitiate at Issy, near Paris, and then took his philosophy and theology at Louvain. "Big Damien," as his brethren familiarly called him on account of his robust build, distinguished himself by his pursuit of holiness as well as by his zeal and success in study. He was quite the Father Damien of later days, who shrank from no sacrifice and could practise heroic virtue.

It was by chance, we might say, that Providence led St. Francis Xavier to the heathen missions. Father Bobadilla had been appointed to go to the Indies, but when the time of departure drew near, he fell ill of a fever, and Francis Xavier stepped into his place and became the great Apostle of India and Japan. In a similar way Father Damien came into his own field of labor. His brother Pamphile, with other missionaries, was appointed to go to the Sandwich Islands in 1863. All was ready for their departure and the tickets were bought when Pamphile was stricken with typhus. Damien immediately wrote to the superior-general of the Congregation humbly asking to go in his brother's place, "and in this way," he urged, "the fare for the voyage will not be wasted." The petition was granted, although Damien had not yet received major orders. His joy at the news was without bounds. The preparations for departure were made rapidly. He took leave of his parents at the pilgrimage of Montaigu and from the port of Bremen he wrote a letter full of the apostolic spirit of faith and at the same time full of tenderness for his parents.

After a voyage of five months the missionaries landed at Honolulu, the capital of the Island Kingdom.

During Pentecost week Damien was ordained and was then stationed on the island of Hawaii, here to give the first proofs of his apostolic zeal. In his first letter from Hawaii to his brother, he wrote:

"If God, Our Lord, would send us a holy priest like the Curé of Ars, these strayed sheep would soon be brought back again. Here in this wide region of Puna (a district of Hawaii), I have longed for that holy and pure love of God, that burning zeal for the salvation of souls, which enflamed a Vianney, Curé of Ars. Oh, dearest brother, I beg of you, pray yourself and get others to pray for me and for my poor flock that the Divine Redeemer may enkindle in our hearts that fire which He brought to earth and so earnestly desired to be enkindled. How unwearyingly would I then visit the sick and the old to baptize them in water and the Holy Ghost before they pass to another life. How zealously I would look after the children and ignorant to preserve them from the influence of heretical preachers."

His desire was fulfilled. Father Damien himself became that zealous apostle, who for nine long years traversed the mountains and valleys of Hawaii to enkindle in the hearts of the Kanakas the fire of divine love.

The frightful plague of leprosy afflicted the inhabitants of the Sandwich Islands. To combat the evil effectively the government in 1865 ordered that all persons infected with leprosy should be transported to the north coast of the little island of Molokai, so that they might be separated from all intercourse with the rest of the people. It seemed a cruel expedient, but it was the only means of rooting out the plague. The life of the poor exiles was the most disconsolate imaginable. Since their numbers continued to increase, the bishop of Honolulu desired to give them a regular pastor so that at least the consolations of religion might lighten their joyless lives. But how could he require any of his priests to accept so heroic a sacrifice. Hardly had Father Damien heard of his bishop's desire than he voluntarily offered, as he said, "to be buried alive with the unhappy victims of the plague."

On May 10, 1873, Father Damien landed on the island of dread and death with the fixed resolve of giving himself to his children without reserve and of never after forsaking them. The number of lepers in Molokai was at the time between 800 and 1000, of whom about a half were Catholics. It is well known how hideous the horrible disease makes the human body. The hopeless exile and dull despair had also most disastrous results on their morals. The sight of this twofold misery excited in Damien's noble soul the heroism of a practical love for God and his neighbor. We learn from himself what was the sacrifice he was obliged to make. On November 25, 1873, he writes to his brother:

"Even the breath of the lepers is so foul-smelling that the air is tainted with it. It comes hard on me to live in this atmosphere. One day while I was celebrating Mass, I thought I would suffocate and I was almost unable to restrain myself from rushing out to take a breath of fresh air. But the thought of my Lord before the grave of Lazarus restored me. My sense of smell is already somewhat dulled, so that it is not quite so hard for me to enter the pestilent dwelling-rooms of the poor sick people. Of course, there comes upon me now and then a feeling of loathing, especially when I must hear the confessions of the sick whose wounds are already full of worms similar to those which consume bodies in the grave. I have often been in great perplexity when I wished to give Extreme Unction because there was not to be found free space between the wounds. There are no physicians here, in fact they could be of no use."

In these comfortless surroundings, where everything was infected with corporal and spiritual foulness, Father Damien worked the miracle of his charity for his fellow-man with a truly heavenly patience, magnanimity, and self-denial. He performed for these lepers the meanest services. He was their physician, priest, judge, builder, carpenter, grave-digger. He built, for the most part by himself, between three and four hundred houses, and made fifteen to eighteen hundred coffins. For the sick he provided occupation, distraction, and amusement and, above all, the necessary sustenance. He was at his best in the office of consoler, especially in presenting the consideration of the life hereafter. The unhappy beings were not insensible to this self-sacrificing charity. They saw what a sacrifice the Servant of God had made—in what great danger of infection he had placed himself in charity to them. Father Damien therefore soon possessed among them the greatest authority and confidence. There was going on visibly a regeneration in morals, many conversions occurred, the people became reconciled to their fate and looked in the face of death more cheerfully. In a short time the heroic priest had transformed conditions in the leper colony. Though surrounded only by misery, Father Damien felt so happy in his hardships that he would exchange with no one. He attributed his success to the prayers of his brethren and his kindred.

For twelve years he had given the consolations of religion to this desert island with unwearying patience when he began to show symptoms of infection. The plague could destroy his body, but not the heroism and cheerful sacrifice of his great soul. "If I could have health at the price of leaving the island and my work, I would not take it," he said to his physician. After four years the disease had done its work and the hero and martyr of charity died on April 15, 1889.

The whole world, Catholic and non-Catholic, had long before manifested its admiration of Father Damien. Anglican ministers preached his praises from their pulpits, gathered collections for him, and corresponded with him. One of them asked what was the secret of his strength for such heroic work. Father Damien answered that the continual presence of Christ in the Blessed Sacrament and the daily reception of the Holy Eucharist alone gave him strength to endure. At the news of Father Damien's glorious death newspapers of all opinions were filled with enthusiastic praise of him.

"In Birmingham," says an eyewitness, "the first who saw a picture of Father Damien displayed in a shop window manifested the old, deep-rooted hatred. But this involuntary dislike lasted only a moment. When they learned that it was the hero of Christian charity, the people gathered about the window in such crowds that the police were obliged to disperse them to open the way for traffic."[73]

The well-known "Daily Telegraph" wrote:[74] "Father Damien is dead. What sorrowful news, and yet it arouses in the heart quite other sentiments than those usual on the death of a distinguished man. So pure and noble was the soul of this man that the death itself does not excite the usual expression of grief, but makes us feel on the contrary something of that true Christian joy which those may well experience who are permitted to be present at the release of a friend of heaven and of mankind. If ever a soul freed from the yoke of earth and hastening from this world will be received with celestial greeting in the Hereafter, surely to this one will the words be said: 'Well done, thou good and faithful servant, enter thou into the joy of thy Lord." In this our century of unbelief and self-seeking we have gazed with wonder upon the simple priest who, by his boundless love of his fellow-man, by his complete dedication to a dreadful vocation freely chosen, has won for himself the acknowledgment and gratitude of the whole civilized world."

In England a committee of men of various beliefs, with the Prince of Wales, afterward Edward VII, at their head, was formed to gather funds for a monument to Father Damien. In Louvain also and at Molokai the memory of the Apostle of the Lepers is to be commemorated by monuments.

But greater than monuments is the memory of the example of his heroic virtue. One of his biographers says with justice:[75] "In him lived again the heroism of the first Christian century in the blood-soaked arena. But he went beyond this. A man would think it a favor to be thrown among wild beasts to be devoured in comparision with even one long year of life in the poisonous atmosphere of a leper place. And Damien, the champion of Christ, lived many years amongst the lepers of Molokai. Uninterruptedly he remained in the midst of these sick people who would be avoided by another sane man as the pest itself. He had consecrated his service to them, bound their wounds, soothed their pains, awaked their trust in the Divine Master and quickened their hope in eternal life; he was with them at the moment of death, laid their dead in the coffins with his own hand and accompanied them to their last resting place."

It is certainly not too much to hope that the Church will honor the hero of Molokai on her altars so that his example may encourage imitation in these days which so need the Apostle of Charity, and that all the world may recognize the supernatural strength that dwells in Christianity.*

*"Die Katholischen Missioner" (1896, 142 sq.) gives an account of the heroic death of the Rev. Don Michael Unia of the Salesian Society, founded by the Venerable Don Bosco. Don Unia, like Father Damien, devoted himself entirely to the service of lepers in Columbia.

Venerable Don John Bosco

29. One day Venerable Joseph Cottolengo* met a
young cleric. After they had exchanged a few words,
Cottolengo said: "You are an excellent man, come into
the Little House of Providence and work will not be
wanting to you." The one thus invited was the Venerable Don John Bosco.[76] The inscription over the
entrance of the "Little House": *"Charitas Christi
urget nos"*—"The Charity of Christ presseth us"
(2 Cor. v. 14) made a strong impression on him, and
when he came into the reception room and read above
the picture of the Blessed Virgin the words: *"Infirmus
eram et visitastis me"*—"I was sick and you visited
me" (Matt. xxv. 36), he was moved to tears. While
going through the institution Don Bosco was highly
edified and deeply impressed by everything he saw and
heard. But one thing filled him with distress. He
saw so many poor young people in the infirmary, who
lay there wasting away and hopeless. It was the first
time he clearly realized that vice alone had devoted
them to death in the springtime of life. "You must
save the young from vice," said a voice within him.
This thought indeed often enflamed his heart, but now
it was his fixed purpose to work out this noble end in
effect.

When Don Bosco was departing, Cottolengo took
hold of his sleeve and said: "The cloth of your cassock
is too weak and thin. You must get a cassock of
stronger and better wearing cloth or it will be torn.
The time will come when many people will be hanging
on by it." Cottolengo prophesied truly. Don Bosco
is one of the greatest apostles of youth, the most successful teacher of the nineteenth century. And not
merely this—he is a saint.

In Don Bosco's life the power of the supernatural

*See pages 68 sqq. above.

becomes, so to speak, tangible. A brief glance at his achievements will convince us.

John Bosco, the son of simple farming people, was born at Becchi, a village in the district of Murialdo, province of Turin, on August 15, 1815. He was a very lively boy, eager to learn and skilful in everything he undertook. His father died when John was only two years old, but his mother was a truly remarkable educator and knew well how to develop the good dispositions of her children. As a boy John displayed a strong inclination to piety, of which he made absolutely no concealment. His apostolate among the young began even before he had begun his studies. As he tells us in his notes, he had a vision when he was nine years old in which his future vocation was clearly sketched before him. Afterward the vision often returned and with increased clearness. He used to gather the boys of the neighborhood and entertain them with games and pleasing stories, but he always added an instruction in catechism and ended with a prayer or hymn.

In 1826 a priest of the neighborhood, Don Calosso, undertook to instruct John Bosco in Latin, but unfortunately the teacher died two years later and the study was interrupted. After two years more, however, the widow Bosco succeeded in overcoming all difficulties and sent her son, then fifteen years old, to the public school at Castelnuovo, and in the year after, to the college at Chieri. Bosco's principles on intercourse with his schoolmates at this time are interesting, and give us an insight into his character.

He writes: "I had divided my schoolmates into three classes—good, indifferent, and bad. Absolutely to avoid companionship with the bad as soon as I learned them to be such; to converse with the indifferent, if politeness and decency required; to admit companionship with the good but friendship only with the best, if I found any such, was my resolute determination."

The first to approach him were the bad, and they met with an energetic repulse. Among the rest he soon won respect; they sought him by preference. He established a union, "Cheerfulness." Every member was obliged to contribute to the promotion of cheerfulness by means of books, amusements, and games. Whatever caused sadness was penalized. Whoever did not perform his scholastic and religious duties, whoever swore or used bad language was expelled from the union. John was the soul of it. He took care that religious instruction was had and frequent reception of the Sacraments. On Sundays and feast-days, though still a student, he devoted himself to the boys of the city.

On October 30, 1835, Bosco entered the seminary of Turin and on June 5, 1841, he was ordained. For further improvement he now went to the Practical Seminary for Young Priests, the Institute of St. Francis of Assisi, where his trusted friend and confessor, Venerable Joseph Cafasso, was at work.* The latter also had spiritual charge of the prison. Don Bosco often accompanied him and thus became acquainted with a great deal of the misery into which vice plunges mankind. He would prevent vice with all his strength—but how?

On December 8, 1841, while Don Bosco was vesting for Mass, a ragged urchin slipped into the sacristy. The sacristan harshly ordered him out. But Don Bosco asked the intruder to stay till after Mass. He then found by questioning that here was a parentless boy of fifteen who could neither read nor write and knew little or nothing of religion. Don Bosco began forthwith to give Bartholo Garelli—this was the boy's name—some religious instruction, and when the lad

*See page 73.

was departing, he asked him to return soon. Garelli had never in his life been treated with such friendliness and cordiality. He soon returned, but not alone, bringing with him other comrades as poor and ignorant as himself. In two months there were twenty who regularly gathered in the sacristy of St. Francis of Assisi. Such was the origin of the Oratory of St. Francis of Sales.

The crowd growing from Sunday to Sunday soon numbered three hundred. Don Bosco now devoted the greater part of the day to them, prepared games, made excursions and arranged for church celebrations in common. He was not without his difficulties, however. He was obliged often to change his meeting-place and when he could do so no more he held forth in the open air in the Valdocco quarter. He was at length able to buy a shed which he changed into a chapel.

The attachment of the boys to Don Bosco and their confidence in him were wonderful. Though only wild and utterly neglected street arabs, they were perfectly submissive to his will. Many people, of course, shook their heads at it, and complained to Cavour that the enterprise was dangerous. Some even considered Don Bosco insane and endeavored to have him confined in an asylum. But the great friend of youth, Archbishop Fransoni, always protected him and he did not lose courage. The work made giant strides. In 1847, supported by his admirable mother, Don Bosco erected, in Valdocco, a boarding-school with a manual training department. The institution increased year by year. The means for the new building were supplied entirely by voluntary contributions, often in a miraculous way. New oratories were erected in two districts of the city and entrusted to the care of priests of a spirit like to his own.

Don Bosco had next to consider the obtaining of competent assistants. Many of the boys who had enjoyed his admirable training showed talent and a desire for the priesthood and wished to assist him in his opportune labors. Thus was naturally evolved the design of forming a religious society. He called it "The Pious Society of St. Francis of Sales." Don Bosco considered the gentleness of the holy bishop of Geneva an ideal for apostolic effectiveness. When he afterward extended his care to girls, a congregation of women was founded under the title of "The Daughters of Mary, Help of Christians." Both congregations developed rapidly and received the Papal approbation in 1874. To these was finally added a sort of third Order—the Salesian Co-operators.

The fame of Don Bosco had long passed beyond Turin. In one Italian city after another his sons founded oratories. Foundations in Austria, France, and Spain soon followed and in 1875 there set out the first expedition to Argentina. They have since spread over the whole of South America. At present the Salesian Society numbers 4200 members and 298 residences. The women's branch has over 2000 members and 250 houses.[77] The sons of Don Bosco must be reckoned among the most active apostles who are working to heal the evils of the new century by practical Christianity.

Don Bosco stands out particularly great as an educator. Even such modern infidels as Cæsar Lombroso are astonished at his success. Hundreds of wild street arabs waited upon his slightest wish, followed with the most exact punctuality a daily order and all this almost without any use of punishment. What we hear related of the fidelity and zeal of his pupils is almost incredible. One of them, Dominic Savio, died at fifteen in the repute of sanctity and the process of his beatification is already begun.* But not only under his personal guidance were Don Bosco's boys so exemplary—they

See pages 250 sqq.

remained the same in later life, especially in the fulfilment of their duties to the Church and to their country.

If we would learn the secret of this success we must at once admit Don Bosco's profound understanding of the souls of the young. He knew that radically every one has noble traits and that it is the environment, bad example, and evil reading that awaken the sinful passions. Therefore, it was always his first endeavor to guard the young from moral contagion. He treated each one according to his individual character to develop the germ of goodness in it and was a declared enemy to mechanical imitation of models. He carefully avoided every artificial formality and all harshness as hindering true confidence from growing up between superior and subject. On the contrary he was always communicative and amiable. He won authority by fatherly love and condescension. Almost all his pupils went to confession to him.

Another aid to his educational skill was solid instruction in religion. With many who follow the paths of vice and are estranged from the Church the chief cause is ignorance in religious matters. In books, periodicals, and in daily conversation they meet with a thousand objections which are begotten in ignorance. Don Bosco was fully convinced that religion alone can give men moral support and that no natural maxims can suffice and endure against the allurements of sin. Therefore he most severely condemned the separation of religion from education. "Frequent confession and communion and daily Holy Mass are the foundation on which is supported the education of youth from which threats and punishment should be as far removed as possible," he said.

It was chiefly his divinely inspired devotion to his pupils that made the young idolize Don Bosco. Only a man whose very life is penetrated by the worth and beauty of a youthful soul for which Christ poured out his Heart's blood has this unceasing, unselfish spirit of sacrifice. An apostle of youth must renounce his own comfort. And Don Bosco was a saint. Without dwelling on his heroic virtues, let us merely mention that eye-witnesses relate many miracles worked by him. One recalls involuntarily the miracles related in the life of St. Bernard of Clairvaux. With Mary, Help of Christians, his prayers were most powerful. No sickness was so stubborn, no sinner so hardened that Don Bosco's prayer was in vain. He may justly be called the *"thaumaturgus"* (wonder-worker) of the nineteenth century.

A panegyrist calls Don Bosco "the representative of the Church in the century of machinery and expansion." The ideal of a priest is truly incorporate in him. *"Da mihi animas, cetera tolle,"* he often repeated —"Give me souls, take the rest"—noble words of a Christian ideal as contrasted with the egoistic spirit of the age. Don Bosco had a deep insight into the needs of his time. He was in touch with all the elements of social life. His keen spirit of enterprise knew how to use all the weapons which modern circumstances demanded in warfare against enemies that endangered the temporal and spiritual welfare of the young. Three things in particular he kept before his mind—the school, labor, and the press. His opportune manual training and industrial schools sent into every position of life thousands of youths whose main business was the fulfilment of their religious duties. His Sunday oratories and evening schools saved innumerable souls from peril and gave them the necessary knowledge and the healthiest recreation for soul and body. *"Servite Domino in lætitia"*—"Serve ye the Lord with gladness" (Ps. xcix. 2) was a maxim with him and he never neglected the encouragement of youthful gaiety.

On January 31, 1888, this great life came to an end. The whole Catholic world mourned in his death the loss of a saint and a great benefactor. Even the hostile press found only words of praise for the noble Don Bosco. He was buried in the mission house of Valfelice near Turin, since the government would not permit his interment in the church of Mary, Help of Christians, which he himself had built. His funeral cortège was one of the most magnificent the world has ever seen.

No one was surprised when Don Bosco manifested his universally known goodness after his death. The necesary documents for the process of his beatification were soon prepared. In 1907, Pius X published the decree opening the Apostolic process.

Venerable Dominic of the Mother of God

30. Pope Gregory the Great sent monks to England to convert the Anglo-Saxons to the Church. Among recent Popes another Gregory sent messengers of the Faith from Italy to England to win back our separated brethren to the Church by word and example. St. Augustine of Canterbury, the envoy of Gregory I, received King Edelbert into the Church. The envoy of Gregory XVI, who received into the Church a prince of the spiritual kingdom, John H. Newman, was a modest Passionist, the Venerable Dominic of the Mother of God (*a matre Dei*).[78] Providence chose a worthy instrument and the Church has already undertaken his beatification. The family name of the Venerable Servant of God was Dominic Barberi. He was born of poor country people on June 22, 1792, near Viterbo. But he lost both parents at an early age, had scarcely any elementary training, and had to work for an uncle, tending cattle and laboring in the field. A companion taught him to read and a friendly Capuchin took an interest in him. Dominic devoured all the books he could lay his hands on. Fortunately there were only good ones which tended to nourish his

sense of the ideal and his deep piety. When twenty-two years old he joined the Congregation of the Passion and took the name of Dominic of the Mother of God. After ordination to the priesthood he was placed in the most important offices of the Order and also labored as a missionary preacher. In 1840, Father Dominic established the first Passionist residence in Belgium and in 1842 did the same in England, at Aston Hall, Staffordshire. He labored only seven years in England and died on August 27, 1849, at a little railroad station near Reading. But his brief time of activity produced the most consoling results. Many distinguished converts made their confession of faith to him, among them, besides J. H. Newman, were two of the latter's companions, E. S. Bowles and R. Stanton, John Dalgairns, and others. In 1846 he had the happiness of receiving into his own Congregation the convert George Spencer, who, under the name of Father Ignatius of St. Paul, was most successful in his labors.

Venerable Joseph Amand Passerat

31. When St. Clement Hofbauer lay dying he said to his younger fathers: "Be consoled. So far you have had in me an imperfect master. Soon I shall send you my great Frenchman, who will teach you how to pray. If you do not become holy under his instruction you never will." This man who was known among his brethren as "the great man of prayer" was the Venerable Joseph Amand Passerat.[79] His great devotion to prayer explains the success of his labors for the salvation of souls as well as for his own perfection.

Passerat's youth fell within the stormy times of the French Revolution. He was born on April 30, 1772, at Joinville, in Champagne. After completing his classical studies he began his higher studies in Paris. But he recognized in time the dangers which threatened both his faith and his life and chose rather to live in his paternal home than to stay in the metropolis. Even here, however, he did not escape the bloodthirsty "comrades" of the Revolution and when he refused to take the oath of the Constitution he was thrown into prison. When the war broke out they removed him from confinement and pressed him into service. At length after two years he was released and he departed from the dangerous soil of his country. The next year we find him a student of theology in Vienna and Würzburg. In the meanwhile he had heard of Hofbauer's great work at Warsaw. He set out to visit the great man and asked to be received into his Congregation. The Saint was not long in discovering the tried virtue of the novice and permitted him to take his vows the same year, 1796. After his elevation to the priesthood in 1797, Passerat was appointed to teach theology and church history to his younger brethren, and soon after became novice-master. Later on we find him in Switzerland, where he established many residences of the Redemptorists. After Hofbauer's death he labored with great success at Vienna and, as vicar-general of the Congregation beyond the Alps, did very much for the interior strengthening of the spirit of the Order as well as for its external expansion. Under his direction were established the first houses of the Congregation in Alsace, Belgium, Holland, Bavaria, France, England, and North America. He died in old age at Tournai on October 30, 1858. The last eight years of his life, during which he was paralyzed as the result of a stroke of apoplexy, gave him welcome opportunity to devote himself to prayer, according to his heart's desire.

Francis Xavier Seelos

32. The Servant of God, Francis Xavier Seelos, a Bavarian Redemptorist, did great work for German-American Catholics.[80] He was born at Füssen on Jan-

uary 11, 1819, made his classical studies at Augsburg, and then went to the University of Munich. Shortly after his entrance into the seminary of Dillingen, November 3, 1842, he asked to be received into the Congregation of the Redemptorists. The career of his patron saint presented to him his ideal and he was to have abundant opportunity to put this ideal into practice. In March of the following year he was sent to the United States to found the first North American novitiate of the Redemptorists. On December 22, 1844, he was ordained by the archbishop of Baltimore. A gigantic task awaited the ardent zeal of the young priest; for the country was so extensive, and there were so many immigrants and so few priests. Father Seelos spent the first year of his priestly labor in parish work and in the direction of religious communities. Afterward he traveled through the wide country as a missionary among the people. Everywhere an unmistakable blessing followed his labor. Men observed that in himself, as in all he said and did, there was an expression of most intimate conviction with which his external conduct was in complete accord. And so it came to pass that he soon had everywhere the reputation of a saint. He alone was much astonished at this and called himself a hypocrite who would have to undergo the severest judgment before God for having so deceived men by his conduct. But when we read what his brethren tell of his prayerfulness, his zeal for penance, his spirit of faith, and his profound humility, we can not wonder that God bestowed so many graces upon his labors and worked through him a multitude of miraculous cures. Father Seelos was an apostle who entirely forgot himself and his own interests and whose heart was wholly filled with the Redeemer's compassionate love of souls. If such men accomplish great things in the vineyard of the Lord, it is because they have in themselves something of that attractive power which the Son of God Himself exercised when He was upon this earth.

Like his life, the death of Father Seelos was heroic. The yellow fever had broken out in New Orleans. Contemning death, he visited the dying to give them the last consolations of religion. He was soon a victim of the epidemic and with cheerful resignation he died, aged forty-eight, on October 4, 1867. This noble death attracted the notice of the world to the sanctity of the servant of God.

The "Baltimore Volks Zeitung" wrote: "The Order of the Redemptorists has lost in him a precious jewel, Catholics one of their most zealous missionaries, and the Church a most exemplary priest; but heaven has gained a saint and a martyr. Charity, gentleness, and piety spoke from his countenance and his exhortations in the confessional compelled obedience through love and goodness. He was indeed a man who by his goodness of heart, by his sincere sympathy for all in distress and by his simplicity and affability won all hearts. Father Seelos died of yellow fever, a victim of his divine vocation, a martyr of charity to suffering humanity."

The "Catholic Mirror" said on the occasion of his death: "It is not ours to speak of the interior life, of the mortification and self-denial of Father Seelos, which gave him a singular power over men whether in the pulpit or in the confessional. It is sufficient for us to say that in his congregation, which is not wanting in admirable examples of virtue, none has been more highly revered than Father Seelos."

A New Orleans paper gives him this praise: "No one could see him especially at the altar or in the pulpit without being convinced that the man belonged rather to heaven than to earth."

May the authority of the Church soon declare the sanctity of this son of Bavaria!

Venerable Vitus Michael di Netta

33. Another jewel in the crown of the Congregation of the Most Holy Redeemer was the Venerable Vitus Michael di Netta.[81] His birthplace was in Lombardy, but Calabria was almost alone in the good fortune of being the witness of his richly blessed apostolic labors. Here he journeyed through cities and towns for almost thirty-five years, preaching against sin with fervent zeal and reconciling numberless sinners with God by his winning charity. The grateful people justly bestowed on him the revered title of the Apostle of Calabria. He died at the age of sixty-one on December 3, 1849, at Tropea in southern Calabria.

Venerable Emanuel Ribera

34. The Venerable Emanuel Ribera[82] was likewise a son of St. Alphonsus and was born at Molsetta in Apulia. Although constantly ill he labored much and with great success in the vineyard of the Lord. His death occurred on November 10, 1874.

Peter Donders

35. Dutch Guiana, with its tropic heats, its fever-laden air, its mosquito plague, and its varied and unsympathetic population of Negroes, Mulattoes, Mestizos, Indians, Creoles, Jews, Mohammedans, and Coolies, has little attraction for civilized men. We must, therefore, the more admire the fortitude of the missionary who without any consideration of earthly reward but for love of the souls of this ill-sorted people alone voluntarily chose this inhospitable land as his adopted country. It needed the strength and courage of a saint to cultivate this vineyard for forty-five years with such unflagging zeal, such never-halting energy and constant cheerfulness as did the Dutch Redemptorist Peter Donders. The Church will reward him by numbering him in the ranks of the blessed.[83]

Peter Donders, born October 27, 1809, at Tilburg in North Brabant, was obliged to spend his boyhood in privation and self-denial. From his very early years his heart was drawn toward the priesthood. But three considerable obstacles stood in the way; viz., his parents were very poor, he had poor health, and possessed but little talent. So much the greater, therefore, were Peter's piety, his purity of morals, and his confidence in God. To help his parents he learned the weaver's trade. When he was twenty-two he was received into the boys' seminary at St. Michiels-Gastel as a servant, with permission to avail himself of whatever instruction he could get. It was no small humiliation for a student who was so much older than his fellows to be almost last in everything; but his strong will and his confidence in prayer won him the victory over all difficulties. Twice he asked admission into a religious body and was each time refused. After six years he was admitted into the priests' seminary.

Some years after his ordination to the priesthood his desire to work as a missionary in foreign lands was gratified. On September 2, 1842, he landed at Paramaribo, capital of Dutch Guiana, which mission was then in the care of Dutch secular priests. Great patience and self-sacrifice was required to protect the 4000 Catholics scattered throughout the colony from the dangers which threatened their faith and morals in consequence of their heathen environment and the enervating climate. Donders paid special attention to the young, rightly foreseeing that it is easier to protect them from vice than to reclaim them when once in its power. When yellow fever raged at Paramaribo in 1851, he won the admiration of the whole colony by his heroism, in caring for both the spiritual and the corporal welfare of the sick, nearly falling a victim of his vocation.

Batavia, a remote place in the colony, had been set

apart by the government for the residence of lepers. In 1856 Donders undertook the pastoral care of this difficult post, and persevered here for thirty years, shirking no sacrifice to be all things to his poor flock and to win all to Christ. When the mission of Dutch Guiana was adopted by the Redemptorists in 1865, Donders asked to be received into the Congregation. What was denied to the young petitioner thirty years before was gladly granted to the deserving and saintly missionary. After a year of noviceship at Paramaribo he took up again his post at Batavia.

"There was never a prince, perhaps," we read in a sketch of his life, "who, crowned with fame and splendid success, entered his capital in triumph after his victories and found so great an overflow of joy and happiness as did Donders when, surrounded by his beloved lepers, he again directed his steps to his poor little church."

He went forth to his work with renewed courage and energy. At last, seventy-seven years of age, he laid down his arms to receive, on January 6, 1887, the reward of his holy and mortified life.

John Baptist Stoeger

36. Not alone the missionaries in foreign lands, but also the lay-brothers who pray and work at home, obtain the grace of perfect holiness. The simple and humble Brother John Baptist Stoeger is a recent example.[84] The foundation of his future sanctity was the exemplary Christian training he received from his parents. His father was an ideal of the man who is thoroughly Catholic and shows his deep conviction in his deeds, and the family was a true example of Catholic life. Once the children wished to go to the capital on Corpus Christi to see the procession at St. Stephen's, but the father would not permit it because it was more for the sake of looking at the show than of devotion.

The only son John, born on October 4, 1810, showed himself worthy of such a father. In early boyhood he manifested great pleasure in religious exercises. He was also a great lover of books. His father, with true watchfulness, took care that these inclinations of his soul should bring him only profit. John was not wanting in talent and a desire for study. But his father thought it too costly and dangerous. So at fifteen the boy had to take care of the horses, often driving into the city and in other ways helping in the ordinary work. Nature had given him a cheerful and lively temperament. Still the years which are usually so full of moral peril to others served only to fix deeper in his soul a zeal and love for the Faith and to foster that most beautiful of all the virtues, purity. He knew that angelic life required angelic nourishment and so he often sought the table of the Lord. And since it was hard to attend to this matter in Enzersfeld, he often rose at two o'clock in the morning without acquainting the others of it and went to Vienna to receive Holy Communion.

John was to be the heir of his father's property. But he had long found his treasure in the acre of which the Gospel speaks and his father was much too religious a man to refuse to God the sacrifice of his only son. When twenty-five years old Stoeger asked to be admitted among the Redemptorists at Vienna. After he had spent almost a year as a postulant he was sent to Eggenburg in lower Austria to make the regular noviceship.

Thenceforth John Stoeger was dead to the world. He performed no prominent apostolic work for the weal of his fellow-man save by his life of prayer and labor, but remained hidden from the world for more than forty years, always in the same place—the quiet cloister of Eggenburg, attending to his duties as gardener. Brother Stoeger entered into his vocation with all the fervor and love of which his pure and uncorrupted spirit was capable. Nothing was too difficult or too mean for him if it helped to perfect him as much as possible in his vocation. His fervent devotion in prayer was known to all. But the whole of his day's work was really one unbroken prayer. "This brother," said a missionary, "saves more souls by his prayer than all our fathers by their preaching." Brother Stoeger was quite as zealous in his work as in prayer. He once said: "One must work as if he had always to live and he must pray as if the day was his last." Thus he observed his "Work and Pray."

God always and by preference makes the saints bearers of the cross—sometimes to try them, sometimes to glorify them the more. And Brother Stoeger was not spared the cross. With oncoming age he endured spiritual desolation and abandonment, being especially tormented by a temptation against faith. Should we consider him as doing penance for the weak faith of our days or as giving it an example of steadfastness? To these spiritual afflictions which, however, were often interrupted by hours of consolation, were added great bodily sufferings until the Lord called His faithful servant to Himself, on November 3, 1883. In 1900, after the process of beatification was begun, his remains were transferred from the common graveyard to the chapel of the Redemptorists in Eggenburg.

Charles Dominic Albini

37. The Congregation of Missionary Oblates of the Immaculate Virgin Mary has justly petitioned for the beatification of one of its members, Charles Dominic Albini.[85] The servant of God was a popular missionary distinguished by his personal holiness and his self-sacrificing zeal for souls and glorified by God with miracles both before and after his death.

Before his entrance into the Congregation, Charles Albini was for nine years vicar in his native town of Mentone in the principality of Monaco, and for two years longer, professor of moral theology and director of the seminary at Nizza. At that time (1824), the founder of the Congregation of Oblates, Eugene de Mazenod, with his companions, was conducting a mission at Nizza. Albini became intimately acquainted with this zealous man and was soon quite captivated by his manner of life. He had himself been successful in mission work, especially at Mentone. But it was only after repeated petitions and with a heavy heart that the bishop of Nizza gave Albini permission to enter the Oblates. "If I had four priests like Don Albini," wrote the bishop to the founder, "my diocese would be transformed. Only on condition that he may later on work here as a missionary, will I let him go."

The penitential spirit of the servant of God may be seen from the fact that after entering the Congregation he could not be permitted to practise all the forms of penance he had hitherto used. Superiors were soon so convinced of Albini's virtue that they shortened his noviceship and permitted him after a few months to make his vows. They were not deceived. Albini had unusual success in giving missions to the people, although he spoke French only imperfectly. It was not long before he became famed as a wonder-worker. For a time he had to interrupt his missions and to lecture on moral theology at the seminary of Marseilles, which was in charge of the Oblates.

The culminating point of Albini's activity was during the last four years of his life, 1835-1839, as a missionary on the island of Corsica. The bishop of Ajaccio desired the Oblates for the upbuilding of his clergy as well as for the spiritual regeneration of his neglected diocese. This was a field of labor that suited Father Albini. The people of Corsica were strongly impressed by his preaching and a notable improvement in morals followed. In many places it needed but a word from the servant of God to produce a radical change. Many miraculous events were connected with the appearance of the missionary, so that he became known throughout the island as "the Saint"—a title no one ever contradicted. His companion, Father Guibert, afterward cardinal-archbishop of Paris, wrote: "It is enough to see Father Albini to be impressed with the idea of a saint—of a man who, lost to everything earthly, lives only for heaven, and this without singularity or pretense but with unaffected simplicity and humility."

Unfortunately the zealous missionary was soon to end his journeying. He died at the age of forty-eight on May 20, 1839, at Vico, in Corsica. The activity of the saints, however, is often richer in blessing after their death, and this appears to be true of Charles Albini.

Venerable John Claude Marie Colin

38. On July 23, 1816, the day after their ordination, twelve young priests made a pilgrimage to the shrine of Our Lady of Fourvière to implore counsel and courage for the foundation of a new religious society. The plan was proposed by the Venerable John Claude Marie Colin, but years elapsed before the establishment of "The Society of Mary" was accomplished.[86]

John Claude was born on August 7, 1790, at St. Bonnet-le-Troncy, Diocese of Lyons, of a good Catholic family. After completing his studies in the little seminary he first took up military life. But after a time he found his heart more inclined toward the militia of Christ. At the seminary of Lyons he was the friend and classmate of the Blessed Cure d'Ars. After his ordination he worked nine years as assistant to his brother Peter, pastor of Cerdon. During this period he conceived the design of establishing a congregation and he awaited a favorable moment for beginning a community life. The Congregation of Sisters (Maristines) was first established.

The misery of the villages in the country roundabout —a result of the Revolution—had touched his heart. With priests like himself he gave missions, and thus in effect obtained the end of the society he had in mind. The work was very successful. But he was called from this field and was entrusted with the direction of the seminary of Belley. Still he did not lose sight of the purpose of his life. Missionaries were wanted for Oceania, and since the "Society of Mary" seemed adapted for this work he obtained approbation from Rome in 1836. Among those who first took vows with Colin were his brother Peter, the Blessed Peter Aloysius Chanel,* and the Venerable Marcellin Champagnat. Colin was elected superior-general. The Society extended rapidly and now labors in nearly every country of the globe. Their great success in foreign missions, especially in Oceania and New Zealand, is well known to all. In 1854 Father Colin resigned the office of superior-general to devote all his time and attention to the spiritual upbuilding of the young Society. He lived to have the happiness of seeing his rules approved by the Apostolic See in 1873. He died holily, as he had lived, on November 15, 1875, at La Neylière.

Venerable Marcellin Champagnat

39. A truly striking character was Colin's companion, Venerable Marcellin Champagnat.[87] In him it is also manifest that God chooses the weak and lowly to do things that are great. The clamor of rebellion against throne and altar had already broken out when Marcellin Champagnat was born on May 20, 1789. His parents were poor, but an aunt whom the Revolution had driven from her convent took care to give the boy

*See page 321.

a good training. Until he was sixteen Marcellin had
to work at home and in the fields and his highest aspira-
tion was to follow the calling of his father. But a
priest came to the parish by order of the archbishop
of Lyons to look for boys who might be trained for
the clerical state. It was necessary that the great gaps
opened in the ranks of the clergy by the dreadful events
of the Revolution should be filled. Marcellin was
pointed out to this priest for his modesty and virtue
and was receved as a candidate. For trial they sent
him to a Latin school, where an uncle of his essayed to
instruct him. But the uncle found that his nephew had
little talent and advised him against further study. In
spite of this Marcellin entered the little seminary of
Verrières in the autumn of 1805; but here, too, they
desired him to leave after the first year because of his
poor talent. Difficulties steel the courage and confidence in God of the saints and bind them only the closer
to God. So it was with our good student. He at once
made a pilgrimage with his mother to the grave of St.
Francis Regis, and there implored the grace to be permitted to remain in the seminary. Then he had
recourse to the Most Pure Mother, seat of wisdom, and
to the fervent reception of the Sacraments that he
might obtain the gift of understanding. His prayer
was not in vain and by persevering diligence he overcame all obstacles and at length became a pattern for
his fellow-students in every respect. St. Francis Regis
and St. Aloysius were his favorite patrons during his
whole life. The first year he suffered a great deal from
his companions because, being older and a country boy,
he was rather bashful and awkward, and besides was
backward in his schooling. Marcellin bore these rail-
leries with the humility and amiability of a saint.

While a student he practised on vacation days the
apostleship of charity, especially so after he had taken
up his higher studies. He visited the sick, gathered

the children to instruct them in catechism, and on Sunday afternoons gave religious discourses to adults, who gathered in large numbers from surrounding districts. In 1816, being then twenty-seven years of age, Marcellin was ordained. The spirit that animated him is made clear by the fact that he was one of those who made the pilgrimage to Notre Dame de Fourvière to consecrate their lives wholly to the service of God under the protection of Mary. The saints always exercise a great influence on students. Champagnat in his office as chaplain of Lavalla had often to spend the whole day in the confessional. He was most energetic, however, in his denunciation of wickedness, bad books, dangerous dances, and the like. The young were his principal interest and they in turn soon became aware how well he understood them. The great ignorance of religion which Champagnat met everywhere, especially in the country districts, led him to establish a society for the purpose of instructing the young in religion. Two young students of Lavalla were the first to be won to this apostolic work. A little house was made to serve as a cloister and they lived in great poverty but extremely happy. Champagnat's example and enheartening words dissipated all fears for the future. To extend their influence the little band had recourse to Mary and four other candidates joined them. This was the beginning of the "Little Brothers of Mary." According to the rules given them by their founder, the members were not to become priests, so that the duties of the priesthood might not interfere with the performance of their work. The Society was to engage not only in teaching but in anything that would be of service to the young.

Champagnat understood clearly that the welfare of an Order depends on the spirit which animates the members. Hence he deemed no care too great in advancing the spiritual training of his Brothers. With a kindly simplicity and piety like that of St. Francis of Assisi he showed extraordinary prudence in spiritual direction; and the charity, harmony, and great fervor of the "Little Brothers" justly claimed the admiration of all.

Great undertakings must always battle against opposition. The clergy of the neighboring country thought Champagnat's plan eccentric; and they would have forced his community to disperse, but he sought no other defense, as the acts of his process tell us, than "patience, prayer, and confidence in Mary." Meanwhile, so many candidates applied that a new house had to be built. No one would contribute to it. Trusting in Providence, Champagnat bade his Brothers to begin building, courageously helped in the labor himself, and to the amazement of those who opposed him, the house was finished in a short time. The archbishop of Lyons now became a warm friend of the enterprise and in 1826 the Brothers were able to take their first vows. When the time had come to elect a superior for the Society, Champagnat desired that a Brother should be clothed with this office. Another priest set on foot secret intrigues to secure this office and could not restrain his anger when in spite of a repeated ballot Champagnat was preferred to him. Champagnat retained the direction of the Brothers even after he had joined the Marists in 1836. He desired his Congregation of Brothers to be regarded as a little sister of the Marists. On this account it is often called the "Marist School Brothers." They spread with great rapidity. In 1910 there were not less than 6000 "Little Brothers of Mary," who according to the spirit of their venerable founder, zealously instruct the young in all quarters of the world.

Champagnat had naturally robust health. But his hard life and restless zeal, which knew no relaxation, prematurely consumed his strength. For his own well-being he had the least consideration. Yet he accomplished more for the glory of God and the salvation of souls than if he had saved his strength to reach old age. He died at the age of fifty-one in the novitiate of his Congregation at Vauban, June 6, 1840, but the seed he sowed grows apace and bears its fruit.

Venerable Pierre Julien Eymard

40. There is a Eucharistic movement in the Church. The attraction of the Saviour hidden in the tabernacle appears to grow stronger and to lead mankind to Him as the only true source of joy and consolation. To promote this Eucharistic movement was the life purpose of the Venerable Pierre Julien Eymard, founder of the Congregation of the Most Blessed Sacrament.[88] But before he came to a clear knowledge of this mission and of the ways and means to make it effective, he had to pass through many trials. The first lay in the removal of many obstacles which barred his way to the priesthood.

He was the son of a blacksmith and was born on February 4, 1811, at La Mure d'Isère, near Grenoble. Julian imbibed a love of the Holy Eucharist from his mother's breast, for she was most devoted to the Blessed Sacrament and paid daily visits to the church with her children. These must have been happy moments for the little Julien, who soon manifested a great liking for the church. If he was missing from the house, they were sure to find him on the steps of the altar. Our Lord in the tabernacle knew well how to enlighten the innocent heart of the child and to draw it to Himself. The boy showed a marvelously precocious intelligence of the truths of Faith. When five years old he asked for Holy Communion and made known his desire to become a priest. When at the age of nine he wished to prepare for the feast of the Holy Name of Jesus by confession and was refused by the pastor and chaplain on the pretext of want of time, he set out indefatigably through the deep winter snow and confessed in a neighboring parish. At his first Holy Communion, which he received at the age of twelve, he made a pilgrimage of seventy miles to the distant shrine of Notre Dame du Laus. Along with his great love of the Holy Eucharist, the lily of purity bloomed in him with a serene splendor.

In spite of Julien's manifestation of so clear a vocation to the priesthood his father wished to make a blacksmith of him and would not permit him to study. Some of his schoolmates who were making their studies taught the blacksmith's apprentice the rudiments of Latin on free days. Finally his father's eyes were opened and he sent his son, now seventeen years old, to a cleric in Grenoble. In the following year Eymard entered the novitiate of the Oblates at Marseilles. But he applied himself with such excessive ardor to the duties of his vocation that he became ill and after ten months at the novitiate was obliged to return home. His condition became so serious that he was given the last sacraments. Though all doubted his recovery, he declared with complete confidence: "I shall become a priest." His strength of will won the victory over his illness after two years of struggle. He then asked admission to the seminary of Grenoble and, although he had studied but little and his pastor could not give a satisfactory testimonial of his proficiency, he made a good entrance examination. He ascribed his unexpected success to the special assistance of the Blessed Virgin. Three years later, on July 20, 1834, he had the happiness of being ordained. The daily offering of the Holy Sacrifice now revealed the extraordinary fervor of his devotion to the Blessed Sacrament. When circumstances permitted he spent two hours preparing for Mass and after it he made an equally long thanksgiving. A priest so penetrated with love for the

Eucharist must necessarily have the greatest success in the care of souls. Only after long refusal did the bishop finally permit Eymard, in 1839, to join the Marists. "I have given sufficient proof of my high esteem for the Society of Mary," he said, "in giving it such a priest."

Father Eymard rendered distinguished services to the Order. In 1845 he was provincial of Lyons, then novice-master and superior of the College of La Seyne-sur-Mer. He made veneration of the Blessed Sacrament flourish everywhere and with it the religious life of those under him. But he was to do much more for the promotion of devotion to the great mystery of love. At the shrine of Fourvière he learned that God certainly demanded of him the foundation of an Order whose chief aim should be the veneration of the Most Blessed Sacrament. His biographer tells us of a thrice-repeated vision of the Blessed Virgin, who encouraged him in the work. Another time, during the thanksgiving after Mass, he received a special enlightenment on the same matter. Still he did not act precipitately. Through the Dominican superior-general, Father Jandel, he informed Pope Pius IX of his plan and the latter replied with words of praise and encouragement. After further counsel with men of prudence. Father Eymard believed it his duty to leave the Congregation of the Marists, hard though he felt it to separate from his well-beloved brethren, who begged him to remain with them.

But his time of trial was not yet past. He endeavored to put his plan into effect in Paris. Men looked upon him as a visionary who had been dismissed from his Congregation. The first companions he had won to his design deserted him. Nevertheless, he was able, with the permission of the archbishop, Monsignor Sibour, to establish a small religious residence in 1857 and in the following year he obtained the preliminary approbation of the rules he had composed. The principal end of the Order is to promote the veneration of the Holy Eucharist in one's self and in others. With ardent zeal Eymard now proceeded to the accomplishment of his purpose. Through his endeavors there came into life "The Priests' Eucharistic League," which to-day is spread over the whole world and whose members have greatly promoted imitation of the boundless love of the hidden Divinity. As a Eucharistic preacher Eymard journeyed through the provinces of France to bring the faithful nearer to the central sun of Catholic worship, to warm them in its rays and to charm them by its beauty. He was an eloquent advocate of frequent communion, for he rightly saw in it the best protection against sin.

Besides the Society of Priests of the Most Blessed Sacrament, Eymard also founded a Congregation for women, the Servants of the Most Blessed Sacrament. Both carry on with great zeal the work of their venerable founder. He died after a stroke of apoplexy, on August 1, 1868, at La Mure. When the body was removed to Paris in 1877 it was found still incorrupt. His life proves what a source of joy and holiness there is in the Holy Eucharist for us sinful pilgrims on earth who stand so much in need of encouragement.

Venerable Vincent Pallotti

41. *"Charitas Christi urget nos"*—"The charity of Christ presseth us" (2 Cor. v. 14). With these words St. Paul briefly points out the motive of his unceasing desire to spread the Kingdom of Christ. The same love of Christ to-day inspires men of noble and generous heart with ardent desire to labor for Christ. The life of the Venerable Vincent Pallotti is an eloquent witness of this.[89] It will be sufficient to notice only the more salient features of his remarkable career.

Vincent Pallotti was born on April 21, 1795, at

Rome, and was the son of a rich merchant; but in the Pallotti family the securing of heavenly treasure was of more concern than the amassing of earthly wealth. The father was accustomed to hear two Masses every day and every eighth day to approach the Sacraments. The mother even surpassed him in her deep and interior religious spirit. It is evident that such parents considered the religious training of their children their holiest duty. In reward God bestowed upon Vincent, the third of their ten children, quite extraordinary graces. Were it not confirmed from all sources, we could hardly believe what perfect sanctity was manifest in the little boy, his great hatred of everything that bordered on sin, his careful avoidance of whatever might sully his purity, his fasting and penance which made even his parents afraid, his compassionate love of the poor, seraphic devotion in prayer, apostolic work among his companions—and all this at an age when the light of reason was just dawning.

When Vincent began his studies at the Roman College he was not distinguished for brilliance of intellect or for mental power. But he overcame this disadvantage by his trustful devotion to the Holy Ghost, and he was soon one of the first among the students. Religious exercises suffered no detriment from his zeal in the pursuit of knowledge. No one was surprised when the boy of sixteen entered the clerical state. He had long cherished the thought of becoming a Capuchin. While yet a student he made vows of poverty and chastity and of obedience to his spiritual director. He vowed also never to strive for dignities. His heart was overwhelmed with holy joy when on May 16, 1818, he was ordained. Words can not tell how happy the celebration of Holy Mass made him. He went to confession every morning. His interior fervor of devotion was evident in his countenance, and during Mass the tears often flowed down upon his vestments, and many persons saw him suspended in the air while he was celebrating. No less a witness than Ignatius von Senestrey, afterward bishop of Regensburg, who served Pallotti's Mass at the Roman College, testifies to this.

Since Pallotti's parents were quite wealthy, the young priest at first lived with his family as private chaplain and meanwhile continued his studies. Promoted to the degrees of Doctor of Philosophy and of Theology he accepted the position of private tutor in the department of dogma in the Roman University. He filled this office for ten years. But his ardent zeal for God's glory did not allow him to remain unmindful of the salvation of the souls of others. Wherever opportunity offered for apostolic work he joyfully accepted it. But this did not satisfy him. So in 1829 he resigned his post as teacher and accepted the rectorship of the poor little church of the Holy Ghost. Now began the glorious epoch in the career of Father Pallotti. He soon had the reputation of a divinely favored confessor and director, was obliged to stay all day long in the confessional and when he came home his room was visited by persons of every condition who came to consult with him on the affairs of their souls. Before long there was no name in all Rome so popular as that of Padre Pallotti. He entered into a life of continuous activity as director of spiritual exercises, missionary among the people, and preacher in the public squares of the city. Those who did not listen to his stirring words on death, judgment, hell, and eternity always yielded when he spoke of the motherly love and mercy of Mary. With him it was a necessary part of a preacher's work to inflame the hearts of his hearers with love for Mary, Mother of God.

Many distinguished men were trusted friends of Pallotti's; for instance, Cardinal Prince Odescalchi; Cardinal Aloysius Lambruschini, secretary of state under

Gregory XIV; Blessed Caspar del Bufalo;* and especially the Venerable Bernard Mary Clausi† of the
Order of Minims of St. Francis of Paula. For nearly
twenty years he was the spiritual director of another
saintly soul, the Venerable Elizabeth Sanna.‡

Pallotti had incidentally formed a committee for
the spreading of good publications. It was to be the beginning of his religious establishment. The union produced great results. Its members increased in number
and this suggested to the founder the idea of gathering
his friends into a strict organization for life in the service of the good cause. He found men enough ready
to place full confidence in him. Through the intervention of his friend Cardinal Odescalchi he obtained in
1835 the approbation of the Church for the "Society
of the Catholic Apostleship," as he then called his Congregation. Later on, with the confirmation of Pius IX,
it took the name of *"Pia Societas Missionum"*—"The
Pious Society of the Missions." Its purpose was to
arouse faith and charity among Catholics and to
propagate the same among heretics and infidels; but
the members made only solemn promises instead of
vows, especially a promise of perseverance in the Congregation.

According to the same rules Pallotti organized a
Congregation of women for the religious training of
young girls, and finally a kind of third order to which
persons of all conditions might belong. The influence
and authority of the servant of God grew from day to
day. Men hastened to him in every variety of affairs.
The poorer classes especially claimed his compassion.
He endeavored to help them by organization and permanent settlements. He formed guilds for the various
avocations and established agricultural schools and

*See page 97 sqq.
†See page 183.
‡See page 289.

country savings banks to protect small farmers against usurers.

It is also due to Pallotti that a solemn mission for the people is held in a Roman church during the Octave of the Epiphany. He desired all nations to gather before the crib of the Redeemer; and he therefore had Pontifical Masses said in all the various rites and sermons preached in the principal languages of the world. The closing sermon is always preached by a cardinal and Pius IX in the first year of his pontificate gave this sermon in person.

The Masonic revolutionaries of 1848 threatened the life of the zealous priest and he was obliged to remain concealed in the Irish College. He was not long to survive the triumph of the Papacy, however, and died on January 22, 1850. All Rome mourned in him the loss of its greatest benefactor. So great were the throngs that crowded to see his body that the police could with difficulty preserve order. He had worked miracles during his life, but many more took place after his death. Leo XIII once said that immediately after Pallotti's death he would have a bust of the latter placed in his ante-room so that he would be reminded to ask the servant of God every morning in passing to implore for him the grace of a good preparation for Mass.

Venerable Bernard Mary Clausi

42. Venerable Bernard Mary Clausi, the intimate friend of Venerable Vincent Pallotti, was born on November 27, 1787, at Sisto in Calabria, of one of the first families of the country.[90] After an innocent boyhood he entered the Order of Minims of St. Francis of Paula at the age of fifteen. But before the end of his noviceship the monastery was closed by the Revolution and Clausi was obliged to return home. He was forced into military service, but even as a soldier he

lived like a saint. He afterward became a secular priest and when the condition of the times grew better he again entered the Order of the Minims. The chief scenes of his labors were Rome and Naples. Ardent zeal for souls, great humility in spite of many extraordinary gifts of grace, and serene cheerfulness under every blow of adversity were the indications of his sanctity. In the dreadful interior sufferings of his last years, his friend Pallotti was his loving consoler. He died on December 20, 1849, a month and three days before Pallotti, as he had particularly foretold to the latter. The miracles of Clausi were numerous both before and after his death.

VENERABLE CAJETAN ERRICO, VENERABLE MICHAEL GARRICOÏTS, FATHER FORTUNATUS REDOLFI

43. The Venerable Cajetan Errico died on October 26, 1860, at Naples. The process of his beatification is far advanced. He was the founder of the Congregation of Priests of the Sacred Heart.[91]

The founder of a similar Congregation in France, the Priest Helpers of the Sacred Heart of Jesus, was the Venerable Michael Garricoïts of Gascony.[92] He died of apoplexy on the Feast of the Assumption, 1863 at Betharram, near Bayonne. His Congregation, which follows the rule of St. Augustine, spread not only at home but also in South America.

The servant of God, Father Fortunatus Redolfi— died in 1850—belonged to the Congregation of the Barnabites.

VENERABLE BENILDES ROMANÇON, BROTHER SCUBILIO

44. The Venerable Benildes Romançon, of the Congregation of the School Brothers of St. John Baptist de la Salle, was born at Thuret in the Diocese of Clermont on June 14, 1805.[93] Because of the poverty of his parents he was obliged when a boy to spend most

of his time in tending cattle. But he also employed much of this time in gathering nourishment for mind and heart from pious books. He had to suffer many a jeer and insult from his companions on account of his modest behavior. During a visit to Clermont he saw the School Brothers and was so captivated by their modesty that he at once resolved to join them. Since he had not attended school up to this time, though he was now sixteen, his parents sent him to the School Brothers for instruction. When he first applied for admission they did not wish to receive him because of his smallness of stature. But the novice-master prophesied that "this little man will become the glory of our Institute." After the completion of his noviceship he taught with great success in the cities of Aurillac, Limoges, Moulins, Clermont, Montferrand, and Billom. In 1841, he was sent to establish and direct a school in the town of Saugues. Until the end of his life he here devoted all his powers to arousing in the young and among the people a living spirit of faith. He considered the religious element the most important matter in education. He took great pains to give catechetical instruction an interesting and attractive character. On evenings he gave religious instruction to adults. But he preached far more by his virtuous example than by his words. His school produced many vocations to the priesthood and to religious life. Very many were benefited by the power of the pious Brother's prayers, but in his humility he managed artfully to ascribe the merit of the granting of the prayer to another. At the news of his death the people from far and near streamed in, endeavoring to obtain some relic of him. His grave in Saugues is honored by many miracles.

The servant of God, Brother Scubilio—died in 1867 —belongs to the same Congregation of Brothers of the Christian Schools.

ANDREW BELTRAMI

45. Prayer and suffering made a saint of a young member of the Salesian Society, the servant of God, Andrew Beltrami.[94] "Mary, rather take my child to thyself than that he become wicked," the pious mother of Beltrami used to pray. Mary accepted the boy commended to her care, but not before he had admirably accomplished the purpose of his life. While he was at the public school of Omegna at the northern end of Lake Orta, Piedmont, where he was born on June 24, 1870, it was feared that frivolity would get the upper hand. But this danger was averted when the lively and highly-gifted boy was sent to the Salesian institution at Lanzo. The supernatural element in education which the admirable sons of Don Bosco know how to instil so well, enabled him to master his flightiness. Frequent reception of the Sacraments and the awakening of the spirit of self-sacrifice in well-doing effected in Beltrami a noble development of all the best traits of his character. He was soon a great help to his superiors in the work of education. He particularly endeavored to win and reconcile discontented youths, of whom there are always some to be found in every institution. On days of vacation he found ways and means of practising apostolic work. Through his endeavors a Catholic public library was established in his native town.

After completing his college course Beltrami entered the Salesian novitiate at Foglizzo, but before he finished he had contracted an incurable disease of the lungs. It seemed his gift from Providence to become a model for the sick. For seven years he was to languish in sickness, yet he had strength enough to be ordained and to say Mass every day until his death on December 3, 1897. But they were not useless or unhappy years for him. He published no less than twelve popular ascetical works and there were others ready when he died. One of the latter was a treatise on sickness, in three parts: Sickness in the plan of Divine Providence; The Temptations of the Sick; The Apostleship of Sickness. Beltrami derived from his sufferings all the benefit God designs them to bestow. He rejoiced in his sickness as a special grace. In his notes he says:

"The chains with which I am bound to my room are dearer to me than the necklaces of princes, and I kiss them as precious jewels. At the end of February I celebrated for three days the fifth anniversary of my illness. I said the *Te Deum, Benedicite, Laudate Dominum,* and *Agimus tibi Gratias* to thank God for having deigned to make me share in the sufferings of His Son. Within my little room, where there is nothing of the world, but a foretaste of heaven instead, I am the happiest man in the world." "To die and to be made whole? No, but to live and to suffer." These sayings show us how deeply he had tasted the sweetness of suffering. All who knew him in his suffering bear witness that these sentiments came from his heart. "To suffer and to pray," he called the purpose of his life. Like a true saint he embraced in his prayers the whole world and that he might help them he recounted all lands, all conditions, and the Church in her afflictions. Beltrami's example reveals the strength and happiness faith gives to souls that are stricken down by disease in early years.

Felix de Andreis

46. Among the first Lazarists who came to the United States in 1817 with Bishop Dubourg of New Orleans, was the servant of God, Felix de Andreis.[95] He was from Demonte in Piedmont and had already won distinction in Rome as a preacher and as adviser of high dignitaries in the Church until the time of Pius VII. It was his constant desire, however, to spend his life in labor among the heathen. But though

the servant of God was not to be sent to China as he had hoped, the United States offered all that the ardent heart of an apostle could desire. Bishop Dubourg sent Father de Andreis to St. Louis, to be vicar-general and pastor. There were in this district negroes and Indians who languished in the misery of heathenism, and large numbers of white men who also were sunk in an ignorance almost as deep. But souls are always desirous of salvation if only the word of God be announced to them with charity. Father de Andreis had an extraordinary success in this great field, a success in which the unselfishness of his wonderful zeal played a great part.

The servant of God was also superior of the Lazarist mission in America, novice-master and director of a college. The establishment of a seminary in Barrens was due to his endeavors. Unfortunately this indefatigable man died when only forty-two years of age, on October 15, 1820. Even non-Catholics mourned his death as an irremediable loss.

ALFRED PAMPALON

47. The young Redemptorist, Alfred Pampalon,[96] is a noble flower of sanctity in the New World. He was born at Levis, near Quebec, in 1867, entered the congregation of the Redemptorists at St. Trond in Belgium in 1886 and died on September 30, 1896, at the famous shrine of St. Ann de Beaupré in Canada. Purity and gentleness are the distinguishing traits of his noble character. The maxim with which he constantly aroused his zeal was: "Only a short time and then eternity."

JOHN MERLINI

48. The servant of God, John Merlini, who died in 1873, was one of the first companions and ablest co-operators of Blessed Caspar del Bufalo.

Conrad Birndorfer

49. The servant of God, Conrad Birndorfer of Parzham, in the diocese of Passau, was a Capuchin lay-brother in the convent of Altoetting and died on April 21, 1894. The process of his beatification was recently inaugurated by the bishop of Passau.

John M. Condrin

50. John M. Condrin, founder of the Picpus Society, died 1837.

Lawrence of St. Francis Xavier

51. Lawrence of St. Francis Xavier—died 1856—belonged to the Society of St. Paul of the Cross.

Louis Pavoni

52. The lifework of the servant of God, Louis Pavoni—died 1849—was the foundation of the Congregation of the Sons of the Immaculate Virgin Mary in the diocese of Brescia.

HOLY RELIGIOUS—WOMEN

WOMEN consecrated to God in religious life have won the love and veneration of the whole world by their modest and self-sacrificing labors. But they have also been a joy to the Heavenly Father. Abundant proof of this has been given by the great number of them who have died during the nineteenth century in the repute of sanctity and, in particular, by the heroism of their faith in God and their love for Him in spite of severest trials; by their clear insight into the needs of the times, so that Providence could make use of them in the establishment of great enterprises for the salvation of souls; and by the grandeur of the graces with which God's liberality has endowed so many of them. Though we could gladly dwell longer on the life of each one, we must be content with a concise and brief account lest our sketch should become too extended.

Three of these valiant women have already been declared "Blessed" by the Church; viz., Julie Billiart, Marie Madeleine Postel, and Madeleine Sophie Barat. All three as founders of religious Congregations have rendered immortal service to the welfare of the Church.

Blessed Julie Billiart

1. Over thorny paths, but lovingly and wisely, Providence led Blessed Julie Billiart to the end of her vocation.[97] She was born at Cavilly in Picardy on July 12, 1751. On account of the poverty of her parents she was unable to obtain any superior education. It was her misfortune to become the victim of a nervous disorder, resulting from a great shock, and in course of time it completely crippled her. But sick-

ness does not set limits to the activity of the saints. By her prayer and example and by her wise counsels Julie practised from her sick-bed a beneficent apostleship on all who addressed her from far and near. This was particularly manifest when the assault on altar and throne began in France. But the time came when the crippled Julie was obliged to flee from the bloody-minded revolutionists, who had discovered her to be the chief support of religion in Cavilly. After long and various wanderings, she at last found refuge in Amiens.

The persecution had brought her into contact with a noble and congenial soul, the noble lady Françoise Blin de Bourdon, Viscountess of Gezaincourt. To check the frightful degeneracy of morals caused by the unbelieving era of the Revolution the two friends resolved to found a Congregation for the education of poor girls. Although afflicted until 1802 with her dreadful ailment, Julie Billiart was the moving power of the enterprise, and with the assistance of two priests of the Fathers of the Faith, Father Joseph Varin and Father Anthony Thomas, who later joined the restored Society of Jesus, the establishment of the Congregation of Notre Dame was realized.

This institute spread rapidly and there prevailed in it an excellent religious spirit owing to the enlightened wisdom of Julie. But heavy storms were to break upon its founder. A French priest, the first confessor of the Congregation, interfered too much in the affairs of administration; there came differences with the bishop of Amiens and Julie Billiart fell under grave suspicion. It finally ended in her formal expulsion from Amiens and the abolition of her work in France. The holy woman turned to Belgium, where she had already established many residences. Here, too, severe trials awaited her. But the more frequent the blows of misfortune, the more refined was the gold of her pure love of God and the more solid the edifice of her Congregation. On April 8, 1816, she rendered her noble soul into the hands of the Creator. She had hardly died when the world recognized how great a saint had left it, but it no longer withheld the acknowledgment. On May 13, 1906, Pius X bestowed on her the honors of the altar. Her Congregation continues to work efficaciously in Belgium, Holland, Germany, England, and America.

Blessed Marie Madeleine Postel

2. A heroine in the true sense of the word was the Blessed Marie Madeleine Postel.[98] History can present few women who possessed the great courage and strength of soul shown by the Blessed Madeleine. She was born on November 28, 1756, at Barfleur, a little seaport of Normandy. Even in her earlier years she manifested a truly remarkable sanctity. When, at the age of nine, she received her First Communion, she made a vow of virginity, promising to devote her life to the service of God and the neighbor. From that time she communicated daily and practised the severest penance. Once, when told that two young men were about to fight a duel, Madeleine, then only a school girl, gathered her schoolmates and knelt to pray for the frustration of the wicked deed. Suddenly, and as the first blow was to be struck, the duelists extended hands to each other in reconciliation. The father of one of them went to Madeleine to thank her for her efficacious prayer, for he could not explain the unexpected reconciliation except by intervention from above. When she was eighteen the saintly young woman opened a school for the poor in her native town. The free time of the day and a great part of the night she spent before the tabernacle. What courage and strength she thence derived was proved in the days of the Revolution. She gave priests shelter and protection in her house, kept

the sacred vessels and vestments there and also the Holy Eucharist. In the darkness of night she assembled the faithful in her house or in some other retired place for the celebration of the Holy Mysteries. She went about encouraging the weak, visiting the sick, and secretly bringing priests to them. She even obtained permission to carry the Holy Eucharist to the sick, since it was dangerous for priests to do so. Bailiffs frequently came to surprise the priests or to obtain evidence of unlawful behavior against her; and it was an evident miracle that they always blindly passed the plainly visible door of the secret chapel. For years this intrepid and valiant virgin was the guardian of the Most Holy at Barfleur and took care that the people should not be altogether deprived of the consolations of religion. At length when, in 1801, divine service could again be held in public, she celebrated the first Holy Communion of all the boys and girls whom she had prepared. Unfortunately the new pastor became jealous of the successful activity of Madeleine Postel. In 1805, therefore, she left her native place never to revisit it again.

She found a charitable reception and assistance from a priest in Cherbourg and revived with new zeal her apostolic activity in behalf of girls. Two years later, with three companions, she made perpetual vows. This was the beginning of the School Sisters of Mercy. But only the energy and confidence in God of a Postel could persevere in the work under the storm which arose against them; and finally she had the consolation of obtaining for her sisters the old and quite ruined abbey of St. Sauveur le Vicomte. The venerable woman, now eighty-two years old, worked like a laborer in the restoration of the building to bring back to its pristine splendor the house of God. Her strong faith, her great love of virginity and her practice of penance so severe that nature shrinks from the thought of it are a sharp rebuke to our effeminate generation. She stands before us like a heroine of the days of the martyrs. When she died on July 16, 1846, no one thought of praying for her but only to her. Her beatification took place on May 17, 1908.

Blessed Madeleine Sophie Barat

3. If one desires to see the spirit of a St. Teresa alive in the nineteenth century, let him read the admirable life of the Blessed Madeleine Sophie Barat.[99] He will be placed face to face, as it were, with proof that eminent sanctity is now found in the Church just as in ages past. She was born of simple but truly Christian parents on December 12, 1779, at Joigny in Burgundy. The Reign of Terror brought bitter grief to the Barat family. Their son Louis, then a deacon, was imprisoned in the Conciergerie in 1793 and only the fall of Robespierre saved him from the guillotine. When Louis was ordained to the priesthood he brought his sister Sophie, eleven years younger than himself, to Paris. He took upon himself her spiritual guidance and wisely and skilfully made her familiar with the principles of Christian asceticism. It was at Paris, the center of the Revolution, that the Blessed Sophie was to found a religious Society for the restoration and defense of the Kingdom of God. The devout Father Varin, superior of the Fathers of the Faith, directed her attention to the needs of the Church and to the misery of so many immortal souls that do not love Him whose love is alone able to give them happiness. He enkindled in her a zeal for souls which was to burn ever more strongly into the days of her old age, and which neither sorrow nor a great flood of bitter trials would succeed in extinguishing. On November 21, 1800, Sophie Barat, with several companions, solemnly consecrated herself to the Sacred Heart. Two years later she was allowed to take the vows of her Society

and was obliged to assume the office of superior, which she filled for sixty-two years.

But it was a heavy and sharp-edged cross that was laid upon her shoulders. In the beginning God permitted that the Society of the Sacred Heart should be very severely tried, and this no one felt more keenly than the superior-general. But, as the cold, dull iron sparkles more brightly with light and glow the more it is penetrated by the fire of the forge, so in this fiery trial of suffering the splendid features of the founder's character and her unshakable confidence in God triumphed; and it was her consolation to see her Society spread over the whole world, with nearly 4000 Religious calling themselves her daughters.

Her life was a living and active faith. The truths of faith were her consolation in all reverses of fortune. They alone decided her resolutions. This spirit of faith was so strong in her that it was endowed by God with the gift of miracles. She was also endowed with remarkable enlightenment, prudence, and a farsighted and intimate understanding of the times. There was nothing extravagant in her conduct. Her chief interest was centered in what the Divine Heart so much desires—the honor of the Heavenly Father, or what is practically the same, the salvation of immortal souls. Seeing that especially among the ranks of the wealthy many are alienated from God at an early age, Mother Barat made it a chief aim of her Society to impart to young ladies a good Christian education. As an excellent means toward the realization of this end she encouraged retreats and endeavored to procure that as many as possible might profit by this means of regeneration for mind and heart. Extraordinary favors from heaven were numerous during her lifetime. She had marvelous success in converting obstinate sinners. Very remarkable are the miracles which took place after her death. Twenty-eight years later her body was found to be incorrupt although the coffin was decayed. Nearly one hundred miracles are recorded in detail in the acts of her beatification. She was declared Blessed in 1908, although her death had occurred on May 25, 1865. But God intends for her even higher exaltation. Since her beatification she has further manifested her power to work miracles and the process of her canonization has already been begun.

Venerable Mother Philippine Duchesne

4. In apostolic fervor Venerable Mother Philippine Duchesne emulated her superior, Blessed Mother Barat.[100]   Bishop Otto Zardetti has styled her the Francis Xavier of the Society of the Sacred Heart.[101] The narratives of a Jesuit missionary in Louisiana awoke in the heart of Mother Philippine a true desire of the missions and of martyrdom when she was only eight years old. She was the daughter of a respectable family of Grenoble. When grown up she tenaciously withstood the desire of her parents that she should marry. She was finally permitted to take the veil in the convent of the Visitation; but before she had taken her vows she was obliged to seek refuge with her family on account of the Revolution. During the Reign of Terror she practised works of apostolic zeal with remarkable heroism. In 1801 she attempted to gather the dispersed nuns into the former convent of St. Marie d'en Haut, near her native town. Her attention was soon attracted to the zealous young society of the Sacred Heart, and with her companions she earnestly petitioned Mother Barat for admission. In the beginning of 1805 the union of the two communities took place.

When Bishop Dubourg of New Orleans came to France in 1817 and asked Mother Barat to send some of her sisters to his extensive diocese, Philippine Duchesne finally achieved the desire of her youth, so often expressed to her superiors. In the spring of 1818 she set out with her companions as their superior for the United States. She founded the first American convent of her Congregation at St. Charles, near St. Louis, then in the diocese of New Orleans. The vast uncultured and uncivilized territory offered the sisters a wide and difficult field of labor. But the ardent zeal of Mother Duchesne did not grow cold. She encouraged the others to constant activity by word and example. When seventy years of age she was relieved of her office of superior and sent to the Sugar Creek Indian reservation, to instruct children who were really pagans. The transports of glowing zeal for souls which had filled her mind during the whole of her lifetime are most inspiring. She died at St. Charles, aged eighty-three, on November 18, 1852.

Marie Lataste

5. Another divinely favored daughter of the Blessed Madeleine Sophie Barat is the lay-sister Marie Lataste.[102] She was the daughter of a simple farmer of Mimbaste, near Dax, but was chosen by God for singular favors. By command of her confessor, she wrote an account of the lights bestowed upon her. Every one was astonished at the profound theological knowledge of this quite illiterate young woman. During Holy Mass it was often granted her to behold Our Saviour visibly present. Marie was overwhelmed with joy when she was admitted to the Society of the Sacred Heart. In the third year of her religious life, on May 10, 1847, when only twenty-five years of age, she departed this life smiling and full of gladness, as became a saint.

Venerable Marie de Sales Chappuis

6. A strong and godly soul dwelt in the Venerable Marie de Sales Chappuis[103] of the Order of the Visita-

tion. She had the rare distinction of being a co-founder of a Congregation of priests. She was the daughter of a Swiss hotel-keeper of Soyhières, in the Canton of Berne. The deeply religious spirit of the Chappuis family may be seen from the fact that two of the sons became Jesuits, another died while a student of theology, and four daughters entered Religious Orders. Marie de Sales, when twenty-two years of age, entered the convent of the Nuns of the Visitation at Freiburg, Switzerland, in 1814. She had gone to Freiburg for the same purpose three years before, but separation from her relatives was so hard for her that she soon returned home. The second parting from home again caused her great affliction, but hardly had the gate of the cloister closed behind her when an extraordinary abundance of joy and consolation flooded her soul and removed forever all inordinate attachment to flesh and blood.

With constant and self-sacrificing enthusiasm Sister Marie de Sales entered into her new career. Her superiors were soon able to confide to her the most important offices, and in 1826 she was sent as superior to Troyes to re-establish there the former discipline of the Order. Her prudence and gentleness won for her complete success. Almost continuous re-election to the office of superior in Troyes and in Paris alternately shows how much she was beloved. The repute of her sanctity passed beyond the limits of the cloister and brought many of high rank to the convent gate for the purpose of obtaining the prudent advice and efficacious prayers of Mother Marie de Sales in affairs of importance.* The apostolic heart of the mother-superior sympathized with all classes of Christians. Her favorite study was the writing of St. Francis de

*Opinions are divided concerning some of the means employed by Mother Chappuis for the attainment of Perfection. The question of her personal sanctity, however, remains untouched by this.

Sales, whose ideas she endeavored to spread as much as possible. Conjointly with Bishop Caspar Mermillod of Geneva she founded a Religious Congregation of women, the Oblates of St. Francis de Sales, whose object was to devote themselves to the welfare of women of the working classes. Some years later the Abbé Louis Brisson under her direction organized the Oblates of St. Francis de Sales, for the purpose of giving pastoral care to young workingmen, establishing institutes for boys, and announcing the Gospel to the heathen. At this day both Congregations are in a flourishing condition.[104] Mother Mary de Sales died in Troyes at the venerable age of eighty-two. The numerous and great miracles wrought through her intercession soon led to the introduction of the process of her beatification in 1897.

Venerable Maria Michaela Florez y Lopez de Dicastillo Olmeda

7. A lady of high aristocracy was the Venerable Maria Michaela Florez y Lopez de Dicastillo Olmeda,[105] descended from a distinguished noble family of Spain. She was born at Madrid on January 1, 1809. Her noble sentiments toward God and mankind befitted her lofty birth. Even as a child she manifested a great love for the poor, and whenever she could she favored them with her gifts. After the early death of her parents she divided a large portion of her inheritance among the poor. She established a Society for the support of poor and needy religious women. Nor did she consider it beneath her dignity to stand unknown at the doors of churches begging alms for her clients. The amusements of the world had no attraction for her. As often as possible, even in her earlier years, she withdrew from entertainments given by her family and by the circles in which they moved. Yet she was often obliged to appear in splendid attire

at the functions of the court and at the theater as etiquette demanded. In preparation for this she used to scourge herself, wore a penitential girdle, and took every care against suffering any loss to her soul. Many proposals of marriage were made to her, but she steadfastly rejected all, having long before consecrated her virginity to God. For five years Michaela lived at Paris in company with her brother, who was Spanish ambassador at the court of Louis Philippe. Here, too, her virtue won universal esteem and the king himself was full of admiration for her. She effected a reconciliation between her brother and his wife and brought two Protestant families into the Church. She received Holy Communion every day. Though a lady of the court she did not disdain to search out the poor in their hovels and to console them with exhortations and with alms. The court of Brussels also, where her brother lived for a time as ambassador, was a witness of her virtues. Her zeal in the practice of active works of charity was not enough for her and she spent entire nights in the chapel before the tabernacle and promoted as much as possible the association for the perpetual adoration of the Holy Eucharist.

After her return to Madrid, Michaela founded a Sunday-school for servant girls and a house for fallen women and those exposed to danger. The latter work she confided to the superintendence of secular ladies, but they did not persevere. She then engaged French nuns, but with these too she was unsuccessful. There came disagreements and the nuns went so far as to forbid Michaela to enter the house. The matter was referred to the Papal Nuncio, who decided in favor of Michaela. The nuns were obliged to submit, but now they worked against the servant of God, insinuated that she was insane, endeavored to set the court against her, and even sought to prejudice the inmates of the house against her. Things came to such a pass that the pastor was on the point of withdrawing the Blessed Sacrament from the convent. But these difficulties only increased the courage of Michaela. She had often thought of entering a Religious Order and now she formed the plan of founding a Congregation herself. Thus there came into being the Congregation of the Servants of the Blessed Sacrament and of Charity. Her plans met with great encouragement at court, especially from the queen's confessor, Venerable Anthony Claret.* Within a few years the Congregation had ten houses. The foundress, now known as Maria of the Blessed Sacrament, had prepared for a journey to Rome to obtain Papal approbation of her institute, but news came that the plague had broken out in Valencia. She at once hastened to attend the plague-stricken. She was seized with the plague and died a victim of charity on August 24, 1865. Her life proves that the Church even in our days has the power to make saints of the nobility of the world. Michaela is justly compared to the great Spanish saints of the sixteenth century.

Venerable Maddalena of Canossa

8. The Venerable Maddalena of Canossa shed new splendor on the lineage of the Margraves of Canossa.[106] When the Margravine Maddalena, along with some other ladies, began a life of poverty and devoted herself altogether to works of charity, her relatives were much distressed, fearing that it would bring disgrace to the name of Canossa. But of all who have borne the name in the nineteenth century none has brought more renown to that ancient family than the same Margravine Maddalena by her life and labors as foundress of the Daughters of Charity. She was born on March 1, 1774, at Verona, and after the early death of her father went to live in the castle of her uncle, Jerome of

*See page 49 sqq.

Canossa. At an early age she felt called to the religious life and was received among the Carmelites, but she soon found that the contemplative life was not her particular vocation and returned from the novitiate. In her own family circle she possessed the highest reputation and the administration of the whole household was placed in her hands. She greatly impressed all by her sincere piety, and her abhorrence of everything that could in the least endanger her chastity. When Napoleon was on his Italian campaign he lodged at the castle of the Margrave of Canossa. Eye-witnesses relate that the dignity and grace of Maddalena greatly impressed him. On one occasion she had the misfortune of falling down some steps while he was present. An officer hastened at once to lift her up, but she refused his assistance, and it is said that Napoleon cried out, "Leave her alone. Do not dare to touch her; she is an angel."

The Revolution forced the Margrave to seek refuge in Venice. According to the acts of the process of beatification it was here that her future vocation was first made manifest to the young Margravine by the Blessed Virgin in a vision at St. Mark's. After her return to her home in Verona she rented a house and with a few companions began to lead a religious life. The object of the young Society was the instruction of girls, especially of the lower classes, and the practice of works of charity. The special protection of God was evident. The Daughters of Charity, or of Canossa, as they were called after their foundress, soon spread through the principal cities of Italy in spite of the unfavorable circumstances of the times. Frequently there were great difficulties to be encountered. But when a woman endowed with extraordinary prudence and sanctity is the superior, such difficulties serve only to give internal strength to the Congregation. This was the case with Maddalena of Canossa. Men knew what she had left in the world, they knew the innocence of her life and saw the noble example of her humility and extreme poverty. God granted her extraordinary graces and we can not be surprised that even during her lifetime she was revered as a saint. Her process is already far advanced.

Venerable Rosa Carafa di Traetto

9. The honor of the altar awaits the Venerable Rosa Carafa di Traetto. She was a twin child, born at Naples on April 6, 1832. Her father was the Marquis Joseph Carafa di Traetto.[107] Cardinal Carafa, archbishop of Benevento, was her uncle. She obtained her father's permission to abstain from theaters and concerts, for she had found them not always irreproachable. She received many proposals of marriage from estimable young men, but the love of God had long been master of her heart. Until the death of her father in 1873, she lived with her family; because in the weak condition of her health it seemed inadvisable for her to enter a Religious Order. But three years later she was able to offer her service to the Servants of the Sacred Heart, tertiaries of St. Francis, at Naples. As mistress of novices and superior of those who without vows were affiliated with the Congregation and lived in their families, but especally by the splendor of her great sanctity and her noble name, she brought to the young Society honor and esteem among men and grace before God. Her happy death took place on May 2, 1890.

Venerable Catharine Volpicelli

10. Only four years later, on December 28, 1894, her associate in founding the Congregation, Venerable Catharine Volpicelli,[108] followed the Venerable Rosa to the grave. Father Louis of Casoria was assisted by the Venerable Catharine in the organization of the Servants of the Sacred Heart. Pius X authorized

the inauguration of the process of her beatification on January 11, 1911.

Venerable Bartholomea Capitanio, Venerable Vincenza Gerosa

11. A very sympathetic character is that of Venerable Bartholomea Capitanio,[109] who died on July 26, 1833, when only twenty-six years of age. In her early years she was deeply affected by the life of St. Aloysius Gonzaga. Reading it over again and again she arrived at the fixed resolve of imitating it as faithfully as possible. She would become like the princely son of Castiglione in his angelic purity, zeal for penance, ardent devotion to the Holy Eucharist, practice of prayer, and self-sacrificing charity toward the neighbor. Both those of her own time and those of later generations bear witness that her endeavors were crowned with brightest success.

Bartholomea's birthplace, Lovere, at the north end of Lake Iseo in the Brescian Alps, is not far from Castiglione, where stood the ancestral castle of St. Aloysius. She was born on January 14, 1807, the eldest daughter of Modestus Capitanio, a merchant, and Catharina Canossi, his second wife. The father did not enjoy a good reputation. He was given to drunkenness, and in consequence was very rude and quarrelsome with his wife and children. His religious duties he neglected altogether. But his virtuous daughter, by her prayers and her tactful conduct, succeeded in bringing him to reflection and he sincerely changed for the better. He died a truly Christian death. What the children were unable to learn from the father was supplied by the good example of their mother.

But it was especially an excellent education in the convent of the nuns of St. Clare at Lovere that excited in Bartholomea a zeal for all that is lofty and ideal. She would have been glad at once to enter the Order of her educators, but she could not obtain the consent of her parents. With the consent of her confessor, however, she made a vow of chastity in her seventeenth year.

When she had completed her studies, with the support of the clergy she opened a private school. Her success was extraordinary. She easily won the hearts of her pupils and showed wonderful ability as a teacher. The Austrian Government, to which Lombardy was subject at the time, freely gave her a teacher's diploma after a brief examination. What most captivates the heart of a child and penetrates its spirit most deeply are the truths of religion explained and illustrated in a simple and childlike manner. And herein lay the secret of the ability of the young teacher of Lovere. To this contributed the lofty idea she had of her vocation. It was not merely to obtain means of livelihood but to attain her heart's desire to lead the little ones to their heavenly Friend and to shelter them from missery, both temporal and eternal, that led her to undertake this noble office with so great charity and self-sacrifice. She had the spirit of Aloysius and souls like that of Aloysius she would reproduce in her little school-girls and in all whom her influence might reach.

Bartholomea, under the direction of the clergy of the place, employed herself extensively in the care of the young. A sodality of the Blessed Virgin owes its beginning to her endeavors. She originated the League of St. Aloysius for the girls of Lovere. Its object was the intimate study of the life of that model of youth, with instruction and direction how best to imitate his virtues in the various circumstances and conditions of life. Special care was devoted to a profitable observance of the six Sundays of St. Aloysius. Since the membership steadily increased, the foundress divided the association into three sections, according to the age of the members. Other opportune projects for the benefit of young people were begun or promoted by her.

Meanwhile, the religious vocation attracted Bartholomea more strongly as time went on and especially during the retreat of eight days, which she made each year under the guidance of her spiritual director.

There was living in Lovere at this period another holy woman, the Venerable Vincenza Gerosa, who rivaled Bartholomea in the practice of good works.[110] Vincenza was twenty years older than Bartholomea, but they had become close friends chiefly through their work in the sodality of the Blessed Virgin. While Bartholomea achieved great good as a teacher, Vincenza had won the veneration of the whole city as a nurse of the sick. She established a little hospital for the poor. The enterprising and far-seeing Bartholomea formed the plan of founding with Gerosa's help a religious institute for the instruction of the young and the care of the sick. But some years passed before the paths were smoothed. On the Feast of the Presentation, November 21, 1832, the two foundresses dedicated themselves to God and began a community life. They called themselves Sisters of Charity and placed their enterprise under the protection of Our Saviour, His holy Mother, and St. Aloysius. It is edifying to read how neither of the two desired to undertake the office of superior. Bartholomea declared it was incumbent on Vincenza as the elder, but the latter urged the superior education of her friend and the fact that Bartholomea was the real author of the plan. Their charity and harmony, however made any disorder impossible.

God is wont to bring great works to their accomplishment in ways unexpected by men. So it was in this case. The whole future of the new institute seemed to depend upon Bartholomea Capitanio. Weakened by her severe labors, she was attacked by

also desired the Sisters of Charity of Besançon for his kingdom, so Mother Thouret went to Naples with some Sisters in 1810 to establish there a home for the Congregation. Soon after she went to Rome and obtained the Papal approbation of her institute. But at this time the Sisters at Besançon, instigated by a priest, refused obedience and the bishop, not desiring the Sisters to become directly subject to Rome, took their part. Thus Mother Thouret had the grief of seeing her first foundation in France desert her. But she labored all the more zealously to establish her new work in Naples. Here she died in the repute of great sanctity on August 25 ,1826.

Venerable Catharine Labouré

13. The "Miraculous Medal" of the Immaculate Conception has found devout friends throughout the Catholic world and there is no doubt that it has been the means of great blessings for many. We need not wonder, then, that the person chosen to inaugurate this devotion to Mary was favored with extraordinary graces.

This child of predilection was the venerable Sister of Charity, Catharine Labouré, whose process of beatification was begun by the Apostolic See in 1908.[113] Sister Catharine was born on May 2, 1806, at Fain-les-Moutier, near Dijon, and in Baptism was given the name of Zoe. The world never possessed her heart. From her earlier years she felt an attraction toward the religious life. She met with an obstinate resistance from her father because, on account of the early death of her mother, she seemed to be indispensable at home. To drive the thought of the cloister out of her mind her father sent her to Paris, where one of his sons kept a restaurant. But it was in vain. Paris simply aroused in Zoe a detestation for the ways of the world. The father finally relented and at the age of twenty-four she was permitted to take the religious habit in the convent of the Sisters of St. Vincent at Chatillon-sur-Seine. She was now named Sister Catharine. In the following year, 1831, we find her in the hospital of Enghien at Paris, where she served in the humblest duties for forty-five years until her death on December 31, 1876. It was in the second year of her religious life that Sister Catharine was thrice favored with apparitions of the Blessed Virgin, who commissioned her to have medals made representing the apparition and bearing the legend "O Mary, conceived without sin, pray for us who have recourse to thee." Her director proved rather skeptical and at first had only scoff and contempt for these extraordinary manifestations. But the conviction grew that the sister was not at all a victim of a delusion. The archbishop of Paris, Monsignor de-Quelen, soon became an advocate of the "Miraculous Medal," which now entered upon a victorious course throughout Catholic countries. Among many other remarkable events, the sudden conversion of the Jew, Alphonse Ratisbonne, has an intimate connection with this medal. Leo XIII, after a careful examination of the facts and a scrutiny by the Sacred Congregation of Rites, approved a Mass and an Office commemorating the apparition of the Blessed Virgin of the Miraculous Medal.[114] Though Sister Catharine, in accomplishing the desire of the Mother of God, did very much to spread the Miraculous Medal, she nevertheless found ways and means in her humility to keep secret from the world the fact that she was the chosen soul favored with the apparition of the Immaculate Conception. Yet, while unaware of the many extraordinary favors she had received, her sisters in religion, and all who became acquainted with her, were thoroughly persuaded of her sanctity. At her death there was great emotion among the people and two Sisters were kept busy for a day applying to the corpse of the Venerable Catharine objects of devotion brought by the great numbers of visitors.

Placida Bellanger

14. The servant of God, Placida Bellanger, a Borromean Sister, displayed great heroism during the French Revolution.[115] A revolutionary mob had broken into the hospital of Saint-Dié. Swords and daggers were raised to strike down the superior; but Placida, the youngest of the Sisters, cast herself between the assassins and their victim, caught their blows, and while her face streamed with blood, put the cowardly rabble to flight. Disguised as a servant girl she went out often at night during those terrible days at Saint-Dié to minister like an angel of charity to the misery all about, though a price had been put upon her head and she had already been condemned to the scaffold should she continue in the work of her vocation. Often, too, in later life, Sister Placida gave noble proof of her fearless courage. With the same energy she labored for the perfection of her interior life. It was this that kept her humble and self-sacrificing in spite of the admiration she excited, and these virtues joined with great prudence and amiability made her singularly capable in the practice of her vocation. The extraordinary influence of her sanctity captivated every one who had anything to do with her. Four times she was unanimously elected superior-general of her Congregation. In this office she died at the age of seventy-six, on July 23, 1841, at Nancy.

Bernadette Soubirous

15. In one of the well-known apparitions of 1858, the ever-blessed Virgin promised that she would make her favored child, Bernadette Soubirous, "happy, not in this world, but in the next." What Mary promises

she surely fulfils. On August 13, 1913, Pius X signed the decree inaugurating Bernadette's process of beatification.[116] Every one in Rome has the greatest interest in its happy and speedy promotion. After the last apparition, July 28, 1858, Bernadette disappeared altogether from Lourdes. Her work at the pilgrimage was done, her connection with the Shrine was severed and in her after life there are recorded no visions, ecstasies, or the like, but only trials and humiliations. This shows that she had not been an overwrought, wonder-seeking hysteric.

On July 8, 1866, she entered the convent of St. Gildard of the Sisters of Charity at Nevers. Here she was to be known as Sister Mary Bernard. We may easily understand that she was universally treated with a certain esteem and reverence. But she was not in the least moved by it. On the contrary, she was always rather painfully affected when friends came to see her. She never believed that on account of the heavenly favors accorded her she was entitled to any prerogative above her sisters. All of them were deeply touched by her humility and modesty. God had sent her to the school of the cross that she might learn her own littleness and that her character might be purged of all the imperfection that might cling to it. The Blessed Virgin had not promised her a happy life in this world. Yet there have been probably very few who have enjoyed so profound a peace of mind and so genuine a joy as Bernadette. She died in her thirty-fifth year on April 16, 1879, at Nevers, quite forgotten.

Of the exhumation of her body, September 22, 1909, an eye-witness relates:

"Not the least trace of corruption nor any bad odor could be perceived in the corpse of our beloved sister. Even the burial dress was intact. The face was somewhat brown, the eyes slightly sunken and she seemed to be sleeping. The damp funeral garments were

exchanged for new ones. The body was placed in a
new zinc coffin lined with white silk. Within it was
placed a record enclosed in a glass tube, and giving
an account of the opening of the coffin and of the condition of the body. After this the coffin was again
deposited in the mortuary chapel in our garden."[117]

VENERABLE SISTER MARY OF ST. EUPHRASIA PELLETIER

16. Among those who are most to be pitied are the
victims of seduction. The Church has never been
wanting in zealous persons who have exerted all their
energy in successful combat against this pest of souls.
In the seventeenth century, about 1680, Blessed John
Eudes founded a congregation of women entitled
"Sisters of Our Lady of Charity," whose object was
to devote themselves entirely to the conversion of fallen
women. In the nineteenth century the Congregation received a new life and a broader development
from the Venerable Sister Mary of St. Euphrasia
Pelletier.[118]

She was born of God-fearing parents on the island
of Noirmoutier, off the coast of Vendée, July 31, 1796.
The reading of the life and writings of St. Teresa
excited in her young heart a fervent enthusiasm for
everything ideal and especially for the saving of souls.
Hence the vocation of the Sisters of Our Lady of
Charity proved most pleasing to her, and when she was
nineteen she joined these self-sacrificing souls at Tours.
Only a few years later they elected her superior on
account of her prudence and zeal.

An important event in her life was her call to
Angers in 1829 for the purpose of establishing there
the work of her Congregation. For she soon perceived
the great disadvantage arising from the want of connection between its individual houses. Often these
individual houses had no one capable of directing their

difficult work. The plans of Sister Pelletier won the assent of the ecclesiastical authorities and in 1835 Gregory XVI sanctioned the reorganization of the Congregation under the title "Sisters of Our Lady of Charity of the Good Shepherd." Sister Mary of St. Euphrasia was the first superior-general. Charity is ingenious. Mother Pelletier was ever on the alert for new means to restrain the vice which ruins both body and soul. For the penitents who after conversion showed an inclination toward religious life, she founded a special branch of her Congregation, the "Magdalens," who take the three religious vows, but live according to their own rules separate from the Sisters of the Good Shepherd. For others who, afraid of relapse into sin, have no desire to return to the world and no inclination for religious life, she organized the institute of the "Consecrates," or those who without vows solemnly consecrate themselves to the Mother of God. These live with the children called "Preservates" and efficaciously support the work of the Sisters.

It is always best to endeavor to secure prevention of the vice. Therefore the wise superior-general opened institutes for girls who were in danger. Finally she extended her work to orphanages and also to prisons for female convicts.

It can not be told in a few words how much good Mother Pelletier effected and still works through her daughters, who, animated by her spirit, labor in all civilized countries. Hundreds of thousands of poor creatures, who would have been doomed to the greatest misery, both temporal and eternal, have been regained to human society and to the Church by this work of charity. And especially in our own day, when depravity of morals is so shockingly widespread, the work of the Sisters of the Good Shepherd is eminently apostolic and suited to the needs of the times. It needed the enlightened zeal of a saint to give it vigorous organization and to impart to others the necessary enthusiasm and spirit of self-denial. "After listening to our Mother," said one who heard her speak, "one would go to the end of the world to save only one soul."[119] Without doubt it was the personal sanctity of Venerable Mother Pelletier that drew down so many blessings upon her work both before and after her death. Her earthly life came to its end on April 24, 1868. Her many services for the salvation of souls have assuredly won for her glorious reward in heaven.

Venerable Anne Marie Javouhey

17. A French officer of high rank once boasted that he had embraced the greatest man in France, Napoleon, and kissed the hand of the greatest woman in France, Mother Javouhey.[120] Whence, as the legend goes, Napoleon once said in a pleasant mood: "I know of only two good heads in France—my own and Mother Javouhey's. If she were a man I would make her a general and give her chief command of one of my armies." It is only a legend, but it is evidence of the high opinion universally had of the ability of the Venerable Anne Marie Javouhey, foundress of the Sisters of St. Joseph of Cluny. At the French court, with princes of the Church, and with statesmen, she possessed great influence. Felicité de Lamennais even after his apostasy paid her the tribute of his admiration. Mother Javouhey owed her fame in the eyes of the world to her remarkable skill in organization and the admirable success of her Congregation at home and in the French colonies. When she was superior-general she once journeyed to the Gold Coast and twice to Guiana to organize and develop the mission work of her Sisters. In Guiana she established a settlement for emancipated negroes after the model

of the Reductions of Paraguay. Her influence in the colony was so great that the envious called her the "white queen" of Guiana.

To this exterior activity corresponded a still greater vigor in the work of her own sanctification from an earnest conviction that she must exert all her powers in promoting the cause of God.

Anne Marie Javouhey was a month older than Blessed Madeleine Sophie Barat, and like her was born in Burgundy in the year 1779. Her birthplace was the village of Jallanges. The dreadful days of the Revolution presented her the first opportunity for the exercise of her dauntless zeal, when she showed heroic courage by giving shelter to priests and making possible the celebration of the Holy Mysteries. She gathered the children of the village about her and went among the people while they were at work to instruct them in their religion. She was everywhere welcomed and eagerly listened to. On November 11, 1798, during Holy Mass, which was said at the altar in the house, she made a vow in the presence of the whole family to devote herself entirely to God. Twice she tried her vocation in a Religious Order, but each time when the occasion for taking the habit arrived her whole spirit rose against it and she felt herself obliged to leave. An interior voice told her that she was herself to found a Congregation. Assisted by her three sisters she opened a sort of oratory for poor children. She had considerable trouble in overcoming the objections of her father. The parish priest of Chalons-sur-Saone heard of her effective work and in 1805 called her into his parish to superintend a school. This enabled her to make rapid progress in the organization of her Congregation. In 1812 she acquired an old convent of the Recollects at Cluny, which she transformed into a mother-house. Thus Cluny once more became the center of a Congregation destined to become eminent in promoting the interests of the Church. Mother Javouhey knew how to inspire her daughters with courage and enthusiasm in their difficult vocation. There was no dearth of novices and of applications for new residences, especially since in 1817 she had included the foreign missions within the sphere of her activity. At her death, on July 15, 1851, the Congregation numbered fully fourteen hundred members and to-day, in spite of the persecution in France, there are quite four thousand distributed throughout every nation on earth.

It would be a mistake to think that in this splendid exterior success the Venerable Mother was not obliged to travel over the way of the cross. If hers had not been a truly valiant character and she had not possessed an imperturbable confidence in God, there were times innumerable when she would have given up her efforts. The heaviest trials were those which came from the ecclesiastical authorities. In Guiana she was forbidden the Sacraments for nearly two years; the archbishop of Paris placed her chapel under interdict; and with other bishops who wished arbitrarily to change the constitutions of her Congregation she was obliged to combat strenuously. But never, as the decree introducing the process of her beatification declares, "did she forget in these bitter trials the duty of charity or the respect due to authority, a clear indication of her virtue and sanctity." So great and yet so humble and modest a soul as Mother Javouhey's we seldom meet with in history.

Maria Cherubina Clara Saraceni

18. In silent solitude all unknown to the world the Servant of God, Maria Cherubina Clara Saraceni,[121] worked out her sanctification. She was a native of Rome, the child of poor parents and after a spotless

youth joined the Sisters of St. Clare at Assisi. The
Lord permitted her many sufferings, but enriched her
with extraordinary graces. Her devotion to the Holy
Eucharist and her zeal for the salvation of souls were
most remarkable. If she envied any one it was the
missionaries who could go forth to announce the doctrine of Christ, and therefore she prayed most earnestly
for their success. She died on February 1, 1891,
revered by her sisters in religion for her holy life and
happy death.

ALOYSIA BORGIOTTI

19. The Servant of God, Aloysia Borgiotti, born
at Turin in 1803, was the daughter of a distinguished
advocate.[122] Her eighteenth year was the turning-
point in her life. Inclined to be somewhat frivolous
before this time, her surrender to God was henceforth
without reserve. "No more vanity, no more tepidity,
but only penance and suffering," summed up her new
plan of life, which she followed in grim earnest until
the day of her death. It was not long before she took
a vow of chastity and resolved to become a Sister of
Charity. Her mother and her two brothers were
invalids, so that the whole care of the house fell upon
her; and she practised in her own family the heroic
work of a Sister of Charity. After her mother had
followed the two brothers to the grave Aloysia entered
a pious society that had taken up the work of attending the sick poor who were ashamed to ask for help.
For thirty-one years she sought out the homes of misery and want in Turin, giving material help to great
numbers and to still more the support of spiritual consolation. She manifested a great devotion to the sufferings of Christ. In every sick person she beheld the
suffering Saviour, and for this reason believed that
she could never treat the sick with sufficient charity.

Aloysia was already sixty-two years of age when

she was commissioned to enter the Sisters of Nazareth, which the superior of the Lazarists, Father Durando, was then organizing in Turin, and to take the office of superior. She rendered such important services to the rising Congregation by her experience and the example of her holiness that the title of co-founder is justly due to her. She filled the office for eight years until her death, which occurred after a brief illness.

Venerable Maria de Mattias

20. The Congregation of the Sisters of the Most Precious Blood owes its foundation to the Blessed Caspar del Bufalo and the Venerable Maria de Mattias.[123] The process of beatification of the latter, who died at Rome on August 20, 1866, was begun by the Apostolic See in 1903.

Venerable Maria Juliana of the Blessed Sacrament

21. The Venerable Maria Juliana of the Blessed Sacrament, daughter of a distinguished physician, Fortunato Arenare, died at Naples on October 25, 1857, a victim of heroic charity.[124] According to the acts of the process the young daughter of Marquis Vigo was dangerously ill, and Sister Juliana, who was attending her, offered her life to God for that of the girl. God accepted the sacrifice. The Sister was seized with the child's illness and the latter was restored to health.

Venerable Maria Crucifixa of the Five Wounds

22. The Venerable Maria Crucifixa of the Five Wounds, a member of the Third Order of St. Peter of Alcantara, died also at Naples on December 16, 1826.[125] Many persons of high position, both secular

and ecclesiastical, sought counsel of the modest Religious. During the days of affliction which the Church suffered from the French Emperor, she prayed unceasingly for the triumph of Pius VII. Interior imitation of her Crucified Master was her greatest joy in this life.

VENERABLE ADEODATA PISANI

23. The Venerable Adeodata Pisani brought new glory to the old Maltese patrician family of that name.[126] She was first novice-mistress and then abbess of the convent of the Benedictine Nuns at Notabili in Malta and died at the age of forty-eight on February 25, 1855, with the reputation of great sanctity.

VENERABLE ANNA MARIA LAPINI

24. The Venerable Anna Maria Lapini—died 1860 —rendered great service at Florence to the cause of popular education in Italy.[127] She was the foundress of the Sisters of the Blessed Wounds, a Third Order of the Capuchins, who, in addition to works of charity, devote themselves especially to the education of girls.

PAULA FRASSINETTI

25. In the same direction, but engaged chiefly in higher education, the Sisters of St. Dorothea are laboring in Italy and Brazil. The origin of this flourishing association is an example of the use which Providence makes of accidental circumstances to call into being great undertakings for the benefit of mankind. The venerable foundress of the Congregation, Paula Frassinetti,[128] was born at Genoa on March 3, 1809. Chiefly to recuperate her failing health she went to dwell with her eldest brother, who was the parish priest of Quinto. She undertook the care of the girls in the little town. She soon observed that her words fell on fertile soil. Encouraged by these circumstances

she conceived the idea of gathering others with her
into a conventual society for the education of girls.
She spent whole nights before the tabernacle and practised severe penance to implore God's blessing on her
work. Her prayers were heard, as is proved by her
saintly life, her holy death on June 11, 1882, and the
splendid success of her Congregation.

VENERABLE MARIA ALOYSIA MAURIZI

26. The Venerable Maria Aloysia Maurizi, a member of the Order of Mantellates (Servite Sisters) and
a lady of distinguished Roman ancestry, was born on
September 27, 1770.[129] She received an excellent education. The theater and other worldly amusements
to which her father brought her made little impression
on her deeply religious mind, and it is said that while
present she would secretly say the Rosary or become
absorbed in the contemplation of heavenly things. She
felt the great loss of the family wealth doubly hard,
because it left her without the dower necessary for
entrance into a cloister. And when finally she did
find admission into an Order without it, God sent her
a new trial in a serious ailment of the eyes, which compelled her to return to her home. When the Masturzi
family founded a convent of Mantellates at Rome in
1797, Aloysia was received through the influence of
the Venerable Vincent Strambi. But the invasion of
Rome by the French in 1799 dispersed the small community. Aloysia was not able to return to the little
convent with her companions until 1801. Pope Pius
VII approved the establishment and appeared in person at the first profession on May 21, 1804. Sister
Aloysia was unanimously chosen superior. Our Lord
richly endowed her with the special gift of His favor
toward His elect—the cross. Struggles and difficulties both exterior and interior were not wanting to
her. The more the artist retouches his work the more

beautiful it becomes. Trials refined Aloysia's love of God and brought out more clearly the heroism of her virtue and noble character. Her life offers many examples of extraordinary favors from Heaven. She died on May 9, 1831, and the decree of her heroic virtue was published in 1896.

Venerable Marie Theresia Haze of Liège

27. A new instance in proof of the truth that purity and rectitude of intention are especially important in sanctity is the life of the Venerable Marie Theresia Haze of Liège.[130] Great simplicity, unselfishness, and condescension to those under her, with a lofty nobility of sentiment, generous magnanimity, and unreserved dependence on God, were among the characteristic traits of this rare woman.

Bitter misfortune fell upon the family when the French revolutionaries invaded Belgium. The father, an official under the prince-bishop of Liège, died on their flight to Düsseldorf. The mother was able to recover only a part of the property; but with the devoted help of her five daughters was able to obtain a livelihood by manual labor. Marie Theresia aided by one of her sisters opened a little school. Its great success drew the attention of the clergy to the directress and the other parishes of the city desired similar beneficent institutions. It was thought best that the teachers should be united into a religious Congregation, and the realization of this plan was accomplished by a pious priest named Jean Habets and Marie Theresia Haze. The first profession of the Daughters of the Holy Cross—so the Congregation was named—took place on September 8, 1833. To school work the Sisters soon added works of charity. Germany, England, and the East Indies emulated Belgium in securing the Sisters of the Holy Cross for their cities. The rapid development of the Congregation and the great zeal

of its members are to be ascribed in no small measure
to the prudent and gentle direction of Mother Marie
Theresia. She governed the Congregation until her
death on January 7, 1876, when she was nearly ninety-
four years of age. Her enlightenment in the principles of the spiritual life and the unbounded confidence
every one had in her were truly wonderful. In 1911,
the Church published the decree approving her heroic
virtue.

MOTHER THEODORE GUERIN

28. Cardinal Gibbons declared that Mother Theodore Guerin,[131] first superior-general of the Sisters of
Providence in the United States, was an athlete of
virtue who by her life and teaching had made great
conquests for Christ and His Church. Mother Guerin
was sent to the United States from France in 1840
to establish a residence of her Order in the diocese
of Vincennes, Indiana. She was a highly cultivated
woman of extraordinary endowments. Still more
admirable was her personal holiness, which was proved
by many trials. Her great success in the many undertakings of her Congregation, particularly in the
schools, is justly ascribed to the charm of her noble
and virtuous character. She died on May 14, 1856.
She was honored with a medal from the French Academy, but greater will be the honor to her name by its
enrollment in the list of the Blessed.

MOTHER ELIZABETH SETON

29. A noble jewel of the Catholic Church in North
America is the convert, Mother Elizabeth Seton.[132]
She was the daughter of Richard Bayley, a distinguished New York physician, and in her twentieth
year married William Seton. A deeply religious spirit
and an active charity toward the neighbor were among
the many excellent traits of the young Mrs. Seton. A

residence at Livorno, where her sick husband was seeking restoration of health, gave her an intimate acquaintance with the Catholic faith. Her untainted mind was easily accessible to the truth. After the death of her husband in 1803 she returned to America and soon entered the Catholic Church. This step brought her many trials from her relatives, who left her alone with her five little children. But all the more cordial was the attention she received from her Catholic friends.

Mrs. Seton desired to spend all her strength in the service of the Church. Her first work was the establishment and direction of a Catholic school in New York. Three years later she was invited to Baltimore to establish an institution for the education of girls. Her charity growing ever stronger and purer urged her to alleviate every human misery. Up to that time there were no Sisters of Charity in America. So under the auspices of Bishop Carroll of Baltimore and the missionary Cheverus, afterward bishop of Boston and later cardinal of Bordeaux, Elizabeth Seton united with some other ladies in forming a Congregation under the rule of St. Vincent de Paul. The first establishment was begun at Emmitsburg, near Baltimore. The work at once found enthusiastic friends and supporters. Mother Seton was chosen the first superior. It was no light task in those days to organize a Congregation of hospital Sisters in America. But Mother Seton more than justified the confidence reposed in her. Her spirit of faith and her interior union with God were the chief sources from which she drew energy to fulfil her providential mission. On January 4, 1821, her eventful life came to its close. Her great longing for heaven is expressed in her own words: "If I could behold myself at the last station of this path of suffering and see the downfall of the walls of my prison, I do not know how I could bear my joy. To go home—to be called thither by God's will! What unspeakable happiness!" Truly does she merit to be crowned an American Elizabeth.

Eugenia de Smet

30. The Servant of God, Eugenia de Smet, justly bore during her religious life the name of Marie of Providence.[133] The visible dispensation of Providence is the chief feature of her life. Encouraged by the Blessed Cure of Ars, Eugenie founded the Congregation of the Sisters, Helpers of the Poor Souls, who by prayer and works of charity endeavor to help the souls of the faithful departed. The rule does not impose any habit on the Sisters, so that they may be unhindered in the exercise of their vocation. In the mission of Kiangnan in China the Helpers of the Poor Souls have been particularly blessed in their labors. Many Chinese women have already become co-operators with them. In Europe also the blessing of God rests visibly on the new establishment. The holy life of the foundress came to its close on February 7, 1871.

Therese Martin of the Child Jesus
(The Little Flower of Jesus)

31. The charm of innocence and of youth envelops the life of the Servant of God, Therese Martin of the Child Jesus.[134] She was born at Alençon on January 2, 1873, and died a Carmelite nun at Lisieux on September 30, 1897. By order of her superiors she was obliged to commit to writing an account of her spiritual life. In it she has revealed to posterity what a truly chosen soul was hers and what care she took to preserve unsullied the clean garment of baptismal innocence. In her humility she says of herself: "I have never done things heroically divine. I am nothing but a little weak child-soul over which the good God has bountifully poured His holy grace." But

great was her zeal to permit none of those many
graces to pass unused. Fidelity in little things made
her so pleasing in the sight of God and ever brought
her still greater grace. And God provided that her
love of the cross was no mere sentiment. Her record
shows a great knowledge of the science of the saints.
Her life has excited great interest outside of France.
The bishop of Bayeux, to which diocese Lisieux
belongs, has already opened the preliminary process
of her beatification.

Mother Marie of Jesus
(Marie Caroline Deluil-Martigny)

32. On February 27, 1884, an anarchist broke into
the convent garden of La Servianne at Marseilles,
rushed upon the superior, Mother Marie of Jesus, and
her attendant, and fired five pistol shots at them,
wounding them both mortally.[135]   The superior fell
covered with blood. "I forgive him. All for the
cause" were her last and only words. The assassin
had accomplished the ruthless deed with cool deliberation and out of hatred for religion, as is evident from
a letter he had written some hours before to an anar-
chistic newspaper so that his intention might be clearly
understood.

The unfortunate man had no idea that he was grati-
fying the heart's desire of his victim. To suffer for
Our Lord, even to shed her blood for Him, was the
ardent longing of Marie Caroline Deluil-Martigny
from her very childhood. Often had she offered her
life to Our Saviour in sacrifice for the many crimes
committed against Him by indifference and unbelief.
A short time before her death she had written: "What
deep sorrow seizes one at the sight of the ever-
increasing godlessness of our time and the seducing
triumphs of anti-Christian societies. Oh, could I but
expiate with my blood those insults offered to the

Divine Majesty!" She considered it the purpose of her life to make atonement to Our Lord for the ingratitude of the world.

After mature deliberation and with the assistance of Father John Calage, S.J., she established the Daughters of the Heart of Jesus with the object of manifesting a love of expiation to the Sacred Heart of Jesus. This aim was to be attained chiefly by an imitation of the spiritual priesthood of the Mother of Sorrows. Besides this, the Congregation included as its special work constant prayer for priests, since on the zeal of these the glory of God particularly depends. The first house of the Society was established at Berchem, a suburb of Antwerp, in 1873. This idea of expiatory work met with great approval from Cardinal Deschamps of Malines and from Monsignor Van den Berge. The foundress was soon able to put her plan into practice in her own country. She had long before sacrificed her will entirely to God, and now the Lord accepted also her sacrifice of her life. Her cruel death drew the attention of the world to her hidden life of virtue and won for her work the blessing of God and the favor of many friends. The process of her beatification was begun in 1908.

VENERABLE THEODOLINDE DUBOUCHÉ
(Mother Marie Therese)

33. Environment and education certainly exercise a very great influence on the religious development of a child. In the case of the Venerable Theodolinde Dubouché everything about her tended to extinguish in her every germ of religion.[136] Her parents were altogether dead to the Faith and in her whole environment there was only one clerk of her father's that had the courage to go to Mass on Sundays. If in spite of this Theodolinde felt a great attraction toward God from early years—especially in

the Most Blessed Sacrament—and also had a great abhorrence of everything evil, we must find therein the effect of a truly extraordinary grace. A strong inclination to self-complacency and independence hindered her at first from following immediately the impulses of grace. She had to conceal her religious practices and her visits to the church from her parents. They made it their object to win her to the ways of the world. She was obliged to learn painting and music and to frequent many places of amusement. Of her life up to her twenty-second year she writes: "At this time I lived in the midst of the frivolous, pleasure-seeking world and daily heard the most scandalous stories. The passions were represented to me as an essential element of life from which one can never escape. Yet not only my will, but even my imagination remained untouched by any impure thought. I knew instinctively what was not good for me, what conversation and what reading I must avoid. I can not describe what was going on within me. I sought solitude and entered into a condition of interior recollection that made me blind and dumb. In society and at the play the external splendor and the harmony of the music gave me pleasure. But in these great dangers God kept safe my innocence. Of certain sins I was as ignorant as a child, and my abhorrence of everything that could inform me about that vice, which according to St. Paul should not even be mentioned among Christians, was so great that if I heard a speech of double meaning I was—it is still always the same with me—covered with a cold perspiration. My detestation of all that might offend chastity was so vivid that if in my study of painting when I visited museums or conversed with painters, I met with any unbecoming representation, I turned away with that shock which a gaping wound inflicts upon us."[137]

An impulse toward the magnanimous and the ideal

was manifest in Theodolinde from early childhood and helped her through many dangers. Interior inspirations of grace urging her to devote herself entirely to the service of God became ever more marked and frequent. But her opposition to frequent communion, toward which Our Lord was, as it were, forcing her, ceased only when she was fifteen. She now desired to consecrate herself wholly to works of charity. A priest advised her to become first an angel of charity in her own family. Here, of course, she met with great resistance, but by her increased friendliness and patience she endeavored to give her relatives a better notion of piety. Many sacrifices were to be made before the good work could be accomplished. For a long time Theodolinde's mother had been seriously ill and the Sister of Charity in attendance, urged by the daughter, asked her to receive the Sacraments. Theodolinde writes of this occurrence:

"The prayer of the sister was refused and, in fact, very badly received. I was not home at the time and when I returned a scene occurred that can be explained only by Satan's presence in a soul. My mother denounced me as the author of the proposal, of her sufferings, even of her death. She was so furious with anger that I feared her sudden death. God gave me the grace to remain calm. I knelt at the bedside, begged her pardon, kissed her hands, and then went away. At the feet of Jesus I sought help and strength. My emotion was so vehement that I fainted in the church. But God willed only to try my faith. When I returned home I found my dear invalid calm and well-disposed. She said to me: 'Since you desire it, go at once and bring the priest to me.' "[138]

It was fifty years since her mother had been at peace God, but her conversion was sincere and God vouchsafed the aged woman two more years of life in which to atone in some measure for her long neglect. After continued prayer and penance Theodolinde brought back to God her father, her sister, and a cousin.

The chief trait of her life was veneration for the Blessed Sacrament. The gross ingratitude of so many toward Our Lord's exceeding love in the Holy Eucharist impelled her to a heroic return of love. She perceived how much that coldness grieved the Sacred Heart and, reflecting on the pleasure we feel when in our sufferings we find others who understand us and make every endeavor to have us forget our injuries, she considered no sacrifice too great if only it aroused love for Our Saviour in the Eucharist. She planned the organization of a permanent work. But things developed in a manner different from what she intended. She had been firmly determined to enter the Carmelite Order, hoping thus to find help in her life-work. But difficulties arose on every side. She was frightened when her confessor told her she must herself found a Congregation. Circumstances, in fact, forced her to establish one. In the midst of the Revolution of 1848 she founded at Paris the Congregation of Sisters of Reparative Adoration (Adoration Reparatice), which day and night without interruption adores the Most Holy Sacrament. As in all great works, so in this the beginnings were insignificant and the obstacles great. It required a saint's courage and confidence in God to escape complete failure. Mother Marie Therese, as Theodolinde was now called, showed masterly ability in the training of the souls entrusted to her and filled them with the spirit of sacrifice for the contemned love of the hidden Saviour. This kept the Congregation together and gave it increase in spite of all assaults from without.

Mother Marie Therese also labored with the Venerable Julien Eymard in the foundation of a Congregation of priests of the Most Holy Sacrament* She

*See pages 176 sqq.

likewise endeavored to interest people cf the world in the practice of reparative adoration.

On August 30, 1863, she was called to the vision of Him for whom, hidden under the species of bread, she had worked so zealously. "I see! I see! I see!" she exclaimed, looking toward heaven as her soul left her body.

Françoise Kestre

34. In Belgium the Servant of God, Françoise Kestre—died 1882—foundress of the Apostolines of the Most Blessed Sacrament, labored in a spirit similar to that of Mother Marie Therese.

Louise Therese de Montaignac

35. With true saints, suffering and sickness are not impediments to their activity. The Servant of God, Louise Therese de Montaignac, was not able to walk during the last thirty-three years of her life, constantly suffering excruciating pain, and yet during this very period accomplishing the chief labor of her life—the establishment, upbuilding, development, and direction of a religious Congregation. God frequently chooses the weak to attain great ends and to manifest the omnipotence of His grace.[139]

The Servant of God was born of a highly respected family at Havre de Grace in Normandy in the year 1820. Under the guidance of her aunt and godmother, who had adopted her, Louise received an excellent education. The aunt was skilled in instilling the old and tried principles of Christian piety and took care, moreover, to train her pupil in all that became a lady of her station and in the duties of housekeeping.

Two devotions guided Louise toward sanctity; viz., devotion to the Sacred Heart of Jesus and to the Mother of God. The latter was fostered and developed chiefly by the young ladies' sodality, which gave the

Servant of God both impulse and opportunity to work for the honor of Mary. When sixteen she made a vow of perpetual virginity. She derived strength for this offering from Holy Communion, which, during the following year, she received every day. Afterward, when unable to walk, she wrote:

"When I recall the past from my sixteenth to my forty-seventh year, memory places before me the joys of my soul in the presence of the Most Blessed Sacrament. It was the most powerful attraction known to me. When I had a minute of time I hurried to the tabernacle. I do not remember ever to have withstood the invitation of my sweet Master. This is to me a consolation that surpasses all."

It is not surprising, then, that she endeavored to spread devotion to the Blessed Sacrament and to the Heart of Jesus. In 1845 she induced the bishop of Nevers, where she lived at the time, to introduce in his diocese daily devotions to the Sacred Heart during the month of June. Father H. Ramière, S.J., the well-known director of the Apostleship of Prayer, said of her: "I do not know any one who has better conception of the spirit of the devotion to the Sacred Heart than the lady of Montaignac." The cherished design of the Servant of God was to create a permanent establishment for the propagation of devotion to the Sacred Heart. Several plans failed. Her family had come to reside in Montluçon, and here, while prefect of the young ladies' sodality, intent on practising charity, she found means after some time to open an orphan asylum. Out of this there gradually developed the Pious Society of the Oblates of the Sacred Heart of Jesus, the object of which is propagation of veneration for the Sacred Heart. In later years Louise founded an apostolic school for training candidates to the priesthood. Although after 1852 she was nearly always ill she knew neither rest nor relaxation. When admonished concerning this she answered: "To gain time means to gain souls. I do not believe in saints with folded arms." Consumed by labor and suffering she died on June 27, 1885. The acts of the process recount almost every sort of ailment cured through her intercession.

ANNA CATHARINE EMMERICH

36. The name of the ecstatic of Dülmen, the Servant of God, Anna Catharine Emmerich,[140] is known and honored throughout the whole Christian world. God set her as a shining light for all who seek the truth in these days of unbelief and indifference and as a standing challenge to the rationalistic spirit of the times. It is certain that her marvelous life has brought consolation and courage to many in these days of affliction for the Church and that many have been aroused by it to a life of renewed religious zeal.

Sanctity manifests itself especially in purity of intention and in virtuous action. Extraordinary gifts of grace are not absolutely necessary to it. In Anna Catharine Emmerich all these are abundantly united.

She was born on September 8, 1774, in Flamsche, a farming village near Coesfeld, Westphalia. Her parents were poor. In her earlier years she was obliged to work at home and among strangers as well. She was able to attend school regularly for only a few months; still, people were astonished at her knowledge and her skill in handicrafts. While yet very young she received revelations in matters pertaining to faith and enjoyed visible converse with heavenly persons, especially with her guardian angel, who lovingly instructed her in many things. This was quite an ordinary matter for her, so that she was altogether surprised when she learned that others saw nothing of the sort. Her holiness became manifest at an equally early age. She had the greatest horror of every sin, a tender charity for the neighbor, and she would weep over the misery of others as if it were her own. She found a pleasure in prayer unusual for one of her age and a delight in every kind of self-denial.

No one was surprised that a vocation to the religious life soon developed in this child; but circumstances seemed to be against her being able to follow it. Her parents were by no means willing to part with their daughter; they were not able to give her a dowry, and no convent was found willing to receive her without it. A convent of Poor Clares in Coesfeld needed an organist. So Catharine, now twenty-five years old, obtained permission from her parents to take lessons on the organ from Soentgen, the organist at Coesfeld, with the hope of being received into the convent without the dowry. But she found the family of Soentgen in straitened circumstances, and her charity prompted her to relieve their misery by the work of her hands. Learning the organ was thus out of the question. Through her intercourse with Catharine, Soentgen's daughter Clara developed a religious vocation. She applied to the Augustinian Sisters at Agnetenberg, Dülmen, and being an expert organist was gladly received. But Soentgen informed the Sisters that he would give his daughter leave only on the one condition, i. e., that Catharine also would be received. The condition was reluctantly accepted. Catharine's parents found the sacrifice very hard. When she was leaving and asked for a trifling sum of traveling money, her father, otherwise so charitable and pious a Catholic, said to her: "If you were to be buried to-morrow I would indeed pay the funeral expenses, but for a journey to the cloister I shall give you nothing."

Thus Catharine, already twenty-eight years of age, saw her desire at length fulfilled on September 18, 1802. But if she had hoped to find her life free of care and suffering she would have been grievously disappointed. In Agnetenberg there was little of the spirit of a convent, the rules were in great part neglected, and there was no spiritual direction. The Servant of God was ill-treated by the Sisters, who considered her as useless on account of her weak health. On her entrance she had asked the superior to accept her as the meanest in the house. Only too literally was her prayer heard. She was regarded as a servant girl for the convent. Her piety and the extraordinary conditions to be observed in her only gave these Sisters occasion to think lightly of her. Catharine bore it all very well. One day she complained to Our Lord in the chapel that there was no one who understood her or with whom she could share her feelings. She received the answer: "I am enough for you." In fact the continual nearness of the tabernacle—she was for a long time assistant of the sacristan—the frequent opportunity for prayer, the consciousness of having given all to God by her vows, compensated for all want of regard on the part of others. It is touching to note what love and enthusiasm she had for her vocation, though she met with so little gratification in it.

No one, therefore, felt the blow as heavy as she when in 1811 the convent of Agnetenberg was secularized. The news made her ill; they feared even that her end had come. But the most important period of her life was just beginning. A French priest, Vicar Lambert, who used to say Mass at the convent and had been impressed by her modest behavior, had the sick and neglected Catharine brought to his residence in Dülmen. It was long before her condition improved. Toward the end of 1812 her confessor, Father Limberg, a secularized Dominican, who came to give her Holy Communion, saw on the backs of her hands bleeding stigmata. He told Vicar Lambert of his discovery and both thought it was wise to make nothing of the matter and to keep it secret. Father Limberg had no liking for the visions, ecstasies, and other extraordinary things he noticed in his penitent. Catharine had experienced before her entrance into the convent the pains of the crown of thorns and now were added the stigmata and a doubled cross upon her breast. The bleeding of the wounds was of frequent occurrence, especially on feast-days and Fridays.

In March, 1813, Catharine's former sister in religion, Clara Soentgen, paid her a visit and saw the stigmata. In a few days all Dülmen knew of it. Great excitement arose among the people, some favorable to her, some against her. A young physician, Dr. Franz Wilhelm Wesener, who had lost his faith at the university, visited the sick Sister with the intention of unmasking the fraud. But the first visit was sufficient to convince him of the genuineness of the stigmata and to effect in him a radical reform of his life, especially when the sick person showed herself thoroughly acquainted with the condition of his soul. Under Wesener's direction a joint investigation of the stigmata was held in which the physician Krauthausen, the parish priest Dechant Rensing, Father Limberg, and Vicar Lambert took part. A record of the proceedings was sent to the episcopal court at Münster. A few days later the vicar-general and administrator of the diocese, Clement August von Droste Vischering, afterward archbishop of Cologne, accompanied by the president of the seminary Bernhard Overberg, and the medical consultor, Professor von Druffel, came to Dülmen to make accurate inquiry into the matter and to interfere directly should any suspicion arise from the investigation. To this many other persons were invited. It occupied four weeks and its verdict was in every way favorable to Catharine. It was extremely painful for her to see every one's attention turned upon her, for, as her biographer says, "she was a soul hungry for solitude."[141]   Often she besought Our Lord to remove the visible wounds and leave her only the suffering.

But worse was to befall her. The State undertook to meddle in the matter because stubborn doubters raised a cry of fraud. Governor von Vincke appointed a committee of investigation in 1819. The members came to Dülmen firmly persuaded that they were to deal with superstition and common trickery, and this inspired their treatment of the Servant of God. The head of the committee, Karl von Bönninghausen, forcibly removed her to another house and here kept her prisoner under the closest observation for three weeks. They subjected her to the most painful examination, watching her day and night. They spared neither flatteries nor promises, denunciation nor threats to induce her to acknowledge fraud. She had but one answer—that she was willing to die, but could not say what was not true. The committee acted the part of guard at the sepulcher of Our Lord. But they were obliged to acknowledge the fact of the wounds and their bleeding and to admit that it was as clear as midday that all fraud was absent. They departed ashamed of their rude behavior and their defeat; but there were some members of the committee who afterward audaciously spread a rumor that fraud had been found, though no confirmation or reason was alleged in support of it.

In view of the many observations of numerous witnesses not to be suspected of favor and in consideration of the innocent and wholly unselfish character of Catharine Emmerich there remains not the least doubt of the genuineness of the stigmata. It is another question whether they could be explained by mental suggestion or whether they are to be attributed to a supernatural cause. The biographers affirm the latter. Those who do not agree with them must at least admit that the passion of Our Lord had taken hold of Catharine's mind in quite an extraordinary manner. Yet this would hardly account sufficiently for all the accessory visions.

Catharine possessed in a high degree the gifts of contemplation. The whole life of Christ passed before her mind in clear pictures. She lived in sympathy with Him. Clement Brentano was sent to her by Providence—an event she had long foreseen—to receive an account of her visions. Most extraordinary was her knowledge of the secrets of hearts and of distant events. She was obliged to suffer much and to pray for important events in Church and State of her days, for high Church dignitaries, for certain dioceses, and for particular persons who were wholly unknown to her. She was a secret instrument in God's hand for the salvation of many souls.

We behold in Catharine Emmerich a noble flower of supernatural holiness, a rare miracle of divine grace. We can understand how those who came near to her were so powerfully impressed by the sight of her. Day after day this highly favored virgin displayed from her bed of suffering the deepest humility, the most inspired love of the cross, the most self-sacrificing charity. She had no other interest than the cause of Christ. Her life was an offense to unbelievers—but a consolation to the faithful. She passed from the earth on February 9, 1825. Bishop Hermann Dingelstadt gratified the desires of many when in 1892 he instituted the preliminary work toward the process of her beatification.[142]

MARIA DOMINICA CLARA MOES

37. Very similar to the life of Anna Catharine Emmerich in its vicissitudes and mission is that of the Dominican Sister Maria Dominica Clara Moes of the Holy Cross.[143] It is also a standing miracle of God's

merciful love for His Church and a living protest against the spirit of unbelief. We have here to deal with a person whom God has overwhelmed with extraordinary graces, but whom He has also proved by the severest trials.

Clara Moes was born on October 27, 1832, at Bous, near the Moselle, in the grand duchy of Luxemburg. On the following day she received Baptism and with it the complete use of her reason, and many supernatural revelations.* Very charming is her intercourse with the holy guardian angel, whom she saw almost constantly after that day. This heavenly messenger took care to instruct and educate her, and proved a very strict disciplinarian when she did not punctually comply with his teachings. There are probably few educators who insist so much on the renunciation of one's own will as did the guardian angel of Clara. At his word she made a vow of virginity when only six years old. After this day she voluntarily practised severe penance. At her first Holy Communion, which she received a few months after her ninth year, it was clearly made known to her that she was called to found in her native country a convent of the Second Order of St. Dominic, a work that would encounter the greatest difficulties. She did not then anticipate how these obstacles would rise like mountains in her path and what floods of bitterness would overwhelm her before she could accomplish the work which God had appointed her.

It was a long and thorny path until in 1861 she could at last begin community life with a few friends in a convent on the Limpetsberg in Luxemburg. Rarely has a convent been established in bitterer poverty and with more contradictions on the part of men. But greater trials were in store. The mystical gifts of

---

*At the command of the ecclesiastical authorities, Mother Clara was obliged to reveal all her extraordinary gifts of grace.

Mother Clara had become publicly known and unfortunately rumor had it that a person was permitted to live in the convent against the will of the foundress, and was causing great disturbance by her pretended visions. This gave rise to malicious reports against Mother Clara and fixed upon her the reputation of a fanatical visionary. The ecclesiastical court took cognizance of the matter and a long drawn out investigation was carried on, causing the Servant of God the greatest annoyance. She was obliged to commit to writing all her spiritual experiences that they might be examined in detail. A verdict was finally reached in 1884, and it brought her a splendid justification. During the same year her convent was affiliated with the Order of St. Dominic.

In trials and in gifts of grace the life of Mother Clara is extraordinary. Her struggles with the Evil One recall what St. Athanasius relates of the holy anchorite St. Anthony. She endured all the keen pain of jeer and contempt on the part of men and the bitterness of apparent abandonment on the part of God. And still her thirst for suffering was not satisfied. Her zeal for ignominy and humiliation reached the most heroic love of the cross. God bestowed upon her, therefore, the stigmata of His Son. Visions and ecstasies were frequent with her. Several times, like St. Stanislaus Kostka, she was strengthened by Holy Communion at the hands of angels, and others of her Sisters witnessed the fact, seeing a host laid upon her tongue by invisible hands. She took pains, however, to conceal her extraordinary gifts of grace even from her own subjects.

What she thought of such things we may learn from her own words. Once she imposed a punishment upon a Sister because the latter had shown admiration for her on the occasion of an ecstasy.

"God demands solid virtue from us," she wrote,

"and will not have a Sister fix her heart upon a soul because it is visited by ecstasy. If these extraordinary graces are not viewed from the proper standpoint and do not lead to God and His love, they sanctify neither the soul that experienced them nor those who behold them. To see a person receive Holy Communion in an ecstasy does not justify one in priding oneself upon it. It is true and remains true that only genuine virtue makes a person holy. Any one who extols me on account of my ecstasies I think my enemy and my best friend is she who despises me. That men consider a person thus favored a saint, only confounds me. One single humiliation counts more before God than ecstasies and miracles, were these ever so numerous."[144]

If it be true that genuine saints are afraid of visions while those who wish to appear saints desire them, then Mother Clara was of the genuine sort. She disliked anything extraordinary among her subjects and their training was as sober and sane as possible in harmony with the old and proved principles of ascetics. The Servant of God died on February 24, 1895. All who knew her were persuaded that a saint had passed from earth and the many prayers answered through her intercession prove that this persuasion is well founded.

Venerable Maria Agnes Clara Steiner

38. A brave Tyrolese proved by severe sufferings meets us in the Venerable Maria Agnes Clara Steiner.[145] She was born of poor parents on August 29, 1813, at Taisten in Pustertal, diocese of Brixen, and from her early years was favored by God with extraordinary gifts of grace. She received her First Communion at the age of nine. From this time she strengthened her soul with the Bread of Angels every week and felt such attraction for Holy Mass that she assisted at it every day in spite of a long and difficult

road. The salutary influence she exercised on her companions was much praised. Her religious vocation met with many obstacles. She was sent to an uncle to work in the fields and to tend cattle and she suffered very rough treatment. As soon as she was allowed to return to her mother she made a pilgrimage to Our Lady of Absam, near Innsbruck, and prayed for the favor of admission into the convent of the Franciscan Sisters at Brunech. But such was not the will of God. They were obliged to dismiss her on account of her weak health. When in spite of this she persisted in her desire of entering a convent, the people of her village scoffed at her and looked upon her as half-witted. But her courage was not broken and later on she went to Assisi, where she was received into the convent of the Bavarian Tertiaries. She was soon esteemed one of the ablest and most virtuous Sisters in the house and was entrusted with the care of the novices. She was also highly thought of for her prudence and firmness of character.

Bishop Nicholas Piervisani of Nocera desired to restore the old convent of the Poor Clares in his city. In 1845 he asked the Apostolic See to give him Sister Agnes Steiner for this difficult task. His expectations were more than satisfied. The spirit of penance and mortification, of interior love of God and the neighbor, and of holy cheerfulness entered the ancient walls of the cloister. To other convents also the superior of Nocera extended her beneficent work of reform. How highly her subjects esteemed her is shown by the fact that they wished to give her the office of superior at Rome. The nuns regularly gave her their votes at every succeeding election. To their sorrow she was called away from this earth on August 24, 1862.

At her investment with the habit in Assisi, she had been named Sister Agnes Clara of the Wound in the Side of Jesus. The name was prophetic. Most dreadful trials, at which our human nature shudders, were destined to remind her continually of the sufferings of the wound in the side of Jesus. But she also received extraordinary graces and consolations. One who constantly abides in the wounded side of Jesus will surely partake of its rich treasures. The life of the Venerable Agnes Clara Steiner will furnish abundant material to modern mysticism. On March 18, 1909, Pius X signed the decree introducing the cause of her beatification.

Mother Francisca Schervier

39. A considerable number of new religious Congregations accrued to the Church in Germany. As a rule, those who took part in their foundation were pious persons of prominence. But as far as we know at present the process of beatification has been inaugurated for only one of them, Mother Francisca Schervier, foundress of the Poor Sisters of St. Francis.[146] Her life furnishes such evidence of extraordinary holiness that the hope of seeing her raised to the honor of the altar rests on solid foundation.

Francisca Schervier, daughter of a wealthy needle manufacturer, was born on January 3, 1819, in the ancient imperial city of Aix-la-Chapelle. As a child she was precocious not only in worldly knowledge, but in the understanding of the mysteries of faith as well. God introduced her early into the school of the cross, of interior sufferings and hard trials. It was important for her future vocation that she should learn from her own experience how those suffer who are severely tried. She received her First Communion when ten years old and after that time she kept unshaken her resolution to live only for God. She saw God in His image on earth and it pained her delicately sensitive mind to see so many men starving in misery and suffering. An irresistible impulse to practise charity took hold of her. She went into the huts of the poor, visited the sick, and everywhere left abundant alms, which she obtained partly from her paternal inheritance and partly from what she begged unremittingly from her relatives and friends. There lived at that time in Aix-la-Chapelle a priest who was very active in charitable work, Father Joseph Istas, chaplain at St. Paul's. In him Francisca found the greatest support and encouragement for her labors of charity. On his part Father Istas found no more zealous co-operator than our Servant of God in executing his many plans for the relief of social misery. For a long time she had desired to enter the religious life. One day a friend of hers, Gertrude Frank, declared that it was imperative upon her to establish a Congregation in Aix-la-Chapelle for the practice of works of mercy and that she clearly knew it was the manifest will of God.[147] Francisca showed reluctance and alleged her unfitness; but her friend gave her no rest and finally she proposed the matter to an experienced priest. Though he greatly approved the plan it was not easy to overcome the reluctance of Francisca. In the autumn of 1845 all difficulties were removed, and Francisca began a community life with four companions, who chose her for their superior. The young community, which occupied itself with nursing the sick and the care of the poor people and the girls who were in danger, found much favor because of its great zeal and it soon began to win new members. In 1851 it obtained the approbation of the archbishop under the title of the Poor Sisters of St. Francis. Until her death on December 14, 1876, Mother Francisca was to her subjects the ideal of a superior. Her discreet direction and sound spirituality secured interior solidity to her Congregation. There was a peculiar charm in her character that attracted every one and gave her great influence over the souls of women. The secret of this power was her lively faith and her interior

union with God. She viewed everything in the light
of faith and thus found it easy to inspire her Sisters
to magnanimous sacrifices in their beautiful vocation.
And this spirit brings with it continual joy. In prayer
she sought assistance and light for every need. Hence
she had no objection when some of the Sisters—those
called "recluses"—gave themselves completely to the
contemplative life, endeavoring by prayer to bring
God's blessing on the work of the rest, as when Moses
prayed on the mountain while the people were fighting
with the enemy.

One who loves God as did Mother Francisca must
needs love immortal souls also. It is touching to read
of the pains she took to seek after lost sheep according
to the example of the Good Shepherd. Her bold and
fiery zeal sometimes impelled her to do things that may
be rather admired than imitated.

We must admit that Francisca's young friend, Gertrude Frank, was right. It was God's will that she
should found a religious Congregation. Incalculable
good for the relief of suffering humanity has been
done by the Poor Sisters of St. Francis, who labor
fruitfully according to the spirit of their foundress in
numerous residences throughout Germany and North
America. God has visibly protected their work and
has not failed to grant extraordinary favors through
Francisca Schervier both before and after her death.

MARIA OF THE SACRED HEART
(Countess Droste zu Vischering)

40. When Leo XIII dedicated the whole world to
the Sacred Heart of Jesus at the end of the last century, few were aware that he did so at the suggestion
of a German nun. It was Maria of the Sacred Heart,
born Countess Droste zu Vischering, superior of the
convent of the Good Shepherd at Oporto, who on June
10, 1898, wrote to Leo XIII that it was the desire

of the Divine Saviour to have the whole world consecrated to His Sacred Heart.[148] The letter remained unanswered. On January 6, 1899, she wrote a second time. In the meanwhile Rome had inquired concerning the writer of the letter and had maturely considered the matter. At the beginning of April, 1899, there arrived at Oporto a letter and the decree of the Holy Father declaring that the desired dedication would be carried into execution on the coming feast of the Sacred Heart after a triduum. What is narrated in the biography of Mother Maria was read to Pope Leo and was expressly approved by him.

Maria Anne Droste zu Vischering, daughter of Count Clement Droste zu Vischering, was born in the ancestral home at Münster, September 8, 1863. She was of an extremely lively disposition and her nature was impetuous, but the excellent training she received at home and in the convent school of the Ladies of the Sacred Heart at Riedenburg turned the enthusiasm of the young and talented countess in the right direction. She appreciated clearly the truth and beauty of Christian ideals and devoted herself to them with all the fervor of her uncorrupted mind. When about twelve years old she received Confirmation and resolved to renounce all the pleasures of the world and to become a religious. She burned with zeal to announce Christ to the heathen and lamented that she was not a boy and so could not become a missionary. But her desire to gain souls for Christ was to be gratified, though not in the manner she had imagined in her earlier years.

In her twentieth year, when she was about to follow the divine call, she was seized with a lingering disease. It was a period of interior purification and of great spiritual profit. Her parents permitted her to lead the life of a religious at home as far as was possible. Her overmastering desire was to practise magnanimity toward Our Lord and to serve Him with pure love. This noble intention determined her in 1888 to enter the convent of the Good Shepherd, though before this time she had not thought of this Order. To gain for Our Lord the most unfortunate of creatures and to live unknown to the world was in keeping with the desire of her great soul. After five years her health had so much improved that she was able to join the Sisters of the Good Shepherd at Münster on November 22, 1888. God overwhelmed her with consolation, but at the same time proved the genuineness of her vocation by severe trials. Homesickness, discouragement, anxieties of conscience, and doubts of her vocation pressed heavily upon her. But it was not in the character of Sister Mary of the Sacred Heart to fail in a resolve she had so clearly understood because there were difficulties in the way. These difficulties rather confirmed in her her favorite virtue—magnanimity in serving Our Lord.

Soon after the completion of her noviceship, Sister Mary of the Sacred Heart was given the office of mistress of the pupils, which duty she performed with great skill. At the beginning of 1894 obedience sent her to Portugal, and after a short stay at Lisbon she was appointed superior of the house of Oporto. They expected from her the accomplishment of a difficult task. The convent lay under an immense burden of debt; means of subsistence were altogether wanting; and the loss of the convent was to be feared every day. By her prudence and her confidence in God, which was often miraculously rewarded, Sister Mary of the Sacred Heart not only saved the house from ruin, but soon brought it prosperity and reputation. She labored with superhuman endeavor for the welfare of her Sisters and the penitents, and showed herself a heroic bride of the heavenly King. But spinal disease soon cast her upon the bed of sickness from which she was never to rise. Still her painful ailment did not end her activity, and she was carried to the parlor on a portable couch to satisfy the many who sought her help and advice.

Our Lord had never spared His chosen bride interior trials. Now also her exterior appearance was a picture of misery. Yet thirst for suffering was never quenched. "My Jesus, My Jesus, more suffering—more love" was her prayer. The lights and revelations vouchsafed her during this time were frequent, consoling, and full of profound wisdom. Her biographers not unjustly compare her with St. Gertrude and Blessed Margaret Mary. For her, too, the Heart of Jesus was the fountain of her ardent charity and her heroic wisdom. The response of Leo XIII that he intended to consecrate all mankind to the Sacred Heart of Jesus was the greatest joy of her life.

But she was not to celebrate the day of the consecration on earth. Just when bells were ringing for the eve of the feast and the triduum of consecration had begun at Rome, she departed this life on June 8, 1899, before she had completed her thirty-sixth year. At the news of her death rich and poor hastened to the door of the convent to see once more the face of the revered Mother and to recommend themselves to her protection. The funeral was like a triumphal procession. Six noblemen asked the privilege of carrying the coffin on their shoulders to the grave, an event before unheard of in Oporto, and an immense crowd of the people followed on foot. Leo XIII took information on all the particulars of her death.

The renown of Sister Maria of the Sacred Heart increases from day to day. The story of her life is echoed with joy in thousands of hearts. She is a proof of God's liberality toward those who distinguish themselves by generosity to the Sacred Heart of His Son. We may surely hope that the Church will honor the memory of this daughter of an illustrious house. She is a heroine of whom her people may be proud. God grant that her example may incite others to the same heroic courage.

OTHER HOLY RELIGIOUS—WOMEN

41. The efficacious power of divine grace in the Catholic Church was likewise made manifest in a number of other saintly religious women whose process of beatification has been inaugurated. They are:

The Venerable Emilie de Rodat[149]—died 1852—who, born of a noble family was during her earlier years in danger of becoming lukewarm in her faith, but afterward displayed all the greater zeal and founded the Congregation of Sisters of the Holy Family with the mother-house at Villefranche.

Venerable Pauline Louise Pinczon—died 1820—a member of the Hospital Sisters of St. Thomas of Villanova.

Venerable Marie Rivier[150]—died 1838—foundress of the Congregation of the Presentation.

Venerable Elizabeth Bichier des Ages—died 1838—who, with Venerable Hubert Fournet,* founded the Sisters of the Cross of St. Andrew.

The Servant of God, Marie Madeleine de Bengy, widow of Bonnault d'Houet—died 1858—who as a young widow ministered to the wounded of Napoleon's army and in 1820, with the assistance of Father Varin, founded the Congregation of the Faithful Companions of Jesus.[151]

The Servant of God, Adeline Desir (died 1875), foundress of the Humble Daughters of Mount Calvary; Venerable Philomena of St. Columba (died 1868), a Spaniard, belonging to the woman's branch of the Minims; Venerable Therese Eustochium Verzeri (died 1852), who founded the Daughters of the

*See page 81.

Heart of Jesus in the Diocese of Bergamo; the Servant of God Maria Aloysia of Jesus (died 1875), foundress of an institute under the rule of the Third Order of St. Dominic; the Servant of God, Josephe du Bourg (died 1862), who founded the Sisters of the Redeemer and of the Blessed Virgin; the Servant of God, Maria of the Sorrows of the Blessed Virgin (died 1891), a member of the ancient Order of the Conceptionist Sisters; and the Servant of God Ludovica Borgiotti, co-founder of the Institute of the Sisters of Jesus of Nazareth.

HOLY LAYMEN AND WOMEN

T HE ideal of holiness is not limited to any state of life, and the Church, as a saving power for all men, must be able to provide for all the means of reaching this ideal. She must not be wanting, then, in a holy laity. And, indeed, in the lay world there is no lack of illustrious models of holiness, who, by the inspiring power of their example, incite their fellow-men to heroic endeavor for Christian virtue. If, therefore, many laymen have reached the ideal, especially in the nineteenth century when conditions were so unfavorable to a holy life, no one should fail in the courage needed to fulfil his duties as a Christian.

DOMINIC SAVIO

1. The college boy of fifteen, Dominic Savio, attracts us with the charm of youth. In 1911 the Eucharistic Congress of Madrid sent a telegram to Pius X, begging him to hasten the beatification of Dominic Savio, who, because of receiving his First Holy Communion at the age of seven and his extraordinary devotion to the Most Blessed Sacrament, merited recommendation as a pattern for children and was deemed worthy of the title—"Child of the Holy Eucharist."[152]

The life of this angelic boy proves how wisely Pius X acted in strengthening children early and often with the Bread of Life. His admirable teacher, Don Bosco, has himself written the wonderful life of Dominic.[153] He was born on April 2, 1842, at Riva, near Turin, the son of a blacksmith, and was early introduced to all practices of piety by his parents. The seductive power of evil had no influence on him. On the contrary, he energetically repulsed others who gave him bad example. We can not but marvel at his precocious intelligence of heavenly things, an intelligence matured by divine grace. "He is indeed a boy of whom much may be expected," writes his spiritual guide. "May God open to him a career in which so precious a fruit may ripen." When the boy of seven was told that he was to receive Holy Communion the joy of his heart knew no bounds. From that time he was almost continually in the church to prepare himself worthily for the great day approaching. The seriousness of purpose which he showed on this occasion remained his guiding star during all his life. It was clear that so promising a boy must study and, seeing that his parents were wanting in the necessary means, the priest of the place enabled Dominic to attend an academy in the neighborhood of his native town. At twelve he went to the Oratory of the Venerable Don Bosco in the district of Valdocco, and from this institution he was sent to the college in Turin.

Don Bosco and Dominic Savio soon understood one another. A divinely inspired teacher and a pupil with an unspoiled and generous heart had met. Dominic soon laid hold of two ideas with all the fervor of his ardent soul, he would become a saint and, if possible, save his soul. With tenacious energy he strove for complete self-mastery. Like all saints he gave himself to works of supererogation in prayer and penance. Don Bosco had to curb his zeal. Among his companions in the Oratory and in the college the boy worked like a true apostle. He strove especially to foster among his associates devotion to the Immaculate Conception and the reception of the Sacraments. Such zealous persons are as a rule not liked by the young. But it was not so with Dominic. Not at all obtrusive, no disturber of youthful gaiety, he was a genuine boy, alive with a boy's nature. He did even more by example than by words, which showed to all how earnestly he was trying to be a saint. His youth was not without its difficulties, but they served only to strengthen the more his steadiness of character.

Dominic had reached the sixth class in the college when he was stricken with a disease of the lungs. Don Bosco, filled with anxiety, hoped that a change of air might bring relief, and sent the boy to his parents at Mondonio, where they were then living. But what Dominic had long confidently foretold now came to pass. On the evening of March 9, 1857, he died in the arms of his sorrowing father. The news of his death at first brought grief and mourning to his relatives, friends and teachers, but this soon gave way to joyful conviction that a new intercessor for them stood before the divine throne. Men soon began to ask favors from Dominic and their prayers were not in vain.

Many cardinals and bishops expressed their desire that Dominic Savio be soon raised to the honors of the altar, that he may serve as a pattern and protector for the precarious age of boyhood. But he will also spur on the old to endeavor for virtue. "We old people," writes Cardinal Agliardi, "feel ourselves humbled before such virtue in a fifteen-year-old boy. But he who is yet in the bloom of youth will under the attraction of so great a fragrance of innocence follow likewise in the footsteps of his piety."[154]

Venerable Nunzio Sulprizio

2. The renown of being a bright example for working boys was attained by the Venerable Nunzio Sulprizio.[155] Leo XIII, in his decree on the heroic degree of the virtues of Sulprizio, published on the three hundredth anniversary of the death of St. Aloysius, wrote as follows.

"It is proper that on this festal day, consecrated to the memory of the angelic youth Aloysius, we publish the decree which acknowledges the practice of heroic virtue by the venerable Servant of God, Nunzio Sulprizio. In consideration of the deplorable condition of the times it is truly a matter of importance. The world . . . all mankind finds itself groaning under a smothering burden of all possible evils. In consequence of the spread of false and unsound doctrines, unbelief and godlessness lord it over all. Unbridled immorality is spreading everywhere, after every barrier which so far restrained the lower passions has been swept away. It is inexperienced youth that suffers most from the evil. They grow up without protection and, cast amidst dangers and allurements of all kinds, fall into the craftily laid snare, miserably perishing in vice and corruption.

"The Church, which seeks to protect youth with loving care, deeply mourns this misfortune and with motherly solicitude does all things possible to save them from final loss. Since in this matter example is of more avail than mere words, she seeks to put before her youth for their imitation a pattern adorned with virginal purity. For the last three hundred years the amiable figure of St. Aloysius Gonzaga, the true model and protecting angel of Catholic youth, has shone before them with resplendent light. Gladly have we taken advantage of the three hundredth anniversary of his edifying death to encourage our youth to celebrate this feast with unusual ceremony, and to honor the wonderful achievement of his life. To-day we would direct the attention of the young to a faithful copy of their heavenly patron.

"This is the young working-boy Nunzio Sulprizio. From his earliest years he took St. Aloysius as his model and strove to imitate the saint in the spirit of mortification, of patience, humility, and prayer, so that, rich in merits and although like his model young in years, he died in the repute of sanctity.

"Would that our youth might learn from Nunzio Sulprizio how the angelic virtues of St. Aloysius may be imitated. May they ever be filled with the spirit of interior piety and be devoted to God and their Church, avoiding with the greatest solicitude all intercourse with the wicked and likewise the corruption of the world. This is the dearest and most ardent wish of our heart."

Leo XIII rightly presents Nunzio Sulprizio as a new model for our youth. Our hearts warm toward this amiable young man when we read how earnestly he fought for the angelic virtue in dangerous surroundings—what heavenly patience and gentleness he practised under unjust treatment; and how immovably firm his character remained under the heaviest misfortunes.

He was born on April 13, 1817, at Pesco Sanfonesco, in the Abruzzi, the child of poor parents. At six he was an orphan. A grandmother took loving care of him. But within three years God removed this only support. The bereaved and destitute boy was now brought to a maternal uncle, a blacksmith, a coarse and cruel man, who strove only for earthly possessions. Nunzio was obliged to recompense him by doing the full work of an adult laborer, for which he received no pay. He permitted the boy nothing, not even to go to school, but overloaded the child with work far above his strength from early morning till late at night. Both in summer, when the excessive heat was unbearable, and in winter, when barbarous ill weather in the rough mountain country cut to the bone, he had to go long distances on the errands of his master. The roughest ill treatment was soon added to this. The uncle was a man of violent temper and fell into a fury upon the slightest occasion. Nunzio could not possibly meet all his humors and each time he failed he had to bear severe punishment. The blacksmith seized the first bar of iron or tool at hand and unmercifully struck the boy or flung him on the floor and kicked him until he was senseless. The master had companions scarcely behind him in cruelty to the innocent boy. Yet the worst to Nunzio's mind were the blasphemous and unchaste language and the obscenities of these men he was obliged to hear every day. He often closed his ears or retired to some corner where he might not listen to such conversation. Harsh treatment and insufficient food were sure to undermine the health of the apprentice. The allowance of food was so scanty that Nunzio was forced to beg from compassionate neighbors. He became extremely emaciated and after a time a great ulcer appeared on his left leg. But his heartless uncle paid no attention to it. When Nunzio could no longer walk they forced him to stand all day and work at the bellows; and when his strength failed in this, they bound him fast in the bellows' chain. Even his frequent fainting spells in the smithy made no impression on the coarse mind of his uncle.

In spite of this cruel treatment no one ever heard any complaint from Nunzio, nor did he cast reproach on his tormentor. He never lost his gentleness nor his serenity of soul. When in spite of all the energy of his will he became unfit for work, his uncle allowed him to be removed to the hospital for the poor in the neighboring town of Aquila. It was too late. Careful attention brought some relief to the sick boy, but he could not be cured. There was no accommodation in the place for incurables, and after some time he was dismissed. On his return his uncle burst into a rage, for he had hoped to have been rid of his sick nephew. Torture began anew for the poor boy. Although he was half dead and too much exertion might kill him, he was obliged to work. But undismayed he stood fast to the end, bearing all things with heroic patience. "I will become a saint . . . a great saint and in a short time." With these words he encouraged himself in many a dark hour. To a saint it is most important that he possess steadfastness of character. In the smithy of Pesco Sanfonesco the character of Nunzio stood the test of fire.

At length, after six years of suffering, came relief. There lived in Naples another uncle of the orphaned apprentice, Francis Sulprizio. When the latter heard of the frightful treatment of his nephew he at once took steps to free him from the hands of his torturer. The blacksmith was glad to lose what he called "so useless a workman." Thus far Nunzio had been for the men about him only a body in the way, but now he was to be overwhelmed with benevolent proof of true charity. Francis Sulprizio, corporal in the first regiment of grenadiers at Naples, invited his nephew to come to him and brought the boy to his superior officer, Colonel Felix Wochinger. When the colonel, well known for his deep piety and great charity, saw the emaciated youth, who could move only with the aid of crutches, and learned how innocent had been his life and how inhumanly he had been treated, his heart was moved with a strong affection for Nunzio and he declared that he would care for the boy as a father. They placed the sick boy in the hospital for incurables, Santa Maria del Populo. Caries of the bones had resulted from long neglected wounds. Nunzio soon became the favorite of all in the hospital. On his countenance shone his innocence and in spite of his dreadful pains he was continually cheerful and uttered never a complaint of his misery. Admiration increased when his previous history became known. He dragged himself to the bedside of other patients to console and encourage them. The spiritual advice which he skilfully wove into his ingenuous conversation was particularly efficacious. He was most edifying in his great and tender devotion to the Holy Eucharist and to the ever blessed Virgin. Like all pure souls he was a great lover of prayer. The attendant often surprised him during the night as he knelt absorbed in prayer by his bedside. Colonel Wochinger gave his ward the best of attention, often sending him to the baths on the island of Ischia. After some two years, on April 11, 1834, he brought the sick boy to his own home, Castel Nuovo, to care for him yet more generously, and particularly to have more frequent opportunity of witnessing the heroic virtue of a saint. "How could I complain of the trials which God sends me," he said, "when I see with what heroic courage Nunzio bears his afflictions. How can I delay for a moment to share my abundance with the poor when he, who is almost the neediest of all, refuses what is offered to himself so as to give to others, and in this says so plainly: 'What, shall not the Lord's own also receive?'" The news of Nunzio's departure caused universal consternation in the hospital. No one had ever brought so much consolation and joy to the sick there as did the blacksmith apprentice of Pesco Sanfonesco.

In his new home nothing was wanting to the sick young man that could restore his crippled strength. For a while it seemed as if fresh life began to pulse in his broken body. Nunzio began to plan for the future. He desired to serve God in the religious state. His noble patron placed a private tutor at his disposal to teach him Latin with a view to the priesthood. But it was an illusion. The sickness returned with new strength. The sufferer remained ever like his former self. Just as formerly the bitterest poverty, so now the greatest comforts could not withdraw his heart from God. He endeavored as far as it was possible in the castle to lead a cloistered life. Suffering he had in full plenty, but not enough for his penitential spirit, and he tormented his weak body by voluntary mortifications. Toward the servants, who out of envy often treated him neglectfully, he was love itself, and no word of complaint ever came from his lips to the master of the house. God glorified him even now by extraordinary favors.

On May 5, 1836, Nunzio, then nineteen years of age, was released from his sufferings. With a smile on his countenance, he took his leave of this world. While gazing upon a picture of the Mother of God he exclaimed: "See how beautiful she is," and in a few moments he had departed. The news of his death brought a pilgrimage to Castel Nuovo. A wonderful change was observed in the dead body. The wounds took on a rosy color and exhaled a sweet odor. To satisfy the people the body was exposed for four days, and it was then buried in the church of Castel Nuovo. High dignitaries in the world, among them King Ferdinand II of Naples, journeyed to Rome to beg for the beatification of the angelic blacksmith apprentice. Nunzio Sulprizio is indeed a splendid model for our youth. He was content in spite of extreme poverty, laborious and obedient under a tyrannical master, and a chaste and unspoiled soul in spite of licentious surroundings. A youth of steadfast character, he knew that man's worth is judged only by his inferior spirit; and this interior spirit was summed up in his magnanimity in fulfilling the twofold commandment of love of God and of the neighbor. His life shows that it is not in social condition nor in age nor in health that a man achieves greatness in the kingdom of God.

VENERABLE JOHN BAPTIST JOSSA

3. The Venerable John Baptist Jossa[156] also belongs to the lower classes of the people. He was first a porter in a court of justice in Naples, but gave up his position to have more time for works of charity. He was indefatigable in gathering alms. It is almost incredible what great sums annually passed through

his hands. It was well known that he kept nothing for himself and so the rich gave him freely of their abundance. He could picture so touchingly the miseries of the poor that it was hard to refuse him. He enjoyed great favor in the whole city on account of his voluntary sacrifice. To the corporal works of mercy he added skill in salutary advice, an exhortation to penance and to endeavor for eternal reward. "Hate sin" was the refrain of all his discourse. His life offers an abundance of delightful and interesting adventures. He died on July 4, 1828, at the age of sixty-one. The blessed Francis Xavier Bianchi said long before: "John Jossa is a great saint. At his death men will behold great events." And so it happened.

Léon Papin-Dupont
(The Holy Man of Tours)

4. A man of strong faith and charity in this age of ours so weak in both these virtues, the model of the Christian father of a family who understood how to bring into harmony with the ideal of sanctity all the duties which modern society imposes, was the Servant of God, Léon Papin-Dupont.[157] He was called by his contemporaries the "holy man of Tours," "the wonder worker of Tours." "If this man is not a saint then there are no longer any saints," said a French bishop. This favors the hope that the Church also will approve of the holiness of Léon Dupont.

Léon Papin-Dupont was a son of the Antilles, born on the island of Martinique, January 4, 1797. His father was a descendant of an ancient Breton family, his mother a Creole. Léon was educated first at a school in the United States and then at the college of Pontlevoy in France. Later he went to the university of Paris to study law. Up to this time he had been an exemplary student, but now the free life of the university threatened danger to his religious spirit. By reason of his social eminence and his considerable means Dupont had entrance into the salons of high society. He was a lover of balls and similar pleasure parties and lacked nothing to take his place among the noblest lords of Paris society. His biographer remarks of this period: "He was worldly-minded but not corrupt." A little incident led him to a fundamental change of mind. Dupont himself later called it his conversion.

One day he missed one of his servants, a young Savoyard. The latter afterward gave as an excuse that he had been attending M. Bordier's catechetical instruction. This aroused Dupont's interest. The next time he himself went with his little Savoyard and found Bordier surrounded by a crowd of boys listening attentively to his words. The sight both shamed and strongly attracted the gay student. But from that day Bordier became his friend, and he later induced Dupont to join the fervent Sodality of the Blessed Virgin which Father Delpuits, a former Jesuit, had founded at Paris in 1801. Vigorous religious life was pulsating in the Sodality; it was excellently directed, and had, among others, various sections for charitable work. To these belonged, for example, the instruction of young Savoyard. Léon was soon burning with ardor for the twofold end of the Sodality—his own salvation and the practice of the apostolate.

Many incidents are related which show with what energy he entered into the work. With other sodalists he used to visit many hotels on Fridays and in a way that attracted attention would order in a loud voice a genuine fast-day meal. One day he happened in a house and heard that the goods of the poor family were to be sold because they could not pay their debts. He straightway sent them his fine horse and carriage. Once when in Nantes he wished to approach the Sacraments, as he usually did on Sunday. The priest to whom he desired to confess was much disturbed. He feared a sacrilege. That so gayly dressed a young man should receive the Sacraments was a thing unheard of. Dupont remarked the priest's embarrassment and informed him that he was a sodalist and was accustomed to go to the Sacraments every week. While life at the university usually robbed so many of faith and innocence, it only strengthened Dupont in his religious convictions, and armed his heart against the allurements of vice. As now, so in his later life it was the Sodality of the Blessed Virgin that spurred him on to renewed zeal. But his relations with polite society were not severed on this account. He made it his pride to be known in such circles as a resolute Catholic.

At the age of twenty-four Dupont had completed his university studies. He now returned to his native land and accepted a position in the royal court of justice in Martinique. He made no concealment of his Catholic convictions. His character knew no half measures, and so without fear of men he was everywhere and in everything. true to the noble principles he had learned in the Sodality of the Blessed Virgin at Paris. All his brothers and sisters were dead, so he obeyed the wish of his mother and married when he was thirty years of age. But after five years his young wife was taken from him by death. Her last wish was that Léon might have their only child, Henrietta, educated in the same institution as herself— with the Ursulines at Tours. This induced Dupont, who was now a judge, to resign his position in Martinique and to reside permanently with his daughter at Tours.

At this time Léon was thinking of becoming a priest. But his friends dissuaded him. And they acted in harmony with God's design; for it was his vocation to become a model for the higher classes. He was highly educated, possessed a fortune of about a million of francs, moved in the best circles of society, and combined the polish of a man of the world with the solid principles of a saint. It was not long before Léon Dupont attracted public attention in the city of St. Martin. During the first years of the reign of the citizen-king Louis Philippe, religious sentiment was not a recommendation. It was, therefore, not merely unwonted, but really an event for Tours that so rich and cultured a man should attend Mass daily, communicate almost every day, often serve Mass, and take part in all processions and other ecclesiastical affairs. In society he frowned down every scoffer at religion. He introduced conversation on religious subjects and spoke with such warmth and conviction that his words were never without good result. It was of great advantage to him that he was so genial a companion, a fine conversationalist, and clever in promoting cheerfulness among his associates.

The Servant of God was above all an advocate of frequent communion. Again and again he dwelt upon it in private conversation and in his letters. "The Christian without Holy Communion is a fish out of water," he said. Not only in the lay world, but from the clergy also he experienced much opposition, for the influence of Jansenism was still abroad. A pamphlet written by him was published anonymously under the title: *"La foi raffermie et la piété ranimée dans le mystère de l'Eucharistie"*—"Faith and piety regenerated in the mystery of the Eucharist."

The well-known Jewish convert, Herman Cohen, at the instance of the Servant of God Theodolinde Dubouché,* had founded a league for the nightly adoration of the Eucharist. Léon Dupont, with whom Cohen was very friendly, made a propaganda in Tours for the league. Although his friends tried

*See pages 227 sqq.

to dissuade him at first, seeing that the men of Tours were not much inclined to such matters, he succeeded in enlisting seventy-four members within two months. It was an inspiring sight to see men of all classes, laborers, students, merchants, railway, military, and state officials coming punctually to perform their nightly adoration. Many of them had to make considerable sacrifices, but Dupont's eloquence inspired them to the ideal work. For many it was undoubtedly a renewal of religious life. After the men had joined the ranks for nightly adoration the Servant of God knew how to persuade them to frequent the Sacraments. On favorable occasions he had distinguished spiritual men like the Venerable Julien Eymard,* Father de Chaignon, S.J., Father Herman Cohen and others to encourage the members of the league. In other cities also nightly adoration was established through the efforts of Dupont.

The Revolution had wrought dreadful havoc in France. Many ancient and revered shrines were destroyed, religious practices were in disgrace or oblivion, and religion was banished from public life. Dupont sought to awake in the younger generation a consciousness of what it meant to be a consistent Catholic. Tours was very rich in ancient shrines. He sought out all of them, had them renovated and often visited them to pray at them himself. There was no statue of a saint in the streets or houses of Tours which he passed without reverent greeting. He endeavored to encourage pilgrimages to the shrines of Our Lady and to this end wrote a booklet about these holy places in France. In Tours even the tomb of its illustrious bishop, St. Martin, was forgotten during the Revolution and the saint's basilica had been completely destroyed. A street had been opened across the site and houses built there. Dupont did not rest until

*See pages 176 sqq.

excavations to find the tomb of the great apostle had been made, and when it was at length found he was the most zealous promoter of the building of a new basilica. He displayed great social activity in the work of the St. Vincent de Paul Societies. Three times a week he devoted an evening to the instruction of young working-people and visited the soldiers to see to their instruction and social amusement. Out of his own means he founded in Tours a residence of the Little Sisters of the Poor, who take care of old people; and with the legacy of his friend Bordier he established a house for priests devoted to the giving of missions among the people. Since blasphemy and the desecration of Sunday were two grave faults of the time, he brought the full weight of his influence to bear against them. He organized a league of prayer against blasphemy, cursing, and Sunday-breaking. It was afterward erected into an archconfraternity by the bishop of Langres and approved by Pius IX.

The idea of propitiation incited him to great veneration of the sufferings of Christ and of the Sacred Heart of Jesus. His devotion to the Holy Face obtained a great popularity. He kept hanging in his room a genuine copy of the towel of St. Veronica with a lamp burning before it, and here he often came to pray. One day he anointed the ailing eyes of a lady with oil from this lamp and she was immediately cured. This was the beginning of those many striking events which turned his room into a real place of pilgrimage and gained him the title of "the Wonder-worker of Tours." Whoever studies intimately the inner life of Léon Dupont will not wonder that God, in answer to his prayers, gave help to so many.

The maxims on which he relied most confidently were such as manifest a genuine sanctity. He was thoroughly penetrated with the truths of faith and with unvarying consistency regulated his whole life by its light. Hence proceeded his unwearied zeal for God's honor, his heartfelt devotion to the Holy Eucharist, and the courageous lay-apostolate, which cost him many a sacrifice. When his only daughter, whom he tenderly loved and had carefully educated, died at the age of fifteen, he recited the *"Magnificat"* aloud. The bystanders were astonished at such joy and gratitude. But he replied that he must above all thank God for granting his daughter so beautiful a death and for calling her to Himself before the world could rob her of her innocence.

Another characteristic trait of the Servant of God was his profound humility. In the church, in society, everywhere, he sought to place himself where he would be least noticed. He was quite distressed when conversation was turned upon himself and his affairs. He was rather displeased when others praised him or showed him respect. When, as time went on, he began to attract public attention, it was painful to him. He thought it unjust that men should ascribe any good to him since it was all the work of God's grace.

Léon held the feast of St. Mary Magdalen in high honor, because on that day in 1831 he had received a special enlightenment; viz., how necessary for the attainment of sanctity is the mortification of the flesh. From this time he showed a holy zeal in the chastisement of his body, in forbidding himself enjoyment of the senses, and in denying his own will. In his wide and numerous correspondence he emphasizes over and again the necessity of this old and tried means of Christian ascetics, and makes known the fulness of consolation and of grace it brings with it.

But we must not think that he at once reached the high degree of perfection we find in his later life. Only by dint of constant struggle did he free himself from the chains of the flesh and rise from the depths of worldliness to those serene heights where the favoring sun of eternal truth illumines and warms all things.

The Servant of God died on March 18, 1876. He had put all his affairs in order and desired to be buried as simply as possible. But his burial could not but be a triumphal procession. High and low, spiritual and secular authorities, all must accompany the man on his last journey. The archbishop of Tours at once changed the room of the picture of the Holy Face into a public chapel and soon a congregation of priests had to be established there to care for the many pilgrims to that revered place.

Modern times have need of lay apostles. Léon Dupont has shown what such an apostle can do, finding a hearing with people among whom a priest can scarcely come and meeting with less prejudice than the one who announces God's word by virtue of his office.

Contardo Ferrini

5. Not less interesting than the life of Dupont is that of the Servant of God, Contardo Ferrini,[158] professor of Roman Law in the university of Pavia. On May 27, 1909, Pius X said to the pastor of Suna, where Ferrini lies buried: "I would call a university professor to the honors of the altar with the greatest joy. What a noble example for our days!" A layman, famed in learned circles as an investigator and lecturer of the first rank—a man surrounded by all the comforts of modern life, and yet in the depths of his soul an ascetic almost without feeling for the pleasures and honors of this world, and a most conscientious follower of the maxims of the saints, this man is indeed a glory and consolation to the Church.

Contardo Ferrini was born of a distinguished family at Milan on April 4, 1859. His father, Rinaldo Ferrini, was professor of physics at the Polytechnic Institute and is known by his numerous works on heat and electricity, which have been translated into many languages. Contardo distinguished himself by his diligence and piety during his classical studies in the schools of his native city. He showed a particular liking for the Holy Scriptures, and the better to understand them learned Hebrew and Syriac. He knew the Epistles of St. Paul by heart. At seventeen he went to the university of Pavia to study law, residing meantime at the College of St. Charles Borromeo, or the Borromeum. In the midst of dangers to faith and morals he shut himself up interiorly in God. His letters and notes at this period give a glance into the inner working of his soul. He made use of prayer as the best means of living a pure and joyful life; and communicated to a friend by letters his experience in this regard. How eloquent he becomes when he pictures the joy and consolation he found in his daily meditation. The words of the forty-second Psalm—"God who rejoices my youth"—gave him frequent occasion to consider God as the God of joy and view to all things as reflecting the beauty and amiability of God. At the college where he lived there was Mass only on Sunday, but Ferrini used every day to be present at the Holy Sacrifice in the parish church, and also paid a visit to the Blessed Sacrament in the evening. He made such an impression on the people by his devout behavior that they called him the Aloysius of the Borromeum. He avoided everything that could endanger in the slightest degree his purity of heart. He never permitted himself words, jests, or songs of doubtful meaning and was sensibly annoyed when others indulged in them. Frivolous companions jeered at him for this. But this youthful blushing at shameless language was indeed great praise for him. It was in him a sign of innocence and of victory and, therefore, a precious ornament. Outside of this Contardo was greatly loved by his fellow-students for his cheerful disposition and sociability, and he exercised on doubtful characters a wholesome influence. What consolation he experienced in Holy Communion is shown in a beautiful letter to his sister who was preparing to make her First Communion.

After our admirable student finished his course of four years at the university of Pavia, he received the degree of doctor and obtained from the government, through the recommendation of the faculty, a purse for study abroad. He chose Berlin, whose faculty had won great renown in the school of Frederic Charles von Savigny. On his journey thither in the autumn of 1880 he passed through Leipsic. Here he searched for a Catholic church and finding none, was very sad, as he says in a letter, because the busy city was to him "like a frightful desert." In Berlin Ferrini went at once to the church of St. Hedwig. As he was finishing his prayer for protection and blessing he noticed praying near him a young man of about his own age. To the latter he applied for information. The young man was favorably impressed by the stranger and helped him to find a lodging. During the first days he put himself quite at Ferrini's service and introduced the stranger to other Catholic students. Contardo was quite astonished to find such fervent Catholic life in the northern city. Social intercourse with others in a Catholic students' society was of great benefit to him. In his letters he recurs again and again to the zeal and the good spirit of these students and urges Italians to imitate them. He also praises the frequentation of the Sacraments in St. Hedwig's and the edifying behavior of the soldiers seen there. He forgets to tell how he edified all others by his own example. Prince-bishop Förster of Breslau, in a letter to Archbishop Riboldi of Pavia, who had given Ferrini a letter of recommendation, speaks of him as *"potens in lingua Germanica et in pietate,"* and expressed a desire that more such students if possible be sent from Italy. As had been his custom he daily went to Mass and communicated every Sunday and feast-day. He was enrolled in a conference of the St. Vincent de Paul Society and here he met the professor of botany, Dr. Max Westermeier, with whom he soon formed a cordial friendship. In this way he became acquainted with all Catholic circles in Berlin. He conceived a deep sympathy with the distressed Church in Germany. The strong faith of German Catholics, he wrote, gave him the best hope for the future. During vacations he visited other German cities. Once he went to Copenhagen and in the Canute Chapel there was moved to tears by the fact that in this distant little church he felt so much at home and so united in faith with a foreign people. He found German hymns particularly pleasing and translated many of them into Italian.

At the university, Ferrini diligently attended the lectures of Henry Dernburg, Bernstein, Theodore Mommsen, Charles Ed. Zachariä von Lingenthal, and others. Zachariä in particular gave him many suggestions. It was the latter who directed his attention to Roman-Byzantine law—a field in which he was to achieve universal renown as an investigator. While Zachariä lived they maintained a close friendship and mutual interest in their learned labors and Zachariä at his death bequeathed his manuscripts to Ferrini. From this time our student began to lay the foundation of his fame as an author.

After two years Ferrini left Berlin and spent a year in further study at Paris, Rome, and Florence. In November, 1883, he qualified as instructor in the history of Roman Law at Pavia. Two years later he was appointed extraordinary professor. In 1887 he accepted the chair of Roman Law in the university of Messina, in 1890 was called to Modena and finally in 1894 was unanimously chosen by the faculty of Pavia to the professorship of Law.

After his two years in Berlin, Ferrini became an exceedingly fertile author. Every year he published a multitude of articles and critiques in Italian, German, and French periodicals. He is the author of a series of text-books for the study of law and of many works on the history of law. He is particularly famed for his various researches in archives on the subject of Roman-Byzantine Law. After Zachariä's death he became the chief authority in this branch. The elevation of law studies in the higher schools of Italy is to be ascribed principally to the labors and learning of Contardo Ferrini.

Theodore Mommsen is said to have declared that "what Savigny was to the nineteenth century, Ferrini will be to the twentieth." Once Mommsen was in Milan and inquired in some libraries for Ferrini. When they could give him no information he exclaimed: "Oh, you poor Italians; you do not know your greatest men." After Ferrini's death the university of Pavia erected a monument to him bearing a most laudatory inscription in which, among other eulogies, the title of "Prince of scholars of Roman Law—the pride of the Faculty" was given him.

Worthy of admiration as is the great learning of this man, his lively faith and profound piety were still more so. Neither honors and flatteries, nor the opposition of unbelievers could in the least diminish his religious spirit. Every day without exception he heard Mass and after his arrival at Modena in 1890, he received Holy Communion every day and regularly at the close of each day paid a visit to Our Lord in the Blessed Sacrament, often bringing with him at the end of the lecture some of his auditors. He prayed before and after study, spent a quarter of an hour in meditation every morning and on free days a whole hour.

He obtained material for consideration from the "Meditations" by Father Louis de Ponte, S.J., and prepared the points of the meditation the evening before. His utterances on prayer are golden. "If I have an element of character—" he wrote, "and I believe I possess more than all past, present, and future liberals —I have prayer to thank for it. If my studies have produced fruit, I thank the blessing of prayer for it. Because of the consoling effect of prayer, I waste no time in the theaters, cafés, and the thousand other useless pastimes of an ill-regulated life." "Life without prayer—a consciousness that excludes the precious blessing of God, another place of rest than in the arms of Christ, are to me inconceivable. Such a life must be like a dark night, disheartening and saddening, on which rests the curse of God, which gives no strength to withstand temptations and in which all joy of spirit is wanting. It is a puzzle to me how any one can live such a life." Ferrini's life was truly one unbroken prayer, an elevation of his soul to God. His clear understanding reached always to the last principle of all things. Everything gave him an occasion of admiring the greatness of God. His best prayer-book was God's own creation.

Contardo's father had a country house in Suna, near Pallenza, on the west shore of Lake Maggiore, opposite the well-known island of Borromeo. Here the family used to spend the greater part of the vacations. In his youth Contardo had learned to love this Alpine region. Long tours and mountain-climbing parties were the only pleasures to which he gave himself. For him it was the healthiest recreation after strenuous mental work. But his spirit even more than his body waxed strong in the beautiful Alpine land. We know from his letters and from the accounts of his companions how mightily it inspired his heart to praise God and to admire the Divine omnipotence of Goodness.

When an intelligence so clear, united with so incorrupt a heart as that of Professor Contardo Ferrini, contemplates the splendor of the universe, it fully responds to the thousand voices which announce God's creation and God's beauty. Those high and calm regions of the mountain land especially suited the lofty and ideal spirit of our professor. Hence it was that he felt so much at home there and his soul so filled with praise for his Creator.

Like nature, art also guided him to God. "God breathes," he writes, "in all immortal masterpieces. How often I felt drawn to Him with unspeakable longing when I contemplated the works of art in the museums of Munich, Dresden, Berlin, Vienna, Rome, and Florence. Often when I admired a great masterpiece tears sprang unbidden to my eyes—tears I hope my angel did not let fall to earth."

Modern unbelief, so widespread in higher schools, could never touch Ferrini. There was no doubt or wavering for him. He published a pamphlet on the contradictions of positivism, with particular advertence to the writings of Ludwig Büchner, then widely spread throughout Italy. He exposed the absurdities of unbelief in an incisive and convincing manner. To friends who had difficulties in matter of faith he was an admirable adviser. It is remarkable that this great scholar considered pride the greatest hindrance to the knowledge of the truth. Hence he could never insist enough on humility as the only way to the knowledge of God. In witness of the truth that true learning leads to God, Ferrini is an illustrious example, and one that our university students would do well to imitate.

The daily order which he followed when professor makes known to us how profoundly this admirable man was penetrated with the spirit of mortification and of zeal for souls. We may find recorded there all the acts of self-denial he intended to practise in his meals, in his intercourse with others, and so on. He would behave with modesty and courtesy toward all. The greatest friendliness would be shown to unbelievers and sinners, since it might give them occasion to feel attracted toward our Faith. Before his lectures he prayed that his hearers might profit by them. When the evil deeds of others were recounted he prayed interiorly for their conversion. Every hour he greeted the Mother of God with a Hail Mary and renewed his desire for Holy Communion.

Ferrini was a man of high ideals. We can not wonder, therefore, that he chose for himself the state of celibacy. He is inexhaustible in praise of this virtue. The notes and points of meditation which he gathered for himself indicate the thoughts of his innermost soul. "What are the satisfactions of the world," he asks, "the joys of knowledge, the gratification of our natural inclinations, in comparison with the joys which celibacy brings?" We could gather from his writings a complete bouquet of beautiful sayings on the nobility and charm of chastity. He appears to have acquired his enthusiasm for this virtue from meditation on the prerogatives of Mary. Every day he said certain prayers to Mary, to St. Aloysius and to his patron, St. Contardus, for protection against dangers to his purity. His parents often expressed a desire that he should marry. But his prompt and decided answer made them understand that this question had long been settled. When similar proposals came from other quarters his refusal was still more energetic. Every one praised Ferrini's courtesy. Even unbelievers highly esteemed his knowledge and character. He had no personal enemies. "Companionship with Ferrini," wrote Professor Luigi Olivi of Modena, "was for many, certainly for myself, a school of perfection." The students were attracted by the noble qualities of the man. Many sought his advice, or brought him books of whose

morality they doubted. In 1895 the Catholics of Milan
elected him city councillor.

In his own family circle Contardo was always an
obedient son, ready for any service. Since he had only
three lectures a week when professor at Pavia, he lived
with his people at Milan. His parents survived him
and had the happiness of being permitted to give testimony to the sanctity of their son.

In 1900 he was afflicted with a heart lesion in consequence of his excessive labors. In the autumn of
1902, greatly weakened, he went to the country house
at Suna. At the beginning of October he was stricken
with typhus, and his strength being insufficient to resist
the malignant fever, he died on the 17th of that
month, 1902, aged forty-three. Now became known
the high esteem in which all held the deceased. Letters of condolence from the university professors
praised him as a saint. The people of Suna at once
expressed the desire to see him numbered among the
saints. They had seen him so often among them and
had been edified by the piety, modesty, and courtesy of
the Aloysius of the Ferrinis, as they called him. The
call for Ferrini's beatification ever became more insist-
ent. Laymen, priests, and bishops asked for it, and
there was universal rejoicing when in 1909 Pius X
appointed Cardinal Ferrari to begin the process. Ferrini is indeed a man who merits to be placed before
the modern world of culture as a model. On May 29,
1910, Professor Carlo Meda, leader of the Catholics of
Milan, directed a pilgrimage of Catholic students to
the grave of Ferrini at Suna and there delivered an
eloquent discourse before a large gathering of people,
exhorting them to follow the example of that great
man. If it be true that a Catholic scholar of the laity,
who is devoted heart and soul to his Faith, is of greater
service to the Church than any apology, we have such
a man in Ferrini, universally renowned for his learn-

ing and leading in the world a life of religious perfection—the life of a saint.

Francis Maione

6. God chooses his saints from all classes of men. Even the portionless, whom the world has denied all goods of fortune, may possess an abundance of heavenly riches. Francis Maione was without possessions, uneducated and deformed in body, almost continually ill, and unable to work. But his life was neither useless nor cheerless, and he gave God and men more service than many on whom fortune had bestowed health, riches, and honors. Born in the community of St. Anastasia, diocese of Nola, in Italy, on October 2, 1840, the son of a poor laborer, Francis Maione received nothing from his parents save a good religious training.[159] He never was able to attend a school. In early childhood he was afflicted with rickets, the result of which was a great deformity of the spine and an extreme weakness of body. The poor child could move about only on crutches and his life remained an unbroken series of illnesses. To enable the crippled boy at least to earn a living his father apprenticed him to a shoemaker, but his health grew worse from year to year. When he was sixteen one of his legs was broken and he was taken to a hospital in Naples. All attempts to strengthen his enfeebled body were unavailing and in the following year Maione was removed to the hospital for incurables. He was now seventeen years old, and was to spend here another seventeen years almost continually confined to his bed—years, however, of richest blessing for Maione and for the sick of the hospital.

The Servant of God lay in a ward of one hundred and twenty-seven beds. By his wonderful patience in his great sufferings and by his unceasing cheerfulness

Francis soon gained the respect and good will of all and ere long exerted an authoritative influence over the whole ward. He made no concealment of his deep piety. Every one could clearly see that it was faith which gave him strength to be so happy in his suffering. He looked upon the sick-ward as the peculiar field in which to practise his zeal for souls. His conversation on divine things was interesting and prudent, so that no one found his talks obtrusive or troublesome. His example was an eloquent sermon in itself. Hopping about on his crutches from bed to bed he encouraged his fellow-sufferers to pray and maintain confidence in God and especially to receive the Sacraments. Many a hardened sinner was brought to the hospital and it is known only to God how many were moved to repentance through the efforts of Maione. When he could not rise from his bed he would gather the others about him to listen to his words. How beautiful and attractive is Christian virtue like this! The poor cripple who was only a patchwork of affliction was yet most happy and a messenger of gladness to all around him. Not able of himself to search out the unfortunate, Providence did so for him. There surely dwelt a strong soul in this weak body, for in spite of unspeakable pain he remained constantly content and full of trust in God and up to his last breath was ever busy in caring for the well-being of his sick companions.

On November 21, 1874, this great sufferer passed away. The fame of his sanctity now became manifest. When his body was placed in the chapel great crowds came to show it reverence and to seek for relics. They cut locks of his hair, tore bits from his garments, and the bandages that had bound his wounds were gathered as precious jewels. Miracles were not wanting. A few years later the archbishop of Naples opened the preliminary process of his beatification.

Aloysius Avellino, Joseph Tobini

7. Under quite similar conditions the Servant of God, Aloysius Avellino, showed that poverty and sickness do not stand in the way of sanctity.[160] He came of a poor family in Vico Equense, archdiocese of Sorrento. Want of means forced him to abandon the study of Latin shortly after he had begun it. At eighteen he contracted the gout while working in a quarry. This was the beginning of his sufferings, which endured till the end of his life. But suffering purified him and fitted him to do great things for God and the salvation of souls.

After Avellino had spent two years at home, vainly expecting alleviation of his pains, he was taken in 1882 to the hospital for incurables at Naples. He had a dreadful prospect before him. Almost all his members were lamed and wasted, and along with this he was afflicted with many troubles of the internal organs, which caused him frequent fainting spells. An interior life of faith, however, kept him cheerful in spirit. He knew there was no hope for him on earth, but the allurement of earthly things never took hold of his mind. He placed his hope of joy in the hereafter and, to his heart's delight, he could merit it by his miserable condition. Those who knew him intimately saw that in purity of soul he was a true follower of his patron, St. Aloysius. Like Maione, he practised in the hospital a richly blessed apostolate. One who loves God from his heart can never rest till God's holy likeness is imprinted in many souls. He died April 13, 1900, thirty-eight years of age. It is surprising how quickly the repute of his sanctity and veneration for him spread abroad. Preachers used to place him before their people as a pattern of pure life, heroic courage in suffering, and glowing zeal for God's honor. The manifold exhibitions of heavenly favor through Avellino's intercession lead us to hope for a happy outcome of the process of his beatification, which has already been inaugurated.

In upper Italy there has been gathered the material for the beatification of the advocate Joseph Tobini, commonly called the O'Connell of Italy. He was a noble counterpart of the saintly Contardo Ferrini. He labored much to organize Catholics into societies, to promote Catholic reunions and to encourage the Catholic press. His admirable life has been written by an Italian Jesuit. He died January 16, 1897, father of ten children.

Venerable Maria Clotilda

8. The past glories in saints of princely station. There are not wanting such in the nineteenth century. The Church may yet honor the holy lives of two queens, one of the house of the Bourbons, the other of Savoy.

The parents of the Venerable Maria Clotilda, queen of Sardinia, were the Dauphin Louis, son of Louis XV, and Maria Josepha of Saxony.[161] These two formed notable exceptions in the immoral court of the time at Paris. Unfortunately, they died too soon, but they had taken care to secure a good education for their children. The Princess Maria Clotilda remained steadfast amidst all the allurements of the corrupt life at court and showed an extraordinary predilection for works of piety, which earned for her no little contempt. In 1775, at the desire of her brother, Louis XVI, she married Charles Emanuel, heir-apparent of Sardinia and Piedmont. She found him a congenial husband, in full sympathy with her religious zeal. She did not consider her duty done unless she gave her attendants and subjects a shining example in the practice of every virtue. She daily attended two Masses, communicated several times in the week, sometimes going to the rail with the common people, and practised works of penance. The household servants called her an angel because of her purity and humility. She was an especially zealous promoter of devotion to the Sacred Heart of Jesus.

There were trials to prove her steadfastness of character. Her brother, Louis XVI, her sister, Elizabeth, and other relatives fell under the guillotine. The Revolution sought to deprive her of her crown. In 1796 her husband succeeded his father as Charles Emanuel II, but two years later he was robbed of all his possessions on the mainland, and only in Sardinia could he find refuge from his enemies. Maria Clotilda sustained the courage of her husband through all these dreadful adversities of fortune. She did not live to see the hereditary possessions of her family restored. She died aged forty-two, outside of her kingdom, at Naples, on March 7, 1802. When dying she often repeated: "Oh, this is rest, this is peace! How beautiful is heaven . . . to heaven . . . to heaven!" And she clapped her hands with joy. In 1808 Pius VII instituted the process of her beatification. The year she died her husband abdicated his throne in favor of his brother, Victor Emanuel I. He later on entered the Society of Jesus and died a simple Religious at Rome on October 6, 1819.

VENERABLE MARIA CHRISTINA

9. The Venerable Maria Christina, queen of both Sicilies, was a daughter of the Victor Emanuel mentioned above.[162] Her deeply religious spirit she owed to the example and excellent training of her mother, Maria Teresa of the house of Austria-Este. The latter had taught her children to hold as truly great only what was great in the eyes of God. Maria Christina, youngest of four daughters, was born on November 14, 1812, and lived a happy and innocent youth. Her heart brimmed with a sane enthusiasm for lofty ideals. Prayer and the dispensation of charities were her

delights and the pleasures of the world exercised little influence upon her.

After her mother's death Maria Christina was obliged to live at the court of Charles Albert of Savoy -Carignan, who in the meantime had succeeded to the crown of Piedmont. Here she had much to suffer, since her piety did not please the company of the new master and he himself was jealous of the daughter of Victor Emanuel I. The princess seriously considered consecrating herself to God in a convent, when at this juncture King Ferdinand II of Naples asked for her hand. Her confessor decided that she should accept the proposal, and in deference to the common good she relinquished the state of virginity.

The new queen was received at Naples with great rejoicing. Her first work of charity was the reconciliation of the king with his mother. At the first court celebration she was curt and cold with the ladies who wore dresses too décolleté, while with those more modestly attired she was friendliness and attention itself. This silent rebuke had its good effect. Christina also insisted that Christian morals should receive due respect in the theater. Like St. Elizabeth, she considered it her duty to show herself a mother to the poor. King Ferdinand gave her much freedom in the dispensing of alms, and though she possessed a considerable fortune from her family, she used very little of it for herself. Poor convents and churches, the timid poor of respectable families, and, indeed, every sort of needy persons, never applied to her in vain. If she could not personally visit the sick and prisoners she sent trusted messengers to give them help and consolation. In her leisure she made clothes for the poor, gave dowries to girls without means to enable them to make decent marriages, smoothed the way for others who wished to enter the religious life, and was to orphans a second mother. It was easy to see that the people

idolized their queen. Not less did the people of the
court express unreserved admiration of the virtues of
their noble lady. There were some, however, who were
moved only to envy. The joy of the people reached
its highest when the queen, on January 16, 1836, in the
third year of her marriage, presented them with an
heir to the throne, later King Francis II. But their
joy was soon changed into profound grief. The life
of the child was the death of the mother. She predicted her approaching end, and died on January 31,
1836. The manifestations of mourning in Naples
exceeded all bounds. It was evident that Maria Christina had won all hearts. Soon after her death, men
began to speak of favors and miracles obtained through
her intercession. Seventeen years later, when the
ecclesiastical authorities opened the process of her
beatification, they found her body still incorrupt. She
was in every way a worthy likeness of the great Land-
gravine of Thuringia.

Venerable Anna Maria Taigi

10. The fame of the Venerable Anna Maria Taigi
has already spread throughout the world.[163] The opening words of the decree introducing the process of
beatification of this servant of God are as follows:

"When God wills to show His power and wisdom,
He chooses what is weakest and most foolish in the
eyes of the world to confound its vanity, frustrate the
plans of the godless, and repulse the assaults of hell.
Thus, in our days, when human pride seems to have
conspired with the powers of hell to undermine both
the foundations of the Church and the very principles
of human society, He chose for this work Anna Maria
Jesualda Taigi, who, born of poor but virtuous parents,
married a working-man and, since the care of the family lay mostly upon her shoulders, supported it by the
work of her hands. God selected her to lead souls to

Him, to serve as a victim of atonement, to be a bulwark against the assaults of His enemies and to avert misfortune by her prayers. After he had drawn her away from the current of the world, He united her to Himself by the bond of charity and adorned her with miraculous gifts and with such virtues as exercised a salutary influence upon pious persons, even in the highest stations, and also upon the godless and made the sanctity of the servant of God to shine before all men in the clearest light."

That the words of the decree are not exaggerated, a few facts from the life of the servant of God will make fully clear. Anna Maria was born on May 29, 1769, at Siena, the daughter of an apothecary, Luigi Giannetti. Heavy reverses of fortune had reduced the once distinguished family almost to beggary. In 1775 Giannetti and his wife went to Rome and obtained positions as house-servants. He placed his daughter under the care of religious women devoted to the education of the children of the poor. When Anna Maria was thirteen she was obliged to help in earning the daily bread for the family. She first worked in a factory as a silk-spooler, afterward she was chambermaid to a lady of the nobility. Anna Maria could not altogether resist the allurements of the world, which exercise so strong an attraction upon persons of her age and condition. She longed to taste all the pleasures of life. She had no suspicion of the great danger she was exposed to, and it was only the good example of her parents and her religious training that kept her from ruin.

On January 7, 1790, she married Dominic Taigi, a servant in the Chigi Palace. During the first year of her marriage she still indulged in vanity and pleasure-seeking. But Anna Maria did not find the expected peace. Grace ever knocked harder at the door of her heart. Thoughts of God and of the hereafter continually rose more and more vividly before her mind. She now went to a priest for the purpose of making a general confession of her life. He barely allowed her to complete her confession, gave her absolution and said: "Go! You do not belong among my penitents." This rough treatment caused the poor woman to fall into despondency and anxiety of mind. After a time she picked up courage again and sought another confessor. This time Providence led her to a wise director. It was the decisive hour of her life. She called it her conversion.

She had now put her hand to the plow, never more to look back; and till her death remained the most pliant instrument of grace. Rich gifts of mind and heart adorned her—a clear understanding, a deep humility, a strong and magnanimous character. To these natural gifts was added an extraordinary measure of grace. With all these powers Anna Maria now endeavored to reach the perfection of her state in life. She avoided all finery in dress, all exterior show and rejoiced in appearing poor. She seldom took part in worldly amusement and then only to please her husband. She considered it important that others should notice her change of mind, because she hoped thus to make amends for any scandal she might have given in the past. In prayer she now found an indescribable consolation and in prayer she spent all the time not employed in the performance of her duties as mother and housewife. Frequently she deprived herself of her night's rest to satisfy the longing of her heart for God. There is no sanctity without mortification. Anna Maria Taigi eagerly looked for every occasion to make a victim of herself, though always careful to conceal it from others. Only her director and the duties of her state could set bounds to her zeal for external penance.

She well understood that her desire for prayer and penance should not in the least interfere with her duties as wife and mother. Her husband was a truly religious and good-hearted man, while at the same time somewhat narrow, eccentric, and hard. But she was so much mistress of herself that she could always anticipate his wishes and treat him with the greatest love and friendship. Dominic Taigi has left us a candid declaration on this point:

"It often happened that on my return home I found the whole house filled with people"—he speaks of the time when his wife was already known throughout all Rome—"at once she would leave them all alone—let them be prelates or great nobles who were present—and come to serve me with courtesy and attention. And they realized that her whole heart was in it when she loosened the latchets of my shoes, although I would have prevented her. In a word, she was a consolation to me and to everybody else. She knew how to admonish one skilfully and I can thank her for the amendment of certain faults which I had. She gave me her admonitions with incomparable kindness and gentleness. . . . She was able by her wonderful prudence to preserve a heavenly peace in the family, although we were numerous and had very opposite characters among us, especially when my oldest son Camillus came to live with us at first after his marriage. My daughter-in-law had a very irascible temper and would play the mistress in everything. But the Servant of God was most tactful in keeping every one in the proper place, and this with so great courtesy that it can not be described in words . . . I was often sad, discouraged, and ill-tempered on arriving at home, but she knew how to cheer me and to restore peace by her amiability."

Practically the whole care of providing for the family and the management of the house devolved on Anna Maria. It was not a small family. She had borne seven children, two of whom God took early to Himself. In addition, she had to care for her aged parents. In after years, persons of rank often proposed to make ample provision for her family, but she would never accept anything for herself or hers. She desired to remain in the condition of life in which God had placed her. She was and remained a poor workingman's wife, but one wholly imbued with Christian spirit and therefore the possessor of profound contentment.

The Servant of God let pass no opportunity of promoting the spirit of religion. In the morning she gathered the whole family for prayer. Condition of work permitting, all in the house heard a Mass in the course of the forenoon and frequently received the sacraments. At night the family assembled for pious reading, to which the mother added some instructive religious conversation, ending with the Rosary and night-prayers. She watched over her children most carefully, especially when they were growing out of boyhood and girlhood, encouraging them to frequent Communion and guarding them against dangerous companions. Even when they were about to enter the married state, she would not permit the betrothed to converse together without supervision.

The goodness of God brought it to pass that the extraordinary virtues of Anna Maria became known to the world around her during her lifetime. Her little house became the chief center of attraction in Rome. Princes of the Church, prelates, and persons of high station in the world came and went, asking the intercession of her prayers or seeking her advice. The Venerable Bartolomeo Menochio, Papal Sacristan; the Venerable Vincent Strambi,* and many others distinguished for their sanctity were her intimate friends, and the Popes Pius VII, Leo XII, and Gregory XVI showed the greatest veneration for the poor workman's wife. Many miraculous events, due to her intercession,

*See page 48.

are well attested. God supernaturally enlightened her concerning the state of consciences, the designs of Providence in the afflictions of the Church, the mysteries of faith, and so forth. All was revealed to her in a mysterious sun which was continually suspended before her eyes.

It was the chief purpose of her life to aid the Church by prayer and suffering; and she was consumed with a burning zeal for its interests. She made sacrifices, prayed, and caused others to pray, whenever any important matter was in progress. Sinners were the principal object of her care. She was rich in sufferings. God tried her with dreadful desolation, sent her many illnesses, and permitted her to meet with hatred and persecution. She herself said that it often seemed impossible to bear the torture of the martyrdom any longer. Yet her courageous spirit of sacrifice never wavered.

In spite of such extraordinary graces, Anna Maria Taigi looked upon herself as the least among the people and fit only to serve others. It touches the heart to read of her profound humility. Truly the saints have so lofty an idea of God's majesty that they deem it presumption to desire to be considered anything in themselves.

May we not piously assume that Anna Maria prayed to be permitted to die unhonored? For when she departed this life on June 9, 1837, no attention was paid to her death. But it was not long till her tomb became glorious. High and low revered her as a saint and at length the Apostolic See took steps to inaugurate the canonical process of her beatification. Its completion is near at hand.

Venerable Elizabeth Canori Mora

11. Venerable Elizabeth Canori Mora merited the crown of the saints by patient endurance of a heavy

family cross.[164]   She was born of a distinguished family at Rome on November 21, 1794, and was educated by the Augustinian nuns at Cascia.   Here she made a vow of chastity and conceived the desire of becoming a nun.   But after a few years she quite forgot her vow and at the age of twenty-one married the advocate Christopher Mora.   It proved an unhappy marriage. Her husband led a disorderly life.   His first love of his wife degenerated into jealousy, then into coldness, and finally into hatred.   Elizabeth did everything to win back his heart but in vain.   He contracted debt after debt and became completely ensnared by a bad woman.   Relatives bitterly reproached Elizabeth, as if she was the cause of the sins of her husband.   These trials, however, served only to withdraw her heart from the lures of the world.   She found no help or consolation from man, but God was all the more liberal in giving her strength to bear her heavy cross with patience.

It was now that Elizabeth remembered her forgotten vow, and the thought was for her a new inducement to bind herself intimately to God.   Though it was merely youthful forgetfulness that was to blame, she bewailed her failure to keep her promise during her whole life.

Since her husband paid no heed to their children she sedulously applied herself to bring them up in the fear of God.   In course of time they, too, were to bring much trouble upon her.   In vain she courageously strove to avert from their home the bankruptcy threatened by the reckless life of her husband; but fortunately his parents were still living and saved her from extreme want.   They urged the conscienceless advocate to make the Spiritual Exercises.   This only rendered him more bitter and he maltreated his poor wife in such a way that even her life was in danger.   Her confessor advised Elizabeth to apply for an ecclesiastical separation; but in kindness to the man and her children she would not consent to such a step. At the death of her father-in-law she was excluded from sharing in the inheritance on the plea that her husband had already squandered his portion. But God did not desert His servant and there were compassionate souls to befriend her.

Elizabeth, led by an enlightened zeal, had made great strides toward perfection in the school of suffering. As a valiant woman she persevered at the side of her wicked husband, who repaid her unbroken love and friendship with scoff and maltreatment.

God sends His saints nothing more plentifully than suffering. Besides her family misery, Elizabeth had to bear many interior trials, attacks from the evil spirit, and illness in body. But God also gave her many extraordinary graces and enlightenments. Others highly esteemed her and depended much on her counsel. Herself so sorely tried, she knew how to console and encourage them. She obtained many great favors by her prayers. Her sufferings she offered up constantly and magnanimously for the triumph of the cause of Christ. Her biographer relates among many miracles of her lifetime that when she was seriously ill the Holy Eucharist was administered to her by angels. The servant of God departed this life on February 5, 1825, to receive the reward of her heroic bearing of the cross.

After her death she at last effected the conversion of her husband, appearing to him and urging him to do penance. He afterward entered the Franciscan Order and led a life of severe penance until his death.

Families from whom peace has departed are unfortunately very numerous in these days. The life of the Venerable Elizabeth Mora shows that even in such misery the Church can lead us to lofty sanctity and bestow true peace on our hearts.

Venerable Elizabeth Sanna

12. The Venerable Elizabeth Sanna sanctified herself in widowhood.[165] She was born on April 23, 1788, at Codrignano, in the diocese of Sassari, Sardinia. Her people were simple farmers. After an innocent girlhood she married according to the desire of her parents and became the mother of five children. When her husband died she made a vow of chastity and resolved to consecrate herself entirely to the service of God. In 1831 she desired to make a pilgrimage to the holy places of Palestine in company with some tertiaries of St. Francis. But she traveled no farther than Rome. Here she became acquainted with the Venerable Vincent Pallotti, to whom she disclosed the affairs of her soul. It was truly a dispensation of Providence. The saintly priest made such an impression upon her that she believed she could do nothing more profitable than to remain in Rome and confide her soul to his spiritual direction. She was not deceived. Pallotti became her adviser and guide, and helped her with enlightened prudence in her struggles for sanctification. A poor little house in the neighborhood of St. Peter's became her dwelling-place and she divided her time between works of love for God and works of charity for the neighbor. By her prayers and penance she obtained many favors for herself and others. She survived her director seven years and died on February 19, 1857. The process of her beatification was begun in 1879.

Venerable Caroline Barbara Carré de Malberg

13. Rapid progress has been made in the process of the Venerable Caroline Barbara Carré de Malberg, who died at Lorry, near Metz, on January 28, 1891.[166] She was born on April 8, 1829, the daughter of Francis Colchen, a wine-merchant of Metz, and received in her family and in the convent of the Sisters of the

Visitation a truly Christian education. At sixteen she had finished her studies and showed a seriousness of character unusual at this age. She heard Mass daily, communicated often during the week and was a stranger to worldly amusements. She endeavored to influence her girl friends in the same direction. So people were somewhat surprised when Caroline at twenty married her cousin, Captain Paul Carré, especially since the latter did not attend to his religious duties. But she did this in compliance with the wishes of her parents, at the advice of her confessor and, as she herself said, in the hope of winning her cousin to God.

But she had to make many sacrifices to win that soul. First of all the captain turned a deaf ear to all the prayers of his wife. Then he was a rough soldier, impetuous, and careless. Since Caroline in many things could not conform to his views, he began to treat her as uncultured and narrow. He made no concealment of this before others and censured her in their presence. This caused his delicately sensitive wife the bitterest pain. Yet she held her peace and prayed and showed her husband only the greater love and affection. This conquered the soldier's heart and in the year 1852 men saw the captain again making his Easter duties in Metz. He had not been freed from all his faults of character, it is true, and in the future he gave his wife many occasions of humiliation and opportunity for self-conquest, but from this time he remained loyal to his Faith.

Madame Carré was above all a genuinely Christian mother, leaving nothing undone to plant the love of virtue deep in the hearts of her children. Unfortunately they all died in childhood save one son, and he only reached the age of twenty-nine. But he proved worthy of his mother. He was an army officer and used to profess his Faith openly as such. For exam-

ple, he would take part in the Corpus Christi procession
in his uniform and when in his last sickness he was
about to receive the Last Sacraments, he desired his
comrades to come and see how a Christian officer dies.
The Servant of God was filled with the spirit of faith,
and the power of the supernatural was never a doubtful thing with her. When, for instance, she came home
after Holy Communion, she kissed her children so
that Our Lord dwelling in her might bless them. Her
social position made it incumbent upon her to pay and
receive many visits and to take part in many worldly
festivals and amusements in company with her husband. On such occasions everyone was edified by her
great modesty and simplicity and her efforts to infuse
piety and religion into the conversation, thus to benefit
souls.

Her spirit of apostleship led her to institute a work
which enabled her to scatter blessings everywhere.
With the aid of a zealous priest, the Abbé Chaumont,
she founded at Paris in 1872 a religious league of
pious ladies of the world called the Daughters of St.
Francis of Sales. The aim of the association was
twofold; viz., the sanctification of one's self, and the
salvation of others. It proposed to lead women to
perfection in their station in the world according to
the principles laid down by St. Francis in his "Phi-
lothea." The members were to make it their duty to
see that religion be better practised in their families
and social circles and that, to this end, they should
undertake the formation of good governesses. Finally
they were to afford practical support to the conversion
of women of the heathen. The league won great
approval and to-day is spread over many lands, some
of its members working with great success as catechists
among Mohammedans and the heathen. Canonical
approval of the Society was obtained in 1901. In 1906
it numbered as many as eight thousand members.

Pius X, in a document dated April 13, 1910, gave it the highest praise and expressed his joy at its continual growth.[167] Madame Carré remained directress-general until her death. The position involved a great deal of labor, for evidently she never permitted it to interfere in the least with her duties toward her husband. The care of the association really increased her charity and devotion to God and it was her example that attracted others to it and enkindled their zeal.

Deeply revered and greatly mourned by all, she died on January 28, 1891, in her native place, whither she had returned to seek restoration of her health. Her body rests in Lorry, near Metz. Veneration for her grows from year to year and, on June 23, 1909, the cause of her beatification was introduced.

VENERABLE ADELAIDE CINI

14. The little island of Malta offers for the honor of beatification not only the cleric Venerable Ignatius Falzon* and the Benedictine nun Adeodata Pisani,† but also a laywoman, the Venerable Adelaide Cini.[168] She was the thirteenth child of a well-to-do citizen of La Valetta and was born there on October 25, 1838. Her father was a flour merchant and owned a bakery. A genuine Christian spirit prevailed in the family. Every night the children and the servants recited the Rosary in common. Adelaide wished to consecrate herself to God in a Religious Order, but at the request of her father, who was old, and since all his other daughters were married, she relinquished her desire for the time. Meanwhile she turned her zeal to the care of girls, whom she instructed in religion and encouraged to the frequent reception of the Sacraments. After the death of her father she sought admission into various convents, but without success.

*See pages 84 sqq.
†See page 293.

She drew from this that God's will had ordained her to remain in the world and here to devote her strength to the winning of unfortunate souls.

In consequence of the large number of soldiers coming and going, not the best morals prevailed on the island. Adelaide Cini resolved, therefore, to become the saviour of the unfortunate of her sex. She left nothing undone to find the unhappy victims of sin, to speak to them and bring about their reformation. She had a great gift of persuasion and worked in many a complete and permanent repentance. Out of her family means and aided by a rich East Indian, John Asphar, who lived on the island, she provided for many of these poor women the necessary dowries for making respectable marriages, or she helped them to obtain a position where danger to morals would be less threatening.

Later on she acquired her father's house and changed it into an asylum for orphans and fallen women, calling it the "Institute of the Sacred Heart of Jesus." In the management of this work she was magnanimously supported by the clergy and by her brother Paul and other relatives. She displayed extraordinary skill as the organizer and directress of an institution with so many dubious inmates. It was chiefly her unselfish and devoted charity that gave her such great power over hearts. Like the Good Shepherd she sought after the lost sheep—often with danger to her life. She gave gifts to them and made promises to attract them from the dens of infamy. She searched all parts of the island, even going into the prisons and hospitals, to trace out the unfortunate. She succeeded in having many orphans or illegitimate children cared for by respectable families or she provided for them herself.

She did everything to make residence in her Institute as pleasant as possible. First place was given to religious exercises; and no one could withstand her stirring and heartfelt exhortatious. She herself lived like a mortified Religious. Daily meditation, Mass, communion, the practice of penance, the annual Exercises—she did all without consideration of any earthly reward. Devotion to the Sacred Heart of Jesus—her favorite practice—gives us the key to her heroism in charity for the neighbor. Her strength prematurely worn out in service of the good cause, she died on March 28, 1885. After her death her Institute was entrusted to the Sisters of St. Vincent of Paul. In 1910 the cause of the beatification of this great and charitable soul was introduced.

GEMMA GALGANI

15. A true jewel of the Church, reflecting in splendid hues a fulness of supernatural gifts, was the Servant of God, Gemma Galgani.[169] She was a child of grace, a favorite of God and His saints, an angel in the flesh. The only purpose of her life seems to have been to demonstrate to the world the reality of supernatural power. At first for a few years she was seemingly unnoticed, but now she enjoys in her native land the fame of a popular saint for her virtues and miraculous gifts. The Church, too, has taken the first steps to raise this simple maiden to the honors of the altar.

Gemma Galgani was born on March 12, 1878, at Camigliano, near Lucca. Shortly after her birth the family moved to Lucca, where her father had a pharmacy. The family was thoroughly Catholic and its life a continual service of God. The mother, a daily communicant, was particularly edifying in word and example. Unfortunately she died in 1886. In the heart of none of her children had she implanted the spirit of religion so deeply as in Gemma's. A short time before her death she had arranged to have Gemma receive Confirmation, and it was at this holy ceremony the favored child was given her first extraordinary enlightenment. Gemma now longed with the fervor of a saint to be admitted to Holy Communion, and nothing was to be done but to yield to the impetuous urging that discovered so ardent a love and so mature an understanding. From this time on—her ninth year—she daily approached the table of the Lord and experienced from it such joy and delight that she seemed in paradise. At the Institute of St. Zita, the school she attended, she was much looked up to for her remarkable modesty, her interior piety, and deep knowledge of spiritual things.

In the family Gemma took the place of a mother to the younger children and had the principal part in managing the house. The year 1897 brought her heavy trials. Her father lost nearly all his property and soon died. The poor children fell into extreme want and Gemma herself fell into a serious illness, from which she recovered, by a miracle it seems, only after a year. A kind-hearted lady, who had a numerous family herself, offered to take care of Gemma and to treat her as one of her own.

Very soon the Servant of God was favored with extraordinary graces and communications. She saw her guardian angel almost constantly at her side and could converse with him as with any other person. Visions and ecstasies were frequent and she was endowed with a knowledge of hidden and future things. On the eve of the Feast of the Sacred Heart, 1899, she received the stigmata, and later the wound in the side and those of the crown of thorns. Eye-witnesses tell us that the wounds were a centimeter deep and that full streams of blood poured out from them. It was also given her to share in the interior bitterness of Our Lord's sufferings. Her spiritual director was very distrustful of these extraordinary conditions, and subjected her to severe proofs. But it served only to bring her virtue into clearer light. And she had to make her sacrifice, for though she ardently desired to join the Sisters of the Passion, they would not receive her precisely because of her extraordinary visitations, fearing that such a person might cause too much unrest in the convent.

Still it was not merely for herself that Gemma was favored with this superabundance of grace. She was most zealous for the welfare of the Church and the salvation of immortal souls and by her prayers she obtained a large number of remarkable conversions.

The life of the Servant of God was completely absorbed in meditation of such works of divine love as are manifested in the sufferings of Christ and in the Holy Eucharist. She strove with never lessening zeal to live in accordance with what the Heart of Our Saviour experienced during His life on earth and still experiences in the tabernacle. By degrees she succeeded in ridding herself of all earthly considerations. Sufferings and the cross were her delight. Desire of God consumed her and Our Lord called His beloved bride to her eternal home on Holy Saturday, April 11, 1903. She was twenty-five years of age.

When we read her life we can hardly know whether we are more astonished at the profuse generosity of God toward this innocent soul or at her heroic love for Him. Apart from the many miracles worked through her intercession after her death, Gemma Galgani won so many friends among all classes, from Pope and cardinals down to the poorest of the people, that in her is united almost everything which made the great saints of the past admirable and amiable. She was, as her name suggests, a jewel which God and men are delighted to look upon.

Veronica Barone[170]

16. The Servant of God, Veronica Barone, bears a great likeness to Gemma Galani. She also, during her

lifetime, was the instrument of extraordinary favors from Heaven. The sworn depositions of a series of still surviving eye-witnesses have been recorded in the process of beatification, compelling us to accept as facts the astonishing events of her life. Since her fifteenth year Veronica had almot constant ecstasies and visions, knew the most secret thoughts of others, foretold future events which were unfailingly verified. It is charming to read what is related of her intercourse from her early years with the Child Jesus, the Blessed Virgin, her guardian angel, and the saints. A burning desire for the Holy Eucharist, which she received nearly every day, quite consumed her. During the last seven years of her life she did not as a rule taste any other than this heavenly food. She was permitted to share in Christ's sufferings with both body and soul. In her struggles with the Evil One she recalls to our mind the Blessed Crescentia Höss of Kaufbeuren.

It is not ours to determine the limits between natural and supernatural influences on the extraordinary experiences of this Servant of God. Her biographer makes the excellent remark that "as yet no saints have been canonized by the Church on account of their ecstasies and visions, but on account of their heroic virtues."[171] If the honor of the altar be reached by Veronica Barone it will be above all because of her consuming love of God, her ardent zeal for the virtue of virginity, her constant practice of self-denial, her deep humility in spite of so great gifts of grace—in a word, because of her spotless life. Indeed, it was the unselfishness and purity of her character which won over very many who at first had only contempt for her. They put her righteousness to severe tests. She splendidly bore them all. When but twenty-one years of age Veronica had completed a life rich in grace and in trial and died on January 5, 1878, at her native town of Vizzini in Sicily. It is as if God, through those who are entirely dead to the senses and live only within the sphere of the supernatural, would reproach the modern world for the perversity of its concupiscences and the short-sightedness of its earthly culture.

OTHER HOLY WOMEN

17. To the lay state also belong the Servants of God: Mary Carola Onorio de Vivo (died 1875) at Naples; Paula Elizabeth Cerioli, widow, of the diocese of Bergamo (died 1865); and Philumena Genovesi (died 1865) at Salerno.

THE MARTYRS

THE martyrs have been from of old the pride of the Church. They are the children who have given their lives for their Mother, heroes whose steadfastness moved even their enemies, and gave consolation and courage to their brethren in the Faith. So the Church rejoices in celebrating their memory. To her, martyrdom means something divine. It was no mere human strength that nerved the hosts of children, weak women, gray old men, people of every age and condition to go forth to death so courageously. Often we find among them those who had been but lately converted from heathenism to Christianity. This is the reason why theologians consider martyrdom a proof of the truth of the Catholic religion.[172] In all her centuries the Church has had her martyrs, and the nineteenth century is distinguished for the great number, enthusiasm, and heroism of its martyrs for the Faith.

BLESSED JEAN GABRIEL PERBOYRE

1. We find a true example of a noble-hearted martyr in the Blessed Jean Gabriel Perboyre of the Congregation of the Lazarists.[173] The Lord destined for him a crown of especial glory. By a holy life Perboyre made himself worthy and developed the strong character that befitted one who was to suffer so dreadful a passion. He was born at Puec, in the diocese of Cahors, on January 6, 1802; and even as a boy attracted the attention of all by his unusual piety and love of purity. By a singular dispensation of Providence he was sent to the little seminary at Montauban, and in December, 1818, inspired by the appeal of an abbé for the heathen missions, he entered the novitiate of the Lazarists at the same place. After his ordina-

tion to the priesthood in 1825, he labored for ten years in his own country as professor, superior, and novice-master. Everywhere he left the repute of a saint. At length his heart's desire was gratified and in 1835 he was able to set out for the mission of China. Every one was surprised that his superiors had granted his petition, since he was in such weak health that many feared he would scarcely be able to reach China alive.

On the journey Father Perboyre exercised a true apostleship by his great amiability and piety. The whole ship's crew was charmed with him and at the end of the voyage declared aloud: "This man is really a saint." Macao was reached in five months, but a further difficult and dangerous journey of six months was necessary before Perboyre could reach the field of his labor, the northern province of Ho-nan. A severe illness brought him to the brink of the grave. But it was not yet his time to die. With indefatigable zeal he traversed his mission, everywhere to strengthen the old Christians in their faith and to gain new ones. We can see his zeal in a letter of this time, in which he writes:

"Wherever one goes he finds the earth devastated by sin and defiled by crime. There have been saints who died of grief because God is so offended by men. This may seem surprising, but to me it is far more surprising that all priests, called as they are to purify the earth of the dreadful poison of sin, do not die of grief at the sight of so many abominations."

Unfortunately the holy missionary found his activity greatly limited by the vexations of inimical officials. In the beginning of 1838 he was sent by his superiors into the province of Hu-pe. It was a period full of danger and it was known that at any moment the hatred of the pagans against the Christians might again break out. But "a true Apostle," writes Father Perboyre, "follows his path regardless of all danger as long as he has not the rope on his neck or fetters on his feet." And after the example of the ancient martyrs he endeavored to strengthen his own courage in the Faith and that of his Christians.

The mission was suddenly attacked on September 15, 1839. The missionaries escaped, but a Christian, for the reward of Judas, betrayed the retreat of Father Perboyre. Before various tribunals he was obliged to undergo most painful examinations, during which he was made to kneel with bare knees on iron chains and was heavily beaten with clubs. When this did not succeed in shaking his steadfast faith, the mandarin subjected him for four hours to a most painful torture called "hang-tse," a sort of gallows on which the victim is suspended by the united thumbs of both hands and the tightly stretched pigtail. Many of the onlookers were deeply moved by the firmness of the martyr. At a later trial the enraged judge ordered him to be given forty blows in the face with a thick piece of sole-leather. So violent were the blows that his jaw was crushed and his countenance beaten out of all human semblance. And after this Perboyre had again to endure for half a day the torment of the hang-tse. A short time later, with ten other Christians, cruelly fettered, he was dragged a distance of 140 miles to the capital, Wu-chang. What he had here to suffer, imprisoned with the most abandoned criminals for nine months, is beyond description. His hands and feet were bound so tightly that the blood burst from his fingers and one of his feet began to putrefy. The jailer was moved with compassion and wished to alleviate his torture. But the missionary begged the man not to do so, since it might bring him into trouble. When at length the hour of condemnation arrived, they questioned him anew, urging him to insult the crucifix and to forswear his Catholic faith. Perboyre's invincible constancy roused the tyrants to extreme

fury and every kind of pain and ignominy their diabolical malice could invent was visited upon the
martyr.

Imperial approbation of the sentence of death
arrived on September 11, 1840. He was immediately
led to execution and was hanged on a sort of cross.
His hands were bound to the cross-beams and his legs
were drawn backward. They had chosen for him a
slow and torturing death by strangulation and only
at the third strain upon the rope was his sacrifice
accomplished.

Father Perboyre's strength of soul and the miraculous signs with which God glorified his dead body
made a deep impression on the pagans and numerous
conversions followed. All Christendom, too, was
filled with admiration and astonishment at his heroic
martyrdom. On November 10, 1889, Leo XIII
inscribed the name of Gabriel Perboyre on the roll of
the martyrs and it is expected that his name will soon
be numbered among the saints.

Blessed Francis Regis Clet

2. At the same place as Perboyre, but twenty years
earlier, another Lazarist, the Blessed Francis Regis
Clet, died a heroic death for Christ.[174] He belongs to
the glorious band of seventy-seven martyrs who, in the
Jubilee year of 1900, were declared Blessed by Leo
XIII. With the exception of two, all of these died
within the nineteenth century. The birthplace of
Blessed Francis Clet was Grenoble, and in 1769, when
in his twenty-first year, he joined the Lazarists. After
his ordination he taught moral theology for fifteen
years, after which he became superior of the novitiate
of St. Lazarus at Paris. In the beginning of 1791
three missionaries were to set out for China. An unexpected impediment arising in the case of one of them,
Father Clet urgently begged to be sent in his stead.

His petition was granted. For twenty-eight years he labored indefatigably in preaching the word of God. In 1818, when he had become old and sick, there broke out a persecution of the Christians. On June 16, 1819, the feast of his patron, St. Francis Regis, after celebrating the Holy Mass he was seized along with the Christians with whom he lodged. Dreadful tortures and prison were now his lot and he was dragged to Wu-ch'ang. In spite of inhuman treatment he was always cheerful and consoled and encouraged his fellow-prisoners. The announcement of the death sentence made the countenance of this old man of seventy-three years radiant with joy. The day of his triumph was February 18, 1820.

Among the seventy-seven martyrs above mentioned there are besides Blessed Francis Clet, twelve others who poured forth their blood on Chinese soil. They are Bishop Jean Gabriel Taurin Dufresse, vicar-apostolic of Sze-Chuen; the Franciscan John Lantrua of Triora; Auguste Chapdelaine of the Paris Missions; the native priests, Joseph Yuen (died 1817), Paul Lieou (died 1818), Thaddeus Lieou (died 1823), and August Tchao (died 1815); the catechists Peter Ou (died 1814), Peter Lieou (died 1834), and Joachim Ho (died 1839); the workingman Lawrence Pe-Man (died 1856), and the widow Agnes Tsao-Kouy (died 1856).

Blessed Gabriel Dufresse

3. The Blessed Gabriel Dufresse, of the Paris seminary of the Foreign Missions, began to labor in China in the year 1776. In the beginning he held a difficult post in the province of Sze-chuen, where he was exposed to constant persecution. In 1785 he spent six months in prison, which ended in banishment, but the fearless missionary was soon back with his flock. In 1800 he was made bishop, so that

he might assume the entire direction of the whole mission. It was a time of continual persecution and at no moment were the Christians, or at least the missionaries, sure of their lives. The bishop was obliged to change his place of residence almost every day. In 1815 a weak Christian while on the rack betrayed the abode of Monsignor Dufresse, and so he fell into the hands of his enemies a second time. This time the ardently desired crown of martyrdom was not denied him. He was beheaded on September 14, 1815.

Blessed John Lantrua

4. The Blessed John Lantrua came from Triora in Liguria, and at seventeen was received into the Franciscan Order at Rome.[175] When he was thirty-nine his oft-repeated prayer was granted, and he was sent to China to preach the Gospel. For fifteen years, amidst unheard-of sufferings and hardships, he scattered the seed of the divine word. And the noblest of rewards was bestowed on him. He was taken prisoner and after many tortures courageously endured, he was strangled at Shian-Sa on February 7, 1816.

Blessed Auguste Chapdelaine

5. The Blessed Auguste Chapdelaine obtained the martyr's palm after a comparatively brief period of activity.[176] But he had in earlier years given many proofs of heroic Christian courage. His parents were pious, well-to-do farmers in the village of La Rochelle, diocese of Coutances, where he was born on January 6, 1814. Still they were unwilling to consecrate their son to the service of the Lord, though he prayed for the grace most earnestly and showed by his whole life how well fitted he was for the priesthood. When he was twenty years old, two of his brothers, after a short

illness, died in the same week. His parents saw in this a punishment of their obstinacy and now gave August permission to study. He was ordained at the age of twenty-nine and desired to go to the foreign missions, but the bishop was against this. After eight years of patient waiting he was able in 1851 to enter the Paris seminary of foreign missions and the year after went out to China.

On his first attempt to penetrate into the interior from Canton he was captured by brigands and robbed of everything. For nearly two years he labored with the greatest success in the province of Kwang-si, when he was apprehended at Si-lin-hien on February 24, 1856. At his first trial the mandarin ordered him to be given three hundred blows of the stick, but the executioners were allowed full liberty and they did not cease until the body of the martyr was covered over and over with blood. Not a sound of complaint or suffering came from the mouth of the scourged victim. During the whole night and the following day he was bound in so cruel a way that he could not stir a limb without the greatest pain. But when he was again led to the tribunal in the evening all the pains of his torture had miraculously disappeared. At this the mandarin grew furious. He believed that the missionary had used magic. So they poured warm blood from a dog over his head to dispel the charm and beat his face with a thick leather strap until his teeth were broken. On the next day, February 27, 1856, Chapdelaine was condemned to death and was subjected to a slow martyrdom by the "torture of the cage." When on the following morning the executioners struck off his head, three rays of blood, it is said, streamed heavenward from the wound. But much more must we admire the heroic patience of the martyr in his unspeakable sufferings.

Blessed Lawrence Pe-Man

6. Two days before, the Blessed Lawrence Pe-Man was beheaded on the same spot. He had been converted to the Faith by Chapdelaine and courageously endured every torture without the least wavering.

Blessed Agnes Tsao-Kouy

7. On the first of March, three days later, the Blessed Agnes Tsao-Kouy died by the same torture of the cage. She was thirty years of age, a young widow, and was born of Christian parents. She had been of great service to the missionaries as a catechist.

Blessed Peter Lieou

8. An especially heroic courage was displayed by the Blessed Peter Lieou. When a young man he embraced the Catholic Faith and, making confession of it in 1797, was thrown into prison, but was released through the intervention of a family of great influence. In the year 1814 he was again imprisoned and banished into Tartary. Thirteen years elapsed before he could return home. A new persecution began and the two sons of Blessed Peter were made prisoners. The father feared for their constancy. "I am now eighty years old," he said to his wife, "the mandarins have taken our sons from us and I am afraid our children may not withstand the trial. I will go to encourage them and show them how to be loyal to Our Lord. If the mandarins seize me, so much the better. I can stay near my sons and strengthen their courage by word and example." He succeeded in entering the prison, but was seized and brought before the judge. "If it is a crime to confess the Christian religion," he said at his trial, "then I am more guilty than my sons, for I instructed them in that holy relig-

ion, and therefore it is but fair that I suffer those severe punishments. But if I am not guilty neither are my sons and their wives, and, therefore, you must set them free." The judge cried out angrily: "You have already been exiled for your disobedience to the imperial laws which forbid the Christian religion. The emperor has pardoned you and now you have the effrontery to offend him by persevering in this religion." The old man was then given ten blows in the face and sent to the prison. He bowed to the judge and said: "I thank you for this great favor."

The rest of the Christian prisoners behaved in like manner, so that the astonished heathens exclaimed: "Who has ever seen prisoners that rejoice and glory in their chains!" It was Peter Lieou before all that sustained the courage and joyfulness of the confessors of Christ. While all the others were sent into exile, he alone, after further tortures, was condemned to death. When they brought him to the place of execution on March 17, 1834, he said to the executioner: "Wait but a moment till I finish my prayer." He made the sign of the cross, commended his soul to God, and then said: "I have finished my prayer, now I am ready." One pull on the rope brought an end to this glorious life. Heathens as well as Christians testify that at this moment among other miraculous signs a beautiful crown descended from the heavens upon the head of the martyr and disappeared only some minutes later. The executioner was greatly moved and declared: "This Christian religion must of a surety be a good religion." The Christians began from that time to manifest their veneration toward this steadfast martyr.

The heroic deaths of the other Blessed martyrs of China exhibit similar striking traits of supernatural constancy.

Blessed Dominic Henares

9. The remainder of the martyrs declared Blessed in 1900, numbering sixty-four, belong to Annam. Two of these suffered in 1798, the rest during the period between 1833 and 1853. Among them we find three bishops, the Blessed Dominic Henares, a Dominican, titular bishop of Fesseita; Blessed Ignatius Delgado, titular bishop of Mellipotamo, also a Dominican; and Blessed Pierre Dumoulin-Borie, bishop-elect of Acanthus.

The Blessed Dominic Henares, a Spaniard, began his labors in Tonkin during 1790 and after 1803 was coadjutor of the Blessed Ignatius Delgado, vicar-apostolic of Tonkin.[177] During the reign of the persecutor of the Christians, Minh-Menh, he was thrown into prison along with his catechist, Blessed Francis Chien, and the owner of the house in which he lived. Unfortunately the last mentioned denied his Faith while on the rack.

But the catechist was all the more steadfast, though they scourged him so terribly that strips of flesh were torn out of his body, and then they flung him upon a seat studded with sharp-pointed nails. The judge was amazed to find that the sentence of death was received by both the martyrs with the greatest joy. Their execution, which occurred on June 25, 1838, reminds us of Sixtus and Laurence. A great crowd of the people gathered to see it, and while the heathens wondered at the joy of the confessors, the weeping Christians were consoled by the martyrs themselves. Three soldiers who had been imprisoned for their Faith were brought to the place of execution that they might be intimidated at the bloody spectacle. But the contrary happened, for they cried out to the bishop: "Father, when you have come to heaven forget not to pray for us," and later they, too, obtained the martyr's palm. How great was the childlike piety of the bishop and his desire for martyrdom may be seen in a letter sent many years before to a little cousin in Spain, begging her to offer up his desire to God for him. He believed that such a prayer from the innocent heart of a child could not be left unheard and his hope was not in vain.

Blessed Ignatius Delgado

10. The Blessed Ignatius Delgado had labored for Christ in Tonkin during the same term of years as Blessed Dominic and only a few days later also received the crown of glory. He had been vicar-apostolic of eastern Tonkin since 1799 and under his administration Christianity had made great progress. This old man of seventy-six years was so grievously tortured that he succumbed under his sufferings before the approval of his death sentence arrived. With these two Dominican bishops was also imprisoned the Dominican provincial, Blessed Joseph Fernandez, who was beheaded on July 24, 1838.

Blessed Pierre Dumoulin-Borie and Others

11. Those who knew Blessed Pierre Dumoulin-Borie when he was a college boy would scarcely have anticipated that the rather frivolous young man would at the age of thirty-two obtain a most glorious crown of martyrdom. He had been somewhat spoiled by his companions and gave his parents and superiors a great deal of trouble. But after he had received minor orders a complete change of mind took place. And when he entered the seminary of the foreign missions at Paris he had to encounter great opposition on the part of his mother.

Immediately after his ordination Dumoulin-Borie was sent to Tonkin. During the whole time of his labor here a furious persecution was raging. He neither feared nor avoided the sacrifice. In July, 1838, he fell into the hands of the persecutors. After severe tortures he wrote a touching letter from his prison to his relatives in France showing the noble-minded sentiments with which he was going to death. His appointment as vicar-apostolic of western Tonkin reached him in his prison. Two native priests and two catechists shared his captivity. The heathens were greatly amazed to hear only songs of praise coming from the prison. The Blessed Peter was beheaded on November 24, 1838. On the same day were strangled the two native priests, Blessed Peter Khoa and Blessed Vincent Diem. The two catechists, Blessed Anthony Quinh-Nam and Blessed Peter Tu, died on July 10, 1840.

Six Other Martyrs of the Paris Missions

12. Six other martyrs of the glorious band belonged to the Paris Missions: Blessed François Isidore Gagelin, strangled on October 17, 1833; Blessed Joseph Marchand, who died on November 30, 1833, while strips of flesh were being torn from his body with red-hot tongs; Blessed Jean Charles Cornay, beheaded on September 20, 1837; Blessed François Jaccard, strangled on September 21, 1838; Blessed August Schöffler, and Blessed Jean Louis Bonnard,[178] both beheaded on May 1, 1852. August Schöffler was a native of Mittelbronn in Lorraine.[179] Before he was ordained to the priesthood he entered the seminary of the foreign missions at Paris and, full of zeal for martyrdom, begged to be sent to the mission of Tonkin. At the age of twenty-nine, after scarcely three years' labor on the missions, he received the martyr's palm.

August Huy, Nicholas The, Dominic Dat

13. The rest of the Blessed Martyrs of Annam were partly native Dominicans or secular priests, partly lay people of every station in life. They gave distinguished proof of their zeal for their Faith. The

pagans endeavored to make three soldiers, August Huy, Nicholas The, and Dominic Dat, apostatize, applying the most frightful tortures; but to no effect. In fact, the torturers felt a sort of shame that their means of torment were exhausted. So they gave the unwitting confessors a most intoxicating drink, put them at once to the rack and forced them to utter a denial of their Faith. The poor men were loaded with gifts and set free. But when they were restored to their people they became conscious of what had been done. They at once considered what they should do to repair the scandal. They found a priest, went to confession, received Holy Communion and then presented themselves again before the judge, declaring that they repented of what they had done and again asserting their loyalty to the Christian religion. The judge sent them away, for he had already despatched a triumphant message to the king announcing that he had subdued the obstinacy of the soldiers. But the three were unwilling to be deprived so easily of the crown of martyrdom. They prepared a memorial setting forth the true account of their abjuration and August Huy and Nicholas The made ready for the long journey to Hué to present the document to the king himself. The third confessor was sick and unable to accompany them. Three times the strange petitioners were driven off by the courtiers. At length they succeeded in presenting their protest when the king, Minh-Menh, went out riding. At first the king was stricken with astonishment, but his old hatred of Christians was soon aroused and he straightway ordered them to be seized. They were doomed to suffer a dreadful death. On the 13th of June, 1839, they were taken out in a boat, sawed in two by the soldiers and thrown into the sea. The son of Huy, a boy of sixteen, was compelled to look on the spectacle, but he was not frightened and two days later also died for his Faith. The third soldier, Dominic Dat, was again imprisoned. When urged to save his life he said: "I have already suffered so much for Christ that I will not lose my reward for it. My two comrades have suffered death for the Faith and I hope for the same grace." And soon after he joined his brave.comrades in heaven.

BLESSED MATTHEW GAM

14. The Blessed Matthew Gam bore his martyrdom with unexampled cheerfulness. He was a sailor who secretly brought the missionaries from Singapore to Annam and carried their letters. In the year 1846 he was arrested and dreadfully tortured to force him to apostatize. Once a day they tormented his body with red-hot pincers to make him confess to whom he had brought the missionaries. During the tortures he said, laughing: "My dear mandarins, do not torment me so cruelly, or I may say when overcome by the strokes and the pinching that I brought the missionaries to you." The fearful tortures he endured for a whole year in prison did not break down his cheerful courage. When others pitied him he used to say that he was rather to be envied. He found strength for this love of the cross in almost continual prayer. When he was led out to death a group of Christian women were standing by the road, weeping over his fate. He turned toward them and said: "I am filled with joy. I beg of you not to mourn for me. My fate deserves not mourning but envy." From time to time during the procession a soldier was obliged to read out the sentence. He did so in such a way as scarcely to be understood. At length the martyr cried out to him: "My dear friend, read a little louder so that all may understand I am not a murderer or a robber, but that I am to die for the religion of Jesus Christ." He died at the age of thirty-nine, leaving a wife and children.

Blessed Thomas Thien

15. Blessed Thomas Thien gave a like example of joyful suffering. He was a young seminarian not yet eighteen years of age. When he was brought for the first time before the mandarin the latter offered the young man the hand of his daughter and a high dignity as a reward for apostasy. The Blessed Thomas answered: "My desire is only for heavenly honor and not for that of earth." When just afterward he was bound to a stake and received forty blows of the bamboo he said: "See, my desire is coming to fulfilment, my blood flows for my Faith." When later he was undergoing a dreadful scourging his silvery clear voice was heard between the blows: "Lord, give me courage and strength to suffer for you." He was strangled on September 21, 1838, in company with François Jaccard.

Blessed Simon Hoa

16. The Blessed Simon Hoa was a physician and the president of a village. While he languished in prison he spoke of his imminent death as of a great feast-day approaching. When they brought to him his youngest child, only four months old, he kissed it and said: "My child, you will never smile on me again and you will forget my face, but God will be a father to all."

Blessed Thomas Toan

17. One of the most dreadful of martyrdoms was suffered by Blessed Thomas Toan, a catechist seventy-three years old. He was delivered to two apostate Christians with the command to procure his apostasy, and if they failed they were to die themselves. The apostates were so ingenious in their malice that in a moment of weakness the catechist was ready to do their will. But soon understanding his error he

retracted it. They then placed on him the terrible neck-yoke, bound both his hands above it, stripped his lacerated body and left him exposed for ten days, with a brief interruption, to the fierce heat of the sun and the stings of insects. He was condemned to die by starvation, but the Lord soon called him to the richly merited joy of the martyr.

Joseph Hien

18. Before Joseph Hien obtained the martyr's palm, at the age of seventy, he had been forced to apostatize twenty-seven times. As many times he retracted and each time suffered a dreadful scourging.

These are only a few of the many examples of heroic constancy shown by the seventy-seven Blessed Martyrs, sufficient, however, to demonstrate that they were true and genuine martyrs. During those years there were, it is true, many sad apostasies among the Christians. All conceivable tortures were practised upon them. But this only renders more admirable the constancy of the faithful ones.

Blessed Jerome Hermosilla, Blessed Valentine Berrio-Ochoa, Blessed Peter Almato, Blessed Joseph Khang

19. Again, in 1906, Pius X was able to proclaim the beatification of a number of martyrs. Four of these belong to a period of persecution in Annam, the Blessed bishops Jerome Hermosilla and Valentine Berrio-Ochoa, the priest Peter Almato, and the servant Joseph Khang. The first three were members of the Dominican Order.[180]

The Blessed Jerome Hermosilla was born on September 30, 1800, at Calzada, diocese of Logroño, in Spain. In 1828 he was sent to the mission of Tonkin. After the death of Blessed Ignatius Delgado on June 12, 1838, Blessed Jerome was appointed his successor as vicar-apostolic of eastern Tonkin. He was put to death in 1861. The Blessed Valentine Berrio-Ochoa entered the Dominican Order when a young priest twenty-six years of age and five years later we find him in Tonkin. He was a man of remarkably amiable and magnanimous character and of talents from which the noblest fruits were expected. In June, 1858, two months after his arrival in the mission, he was consecrated coadjutor of the vicar-apostolic of central Tonkin, Venerable Melchior Sampedro. As the latter suffered the death of a martyr only a month later, the whole burden of the difficult office devolved upon the Blessed Valentine. In 1861 the persecution grew worse and he fled from his vicariate into that of eastern Tonkin. Here, with Bishop Hermosilla, he fell into the hands of the persecutors, as did also the priest Almato and the servant Khang. They were dragged to the capital of the province and after frightful tortures the three Spaniards were beheaded on the first of November. The persecutors hoped to triumph over the constancy of the native Khang. They tried every means that cruelty could suggest and almost tore to pieces his scarcely living body. At length they knew that their efforts were useless and he was beheaded on December 6.

Blessed Stephen Theodore Cuénot

20. The year 1909 was likewise distinguished by the beatification of thirty-three martyrs of the nineteenth century. Of these, twenty belonged to Annam and thirteen others to China. At the head of the Annamese band of heroes stands the Blessed Stephen Theodore Cuénot, vicar-apostolic of Cochin-China.[181] He was made bishop in 1835, being then thirty-three years of age. On account of the uninterrupted persecution it was only in disguise and under cover of night that he could penetrate into his dangerous diocese.

He had constant success in adding new members to the Church of Christ. In the autumn of 1861 he was captured along with a considerable number of Christians and was transported in a cage to the capital. But after a few days he died in the prison in consequence of the many hardships he had endured. Some witnesses were of opinion that poison had been administered to him. The death sentence from the king came too late.

BLESSED PETER NERON

21. In the preceding year (1860) Blessed Peter Neron was beheaded on November 3. The son of a poor peasant family, he was born at Bornay in the department of Jura on September 21, 1818. He tended the cattle until his seventeenth year and in all the mischievous pranks of the village boys took the part of principal hero. But something noble lay hidden in the nature of the rough farmer's boy. Through the reading of a pious book a complete moral change took place in him. He became fond of prayer, went frequently to the Sacraments, and used all his influence in urging his companions to a like fervor. A desire to become a priest gradually took possession of him. The parish priest of the place undertook to teach him the elements of Latin, and Neron, now nineteen years old, proved a diligent and virtuous student. When he had reached his thirtieth year he stood before the altar a priest. Two years previously he had been received into the seminary of the foreign missions at Paris. His proved and energetic character marked him the right man for the dangerous mission of Tonkin. Here he labored from 1849 to 1860, under the greatest privations, often not knowing where he could find a safe hiding-place. He excited the greatest admiration as well for his piety and mortification as for his courage. Twice his friends succeeded in freeing him from prison, but the third time the enemy was

not willing to let go its victim. After the usual tortures the Servant of God was confined for three months in a cage. The pagans were greatly astonished at his untroubled cheerfulness in view of his imminent death. He was executed on November 3, 1860.

Blessed Théophane Vénard

22. The reading of an account of the glorious death of Jean Charles Cornay (died 1837) enkindled in the heart of a boy of eighteen years a desire for the life of a missionary.[182] His enthusiasm remained alive through all the dangerous years of study and developing manhood, throughout the tribulations of an apostleship full of sacrifice in a distant heathen land, and became the greater when the martyr's crown gleamed its welcome. This fortunate one was Théophane Vénard, whom the Church now venerates as a blessed martyr. He had come to Hong Kong a newly ordained priest, to prepare for the Chinese mission. His heart bounded with joy when he was suddenly chosen for the kingdom of Annam, where at that time the persecution demanded so many victims. On receiving the glad news he wrote to a friend:

"As often as the thought of martyrdom comes to me it makes me overflow with gladness. It is the good and noble portion that is not given to all. *Exultent in Domino Sancti, alleluia.* I do not dare to pray for so radiant a crown. *Domine, non sum dignus.* But my soul can not refrain from a lively emotion and frequent ejaculatory prayers. *Domine, qui dixisti, Majorem caritatem nemo habet ut animam suam ponat quis pro amicis suis.* (Greater love than this no man hath, that a man lay down his life for his friends. John xv. 13). Remember our prayer; it has an irresistible charm for me—*Regina martyrum, ora pro nobis.* Pray for our friend, who does not forget you for a single day."

Vénard first labored with Theurel, a boyhood
friend, and with Blessed Peter Neron in teaching the
boys at the college of Hoang-Nguyen. In 1857 the
missionaries narrowly escaped death in an unexpected
attack by the heathens. For three years longer Vénard
persevered in seeking after the strayed sheep before he
was made a prisoner. After two months' confinement
he was executed on February 2, 1861. He was only
thirty-one years old. He enjoyed sufficient freedom
in prison to write to his parents and sisters of his sufferings and approaching death for Christ. Here he
again shows the greatness of soul that is filled with
joy because it can make such a sacrifice. He tells his
relatives to shed only tears of joy over the en-
viable fortune of their beloved Théophane. The
Christians also secured for him the consolation of
having a native priest visit him in disguise and finally
a Christian woman brought to him the Holy Eucharist. Holy Communion was ever the strength of
martyrs.

BLESSED ANDREW NAM-THUONG

23. The native martyrs emulated the Europeans by
their constancy in the Faith. As in ancient days, it
happened now that their nearest relatives played the
part of traitors. We find an example of this in the
martyrdom of Blessed Andrew Nam-Thuong. He was
an aged man and the head of a village. His exhortations to a good life had no effect upon his degenerate
grandson. This worthless man lodged an accusation
against his grandfather as a Christian. The old man
gave his people a most heroic example of loyalty. All
attempts to make him apostatize were without effect.
The judges had compassion on his venerable age and
condemned him to exile, but on the journey he succumbed to the hardships of deportation on July 15,
1855.

Blessed Paul Hanh

24. There were some among these martyrs whose previous life had not been irreproachable. The Blessed Paul Hanh was born and brought up a Catholic, but they relate of him that in company with his brothers and some other associates he followed for some time the life of a brigand. All the more must we admire the power of grace in him, for when he was accused of being a Catholic he showed a wholly unlooked-for courage and his martyrdom was certainly not made an easy one for him. All the dreadful tortures which the cruelty of the persecutors had invented were employed on him. They were humiliated by their inability to master this ill-reputed young man. He met his death without the least wavering of his faith.

Blessed Francis Trung

25. Blessed Francis Trung, captain in the king's army, did not rank among the more zealous Christians, but the persecution discovered how deeply rooted was his faith. Neither threats nor tortures nor the penalty of death could tear it from his heart.

Blessed Michael Ho-Dinh-hy and Others

26. Serious charges might be made against the former life of Blessed Michael Ho-Dinh-hy. He was a mandarin of high rank and held a distinguished position in the court. For some years before his glorious end, however, his life was free from blame and he won great merit by protecting the Christians. Envious persons accused him of being a Catholic. He was made to suffer the full rigor of the law and all the fury of the tyrant. They desired to make an example of an official who had failed in loyalty to his king. But Michael remained loyal to the King of kings until his death.

The Church has no hesitation in pronouncing these men Blessed. She is convinced that voluntary death for Christ wholly atones for every former fault.

Nevertheless, the majority of these martyrs were during their lives not merely exemplary but even holy Christians. Thus, for instance the native priests Peter Luu, John Hoan, Peter Qui, Paul Tinh, and Lawrence Huong; the married men Matthew Dac and Emmanuel Phung; the married women Agnes Thanh and many others.

Blessed Jean Pierre Néel, Lucia Y

27. Among the thirteen martyrs of China we find a European, the Blessed Jean Pierre Néel. In a very short time he made many conversions in a village of the province of Kwei-chow. Here he was suddenly made prisoner in February, 1862, along with his catechists, Blessed John Tchen and Martin Uh, and his host, Blessed John Chang, a mandarin. The fiends tied him by the hair to the tail of a horse and made savage jests at his endeavors to keep pace with the galloping beast. They did not delay, however, for on the same day the martyr was beheaded. John Chang was kept to the last. He had been baptized only two days before. They reminded him of his children, whom he would leave orphans. He answered only: "I am grieved for them." In this neophyte grace was stronger than love of life or of flesh and blood.

On the following day at the same place the maiden Lucia Y was beheaded for her Faith. She had assisted the missionary as a catechist.

Joseph Chang, Paul Chen, John B. Lô, Martha Wang

28. The Blessed Martyrs Joseph Chang, Paul Chen, John B. Lô, and Martha Wang were led to a glorious death at Tsingay on July 29, 1861. The first two were

young seminarians who were taken prisoners along with the servant John Lô in a sudden attack on the seminary. From prison they wrote a noble letter to their bishop, telling of their sufferings and showing their courage for the sacrifice. The widow Martha Wang acted as their messenger.. In spite of threats and insults she often entered the prison to provide relief for the prisoners. When the confessors were led out to execution the soldiers noticed Martha, who was washing clothes in the river. They halted the procession, seized the good woman and accused her: "You, too, are a follower of this religion, either renounce it or go with these." "Then I will surely go with them," she promptly answered. The onlookers were amazed at her fearless spirit. Thus Martha Wang, for her service to the martyrs, obtained a martyr's crown. In a few moments the four had won the noblest of victories.

BLESSED PIERRE LOUIS CHANEL, BLASE MARMOITON

29. The Marist Father Pierre Louis Chanel will share in the honor of the altar with the apostolic men who made fertile with martyrs' blood the islands of the South Sea.[183] As a boy, a seminarian, and a parish priest he ever enjoyed the repute of a saint. Desiring to accomplish great things for God, he joined the newly founded Society of Mary in 1831. The founder, Venerable John Claude Colin,* promoted him forthwith to the most important offices. After five years the new Society was able to send some missionaries to the heathen. Father Chanel was appointed superior of the fortunate band. Their destination was the Gambier Islands in the Pacific. The long voyage, including a journey across South America, lasted nearly a year. Their first station was established on Walli Island. In December, 1837, Father Chanel set-

*See page 171 sq.

tled on the still entirely heathen island of Futuna. The work of the mission progressed satisfactorily, owing not a little to the self-denial of the missionary. He overcame himself so far as to follow as much as possible the customs of the islanders and thus won their hearts. The skilful assistance he was able to afford the sick greatly increased his reputation.

But the rapidity of the spread of Christianity soon brought the enemy upon the scene. The royal dignity was closely involved with the heathen religion of the Futunans and the jealousy of the king was at once aroused. When the king's son was received among the catechumens and in spite of all threats persevered in his resolve, open enmity broke out. Father Chanel could not abandon his flock in the moment of danger, and on April 28, 1841, a band of warriors sent by the king fell upon him in his dwelling and with a few blows of their clubs put an end to his life. The saying of Tertullian that the blood of martyrs is the seed of Christians was again splendidly verified in the case of Blessed Chanel. The news of his death made the deepest impression on the catechumens and strengthened their constancy. Three years later the whole island had become Catholic, and even the slayers themselves received the grace of the true Faith.

The Marist Congregation counts yet another martyr in the South Seas, who is to be declared Blessed, the lay-brother Blase Marmoiton, who was put to death by the heathens in New Caledonia in 1847.[184]

José Marie Diaz Sanjurjo, Melchior Garcia Sampedro

30. Besides those already mentioned, the kingdom of Annam still presents us with an immense roll of martyrs. The Church in Annam was truly a church of martyrs in the nineteenth century. Its foundation in the first half of the seventeenth century was due to

the zeal of the Jesuit, Alexander de Rhodes, and in 1820 it numbered about four hundred thousand Christians in the two provinces of Cochin-China and Tonkin.[185] But when King Minh-Menh ascended the throne he set himself the task of extirpating the Christian religion. During the decade following 1830 the blood of martyrs flowed in streams. Minh-Menh's son and successor, Thiö-Tri (1841-47), issued no new edicts, but individual executions of Christians still occurred. Under his successor, Tü-Dük (1847-83), the summit of the persecution was reached. For decades they raged against the outlawed Christians with the grossest cruelties. They had them tortured, sawed to pieces, strangled, drowned, burned, beheaded, trampled by elephants, or banished. All manners of death were inflicted on them—whole villages were massacred or completely pillaged and still Christianity increased. It is true that many weak souls apostatized and trampled the cross under foot, but in general there prevailed a genuine enthusiasm for martyrdom. How great was the number of martyrs would be hard to determine, but they certainly amounted to many thousands.

We have given some instances of the constancy of the martyrs already declared Blessed, but the courage of these others was in no wise less. There is in progress a great process for the beatification of 1743 persons, all of whom died between 1856 and 1862. At the head stand the names of two vicars-apostolic of Tonkin—José Marie Diaz Sanjurjo and Melchior Garcia Sampedro, both Dominicans. The rest are all natives, people of every class and age.[186]

"The cangue (neck-yoke) and the chains I bore," writes Bishop Sanjurjo from prison, "are precious jewels binding me to Christ. My soul leaps with joy that at last I can give my blood to the last drop in union with the adorable blood of Our Redeemer . . . the days I have yet to live are not many. If I am cast among the leopards that surround me, may heaven receive it in atonement for my sins." A few days afterward, he was beheaded, on July 20, 1857, and his remains were cast into the sea. The head was recovered by the Christians.

The Venerable Sampedro was put to death a year later. They stretched him on the ground, bound his hands and feet to stakes. His hands and feet were first cut off and finally his head. To increase his torment they used dull axes. They began to hack off the legs above the knee and ten or twelve strokes were needed for this, five or six for the arms, and the head was struck off only after fifteen blows.

PAUL BAO, DOMINIC DUYET, PETER THAE, PETER TUAM, DOMINIC NINH

31. Even boys gave sublime examples of fortitude. "I must not pass over in silence," writes Bishop Sampedro shortly before his martyrdom, "the noble combats which some of our young people and pupils of our houses have fought. They withstood all the tortures used in this tribunal, the pincers with which strips of flesh were torn from their bodies and the sharpened nails on which they had to kneel not excepted. Finally, the name of God, whom they would not deny, was burned into their cheeks and they were sent laden with chains into a far exile." During the torture of the pincers, which were now cold, now red hot, the victims were bound fast on the ground. Then the executioners would pull a strip of flesh from the body of the tortured one, tearing it violently back and forth until the piece came off. This horrible torture was often repeated.

On July 24, 1859, five pupils from an orphanage won the martyr's palm—Paul Bao, Dominic Duyet, Peter Thae, Peter Tuam, and Dominic Ninh.[187]

"Stamp on the cross with your feet and I will assure you fortune," said the mandarin, smiling. "We may be put to death," was the answer, "but we will not cast under our feet the Lord we adore." "Who gives you food?"—"Our Lord Jesus Christ."—"But who keeps you living?"—"God alone, who gives life, can do that." This excited the anger of the judge. "Your folly," he exclaimed, "is not worthy of death, but since you have thus spoken, you shall die and learn that your death is in my hands." The boys clapped their hands for joy and cried: "So we may go to our home." The furious mandarin ordered Peter Thae and Peter Tuam to be bound hand and foot with strong cords and dragged on the ground to the place of execution. Then he had ropes tied to the necks of the remaining three and made them run after the executioner, who choked them cruelly. When the first two came to the place of execution where they were to win the palm of martyrdom they were covered with wounds from the dragging and colored the earth with their blood. An elephant was now brought to kill them. The beast, enraged by the soldiers, rushed upon Peter Thae, threw him twice into the air and then crushed him under its feet. Next it seized Peter Tuam and in like manner ended his glorious combat. The death agony of the others was longer. The soldiers seized the ends of the ropes which were noosed to the three young confessors, tightening and loosening them, prolonging the torture for half an hour. At length they were strangled. Who gave these children such strength?

Wholesale Murders

32. "The heads of Christian communities," writes a missionary,[188] "have most to suffer. On December 31, 1859, 90 Christians were brought before the tribunal. Bound hand and foot they were first so

beaten that the blood flowed copiously and the flesh was torn in strips from their bodies. Incessantly the mandarin shouted at them: 'Trample on the cross!' and to the executioner he cried: 'Strike on with all your might until they are dead.' A few apostatized. The others endured 60 strokes of the bamboo. Unable to move from the place, they were dragged to the prison. After two days the same torture began anew. On the torn and bloody bodies fell 42 strokes of the bamboo. After another two days, 45 more. Then in turn came blows with a hammer, with which their legs were crushed, and after this they were made to sit on pointed nails. Their tormentors were determined to force them to apostatize or to kill them with excess of pain. More unfortunately fell away, but the majority—and among them a man of sixty years—remained unshaken."

Another missionary writes:[189] "The Prefect himself wished to give his subordinate officers an example in torturing Christians. So he brought hundreds of Christians from all parts of the province and practised on them the most cruel slaughter. On May 18, 1862, he had 21 beheaded; on the 22d, 43; on the 26th, 67; an equal number on the 27th; and others on the following days, but 224 victims still remained. Tired of cutting off heads, he left them two days without food. On May 30 he caused 112 to be drowned in the river singly and by fives. The remaining 112 met the same fate on May 31.

"This example in the capital found only too eager imitation in many districts. Thus, on May 27 and 30, 56 Christians were beheaded in the chief town of San; on the 29th, 96 in Cham-Dinh; in Quinh-Toi many Christians were crowded into the prison, the place was set on fire and all perished in the flames. Some had succeeded in breaking their neck-yokes (cangues) and chains and were taking to flight, but the burning place was surrounded by order of the mandarins and the executioners drove them back with blows of the sword and thrust of spear into the flames. At Dri-Jen, it is said, 150 neophytes were to have been beheaded, but the executioners were new to the work, and after they had cruelly mangled some twenty they threw the rest into the river. Since the stream is not wide there, many succeeded in reaching the shore. They were recaptured, bound two together hand and foot, so that the feet of one were tied to the neck of the other, and drowned in a deep well.

"Amidst all this slaughter there is one consoling fact: Among the thousands of confessors there have been only six apostates. These dreadful executions forced cries and groans from the victims, indeed, but the Faith spoke as strongly as the pain. Everywhere were to be heard praises of Christ, hymns to the Blessed Virgin, and the Litany of the Saints, which the martyrs recited in response to one another as they did before in the churches. 'God be glorified in His saints.'"

The Christians of the village of Ba-Giong sought to find safety in flight.[190] Since they were already surrounded by the executioners there was no way left for them but to wade through a marsh three feet deep. They started out in the middle of the night, carrying their sick and children. Unfortunately their enemies soon discovered the disappearance of the brave people and hurried after the fugitives in boats. The greater number, especially old people and women, were captured. The men were beheaded on the following day, for they refused to trample on the cross. The same fate was reserved for the women and children, but the crowd of onlookers, tired of gazing on such a bloodthirsty exhibition, revolted against the cruelty of the mandarins and prevented the commands from being carried into execution.

TEN THOUSAND CHRISTIANS PUT TO DEATH

33. The viceroy of Tonkin, father-in-law of the king, desired to win special laurels. He caused graves to be prepared into which the Christians were thrown and securely covered with boards. After eight days he had the board covering taken up and the corpses removed. In one month it is reported he put to death more than ten thousand Christians, burning or drowning or beheading, or having them trampled to death by elephants, sometimes burying them up to the necks and then literally mowing off their heads. The man would be a fit companion for Nero. In other districts the Christians were buried alive or burned *en massé*.

Since all could not be punished by death they devised a complete system of harassing annoyances to make the Christians apostatize—such as causing them heavy losses in money; setting their houses on fire; scattering the faithful among the heathen; and the like.

THE PERIOD FROM 1873 TO 1885

34. After 1863 the persecution in some measure abated, but in 1873 the storm broke out anew. Again the missionaries inform us of superhuman heroism shown by young children.[191] In the vicariate of western Tonkin alone, the villages of twenty-five thousand Christians were burned and pillaged. From southern Tonkin Monsignor Gauthier writes:

"On February 24 the 'Doctor' Cic with his people made ready for a great offering of victims. On the 25th he caused two servants of Father Doan and another Christian to be beheaded and their bodies to be cast into the river. On the same day they burned the villages of Trun-lam, Mo-vinh and Ban-tash. The villagers were massacred. Those who had fled were pursued with bloodhounds and fell on the following day under the swords of the persecutors. I am told that the river is covered with bodies. At this moment the looters have reduced the villages of Hoi-Jen parish to ashes. Here, too, the poor Christians were slaughtered. The chief judge, with a force of eight hundred soldiers, is in the district of Sa-Nam and calmly looks on at the bloodshed. One of the leaders, who murdered two Christians in the open street, boasted of his heroism before the governor of the citadel and was dismissed with honor. He then proceeded with his followers to murder twenty women and children. In many places the cruel persecutors take a whole family —father, mother, and children—tie them together in a bundle with bamboo ropes and then throw them into the river, having first cut off the heads of the men. Often eight or ten bodies thus bound together come down the river. To the astonishment of all, these bodies do not spread any stench of putrefaction. In like manner five parishes, numbering ten thousand Christians, have been completely annihilated."

Similar are the accounts of the massacre of Christians in other districts. Consoling examples of great courage and faith are not wanting.

"Fifty-seven Christians," writes the same Monsignor Gauthier,[192] "were captured by the rebels. Before putting them to death the Doctors (mandarins) announced that all who desired to live should stand up as a sign that they renounced their Faith. One man and four women arose and were thereupon declared free. The others were led to the bank of the river to be thrown into the water. They persevered in prayer calmly, permitted their hands and feet to be bound and were then cast into the stream. Among them was a mother with her infant child. When she saw that the heathens were about to take her child from her she rushed forward and cast herself into the river with the little one to save it for heaven. The 'Doctors' offered another woman her life if she would surrender to them her three little boys, but the noble-hearted mother refused the offer and would rather see her children slain in her arms while she received the death-stroke than give such a price as their souls' salvation. A young man was strongly urged to give up his religion, when his mother rushed up to him and cried: 'No, child, you will not deny your Faith.' 'No, Mother, never and never,' he answered, strengthened by his mother's words. A Christian woman, mother of four little children, told me of her husband who was beheaded while he prayed. When the executioners saw that he calmly persevered in his prayer after he had already received a stroke of the sword they became furious, laid him on his back and sawed off his head. With him suffered a child and a young married couple who had received Baptism only a short time before. All met their death with great joy."

It is related that children from seven to ten years old, to whom life was promised if they would deny their Faith, took their stand beside their parents of their own accord to die with them. Others are said to have snatched their hands away from their pretended rescuers to go to death for the Faith with their parents. The inhuman wretches used generally to sell Christian boys and girls as slaves in China.

The horrors of desolation which the persecution produced were most shocking. Christians were allowed no redress for their losses. Many died of hunger. They were defenseless. "Those days," writes a missionary, "I visited three villages. Meeting only a few women in the first, I asked: 'Where are the men, is there no one coming to greet me?' 'Father,' they answered, 'there are no more men here, all have been beheaded. There are only women and children.' In both other villages I found the same state of things, asked the same question, and received the same answer." The Christian villages were simply nothing more than smoking ruins.

In spite of the persecution, Christianity made continual progress. The heathens could not conceive what bound the people so firmly to a doctrine that offered them while they were on earth a prospect only of persecution, misery, and death.

35. But enough of Christian blood had not yet been spilled. From 1883 to 1885 all the dreadful scenes were reproduced. Many European missionaries, a great number of native priests, and uncounted numbers of the Faithful—there were many thousands—obtained the martyr's palm. The occasion of the renewed outbreak of hatred against the Christians was the war with France, but it was for their steadfast adherence to the Christian faith that the Christians were put to death. Apostates were always given their lives.

The Annamese Christians well knew how to die joyfully for Christ. The most heroic acts are related of these years of combat. "There is certainly not a village in the whole district of Bon-son," writes a missionary in 1888,[193] "where the remains of our martyrs are not to be gathered. Wherever they found Christians they struck them down. The poor Christians could escape death only by flight into the mountains, and even there they were hunted with hounds. Very many perished there from hunger and misery. Their bones can be found up to the highest ridges of the mountains. . . . A quite wealthy Christian named Ngat, of the town of Plük-Dük, tried to save himself. He was twice stopped in the neighborhood of his home. When they asked him the first time whether he was a Christian he answered hesitatingly, 'No,' but on the second occasion when they said to him: 'Then trample on the cross and we will let you go,' he answered, 'Oh, not that! I am a Christian and will never trample upon the cross,' and straightway a spear was driven through him.

"How many dreadful deeds were done without mercy or compassion! In a village of my district they threw all the Christians into a deep well. They had tried to save themselves by flight into a neighboring mountain, but they were surrounded and driven back to the village. They marched in with their crucifixes and rosaries in their hands reciting prayers. The chief of the Christians, a venerable old man, asked the heathens to wait for a moment, and the victims all knelt around the well and finished their prayer. When the executioners showed signs of impatience the old man arose, addressed a few words to his companions and then said to the heathens: 'You may now begin your work.' In another place some thirty Christians had fled into a mountain and had carried with them a statue of the Blessed Virgin. They were captured and burned alive. They ranged themselves around their cherished statue and paid it reverence while the heathens were cutting the wood for the burning. They ceased not to pray to their good Mother till the fire and smoke suffocated them. Death by fire was a frequent fate of the Christians. They were shut up in churches and in private houses and the buildings, packed with human beings were set on fire. Complete extirpation of the name 'Christian' was the aim. No age nor sex found favor. Mercy was a capital offense, and many heathens were put to death for attempting to save the lives of Christians. A heathen official was buried alive with his wife because he had harbored some Christians. Tai, a former superintendent of the village of Hoi-tin, met a similar fate. . . . How many interesting and edifying things I could tell you if only I had the time. The Christians who remained in the country while the rising continued told me every day of such events. Every one of them had lived through a whole history full of tension. . . . The majority of Christians looked on participation in

the abominations of heathenism as something so horrible that they much preferred death; and I believe I
can say that the overwhelming majority of them so
thought. Hence, mothers made every sacrifice to prevent their children falling into the hands of heathens.
A woman named Tho, who was brought up in an
orphanage at Toak-da, fought with all her might
against the heathens who tried to take her child away
from her. In the struggle the child's arm was broken.
'Better so,' she cried, 'since he is now of no value to
you and he will die with me,' as indeed was very soon
the fact.

"In the Christian village of Dai-psinh, in Father
Barrat's district, a young girl of fifteen named Thu
and her little sister for a long time escaped the slaughter. Their father was no longer living and their
mother had married again. Thu lived with her paternal grandfather. A wealthy young heathen adorned
with the rank of Ba-ho, which can be bought at court
for some six hundred francs, was attracted by the
girl's beauty and sought with the most alluring promises to obtain her in marriage. 'No,' she said, laughing, 'I will never live with a heathen.' 'But they will
kill you and your little sister,' he replied, 'if you refuse
my hand.' 'All the better,' was her answer, 'we shall
then go to heaven together and possess far greater
happiness.' 'Have compassion on your little sister.'
'I do indeed have compassion on her, and therefore
certainly desire that she may die with me.' To
frighten Thu, they began to dig a grave. 'They will
bury you alive if you do not accept my proposal,' said
the young heathen. The maiden gave no answer and
calmly allowed them to finish the grave. When the
last shovelful was thrown out, they intimated that she
would now be thrown into it. 'Wait a moment,' she
said, and cast herself on her knees at the edge of the
grave. She said a prayer, then arose and said: 'Go

on, I am now ready.' They threw a mat into the grave. Then she descended and laid herself on the mat, placing beside herself her little sister, who, though only four years old, let it be done without weeping, and Thu said smiling: 'Now you may shovel in the earth, while she covered herself and the little one with a half of the mat. And in truth the heathens filled the grave above the two sisters. A few months ago a heathen came to me and said that he wished to become a convert. I asked his reasons and he answered: 'I have seen the Christians die, and wish to die like them. I saw how they were cast into rivers and wells. I saw them burned alive and pierced with spears. Truly they all died with gladness that astonished me, while they said their prayers and encouraged each other. Only Christians can die thus, and it is the reason why I would become a convert.'

"As has been said, scarcely any of the Christians born of Christian parents purchased their lives at the price of apostasy, and this is why we have so few of them left. The fine Christian community of Shaa-hun three years ago numbered over eleven hundred Christians, about seven hundred of whom were old Christians and four hundred newly converted. Of the seven hundred only five are now living—an old woman, a young man who served as a soldier on the border, the wife of a new convert, and two children, one ten and the other eight years of age. Of the newly converted fifty are still living."

36. Do not these reports sound like copies of the acts of the ancient martyrs? In many regions the Christians crowded, so to speak, to martyrdom, and a man felt jealous when the crown seemed to escape him.

The vicar-apostolic of northern Cochin-China writes:[194] "Twenty-five new converts of the village of Trüoi were arrested, and among them the head man

of the Christian community. When the officials broke
into his house he shouted at them with indignation :
'You bandits! Must I submit to such audacity?' He
endeavored to defend himself, but was quickly disarmed. A Christian who did not see his own family
among the prisoners cried : 'What is to become of my
wife and children? Let my whole family share my fortune, for all are Christians like myself.' His desire was
gratified. Another, whom the bailiff had forgotten,
and who saw the touching spectacle of his brother who
was going in fetters to death, could not restrain the
desire to share his fate and cried out with a firm voice :
'I am a Christian too.' 'Are you speaking the truth?'
asked the persecutors. 'Yes,' he answered, 'and what
is more, I was born of Christian parents. Look!
There stands my wife, the woman with the pallid face
and the babe in her arms. Let us be united in death
as we were in life.' And all three were joined with
their brethren in Jesus Christ.

"Before they were led to the place of execution they
were permitted, at the urgent petition of the chief man
of the Christian community, to make a last visit to the
little chapel where they used to say their morning and
evening prayers in common. There they prostrated
themselves before the altar and recited aloud the litany
of the Blessed Virgin and other prayers. The time was
not long, except to the executioners, who violently put
a stop to their pious devotions. 'Let me take the picture of Our Saviour from the altar,' said the chief
man, 'I will bring it to the place of execution, and it
will help us to die as true children of Our Adorable
Master.' The persecutors granted his request and he
led the procession with the picture of Our Crucified
Lord borne aloft so that all his companions might
clearly see it, and at sight of it sustain the noble courage that animated all till the moment of death. Their
eyes fixed on the picture, the Christians said the Rosary

with touching fervor and animated each other to shed their blood magnanimously for Jesus Christ. Thus they traveled the way of suffering and completed their sacrifice after the example of their Divine Master, while they ceased not continually to praise and adore Him until their tongues, stilled in death, could no longer utter His sacred name."

The history of the martyrs of Annam alone proves that the ancient spirit still lives in the Catholic Church.

CHINA

37. The heathens of the broad Chinese empire showed a like deadly hatred against the Church. Here indeed the persecution was, in a way, more local, but there was scarcely a year when in that or the other province bloody massacres of Christians were not reported. It was not merely hatred of the foreigner, but a genuine religious hate that caused such outbursts of popular fury. They attempted in the first place to force the numerous native Christians, who were mercilessly slaughtered, to apostatize from the Faith. And they regarded the missionaries in the same light, putting them to death chiefly because they were the preachers of a foreign religion.

To make known the heroic struggles of the Church in China during the nineteenth century a few scenes will be sufficient. A noble example is related of the fortitude of a catechist in the vicariate-apostolic of northern Shantung[195] during the Boxer rebellion of 1899-1900.

A catechist of Wan-quen, cruelly beaten and fettered, was dragged before the leader of the "Big Knives" at the under-prefecture of O Shen Pin. "Are you a Christian?" they asked the catechist. "Yes, I am one," he answered. At this they cut off one of his ears. 'Are you still a Christian?" "Yes, I am one." The second ear fell under the knife. "Are you still a

Christian?"   "Yes, I am one."   And with a blow of
the sword his head was struck from his body and the
brave catechist obtained the crown of martyrdom.

Monsignor Ferdinand Hamer

38. One of the most dreadful martyrdoms known to
history was suffered in the province of Kan-su by Monsignor Ferdinand Hamer of the Belgian Missions
(Scheutveld Mission Society), vicar-apostolic of
southwestern Mongolia.[196]   It was at the time of the
Boxer disturbances in 1900.   When the danger was
greatest, the bishop told his missionaries to seek safety
in flight while he would remain with his flock to console and encourage them in their hard struggle by word
and example.   On the 20th of July Monsignor Hamer
and his community became the prey of the Boxers.
"The Chinese Sisters were bound to trees and pierced
with swords and spears.   One of them survived the
dreadful scene, but so mutilated and disfigured that she
scarcely looked like a human being.   The girls and
children were slain until only a third of them remained and these with a number of young women
were dragged away and sold to Mohammedan slave-
dealers.

"Meanwhile, ten soldiers forced their way into the
church to seize the bishop.   He was taken without
resistance, partly stripped of his clothes and dragged
in the roughest manner from the church.   They then
cut off the fingers of his right hand to prevent him
from giving his blessing to the faithful, to which act
the heathens ascribed a mysterious power.   The mutilated hand was then tied up.   They fettered the arms
and legs of the venerable old man and carried him fastened on a pole through the village.   The brutal soldiers then began their sport with the poor victim, often
letting him fall heavily to the ground.   Passing Boxers
tore the hair from his head, and when they found how

painful this was they also tore away his strong, full beard. After this the confessor, along with five other Christians, was thrown on a cart and brought to Mao-tai, three hours' distant. Here the prisoners were so fettered that they could rest only on their knees and at every jolt of the cart they were wounded in the back of the neck by the edge of a knife placed horizontally behind it."

On the following day after a journey of seven hours they reached T'uo-sheng, a city of ten thousand inhabitants, near which there was a place of execution where, shortly before, three hundred Christians had been beheaded and their heads fixed on stakes.

"On July 22," proceeds the report, "began the long succession of tortures which were to precede death. They stripped the flesh off the breast of the confessor so as to fix a chain there. Then he was taken out of the cage in which he had been placed and led through the streets of the city by a rope wound around his head. Above his head was the inscription 'Lao Jang Muo,' i. e., 'old devil of the West.' The people gathering about assailed the confessor with jeers and insults of all sorts. From this place the bishop was brought on a cart to Ho-keu for a like exhibition, and on the way was subjected to one of the most disgraceful tortures. Fettered so that he could not move he was obliged to sit on a sharp instrument which is used in this country for making brooms. Whenever the poor sufferer, on account of the jolting of the cart, seemed about to lose consciousness from the pain, they asked him jeeringly whether he found the seat as good as the carriage-seat on which he made his (apostolic) journeys. 'Much better,' was the answer of the heroic old man. After he had endured unimaginable torment and ill treatment for three days they returned to T'uo-sheng, and from this place he at length went forth on his last journey to the open field before the city. Here they had driven three stakes into the ground in such wise that the upper ends came together in a point. Upon this triangle the bishop was bound fast, and first the flesh was torn from his back with iron instruments. Then they cut off successively his hands, feet, ears, and nose. The mutilated body was now fastened by the legs on the points of the scaffold of stakes in an upright position, and the cotton, soaked with oil and tallow, with which the legs and lower part of the body had been wrapped, was set on fire. The frightful pain forced a few deep sighs from the poor victim. But the wadding, in spite of all efforts to keep it afire, continually became extinguished and the legs were only scorched. This did not satisfy these devils in human form. They finally slashed open the body of the confessor, tore out his heart, roasted it, and forced a beggar to eat it, giving him five hundred sapecks. Probably they had some superstitious notion in this. The fat of the intestines was removed and sold as medicine to the heathens. Finally the head was cut off and fixed on a stake, where it remained for many days. According to another account, Monsignor Hamer spoke only once during all these cruelties, saying, "I forgive you and will pray for you.' "[197]

What greatness of soul such heroism argues! It is thus that true martyrs die. The first of them, Stephen, gave the example, and he learned from the cross of his Master. Such heroes are a glory of the world to come. Nimeguen, the native town of Monsignor Hamer, has erected a monument to him; and the Church, it is hoped, will soon number him among her Blessed martyrs.

A few days before Monsignor Hamer, and almost in as dreadful a manner, the Franciscan bishop, Antonine Fantosati, vicar-apostolic of southern Hu-nan, with his companion, Father Joseph Gambaro, O.F.M.,[198] suffered death for Christ. Of the same mission was the Franciscan, Cesidius da Fossa, who only a short time after he arrived in China was wrapped in linen soaked in petroleum and then burned alive.[199] Father Joseph Segers of the Scheutveld Congregation was first half strangled by the Boxers and then buried alive.[200] With like cruelty many other missionaries and native Christians were put to death.

OTHER PERSECUTIONS

39. "Most consoling to us," writes Father Ignatius Mangin, S.J., missionary in southeastern Tcheli,[201] "was the constancy of our Christians. The number of apostates was very small, and in these cases the apostasy was for the most part merely external. Almost all repented and accepted public ecclesiastical penance." Three months later, on July 22, 1900, Father Mangin and his community were attacked by the Boxers and over two thousand Christians were killed or burned. Father Mangin himself, while on the altar-step, received a blow of the sword that struck off his head. His companion, Father Paul Denn, was killed in his room while kneeling at his bedside. In the same district two Jesuits, Fathers Remy Isoré and Modest Andlauer, an Alsatian, were killed with spears in the chapel.

Most interesting examples of fortitude, which also prove that here there was question of persecution for the Faith, are reported by Father Gaudissart, S.J.[202] He brings out many circumstances showing that Christians had to suffer frightful tortures because they would not deny their Faith. He then proceeds: "Some days later one of my Christians, while confessing the Faith before the same tribunal, died gloriously under the scourge. The acts of these martyrdoms have an entirely official character, and it forms a noble page in the history of this persecution. Here is the fact. U-Wenn-Yinn was mayor of the Christian portion of his village. They dragged him before a mandarin, and the latter cited him before his tribunal. The future martyr, who well foresaw that it was a matter of life and death for him, knelt before his old mother to take his last leave of her before being led away by the servants of the court. The heroic woman said to him— they are admirable words—'If you die for your Faith, the good God will take care of us. So have no fear for me or your children. But if you deny your Faith, never show yourself to me again. I could never again call you my son.' 'Mother,' he answered, 'be at peace. With God's grace I shall not deny the Faith.'

"'Are you a Christian?' asked the mandarin. 'It is no longer permitted, and you must change your religion.' 'That I can not do—it is impossible.' 'Then strike him!' And the court menials began forthwith to apply the tortures of blows with the club and beat him until he lost consciousness. When he revived the mandarin asked him anew: 'Are you still a Christian?' 'Yes, I can not deny my Faith; it is impossible.' A second time the mandarin ordered him to be beaten, but without effect. He now tried another torture. After asking the same question and receiving the same answer he ordered the hero of faith to be suspended in the wooden cage. The confessor prayed constantly and fervently 'to die like Christ.' He had previously made to the mandarin and the executioners a declaration as noble as it was heroic. 'If in consequence of too great suffering I can speak no longer and you see me moving my lips, do not think that I am trying to deny my Faith. It will rather be a prayer I am trying to say.' In fact, after some moments of torture in the cage they saw him moving his lips. The executioners, believing they discovered in the change of his countenance that he was now near death, hastened to let him down, but too late. U-Wenn-Yinn had already received the glorious palm of martyrdom, and surely it was a martyr's death of whose genuineness none can doubt.

"Yet another glorious instance. . . . A Christian of Li-Kao-Echoang had long defended himself against a band of the 'Big Knives' who were trying to set fire to the church of the village. At last he was taken. 'Are you a Christian?' they asked. 'Certainly I am.' 'If you renounce your belief we will set you free.' 'I do not deny my Faith, and you may not only chop off my head, but cut my body into several pieces, too, and every piece, if you ask it, will answer you it is Christian.' After this bold confession of his Faith, he received his deathblow."

A like answer was given by the Chinese priest Wu, who was killed in eastern Mongolia. "If every day you cut off an ounce of my flesh, in two weeks you would get a pound, but then whatever remains would be what I am—a Christian."[203]

A young Belgian Franciscan, Father Victorin Del Brouck, came to his glorious end on December 11, 1898, in southern Hu-pe.[204] One of his catechumens was urged by the executioners to deny his Faith. "Apostatize?" he said; "never. I am and I remain a Christian. Though I have not yet been baptized, I know that there is a baptism of blood, and it is enough for me. I remain a Christian." At this courageous confession they first plucked out an eye, then cut off a foot, and finally beheaded him. Seventy Christians of the same place had sought refuge in a cave, but were betrayed by a false brother. Their enemies built a great fire before the cave to suffocate the fugitives with the smoke. They were only too successful. Only two of the Christians were afterward found alive, and the heads of these were stricken off.

40. Similar scenes of horror were often repeated in the history of the Chinese missions. For the most part they offer a splendid testimony to the fortitude of

youthful Christians. The following incident is related of the year 1884 :[205]

"In the village of Siao-sui-liang, in the Mandarinate of Ho-yen, there lived a distinguished family of catechumens—father, mother, and a boy of sixteen. All three had asked me to baptize them on the Feast of the Assumption, but I postponed it till Christmas, so that they might be better prepared. But on the 17th of September the heathens suddenly and without any provocation on the part of the family surrounded the house, broke in the doors, seized the father and son, bound them, hung them up by the arms and beat them for a long time with all sorts of instruments. On the following day they came again to our catechumen and demanded that he renounce his religion or they would subject him to the worst torments. On his decided refusal to apostatize they again seized him (during the night he had sent his son to a distant Christian village), hung him up again and scourged him unmercifully. After he had suffered the torture for an hour they unbound him and went off. One would think that this had been cruelty enough. But not so—on the third day they came again and commanded the catechumen to renounce his Faith or prepare for death. The scourged and half crippled man declared with firm resolution that he could never adore their gods and was ready to die. Enraged at this, they furiously rushed upon him, bound him as on the previous days and repeated the torture. Some beat him with bamboo staves, others struck him with iron tools, others assailed him with bricks and tiles until he lost consciousness. The murderers then cut his bonds, leaving him on the floor for dead and fled, frightened at their own crime. After a few hours the poor dying man— shall we not call him martyr?—showed signs of life, but could utter no intelligible word, and gave up his soul to God six hours after the torture. Surely God received him into His favor, and the blood which he poured out for his Faith supplied for the water of baptism."

In the same year the heathens put to death a most zealous catechist in the province of Sze-Chuen. Through his efficacious zeal some thousands had been converted to Christianity.[206] He was slain in front of the church, receiving more than a hundred knife-blows. Before his last breath he once raised himself as far as he could, tried to fold his hands on his breast and cried: "My God, I thank Thee for the grace of being permitted to die a martyr near the house of God I helped to build. My God, forgive my sins, I place my soul in Thy hands." With these words his noble soul made its flight to heaven.

The examples cited, which might be increased by many others, are sufficient to show that in China there was no want of steadfast and joyful martyrs during the nineteenth century.

KOREA

41. The soil of Korea has drunk deep of the martyr's blood. And the blood of martyrs flows only from heroic hearts in which pulses a supernatural life.

Korea offers a rare example in the fact that her Christianity found entrance not through foreign priests, but through native teachers.[207] Toward the end of the eighteenth century some Chinese manuscripts on the Christian religion fell into the hands of a few Korean philosophers. They were astonished at the clearness and beauty of the doctrine set forth in these writings. In 1783 one of them went with one of his followers to Pekin, where he became acquainted with Christians, received instruction, and was baptized. On his return he administered holy Baptism to his friends, and these soon became zealous apostles of the new doctrine. There were many persons of high

rank among the new Christians, so that the young
Christian community soon attracted the notice of the
court, which began to oppose it by means of penalties.
But these measures were of little avail. The Koreans
seemed to have a predilection for Christianity. The
heroic death in 1791 of two young doctors of letters,
Paul Jun and James Kuën, both of noble descent,
excited veneration for Christianity and won many
adherents in spite of prisons, exile and death.

Yet it was a flock without a shepherd—their number is said to have been over four thousand—they had
received only the sacrament of Baptism and were but
imperfectly instructed. No priest had so far set foot
on Korean soil. At last, in 1794, the young Chinese
priest James Tsiu[208] (Tjyu) came over the border in
disguise. The joy of the Christians was indescribable,
and they brought the Lord's messenger to Seoul, the
capital of the country. Now at last they could partake
in all the graces of Christianity, and their zeal grew
and their numbers increased. But the government was
soon on the priest's track. Those who had given him
support or lodging were punished with death. For
five years James Tsiu continued to perform the duties
of his office with unwearying zeal. But in 1801 he fell
into the hands of the persecutors and was beheaded
on May 31 in Seoul.[2]

42. With him many others obtained the martyr's
palm, among them persons of high rank. Of these
were: Josaphat Kim-Kensiuni,* a young man of twenty-six, belonging to one of the first families in the land.
He was beheaded at Seoul the day after Father Tsiu.
His family considered itself disgraced by him and
deprived him after his death of his title and his privi-
leges; the doctor of letters, Ambrose Kuën, who was
lying wounded in prison; the highly cultured August

*The spelling of Korean proper names varies in different
reports.

Tieng, who enjoyed a most distinguished reputation; and his son Charles, a young man of twenty; Aloysius Ni-Tanueni, who had made many conversions among the country people; Augustine Niu-Hang with many members of his family—among them his daughter-in-law Lutgard, who with her husband had embraced a life of continence after their marriage, and many others. Two princesses were put to death by poisoning. The noble lady Columba Kang, who had rendered great service to the young Christian community, was executed on October 4, 1801, with four other Christians. Her stepson Philip soon after suffered the same fate.

The accounts also tell us of very many apostasies. This is not to be wondered at, since there had been no regular pastoral care of the Christians. James Tsiu was the only priest in Korea, and during his five years there could labor only under the greatest precautions. We ought rather be surprised that Christianity had already struck its roots so deep that the converts were striving after the Christian ideal with so much zeal, and were glad to be permitted to suffer for Christ. The cruelty of Korean tortures far surpasses all imagining. How often it is related that the confessors died in consequence of excessive torture! And then a horrible imprisonment; cold, tormenting hunger and thirst, filth and vermin, contagious disease were to be expected by those who, half dead and covered all over with wounds, were brought to prison from the torture. Even many who were regarded as zealous Christians had not the strength to remain steadfast under all these afflictions. Indeed, their apostasy was in great part only exterior.

43. After the death of James Tsiu, thirty-five years passed by before any priest could get into Korea again. In the meantime Christianity made continual progress in spite of constant persecution. Banishment and exe-

cutions were not infrequent, and it is deeply touching to read how zealous was the shepherdless flock and how they sent letters to the bishop of Pekin and to the Holy Father begging them to send priests.

In 1815 measures against the Christians were again made more severe. At Morai-san lived a zealous Christian named Alexis Kim-Sioui, who was a cripple and earned his livelihood as copyist.[209] On Easter, 1815, many Christians were seized in Morai-san. Hearing this, Alexis began to weep aloud. "What are you crying for?" asked a servant belonging to the tribunal. "I, too, am a Christian," said Alexis, "but since I am a cripple they do not care to arrest me, and this is why I weep." "Oh, if that is your wish, you can nicely come along with us." Beaming with joy the poor cripple joined the ranks of the shackled crowd. He would not be overlooked in heaven as he had been on earth. He was brought to Tai-ku, the chief town of the province, bore all the tortures unshaken and answered with great cleverness the judge who jeered at his belief in a crucified God. After two months in prison he was freed from his sufferings by death.

Among those imprisoned at Tai-ku Andrew Kim-Kiei took the part of a leader.[210] Having led a sort of hermit's life before this time and being practised in all exercises of piety, he knew well how to rouse the courage of the others. He changed the prison almost into a religious house, so that even the heathens admired the behavior of the prisoners. When Andrew was brought to Tai-ku there met him before the tribunal a woman who had just been set free. Andrew asked her what it meant. "I have denied my Faith," was the dejected answer. "But you have lost your finest opportunity," said the confessor. "What have you now to hope for if you die? Certainly you are now free, but how many years will you live?" "I am free, it is true, but how can I know whether I shall die to-day or to-morrow?" "Very well," replied Andrew, "then is it not a thousand times better to choose a good death to-day?" He soon succeeded in persuading her so that she repented the false step and desired to make all right again. Although the bailiffs insulted her, buffeted her, and thrust her back, she went on with Andrew to the tribunal. "What are you coming back here for?" inquired the judge. "I have already set you free." "So it was," she replied. "I was so weak in bearing the torture that I denied my God and so committed a dreadful sin. I repent of it, and therefore I have returned. Kill me if you will. I am now more a Christian than I was before." The mandarin treated her as a fool and chased her out, but she returned and with a louder voice again retracted her apostasy. This time they bound her and beat her so terribly that pieces of flesh were torn from her body, and while they were carrying her back to the prison she died.

Andrew was obliged to languish in prison for more than a year, and then, with six other Christians, he was beheaded. Among them were two women. A last attempt was made to shake their constancy on the place of execution after the heads of the five men had fallen. "Only a word from you," concluded the warning of the mandarin, "and you are safe." "How can you be so inconsistent?" said one of the women. "According to you the men must honor God as their Most High Father, but not the women. Do not waste words. I expect to be treated according to the law." "If Jesus and Mary call us and invite us to heaven," said both, "how can we apostatize and, to save this temporal life, lose true life and eternal happiness?" In a few moments both were in possession of the true life.

The following year also witnessed many courageous and inspiring martyrdoms.

44. Finally, the French missionary, Venerable Peter Maubant, and soon after him the Venerable James Chastan succeeded in entering Korea in 1836. In December, 1837, the vicar-apostolic appointed for Korea, Venerable Lawrence Imbert, arrived also. The activity of these self-sacrificing missionaries gave the Catholic movement new life, but it soon brought on the severest persecution of all. The government set a high price on the heads of foreign priests and the imprisonment and executions of native Christians increased from day to day. Monsignor Imbert fell into the power of his enemies in 1839. From prison he sent word to his two companions and asked them to surrender voluntarily to the court of justice. He hoped thus to put an end to the cruel slaughter of so many Christians. Both missionaries made the heroic sacrifice and voluntarily presented themselves before the astonished judges. Before going they sent a farewell letter to the Paris Mission Seminary. In it they say:[211]

"To-day, September 6, a second order from Monsignor Imbert arrived. He tells us to prepare ourselves for martyrdom. We have the consolation of setting out after having once more and for the last time celebrated the Holy Sacrifice. What a joy it is to be able to say with St. Gregory: *'Unum ad palmam iter; pro Christo mortem appeto'* (only the path to the palm now; I desire to die for Christ). If we have the happiness of obtaining this noble palm *'quæ dicitur suavis ad gustum, umbrosa ad requiem, honorabilis ad triumphum'* (which is sweet to taste, spreading shade for rest, and honorable for triumph); then thank the Divine Goodness a thousand times for it and forget not to send help to our poor neophytes who again become orphans. If the joy we feel at the moment of departure could be diminished it would be at the thought of having to leave such zealous neophytes of whom we have been pastors for three years and who love us as the Galatians loved St. Paul. But we depart for a feast too great to permit the feeling of grief an entrance into our hearts." Truly these men were worthy of a martyr's crown. On September 29, 1839, after the usual trial and tortures they were executed along with their bishop at the gates of Seoul.

45. The tyrants now raged furiously against the shepherdless flock. The reports give us a multitude of touching scenes of steadfastness and joy in martyrdom. We can not help shuddering when we read what John Tsoi[212] had to suffer. No torture that Korean cruelty could devise was omitted. They hanged him for half a day by the feet, beat him during a whole night till he was unconscious and his body was one great wound, so that the entrails were partly exposed and his bones crushed, and through it all the confessor remained calm and cheerful, thinking only of becoming like to his crucified Saviour. On October 6, 1839, his head fell under the executioner's axe. He was twenty-nine years old.

How God strengthened and consoled the martyrs is shown by the words of Barbara, wife of the catechist, Augustine Pak.[213] While she was languishing in prison with her husband and had already endured many torturings, she said: "Formerly I trembled when I only heard men speak of martyrdom. But the Holy Ghost has deigned to give a great grace to a sinner such as I am. I have no longer any fear and am filled with gladness. I had no thought that the reality would be so easy." She awaited the deathblow with eagerness and counted on her fingers the days before her execution.

When Joseph Nim-Kun[214] groaned under the excruciating torture of the distortion of his limbs, the executioners said to him: "If you let me hear you groan again I shall take it as a sign of apostasy." Joseph overcame his natural weakness and did not permit a groan to escape him till he became unconscious. The moment they brought him among the other prisoners he awoke, smiled and said: "I do not know whether I suffered much. I felt nothing," and soon he began to console the others and to care for their wounds. But he had still great sufferings to bear before he won his crown.

Protasius Tsieng-Kuk[215] had, in consequence of his terrible sufferings in prison, the misfortune of denying his Faith, but he had scarcely returned to his home when he realized his error. Day and night he bewailed his sin and could not rest until he could again present himself before the tribunal. They would not admit him, but at length he managed to attract the attention of the mandarin. The latter was furious at his retraction and had him so beaten that he died the night following in prison.

In like manner many others made amends for their apostasy by a renewed confession of Faith.

46. The martyrdom of Peter Niu-Tai, a boy of thirteen, who in many ways resembles Saints Pancratius and Venantius, created the greatest astonishment.[216] He was the son of a martyr, but his mother and sister were obstinate heathens who made it a real martyrdom for him at home. The boy desired to follow the example of his father and presented himself to the mandarin as a Christian. No tortures were spared to intimidate the courageous boy and to weaken his strength. One day a guard used his copper whistle as a hatchet and hacked out a piece of flesh from the upper part of the boy's thigh. "Now will you remain a Christian?" was the mocking question. "Quite surely," replied Peter; "there is nothing that will prevent me." Then the demon took up a glowing coal and ordered the child to open his mouth. Without hesitation Peter opened his mouth as wide as he could. But the monster at the last moment desisted, frightened by the devilishness of

his own act. The young confessor was examined fourteen times and each time tortured. Besides this he received six hundred strokes of the rod and forty heavy
blows with a broommaker's tool. His body was one
wound, his bones were broken and shreds of flesh hung
loose upon him, yet all this could not disturb the look of
calm and joy upon his countenance. He seemed to
laugh at his wounds and even took hold of loose hanging strips of flesh and tore them off as if they did not
belong to his body. Did God relieve him of the feeling
of pain? It surely seemed so. The executioners themselves were amazed, though they were furious at his
fortitude. They say what a powerful impression this
spectacle would make on all, and so, not daring to
behead the boy publicly they strangled him in
prison.

A young girl, Anastasia Ni-Pong-Keumi, not yet
twelve years old, also put heathen cruelty to shame.[217]
At first they tried only to scare the brave child with
threats. Anastasia's mother, who was likewise a prisoner for the Faith, now used every means to encourage
her daughter's constancy. Once the mother, pretend-
ing, said: "I am almost sure you will surrender." The
little girl denied it energetically. "But if they merely
show you the instruments of torture you will give way,
for you have not the strength to stand firm." Anastasia asserted her firm will all the more. "Well, we
shall see what you can do," concluded her mother.
Anastasia proved herself right. At first the executioners avoided torturing the weak and innocent child,
but tried everything likely to change a child's heart.
They would have been contented with even a doubtful admission that could be construed into an apostasy before the judge. But no such word was uttered
and even the torture could not shake her firmness. To
avoid a sensation they secretly strangled her. Her
mother soon shared with her the martyr's crown.

Barbara Ni was in her fourteenth year when she died in prison from her sufferings under the torture.[218]

47. The great veneration of the young Korean Christians for virginity is very surprising. Before these days this virtue was absolutely unknown in Korea. According to the custom of the country an unmarried woman had no right to protection. For this reason many had to resist even their Christian relatives if they desired to remain virgins. It was much worse if part of the family was heathen, or if there were a heathen suitor. The acts inform us of many instances in which virgins could save themselves only by flight from their father's house. It was the great insecurity of their lives that taught Christians thus to appreciate the value of imperishable goods. Many of these heroines suffered death for Christ.

We have already mentioned Lutgard, who from her prison wrote triumphantly to her mother that she and her husband, John Niu-Hang, had vowed virginity on the first day of their marriage and that now, after a happy life of four years together, they were together to receive the martyr's palm.

When Julietta Kim-Si was seventeen her parents wished her to marry.[219] She knew no other way of helping herself than to have her head shaved smooth and thus be beforehand in repelling every suitor. Later she died a virgin martyr.

Most glorious and wonderful is the martyrdom of the two sisters Columba and Agnes Kim.[220] They were five times put to the rack and beaten with heavy staves. No groan of pain escaped them, only the names of Jesus and Mary passed their lips, and they appeared to be filled with joy. Angered at this, the judge, who ascribed it to witchcraft, had some symbols cut in their backs to dispel the charm. Then he gave them thirteen stabs with a red hot awl. The sisters did not seem to feel it. He now asked them why they had not chosen a husband before this. Columba was twenty-six and Agnes twenty-four. The elder sister answered that in the eyes of Christians virginity was a state of perfection and they had chosen it to please God the more. The shameless judge determined to rob them of this virtue they prized so highly. He first had them scourged by the bailiffs, who meanwhile uttered the most filthy language that could come from corrupt hearts. Then he ordered the two heroines to be taken into the prison of common criminals and delivered to these lecherous ruffians. But Our Lord did not abandon His loyal brides. He bestowed on them a superhuman strength so that each one seemed stronger than ten of the lewd crowd which they successfully kept way from them. The men at length were stricken with a great awe of these unconquerable virgins and gave up the attack. For two whole days the two sisters were obliged to remain with this horrible company, and then were brought to the prison of the women. After new tortures and further imprisonment both won the twofold crown of martyrdom and virginity.

In like manner triumphed the virgins: Agatha Tsien, whose most wicked enemy was her heathen brother; Lucy Kim-Panmul, who had vowed her virginity to God when she was fourteen; Mary Ouen; Elizabeth Tieng; and others. One discovers remarkable resemblances to the acts of the early martyrs.

48. In 1846 fell the head of the first native Korean priest, the heroic Andrew Kim. His father Ignatius and many other relatives had died for the Faith. Andrew, with two other boys, was sent to Macao by the missionary Father Maubant to study for the priesthood. It was chiefly due to their resoluteness that in 1845 Monsignor Joseph Ferriol and Antoine Daveluy were able to enter Korea with them. Only a year was spared to him for the preaching of the Gospel to his countrymen.

The process of beatification is in progress for more than eighty of the martyrs of this glorious period of the Church in Korea.

49. The persecution gradually lost its sanguinary character. Christians increased rapidly. But in 1866 the storm broke out afresh. This time it seemed it would not cease until the last Christian was gone from Korea. In the first year fell the heads of the two vicars-apostolic, Monsignor Simeon Berneux and Monsignor Antoine Daveluy, and of the seven missionaries—Peter Dorie, Simon de Bretenières, Bernard Beaulieu, Charles Pourthié, Michael Petitnicolas, Peter Aumaître and Martin Huin. Only three missionaries escaped the toils of the persecutors. A dreadful slaughter of Christians began. Again we behold multitudes gladly suffering torture, prison, and death for Christ.

Along with the two missionaries Pourthié and Petit-nicolas were beheaded an old man and a youth, Mark Tieng and Alexis Ou, both ornaments of the Church in Korea.[221] Mark Tieng, a descendent of a noble family and professor of Chinese, was an accidental witness of the martyrdom of the Venerable Imbert, Maubant, and Chastan in 1839. The calmness and cheerfulness with which the martyrs received the death-blow were to him incomprehensible. It made him curious about the doctrines of Christianity. He bought books about it and soon the work of grace was complete. On account of his learned training he was made catechist in Seoul. Here he gave inestimable service to the mission and not least by his noble example in practising works of charity toward the neighbor. Every one considered him a saint. Monsignor Berneux used to say that he would be glad to exchange places in heaven with Mark Tieng. The executioners were aware of Tieng's great influence among the Christians, so they tortured him with a double cruelty, as they expressly avowed. The death of this old man of seventy-three was as edifying as his life.

Alexis Ou was the son of a doctor of letters, and because of his talent was educated by his father with especial care. In 1863, after he had finished his studies, he met a catechist, and from him learned for the first time something of the Christian religion. As soon as its truth and beauty became clear to his mind it filled his young heart with enthusiasm. He had now to sustain a bitter struggle with his family. Hitherto the favorite of his father, he was now obliged daily to suffer insults, ill-treatment, and blows. They finally gave him to understand that it would be well for him if he nevermore crossed the threshold of his father's house. Alexis went to Seoul and found welcome with Mark Tieng. By his patient suffering and his prayers he effected the conversion of his whole family. At the outbreak of the persecution his father called him back and desired to be instructed. Not less than twenty persons were there, ready to receive Baptism, and soon afterward his father died a Christian death. Alexis could not remain long unknown to the persecutors. At the first trial he suffered the torture of the rack and his bones were laid bare with wounds, but at the second trial in a moment of weakness there escaped him a sign of surrender and he was immediately set free. He had hardly left the tribunal, however, when tears of repentance poured from his eyes. "Woe to me," he said, "I am lost. To whom shall I now confess and obtain forgiveness?" He knew that the priests were all in prison. He quickly made his determination, bound up his wounds, took horse and started for Seoul. They tried to keep him back, but he replied: "Let me go before it be too late. I will confess my sins in the capital, where I am known to the Christians and all shall be witness of my infamy and my repentance." In Seoul he wished to stop at

Mark Tieng's, but found the house beset by the officers. Then and there he declared aloud that he was a Christian, was apprehended, and to his joy was brought to the prison in which was confined Monsignor Berneaux, who had baptized him scarcely three years before. Strengthened by sacramental absolution and the consoling words of the bishop, he now heroically suffered much more grievous pains than before. "Young man, you have only to say one word as you once did and your life is saved," they told him. "Oh, at such a price I would not live," was his decided answer, and even as bravely as the missionary and the old man he went to the place of execution and bowed his young neck to the sword of the executioner.

The accounts give many more examples showing the heroism of the martyrs of this period. The process for the declaration of the martyrdom of a considerable number of confessors is already in progress.

50. Another period of years passed before new missionaries found entrance into Korea. At the end of 1877, Monsignor Ridel crossed the boundary, but in January, 1878, he was languishing in prison. It pains the heart to read what the bishop relates of the treatments and sufferings of his companions, and yet it needed only the word of denial of the Faith to be freed from all these tortures. Certainly the human will possessed not of itself the strength to remain steadfast through these long sufferings.

Monsignor Ridel, who was transported to China in 1878, writes from prison of a striking example of desire of martyrdom.[222] A young man of twenty, named Pak, voluntarily announced himself a Christian and the son of a martyr. "I have heard," he said, "that you have imprisoned the bishop, my master, and other Christians. Well, I, too, am a Christian from my infancy. You were not fortunate enough to catch me, so I offer myself of my own free will. You put my father and mother to death in 1868. I was then ten years old, but my heart has kept their counsels. I adore God, the Creator of heaven and earth, who rules and governs all things, who gives us support and sustains our life. He has suffered for me, and I will suffer for Him. I long for the rack. I hunger and thirst for sufferings. If my arms and legs be broken in pieces my life belongs to God." They looked upon him as an idiot and drove him away. But he returned, and the judge gave orders to put him with the other prisoners. We can not but remember the desire of Ignatius of Antioch to be consumed for Christ. At last, after 1880, the Christians were no longer outlawed.

The history of the Korean persecutions forms one of the most noble and glorious pages in the history of the Catholic Church. We can readily agree with the martyr-bishop Daveluy when he writes: "I am convinced that the history of the martyrs of Korea will be an astonishing revelation of Divine omnipotence and goodness."[223]

JAPAN

51. The Christian communities of Japan which, in spite of laws hostile to their Faith and the strictest seclusion from Europe, remained true to that Faith without bishops or priests for more than two hundred years, were obliged in the nineteenth century to give new proof of their constancy.[224] It is certain that a series of executions took place at the beginning of the century. In 1856 a persecution again broke out at Nagasaki. Ten of the confessors died in prison as a result of maltreatment. The rest, who after two years were set free, were so broken by sufferings they endured that they did not long survive.

In 1859 Japan opened to Europeans a few ports, and in these numerous missionaries soon took up their residence. In 1865 they discovered near Nagasaki the remnants of the Christian communities which had formerly suffered through sanguinary persecutions. From 1867 to 1873 the ancient hatred of Christians once more blazed forth. It was particularly directed at the native Christians. At first every sort of annoyance was made use of to prevent them from practising their religion, but it finally passed into imprisonment and the torture. Cruel treatment in the prisons brought release to many by a speedy death. Out of one hundred and ten prisoners from Omura, for instance, seventy died during one year. The victims of Fusakasima, about two hundred in number, were so closely crowded together that they could only stand upright. A catechist was, like St. Laurence, placed on a red hot gridiron. He remained steadfast and was able to say to his family: "Let us implore together the grace of remaining loyal to Our Lord. No matter what happens to me let it console you . . . even if my body is only one great wound . . . for my pain is less than you can imagine. God is giving me assistance."

Later on they proceeded to transport the male population—especially from the valley of Urakami, near Nagasaki, where very many Christians dwelt—to a distant island. Here they suffered the extremest privations and were condemned to the hardest forced labor and driven to the pagoda with the lash. In Iwano, out of sixteen so deported, eleven died in a very short time. They were stripped of their clothing, bound hand and foot, and thrown out on a frozen pond. The only nourishment they had was some spoiled fruit once a day. Finally the women and children also were banished from Urakami.

Yielding to the influence of European diplomacy, the Japanese government at the beginning of 1873 permitted the surviving confessors to return to their homes and live according to their Faith.

Uganda

52. A heroic and joyful martyrdom for faith and morals was endured in 1886 by a band of young men in the kingdom of Uganda in Equatorial Africa.[225] Mwanga, who at the age of eighteen became king in 1884, at first showed favor to the Christian religion and permitted the return of the missionaries who had been banished from the country by the hostility of his father Mtesa. The people seemed all ready to accept Christianity. But the prime minister, a fanatical heathen, succeeded in filling the heart of the king with anger against Europeans and hatred for the Christian religion. One of the chief officers of the court, Joseph Mkasa, a zealous Christian and a former confidant of the king, happened to contradict the latter in some slight matter. He was soon to pay for his hardihood with his life. In the service of Mwanga, who was a pagan, there were many Christians especially among the pages. The missionaries gave high praise to the chief page, Charles Luanga, a young man of twenty, who possessed great influence over his comrades and used it to inspire their hearts with love for Christian doctrine. The capricious king, urged on by his evil demon, soon began to nurse anger against his pages because they professed a religion other than his. His anger was increased, as Monsignor Livinhac writes, because they energetically refused to commit with him that sin for which God destroyed Sodom with fire and brimstone, and he proceeded to vent his fury upon them without delay.

The first victim of Mwanga's rage was the young page Denis Sebuggwao, who was explaining the catechism to one of his companions when the king happened to meet him on an evening walk. "What are you doing there?" asked Mwanga. "I am instructing my friend in catechism," answered Denis. This roused the irritated monarch to fury. "Wait; I will drive out your impudence," he cried, and drove his spear through the little catechist.

This was the signal for a general persecution of the Christians. That same night, May 25, 1886, the king held a council of war with his prime minister and determined on the annihilation of the native Christians. Next morning all exits from the king's house were closed. The pages of Charles Luanga's division were the first to appear before the king. He reprimanded them severely and said: "Those who pray shall stand on this side." At once Luanga with the little catechumen Kizito by the hand sprang to the place indicated. All the rest who were Christians followed his example. At a sign from the king the bailiffs leaped upon the young confessors and bound them fast to one another so that they could scarcely walk. "I still see," wrote Father Laurdel, who that morning went boldly to the palace, "the young Kizito laughing at the strange situation and submitting himself to be led to prison with as cheerful a mien as if he were going out with his companions to play." Then another division of pages was summoned, among whom there were likewise some Christians. These shared the lot of the first division. There were about twenty of them between the ages of eighteen and twenty. Kizito was the son of one of the chief officials of the kingdom. He had besieged the missionaries with petitions for Baptism and would not leave them until they had appointed a day for it. But the boy was not to live to that day, and received the longed-for water of regeneration in prison the night before his martyrdom.

Charles Luanga, whom they had separated from the rest so as to be able to effect their apostasy the more easily, was the first to obtain the palm of martyrdom. They burned him with a slow fire, beginning at his feet. The executioners said mockingly: "Now let your God come and free you from the fire." The martyr calmly replied: "You poor blinded men, you do not know what you are saying. At this moment it is as if you were pouring water over my body, but the God whom you now insult will one day cast you into fire that will really burn." Without a groan the steadfast youth endured his dreadful martyrdom.

The three youngest of the pages, Simeon Sebuta, Denis Kaminka, and Uélabé, still catechumens, excited the compassion of the executioner, who had never put such innocent children to death. He said to them: "You have only to declare that you will not pray any more and the king will release you." "We shall pray as long as we live," was the resolute answer. The official, hoping that the sight of the dying torments of the others would terrify them, had them conducted to the hill opposite Rubaga, where the cruel scene was to be enacted.

Here there was a great heap of dried rushes. The executioner made bundles of these, and in each bound one of the pages. When Simeon Sebuta saw that no bundle was prepared for him, he cried out: "Where is my bundle? The others have one and I must have mine." So the three boys had to be bound up in rushes like the others, but were put on one side. When all the bundles were ready they were piled in a heap.

Among the victims was the son of the chief executioner, Mbaga Tuzindé. The unhappy father used every effort to obtain a word from his son that could be construed as an apostasy. But in vain. The preparations for the burning did not impress the boy, and he suffered himself to be tied into one of the bundles without a word. At the last moment his father made another attempt. "My son, permit me at least to hide you secretly. They will not notice it." "Father," answered the son, "I will not be hidden. You are the servant of the king. He has commanded you to kill me. If you do not you will bring trouble upon yourself. I wish to spare you this. I know the reason for my death. It is my religion. Father, put me to death." To save his son at least from the frightful death by fire, the official ordered one of his servants to kill him with a heavy blow on the neck with a club. The body was again wrapped in rushes and laid with the rest.

They now set fire to the bundles, beginning at the feet of the victims. They wished to burn them as slowly as possible, hoping that excessive pain might cause them to abjure. But to no effect. When the flames encircled the living sheaves, the brave confessors began with loud voice to pray together. After half an hour there was nothing left but a heap of ashes with the half consumed bodies.

The three youngest still remained, contemplating the smoking remains of their companions and waiting impatiently for their own martyrdom. "Only be quiet," said the officers, "we will finish the feast with you if you remain obstinate, but if you renounce your religion we will save you." The executioner now used every endeavor to change the hearts of the three boys. It was a mystery to him that young people full of gladsome life could show such contempt for death. His eloquence failed, but he could not find it in his heart to give these innocent heroes to the flames. He had them taken from the bundles and brought back to prison. The pages were inconsolable. Their dearest hope was frustrated. "Why will you not put us to death?" they said to the officials. "We are Christians like the rest and they have been burned. We have not denied our Faith and we never will. And it is all useless for us to be spared any longer." But the executioner was deaf to their imploring prayers. It seemed that it was God's will to leave these three confessors alive so that later they could testify as eye-witnesses to the glorious end of their admirable comrades. The chief executioner

excused his conduct to the king, saying that he had
hopes of soon bringing the three young pages to their
senses. Mwanga reprimanded him, but gave him no
command to put them to death. They remained steadfast and even persuaded their jailer to accept the Christian Faith.

We involuntarily ask ourselves what it is that gave
such strength to young people who were but newly converted and at an age when the passions are developing,
that they withstood the demands of a lascivious king
and maintained so great a desire for the crown of martyrdom and virginity. The beatification process of this
noble band is already far advanced and also of another
list of their countrymen who died for the Faith at that
time.* The latter also gave striking proof of their
fortitude. Mathias Murumba, formerly a Mohammedan, after his baptism in 1882 had led an exemplary
life.[226] At the outbreak of the persecution he was
dragged before the heathen tribunal. "Is this
Murumba," asked the judge, "that in his old age has
accepted the Christian religion?" "Yes, it is I." "Why
do you pray?" "Because I desire to pray." "You
have sent away all your wives. Do you prepare your
meals well by yourself?" "Am I cited on account of
my leanness or on account of my religion?" "Take
him out and kill him." "That is just what I desire."
"Cut off his hands and feet," cried the judge furiously,
"then cut a slice of flesh from his back and fry it before
his eyes. Your God," continued the judge, laughing
contemptuously, "will free you?" "Yes, indeed,"

*Die Kath. Missionen, 1909-10, 176 sq.—The Decree of the
Sacred Congregation of Rites for Aug. 14, 1912, gives the follow-
ing twenty-two names: Dionysius Sebuggwao, Carolus Luanga,
Bruno Séronkuma, Mgagga, Gonzaga Gonza, Mathias, Murumba,
Andreas Kagwa, Noe Maaggali, Josephus Mkasa Pontianus
Mgodwé, Athanasius Badzekuketta, Jacobus Buzabaliao, Kizito,
Ambrosius Kibuka, Kyavira, Achilles Kiwanuka, Adulphus
Rudigo Mkasa, Mkasa Kilwanwu, Anatolius Kiligawajjo, Mbaga
Tuzindé, Lucas Banabakintu, Joannes Maria Mzée.

replied Mathias, "God will free me, but you will not see how He does it. He will take my soul from you and leave in your hands only the dead husks."

With brave step and beaming with joy, Mathias followed the executioner to the place of execution. They led along with him to death his friend Luke Banabakintu. The shocking sentence of the judge was carried out. They struck off Murumba's hands and feet, cut pieces of flesh from his back and broiled them before his eyes. The martyr suffered all this without a groan. To prolong his torture the executioners bound up his mutilated members to stop the flow of blood. After three days his soul fled to heaven. His friend Luke was beheaded at one blow.

One of the most influential among the Christians was Andrew Kagwa, formerly counselor of the king and said to have had chief command over the army. The prime minister took occasion to accuse him of his Christianity before the king. A few hours later Andrew stood before the judge and his head fell under the sword of the executioner. Short shrift was likewise given to the soldier James Buzabaliao, who had attempted to persuade the king himself to accept the Christian Faith.

The young man Noe Maaggali was slain with spears for his Faith by emissaries of the king in the house of Mathias Murumba. During the looting of the house, Noe's sister Mary Matilda, unmarried and still a catechumen, hid herself, but when she saw what was happening she presented herself before the band of plunderers and said: "You have slain my brother because he prayed. I pray as he did, so kill me too." The men were astounded at such a petition and their leader bade them not to kill her, but to take her with them as prisoner. The heathen judge was charmed by Matilda's bold courage and admirable qualities, and hearing that she was unmarried sought to save her so that he might afterward make her his wife. But the young woman answered: "I am not here to look for a husband, but to die for my religion." Yet the judge would have compassion on her and forbade the announcement of her arrest to the king. He managed to have her brought secretly to the missionaries and put in a safe hiding-place.

After a year Mwanga's fury seemed to have disappeared. He could not but see that Christians were becoming more numerous the more he raged against them. To-day Uganda is the pride of the missionaries. In no other mission country is a universal tendency toward Christianity, reception of the Sacraments, and especially toward the spiritual life as marked here.[227]

Massacre at Damascus

53. During the frightful massacre by the Mussulmans at Damascus in 1860 thousands of Christians were slaughtered. The majority of these were given a choice only between death and apostasy. An eye-witness gives some examples of heroic fortitude.[228] "The grand sheik Abdallah-el-Halebi sent two Moslems to Francis Mussa Becki, a wealthy Christian. Two months before he had loaned one hundred and sixty thousand francs to Abdallah. The two assassins demanded from the venerable old man either apostasy or death. 'Let Abdallah keep my money,' he replied, 'but leave me my Faith. I can not deny my God. From Him I have learned not to fear those who can kill my body, but rather him who can destroy both body and soul.' Then he fell upon his knees and began a prayer. He ended it in heaven, for a blow of the sword struck off his head.

"An old man of eighty was commanded to become a Mussulman. Like St. Polycarp, he answered, 'I have served Jesus Christ for eighty years. At the end of my life I will not desert Him.' These noble words were his last on earth.

"The following incident shows to what a degree the fury of a Moslem can go. A Turk who was in his death agony heard that the Christians were being slaughtered. His vitality seemed to revive. As a last favor he desired that a shackled Giaour (Christian) be brought to where he lay. A Christian was dragged thither. 'Dog, renounce your Faith.' 'Never!' The furious Mohammedan raised himself, placed a pistol against the Christian's forehead and killed him. Then he sank back and a few moments later was a corpse.

"A mother, hard pressed by the persecutors, tried to escape with her five children in the general tumult. They caught her and asked if she would apostatize with her children. 'We are and we remain Christians,' was her answer. They compelled the unfortunate mother to sit down and used her knee as a block for the beheading of her children. Streaming with the blood of her little ones and fainting with pain she sank unconscious on the ground. The brutes revived her with cold water and again asked her to apostatize. She shook her head and her last child was destroyed before her eyes. Then she herself received the saving blow.

"Another time we met a poor mother with her child in her arms. She had disguised herself, but her uneasiness and haste betrayed her. 'Apostasy or death.' 'Then death!' They tore her child from her and nailed it with large nails to a gate. A dagger-stroke killed the mother."

God alone knows how many during those days sealed their faith with their blood.

Many Franciscans who suffered death in Damascus at the time are named in a process of beatification which completed its first stage in 1885. Among them is a Tyrolese, Venerable Father Engelbert Kolland from Ramsau in Zillertal.[229]

Russia

54. The Catholic Church in the empire of the Czar can tell not only of much woe and oppression, but also of heroic steadfastness in the Faith. During the first (1773) as well as the second (1793) partition of Poland, Catherine II solemnly proclaimed full religious freedom to Catholics of both rites (Poles and Ruthenians). What she meant is evidenced by the fact that she forced under the knout about eight millions of the Ruthenians to be incorporated in the Russian Church, closed numberless churches and monasteries and abolished all Ruthenian bishoprics except one. Only death prevented her from wholly annihilating the Ruthenian body. Czar Nicholas I, 1825-1855, thought it belonged to him to complete the work. The Polish insurrection in 1830 gave the desired occasion of including in the persecution the Catholics of the Latin rite. Many churches and monasteries were taken from them, the bishops and priests who remained faithful were sent into exile and condemned to hard labor, and all this to force the people to accept the schism. Russian Catholics fared little better under the successors of Nicholas I. The persecution of the United Ruthenians in the diocese of Chelm under Alexander II is one of the severest in history.[230]

Some scenes from this dissimilar strife will show what superhuman strength was manifested by the brave confessors. Pius IX justly declared on May 17, 1872, that this fortitude was "a spectacle before God and angels and men."

"The still loyal Basilian monasteries were broken up, and the 'obstinate' monks were thrown into subterranean dungeons, while apostates who had gone over to the schism were made their jailers. It went so far that they allowed the heroic confessors to die of hunger, as was the case with Father Slobotski, who was seventy-four years of age. Other priests were shut up in burial vaults by the apostate Bishop Zubko. The persecutors tried to deprive the dead of the people's veneration by spreading the calumny that they had died of drunkenness. Laymen also as well as the priests stood out against the commands of the Synod and died for their Faith. One example out of many will show how they persecuted such 'rebels.' On Monday of Holy Week, 1841, a battalion of infantry, under the leadershp of the under-governor and numerous agents of the police, surrounded the town of Dudakovitz, in the district of Mohilev. The inhabitants were kept without food until Good Friday. Then the town was set on fire and three hundred of the chief people of the town were flogged because they refused to apostatize from the Catholic Faith. Two hours after this barbarous act, all thus beaten were dead.[231].

"Miserable place-hunters, who sought to curry favor with the higher authorities, sought in 1868 to enroll under the schism the Catholics of twelve villages in the Sludski district of the government of Minsk.[232] To this end a district inspector and a clerk went from house to house and wrote down the names of the residents under the pretext that a revision would soon come from Minsk. As a result half of the villagers found to their great surprise that they—four hundred men—were become Russians. They protested and declared in vain that they never thought of denying their Faith. To this day they are counted as orthodox, although they have never set foot in an orthodox church. To make them complain, nine of the most notable were confined in prison for nine months. I here give the names as martyrs and confessors so that they may be handed down to posterity: Michael Shagun; Casimir Chodor; Anton, Peter, Ignatius, and Stephen Kalecinski, the last dying in prison a martyr for his Faith; then Joseph Kanchelechic and Victoria Kanchelechic with her infant child, all from the town of Medwedicz. Since this produced no effect, two hundred men were chosen from the four villages of Poczkan, Kanjuki, Gaslaicin, and Potapowichi and were taken to Podlessia, shut up in a barn, and the following morning were led to the Russian church, where they were to receive Holy Communion. They all refused. Some said they had eaten; others that they had smoked their pipes all night, that they had chewed tobacco; but it was no use. Two policemen held the hands of each; a third the head. Then a blow on the chin, the mouth opened, and the Communion was placed in the mouth of the poor men. . . .

"They would also take the churches away from the Catholics. . . . But the people objected and again four of the principal men were shut up for three weeks. Then Cossacks came to quarter in the village, and they ate up everything and remained so long that there was absolutely nothing left to be squeezed out. The four men were sent to Warsaw for two years, but were pardoned before the end of this time. The Russians could not take possession of the church, however, for the Catholics had left the Blessed Sacrament there, and the Russians did not dare to take it away. And so it is there to this day, although nineteen years have passed. At first the people of the community used to pray before the closed doors until Prince Trubetskoi, governor of Minsk, strictly forbade it.

"In Spicklos the faithful opposed the schismatic clergy and refused to surrender the keys of the church. After a time the chief of the district came with an armed force, installed the clergymen, and with the help of the soldiers forced the community to be present at the service. The quartering of one hundred Cossacks and a heavy fine came next, and the Cossacks withdrew only when at the point of the lance they had procured a petition for one of the schismatic priests. In Polubiecz also they tried to force a schismatic clergyman upon the people. Only one man, who received one hundred lashes, apostatized. A second was beaten to death. A third who guarded the entrance to the church was slain with a lance. A certain Godlenski from Lokovitz was kept nine days on three-quarters of a pound of bread and a quarter of a liter of water in a cold dungeon without light, so that when freed he was almost dead. In Pratulin the troops fired on the people who refused to apostatize. Nine men were killed and four died of their wounds. The brains and hair of one were spattered on the church wall. This heroic deed was performed by a Captain Stein. A young boy, who had been shockingly maltreated, was brought to the hospital. Next day the captain came to see if he was living. The boy thought that they were going to beat him again and said: 'Do what you are ordered. I can only pray that you may kill me.' A woman named Kraiczica was urged to apostatize. When she refused to subscribe they said: 'Subscribe or go to Siberia.' 'I will go to Siberia.' 'Then we take your little child from you.' 'Take it,' she said, and blessing it gave them her child.

"The American consul, Mr. Jewel, informed his minister, Mr. Fish, on February 23, 1874, that the customary allotment of lashes was fifty for men, twenty-five for women and ten for children, but it was increased now so that women often received one hundred blows of the knout. Very many were beaten to death. This happened just a short while ago in the case of a girl who remained loyal to the end. The 'Naska Shisu' (a Russian newspaper) has published the fact that people were often buried up to the neck in the earth. In the village of Uszimow the district chief, Tur, furnished a counterpart of this by driving all the villagers up to their necks in an ice-cold pond. Only when they had stood in the water up to the neck did he allow them to return. Captain Klemenko of

Kurnik surpassed him by making all the villagers stand out in the open air at a temperature of 16° R. (—4° F.) and put them out without any clothing in the wind at night and strictly forbade them to make any movement. The guard of soldiers was relieved every two hours. The same thing was done by Kalinski, district chief of Siedlce. But it was only 12° R. (57° F.), and he avenged himself on the people by allowing the Cossacks to plunder their homes. In Wlodawa the hetman of the Cossacks forced the inhabitants to sign a schismatical declaration. When they refused he had them beaten till the blood flowed, but slowly, and three women died where they were scourged. In the village of Kodnia the people were shut up for three days and three nights in the graveyard. If any one in compassion dared to bring nourishment to the sufferers she was struck down and killed on the spot. In Grodno they threw a mother into a pigsty, took her children away, and baptized them in the orthodox church. Cossacks were everywhere quartered on the so-called 'obstinates,' ate up everything eatable, and what they could not eat they destroyed. A poor man from Viesk told me that they anointed the hoofs of their horses with the best pieces of bacon. If the people had been robbed of everything else, they took not only their cattle, but even their clothing and beds. It came to pass that even the Jews would not buy such things and were punished, because, being merchants by profession, they were declared obliged to buy. The poor people by such plundering and quarterings were brought literally to despair. So it happened that on December 10, 1874, a young farmer of Klodno shut himself up in his barn along with his wife and children and set it on fire. When the fire was extinguished they found his half consumed body kneeling as if in prayer. Nine rubles lying on the table in the house were all he had left.

Leroy-Beaulieu relates that one of his friends saw a mother dash her child against the wall and kill it when they attempted to take it from her to make it a Russian."

How dreadful must their afflictions have been, when the poor people in despair could take such means to save themselves and theirs from the persecutors. Similar scenes were repeated not in isolated places merely, but throughout the whole governments of Minsk, Volhynia, Mohilev, and wherever there were Catholics.

The poor people were plundered of everything— churches, priests, sacraments, property, and political freedom—but in spite of it all they did not desert their Faith. When the year 1905 announced religious toleration, hundreds of thousands streamed back to the ancient Mother Church, who till now had not dared to practise their Faith openly. Unfortunately this toleration was not meant in earnest, and the Russians shortly began again to restrict freedom of conscience. May the day of freedom dawn soon upon this people who have displayed a heroism which reminds us of the days of the Catacombs.

THE PARIS COMMUNE

55. On May 24, 25, and 26, 1871, the archbishop George Darboy, many secular and religious priests and laymen fell victims to the Paris Commune. The process of beatification has been inaugurated in the case of some of these, namely: The Dominicans Father Raphael Captier, Father Bourard, Father Delhorme, Father Cottrault, Father Chatagneret; the Jesuits Father Pierre Olivaint, Father Leo Ducoudray, Father Jean Caubert, Father Alexis Clerc, Father Anatole de Bengy; the priest, Father Mathieu Planchat of the Parisian Vincentian Brothers, and his companions in the Faith.[233]

SPAIN—FATHER FRANCISCO CRUSATS

56. The hatred of Spanish revolutionists for religion gave the martyr's crown to the Servant of God Father Francisco Crusats.[234]. The expulsion of Queen Isabella in 1868 aroused the fanatical instincts of a godless mob in the town of Reus in Catalonia. They determined to take revenge on the missionary who had combated vice and religious indifference with such grand success. On the evening of September 30 the nefarious band rushed against the neighboring town of Selva and stormed the residence of the sons of the Immaculate Heart of Mary. Father Crusats fell into their hands. With diabolical curses and imprecations they struck the missionary and pierced his throat with daggers until he fell unconscious. During this cruel martyrdom Father Crusats prayed God to forgive his enemies. It had long been the desire of his heart to shed his blood for Christ. His manuscript papers are witness to this. He had prepared himself for martyrdom by a holy life. He was greatly loved by his brethren for his ability and his humility. He especially was esteemed by Venerable Anthony Claret,* founder of the Congregation. As a missionary among the people, he contributed greatly to the good reputation of the young Society. He added to it still more by his glorious end. Both clergy and people were persuaded that he died a true martyr.

PERU—FATHER PETER MARIELUX

57. There is a special providence of God safeguarding the secret of confession. Else dejected hearts would fail in courage to seek new strength in the consoling sacrament of Penance. St. John Nepomucene is not the only priest that preferred to suffer all tortures rather than betray the secret of confession. A similar glorious martyrdom occurred on September 23, 1825,

*See page 44 sqq.

in the citadel of Callao in Peru.[235]   It was at the time
of the wars between the Spanish colonies and their
motherland.   The governor Rodil had discovered indications of a conspiracy.   After a brief investigation the
accused were condemned to be shot.   They were permitted to seek reconciliation with God from the military chaplain, Father Peter Marielux, a native Peru-
vian of the Order of St. Camillus de Lellis.   The
suspicious governor, afraid that he had not discovered
all the guilty and observing that the condemned took
their hard lot calmly after going to confession, concluded that Father Marielux had been informed of
all the circumstances of the plot.   In the name of the
king he demanded that the priest name all the persons
who had taken part in the conspiracy.   "My General,"
answered the courageous confessor, "you ask the
impossible.   I will never risk the salvation of my soul
by revealing the secret of any one who comes to me
for confession.   And if the king himself were here
present to give me such an order, God would prevent
me from obeying it.   "Monk," cried the rough soldier, "tell me all or I will have you shot."   "If God
wills my martyrdom," was the calm answer, "may His
holy will be done.   A minister of the altar can never
reveal to any one the secret of confession."   The com-
mandant became furious.   He upbraided the priest as
a traitor to king and fatherland.   "I am loyal to my
king and my flag," replied the priest, "but no one has
a right to demand of me that I become a traitor to my
God.   It is forbidden me to obey you."   Rodil then
called four soldiers and ordered them to level their
muskets at Father Marielux.   A last delay was granted
to give him opportunity to avert the execution of the
death sentence.   "For the last time I command you in
the name of the king to give me the information."
"In the name of God, I refuse to do it," answered the
steadfast martyr.   "Fire!" came the command, and

with several bullets in his breast the victim sank down dead. They could take the priest's life, but they could not take from him the secrets confided to him in confession. These had gone with him to the host of blessed martyrs. The name of Marielux will be a glorious star in the heaven of the saints of the Church.

In many other parts of Europe as well as in lands across the seas hatred of the Church demanded its blood-stained victims. But the examples adduced are sufficient to prove that there dwells in the Church the same power as of old to strengthen her children for heroic martyrdom.

RETROSPECT

A GRAND review of heroes—these favored sons and daughters of the Catholic Church—has passed before our mind. Real heroes of the spirit are they, shining stars lighting for their fellow-men the road to the heights, characters tried in tempests, men of the noblest mind and undreamed-of depths of heart, who felt another's weal and another's woe as if it were their own, souls like pure crystal in which the rays of eternal beauty are mirrored back with most enchanting splendor.

It was a long and illustrious array, but our work can be only incomplete and imperfect. All conditions of men are represented in this hall of fame, priests and religious naturally most of all. But nearly all classes of laymen, too, can show their victors in the glorious combat. No age is wanting, from tender childhood up to old age. Neither the thoughtlessness and passion of youth, nor the cares of life, nor sickness and ill health can hinder the attainment of sanctity.

Neither can sin nor imperfection. That no one may despond because of his own sinfulness Our Lord has in these days of ours lead even to the heights of sanctity those who had not been always loyal to Him. Entanglements of sin, thorn-hedges of deep-rooted defects were to the heroes of the cross only barricades to be conquered on the pathway of light. They were not born saints, they had to struggle to become such. We were able to say only a little of their deeper growth and their interior life, but what we have related will give some insight into the great spiritual struggles of their lives. Some had a hard combat against their natural dispositions. Against others the Evil One was permitted to let loose the whole fury of his hatred for

God and men. Others, again, were the targets of continual mockery and persecution on the part of their fellow-men, often of those from whom they had the best reason to expect assistance, or they were surrounded by every affliction and misery peculiar to the modern world. But they were all bearers of the cross. They did not cast off the burden when it grew too heavy for their shoulders; they were not discouraged, black as might be the night of suffering that spread over them. They said with the Apostle: "I can do all things in Him who strengtheneth me" (Philipp. iv. 13). This dauntless confidence in God was the ever-flowing fountain of their untiring activity and unyielding energy, wherein was hidden the secret of their success. And therefore they remained a mystery to the world.

Miracles and extraordinary favors are not required for personal sanctity. They are the special gifts of God. The lives of many servants of God recorded above know nothing of such extraordinary gifts of grace; and yet God deigns to show that His power of working miracles is as great as in former days, that He is to-day as liberal in dispensing His gifts. Nearly everything we admire in the early saints we meet with in the saints of these days also. We find great wonder-workers among them, men of great prayer who experienced in themselves all that is known to Christian mysticism, souls which here on earth enjoyed a visible intercourse with the inhabitants of heaven. In general it has seemed that God willed to increase the signs of a supernatural world against the increase of infidelity. To instance only one—what century has been the witness of so many extraordinary events as have been seen at the grotto of Lourdes? We read not seldom in the writings of our adversaries that Catholics have nothing that is interior, that they have only exterior ceremonial and submission to a rigid dogma. This is again one of those monstrous assertions which betray a complete ignorance of Catholic life. Indeed, the simple Catholic people possess more warmth of faith and more of the interior life of faith—not to mention the fact that their thoughts, will, and feelings are more penetrated by the truths of faith—than is the case where religious sentiment is at the mercy of subjective freedom of choice in the matter. Such an immersion in the depths of divine truth, such a living participation in the great works of divine love and sympathy with them is altogether unknown to our adversaries. It is no mere fit of feeling, no imaginative ardor. but the effect of facts whose truth is immovably established. Only on such a foundation is a living faith possible. And the faith of our saints was a living faith. It was not an empty word, not a sweet reverie; it was life and deed. They have practised effective charity; they have crucified their flesh with its evil concupiscences; they have with glad hearts made sacrifices for God's cause, sacrifices at which nature shudders; and they have defended this cause with all their powers, even offering their heads to the sword of the executioner for it.

Thus the Church in the nineteenth century has proved herself a true mother of heroes. She is the home of saints. There still lives in her that divine fervor and burning love of poverty with which a St. Francis renewed the face of the earth, that Christian idealism with which a St. Bernard by his words of flame inspired the whole of Europe, that zeal for souls which glowed in a St. Ignatius and a St. Francis Xavier. Camillus de Lellis, Vincent de Paul, and so many other heroes of charity still find zealous imitators. The amiability and kind-heartedness of a Philip Neri are not alien to the modern saint. We meet those also who practise the severest penance after the example of a St. Peter of Alcantara or a John of the Cross. We meet women, too, who seem to rival in their greatness of soul the great saints, Catherine of Siena, Teresa, Elizabeth of Hungary, and Frances de Chantal. Nor has love of the lily of virginal purity disappeared, of which the ancient Doctors of the Church spoke so eloquently, for which the martyrs sacrificed their lives, for which Aloysius exchanged his coronet and all the emoluments of the great ones of earth. Nor is the race of martyrs extinct in the Church. The Christians of the nineteenth century, like their forefathers of the blood-stained amphitheater, knew how to die heroically for their Faith. And finally, the Church is glorified by that tenderest trait of true sanctity, the celestial bloom of interior devotion to the Blessed Virgin. True knowledge of Christ and heartfelt love of Him bring with them of necessity the highest veneration for His holy Mother.

It is a grand review, that of the saints of the nineteenth century who have passed before us. "Star differeth from star in glory" (1 Cor. xv. 41). Stars of various splendor, their true human individualities purified and made glorious in the school of Christ. Sanctity did not destroy their characteristic personalities, but made them nobler. "But if it [the grain of wheat] die, it bringeth forth much fruit" (John xii. 25). Amid their variety shines the great eternal unity, incomparably beautiful, Jesus Christ, the model and fountain-head of their holiness. The view of them makes known to us the son of God revealing Himself constantly and forever living in His Church.

Justly, therefore, does the Vatican Council point out to the world the extraordinary holiness of the Church as a proof that Jesus Christ lives and works in her. The saints of the Church are jewels to be found only in the treasure of the true bride of Christ.

LIST OF NAMES

(Those who have been proposed for beatification and canonization, arranged according to the year of their death)

CONFESSORS

1801. *Didacus of Cadiz,* Bl.
1802. Simon Philippovic, Ven.
  Maria Clotilde of Savoy, Ven.
1803. Aloysius a SSmo. Crucifixo, Ven.
  Jesuald of Reggio, Ven.
1804. Anthony Sylvester Receveur, Ven.
  Francis a Laculibero, Ven.
  Generosus a Premosello, Ven.
1811. Joseph Pignatelli, Ven.
1812. *Aegidius of St. Joseph,* Bl.
  Vincent Morelli, Ven.
1813. Dominic Anthony Galli, Ven.
1815. *Leopold von Gaiche,* Bl.
  Francis Xavier Bianchi, Bl.
  Julie Billiart, Bl.
1820. *Clement Hofbauer,* St.
  Joseph Picot de Cloriviere.
  Felix de Andreis.
  Pauline L. de Pinczon, Ven.
1821. Elizabeth Seton.
1823. Bartholomew Menochio, Ven.
1824. Vincent Strambi, Ven.
  Anna Catharine Emmerich.
1825. Elizabeth Canori Mora, Ven.
1826. Jeanne Antide Thouret, Ven.
  Maria Crucifixa of the Holy Wounds, Ven.
1828. Ignatius Jennaco, Ven.
  Dominic Lentini, Ven.
  John Baptist Jossa, Ven.
1829. Aloysius Solari, Ven.
1830. Magin Catalá.
1831. Vincenzo Romano, Ven.
  Maria Aloysia Maurizi, Ven.
1832. Francis of Ghisoni, Ven.

MARTYRS

1801. James Tsiu and Companions, Martyrs in Korea.
  The Martyrs in Japan.
  Various persecutions in China during nearly the whole century.

1814-1856. *The Seventy-five Blessed Martyrs of Annam and China.*
1815-1880. Almost continuous persecution in Korea.
1820-1841. Persecution of Christians in Annam under Minh-Menh.

1825. Peter Marielux.

1830. Beginning of persecution in Russia.

1833. Bartholomew Capitanio,
    Ven.
1834.   Andrew H. Fournet,
    Ven.
1835 Louis Baudouin, Ven.
    Maddalena of Canossa, Ven.
1836. Nunzio Sulprizio, Ven.
    Maria Christina of Sicily,
    Ven.
1837. *Caspar del Bufalo,* Bl.
    Anna Maria Taigi, Ven.
    John M. Condrin.
1838. Marie Rivier, Ven.
    Elizabeth Bichier des Ages,
    Ven.
1839. Carlo Albini.
1840. *Stephen Bellesini,* Bl.   1840.   *Gabriel Perboyre,* Bl.
    Marcellin Champagnat, Ven.
1841. Francis Mangano, Ven.   1841.   *Pierre Louis Chanel,* Bl.
    Placida Bellanger.
1842. Joseph Benedict Cotto-
    lengo, Ven.
    Paul of Recanati.
1844. Henry Thyssen.
1846. *Marie Madeleine Postel,*
    Bl.
    Anthony Gianelli, Ven.
1847. John Baptist Guarino,   1847. Blase Marmoiton.
    Ven.   1847-1883. Persecution in An-
    Vincenza Gerosa, Ven.   nam under Tüe Dück.
    Marie Lataste.
1848. Anthony Pennacchi, Ven.
1848.   Bernard Mary Clausi,
    Ven.
    Dominic of the Mother of
    God, Ven.
    Vitus Michael di Netta, Ven.
    Louis Pavoni.
1850. Vincent Pallotti, Ven.
    Fortunatus Redolfi.
1851. Placidus Bacher, Ven.
    Anne Marie Javouhey, Ven.
1852.   Francis Mary Paul
    Libermann, Ven.
    Philippine Duchesne, Ven.
    Emilie de Rodat, Ven.
    Teresa Eustochium Verzeri,
    Ven.
1853. Caspar Bertoni, Ven.
    Andrew Ph. Garcia.

1854. John B. Muard, Ven.
Modestinus a Jesu et Maria, Ven.
1855. Adeodata Pisani, Ven.

1855-1862. The seventeen hundred and forty-three Venerable Martyrs of Tonkin.

1856. Lawrence of St. Francis Xavier.
Mother Theodore Guerin.

1856. Persecution in Japan.

1857. John Hám.
Andrew Soulas, Ven.
Paul Capelloni, Ven.
Dominic Savio.
Juliana of the Most Blessed Sacrament, Ven.
Elizabeth Sanna, Ven.
1858. Joseph Amand Passerat, Ven.
Marie Madeleine de Bengy, Ven.
1859. *John Baptist Vianney,* Bl.
Charles of Abbiatecrasso.
1860. John N. von Tschiderer, Ven.

1860. The Massacre of Damascus.

John N. Neumann, Ven.
Justin de Jacobis, Ven.
Joseph Cafasso, Ven.
John M. R. de Lamennais, Ven.

1861. *The Blessed Hermosilla and three companions in Tonkin.*

Cajetan Errico, Ven.
Anna Maria Lapini, Ven.
1862. *Gabriel of the Mother of Sorrows,* Bl.
Benildes Romançon, Ven.
Anna Clara Steiner, Ven.
Joseph Dubourg.
1863. Michael Garricoïts, Ven.
Marie Thérèse Dubouché.
Francis of Collodio.
1864. Jacques Desiderius Laval.
Nicholas John Olivieri.
1865. *Madeleine Sophie Barat,* Bl.
Michaela Florez, Ven.
Paula Cerioli.
1866. Marianus of Rocca Casale, Ven.
Francis Croese, Ven.

Anastasius Hartmann.
Maria de Mattias, Ven.
1867. Francis X. Seelos.
Brother Scubilio.
1868. Pierre Julien Eymard,
Ven.
Louis Ed. Cestac, Ven.
Marie of St. Euphrasia
Pelletier, Ven.
Philomena of St. Columba,
Ven.
1870. Anthony Claret, Ven.
1871. Cherubina Saraceni.
Maria of the Divine Provi-
dence.
Matthieu Planchat.
1873. Aloysia Borgiotti.
John Merlini.
1874. Emanuel Ribera, Ven.
Francis Maione.
1875. John Claude Colin, Ven.
Benvenuto Bambozzi, Ven.
Ignatius Falzon, Ven.
Marie de Sales Chappuis,
Ven.
Adeline Desire.
Maria Aloysia of Jesus.
Maria Carola Onorio.
1876. Marie Thérèse Haze,
Ven.
Catharine Labouré, Ven.
Agnellus Coppola.
1877. Leon Dupont.
Francisca Schervier.
1878. Pius IX.
Veronica Barone.
1879. Antoine Chevrier, Ven.
Bernadette Soubirous.
1882. Paula Frassinetti, Ven.
Françoise Kestre.
1883. John Baptist Stoeger.
1884. Francis Jos. Rudigier,
Ven.
Louis of Casoria, Ven.
Marie of Jesus (Marie Caro-
line Deluil-Martigny).
1885. Adelaide Cini, Ven.
Louise de Montaignac.
1886. Joseph of Palermo.
Michael Angelo Longo.

1867-1873. Persecution in
Japan.
1868. Francisco Crusats.

1871. The Martyrs of the
Paris Commune.

1885-87. The venerable martyrs of Uganda.

1887. Peter Donders, Ven.
1888. Don John Bosco, Ven.
1889. Damien De Veuster.
1890. Rosa Carafa di Traetto, Ven.
1891. Caroline Carré de Malberg, Ven.
  Maria of the Sorrows of the B. V. M.
1893. Pascal Attardi, Ven.
1894. Catharine Volpicelli, Ven.
  Conrad Birndorfer.
1895. Paul Ginhac.
  Dominica Clara Moes.
1896. Alfred Pampalon.
1897. Thérèse Martin of the Child Jesus.
  Andrew Beltrami.
1898. Peter Lopez.
1899. Maria of the Sacred Heart.
  Joseph Giraldi.
1900. Aloysius Avellino.
1902. Contardo Ferrini.
1903. Gemma Galgani.
1905. Valentin Paquay.

1898-1900. The victims of the Boxer rebellion in China.

The number of confessors is 174, of whom 111 are men and 63 are women. Thus far one has been canonized a saint and eleven have been beatified.

The number of martyrs reaches many thousands. Of these, 114 have been already beatified.

LIST OF AUTHORITIES

(Those Cited in the Work and Others Added for Reference)

[1] Denzinger-Bannwart, Enchiridion Symbolorum, Twelfth Ed., No. 1794.

[2] Chr. Pesch, S.J., Prælectiones Dogmaticæ I, No. 409.

[3] Jos. Laurentius, S.J., Institutiones Juris Ecclesiastici, Second Ed., No. 721 sq.

[4] Piusbuch, by F. Hülskamp and W. Molitor—Stimmen aus Maria Laach, XIV (1878), 225 sqq.—Mgr. Bernard J. O'Reilly, LL.D., Life of Pope Pius IX.

[5] Ludwig Koesters, S.J., Maria, Die Unbefleckt Empfangene, 236 sqq.—Hist. Polit. Blätter, Bd. 36 (1855), 162 sqq.

[6] Loc. cit. 241 sq.

[7] Analect. Eccl. 1907, 490—Stimmen aus Maria Laach, LXXVIII (1910), 117 sq.

[8] Mitteilungen ueber das Leben und die Tugenden des Dieners Gottes Joh. N. v. Tschiderer, Fürstbischof v. Trient.—Leben des Ehrwuerdigen Dieners Gottes Johann Nep. von Tschiderer, Fürstbischofs von Trient, von Msgr. Anton Tait, deutsch v. P. Leo Schlegel, Zisterzienser von Mehreran—Joh. N. v. Tschiderer, von Leo Oettel—Sacra Rituum Congr., Tridentina, Beatif. et Canonis. Venerabilis Servi Dei Joannis Nep. de Tschiderer, Episcopi Tridentini, Nova Positio super Virtutibus—Catholic Encyclopedia, Vol. XV, p. 79.

[9] C. Flumser, Der Ehrw. Tschiderer als Kgl. Bayerischer Theologieprofessor, Passauer Theologisch-praktische Monatsschrift, Bd. 17 (1907), 216 sq.

[10] Leben und Wirken des Bischofs Franz Joseph Rudigier von Linz, bearbeitet von Konrad Meindl—Sacra Rituum Congr., Lincien., Beatif. et Canonis. Servi Dei Francisci Josephi Rudigier, Episcopi Linciensis, Positio super Introductione Causæ.

[11] Analecta Eccl. 1897, 109 sqq.—Joh. Nep. Berger, C.SS.R., Leben und Wirken des hochseligen Joh. n. Neumann, Bischofs von Philadelphia, Tr. Grimm—Magnier, Short Life of Bishop Neumann—Clarke, Lives of Deceased Bishops in U. S., Vol. II, p. 431 sq.—Shea, History of the Catholic Church in U. S., Vol. IV, p. 397 sq.—Funeral Obsequies of Right Rev. John N. Neumann—Ave Maria, XXX, 181—The Catholic Church in the U. S. A., Vol. I, p. 236—Amer. Eccl. Review, XVI, p. 393 sq.; XXIII, 315 sq.; XXXIII, 182 sq.—Catholic Encyclopedia, Vol. X, p. 773.

[12] Compendium Vitæ Servi Dei Joannis Hám, Episcopi olim Szatmariensis.

[13] Kirchenlexicon, 2. Aufl. XI., 864 sq.

[14] Card. Wiseman, Recollections of the Last Four Popes.

[15] Luigi Rodino, Vita del Servo de Dio Antonio Maria Gianelli, Vescovo di Bobbio—Civiltà Cattolica 1894, IV, 444 sqq.

[16] Analecta Eccl. 1900, 18 sqq.—E. Guelfi, Vita del Ven. Servo di Dio Ant. M. Claret, Arcivescovo, etc.

[17]Otto Braunsberger, S.J., Rückblick auf das Katholische Ordenswesen im 19. Jahrhundert.

[18]Sacra Rituum Congr., Abyssin., Beatif. et Canonis. Servi Dei Justini de Jacobis, etc. Positio super Introductione Causæ—Analecta Eccl. 1905, 127 sq.—Gab. Larigaldie, Le Venerable Justin de Jacobis, Prêtre de la Mission, Premier Vicaire Apostolique de l'Abyssinie.

[19]Adrian Imhof und Adelheim Jann, O.M.Cap., Anastasius Hartmann von Hitzkirch, Bischof von Derbe, Apostolischer Vicar von Patna und Bombay. Ein Lebens und Zeitbild aus dem 19 Jahrhundert.

[20]Le Bienheureux Curé d'Ars, par Jos. Vianney—Leben des Pfarrers v. Ars Joh. Bapt. Vianney, von Alfred Monnin, übersetzt von. J. Th. Rieforth, 2 Bde., 2 Aufl.—Dasselbe, nach der 18 Aufl. übersetzt von Dr. Albert Sleumer—Joseph Vianney, Blessed John Vianney, Curé d'Ars—Monnin, The Curé of Ars—Catholic Encyclopedia, Vol. VIII, p. 326.

[21]Loc. cit. II, 4 sq.

[22]Analecta Eccl. 1905, 209 sq.—Sacra Rituum Congr., Montispessulana, Beatif. et Canonis. Servi Dei Andreæ Soulas, etc.—Positio super Introductione Causæ.

[23]Vie du vénérable Louis Marie Baudouin, par l'Abbé Pierre Michaud—Michaud, Life of Venerable Louis Baudouin.

[24]Don Gastaldi, Der ehrw. Diener Gottes Don Joseph Benedikt Cottolengo—Don Gastaldi, Life of Venerable Joseph Benedict Cottolengo—The Month, Vol. LVI (1886), 339 sq.—The Ven. Jos. Ben. Cottolengo, by Mary Eliz. Herbert—"Charitas," IV (1899), Nos. 2, 3—Das kleine Haus der göttlichen Vorsehung in Turin und sein Gründer Joseph Benedikt Cottolengo, von Dr. Konrad Gröber.

[25]Sacra Rituum Congr. Beatificatio et Canonisatio servi Dei Josephi Cafasso. Positio super Introductione Causæ—Civiltà Cattolica, 1895, 191 sqq.—Analecta Eccl. 1907, 154 sqq.—A. Anzini, Vita del Ven. Cafasso.

[26]Analecta Eccl., 1909, 284 sq.—Sacra Rituum Congr., Neapolitana, Beatif. et Canonis. Servi Dei Placidi Bacher. Positio super Introductione Causæ.

[27]M. Meschler, S.J., Leben des hl. Aloysius von Gonzaga, 12. Aufl. 256 sq.

[28]Analecta Eccl. 1895, 112 sq.

[29]Analecta Eccl. 1898, 112.

[30]Sacra Rituum Congr. Policastren., Beatif. et Canonis. Servi Dei Dominici Lentini, sac. sæc. Positio super Introductione Causæ—Analecta Eccl. 1905, 406 sqq., 465 sqq.; 1906, 28 sqq.—G. Rossi, Cenno biografico del Sac. D. Lentini.

[31]Acta Apostolicæ Sedis, 1910, 414 sqq.—Sacra Rituum Congr. Neapolitana, Beatif. et Canonis. Servi Dei Pascalis Attardi, sac. sæc., Positio super Introductione Causæ.

[32]Analecta Eccl. 1906, 214 sqq.

[33]Ibid., 1906, 446 sqq.—Sacra Rit. Congr. Veronen. Beatif. et Canon. Servi Dei Gasparis Bertoni, Positio super Introductione Causæ.

[34]"Charitas," III (1898), 56 sq.—Acta Apostolicæ Sedis, 1913, 309 sq.

[35]Kirchenlexicon, IV, 1640 sq.

[36]Analecta Eccl. 1908, 195 sq.—Sacra Rit. Congr., Beatif. et Canon. Servi Dei Ludovici Eduardi Cestac, etc. Positio super Introductione Causæ.

[37]Kirchenlexicon, VII, 1365 sqq.—Acta Apostolicæ Sedis, 1911, 165 sq.

[38]M. Heimbucher, Die Orden und Kongregationen der Kath. Kirche, III, 359.

[39]Analecta Eccl. 1904, 255 sqq.—Sacra Rituum Congr., Meliten., Beatif. et Canonis. Servi Dei Ignatii Falzon, clerici sæc., Positio super Introductione Causæ.

[40]Ein oesterreichischer Reformator. Lebensbild des heiligen P. Klemens Maria Hofbauer. Von P. Adolf Innerkofler, C.SS.R. 2 Aufl.—Stimmen aus Maria Laach, LXXVIII, 1 sqq.—Klemens M. Hofbauer, ein zeitgemässer Heiliger, von. M. Meschler, S.J.—Haringer, Life of St. Clement Mary Hofbauer, tr. by Lady Herbert.—Catholic Encyclopedia, Vol. IV, p. 44—Rev. O. R. Vassall Phillips, C.SS.R.—Life of St. Clement Mary Hofbauer.

[41]Analecta Eccl. 1905, 3 sqq.—Vita del Beato Stefano Bellesini, parroco Agostiniano, per Paolo Billeri del Medesimo ordine.

[42]Analecta Eccl. 1894, 151 sqq.—P. Damase de Loisey, Le Bienheureux Diégo-Joseph de Cadix.

[43]Analecta Eccl. 1893, 73 sq.; 105 sqq.

[44]Analecta Eccl. 1893, 54 sq.

[45]Vita del Bl. Gaspare del Bufalo, descritta secondo i processi, da Mons. Vinc. Sardi.—The same translated into German by Conradi and Gregor Jussel, C.PP.S.—Sacra Rit. Congr. Beatif. et Canonis. Venerabilis Gaspare del Bufalo, etc., Positio super Miraculis.

[46]Sacra Rit. Congr. Pinnen., Beatif. et Canonis. Servi Dei Fr. Gabrielis a Virg. Dolorosa, etc. Positio super Introd. Causæ; Pos. super virtutibus; Pos. sup. Miraculis.—Analecta Eccl. 1896, 305 sqq.; 1908, 231 sqq.—Germano di S. Stanislao, Vita del B. Gabriele dell' Addolorata.—Marcolinus Houtmortels, O.P., Ein Aloysius unserer Tage, der Ser. Gabriel v. d. schmerzhaften Mutter—Hyacinthe Hage, C. P., Life of Venerable Gabriel of Our Lady of Sorrows.

[47]Der Sendbote des göttlichen Herzens Jesu, 1889, 45 sqq.

[48]Leben des im Ruf der Heiligkeit gestorbenen P. Heinrich Thyssen aus den Orden des hl. Franciskus; Nach dem Flämischen herausgegeben v. P. Corbinian Wirz, O.S.B.

[49]Sacra Rituum Congr., Neapolitana, Beatif. et Canon. Servi Dei Lud. a Cesaurea, etc. Positio super Miraculis.—"Charitas," IV (1899), 129 sqq.—M. Le Monnier, Vie du Louis de Casoria.

[50]Charles Tyck, Notices Historiques sur les Congregations et Communantés Religieuses du XIXme Siècle, 260 sq.

[51]Analecta Eccl. 1897, 155.

[52]Acta Sanctæ Sedis, IV (1868), 214 sq.

[53]Analecta Eccl. 1898, 293 sq.

[54]Analecta Eccl. 1896, 67 sq.

[55]Analecta Eccl. 1897, 331 sqq.

[56]The Catholic Encyclopedia, Vol. IX, p. 530.

[57]The Cath. Fortnightly Review, June 15, 1906.

[58]Acta Apost. Sedis, 1912, 27.

[59]Aperçus sur la vie et les vertus du serviteur de Dieu, le Père Valentin Paquay, O.F.M. D'Apres le Flamand, du R. P. Remacle Moonen, O.F.M., par le P. Léopold Quinot du même Ordre.

[60]P. Jos. Ant. Kessler, O.M.Cap., Der Ehrw. P. Jesuald von Reggio aus dem Kapuzinerorden.

[61]Jos. Bouchard, Vie du R. P. Muard, fondateur des Pères de Montigny.

[62]Leben des Ehrw. Dieners Gottes P. Joseph Maria Pignatelli aus der Gesellschaft Jesu, von P. Gabriel Bouffier, S.J.—Catholic Encyclopedia, Vol. XII, p. 82.

[63]Bouffier, Loc. cit., 10 sq.

[64]Histoire du R. P. de Clorivière de la Compagnie de Jésus, par le Père Jacques Terrien, S.J.

[65]Sacra Rit. Congr. Beneventana seu Januensis, Beatif. et Canon. Servi Dei Aloysii Solari, etc., Positio super Introductione Causæ—Analecta Eccl. 1907, 201 sqq.—Salv. Casagrandi, S.J., De Claris Sodalibus Provinciæ Taurinensis Soc. Jesu Commentarii, 297 sqq.

[66]Analecta Eccl. 1907, 202.

[67]Analecta Eccl. 1909, 380 sq.—Sacra Rituum Congr., Neapolitana seu Ferentina, Beatif. et Canon. Servi Dei Pauli Capelloni, etc., Positio super Introductione Causæ.

[68]Calvet, Life of Father Paul Ginhac.—Le Père Paul Ginhac de la Compagnie de Jésus, par le Père A. Calvet, S.J. 4th ed.— The same translated into German by Otto Werner, S.J.

[69]Sacra Rit. Congr. Parisien, Beatif. et Canon. Ven. Servi Dei Francisci M. P. Libermann, etc.—Positio super Virtutibus.— Acta Apost. Sedis, 1910, 487 sqq.—Leben des Ehrw. P. Libermann, von Card. Joh. B. Pitra. Nach der 4 Aufl., übersetzt von. J. Müller. —J. Heilgers, Das Ideal des Priesterthums. Briefe des Ehrw. P. Libermann.—By the same author, Die Gründung der Afrik. Mission durch den Ehrw. P. Libermann.

[70]Echo aus Knechtsteden, 1909-1910, 99 sqq.—Die Katholischen Missionen, 1895, 71.

[71]Der Sendbote des göttlichen Herzens Jesu, 1899, 214.

[72]Hedwig Schätti, P. Damien, der Apostel der Aussätzigen auf Molokai. 2 Aufl.—C. von Falser, Leben und Wirken des P. Damien de Veuster. 1892.—Die Katholischen Missionen, 1887, 22 sq., 92 sqq., 119 sqq., 144 sqq.; 1888, 155; 1889, 176 sqq.— Tauvel, Father Damien—Clifford, Father Damien—Stoddard, Father Damien, the Martyr of Molokai—Catholic Encyclopedia, Vol. IV, p. 615.

[73]C. von Falser, l. c. 148.

[74]Quoted in Der Sendbote des göttlichen Herzens Jesu, 1889, 274.

[75]C. von Falser, l. c. 121.

[76]Salesian Bulletin, 1908, 1909—Don Bosco, der Stifter der Salesianergenossenschaft, von J. M. Villefranche—J. B. Mehler, Don Bosco und seine sozialen Schöpfungen, 2 Aufl.—Eugen Mederlet, Don Bosco, ein Apostel der Jugend im 19. Jahrhundert—Filippo Crispolti, Don Bosco—Don Bosco's Apostolate and Other Sketches—Villefranche, Life of Don Bosco—Kirchenlexicon, Vol. X, p. 1558—Catholic Encyclopedia, Vol. II, p. 689.

[77]M. Heimbucher, Die Orden und Kongregationen der Kath. Kirche, III, 494 sq.

[78]Catholic Encyclopedia, Vol. V, 113—Acta Apostolicæ Sedis, 1911, 320 sqq—Devine, Life of Father Dominic of the Mother of God—Camm, Father Dominic and the Conversion of England (Eng. Cath. Truth Soc. Pub., 1900)—See supplement to Oratorian Life of St. Paul of the Cross.

[79]Sacra Rituum Congr., Tornacen. seu Vindobonen., Beatif. et Canonis. Servi Dei Josephi Amandi Passerat, etc., Positio super Introductione Causæ—Analecta Eccl. 1901, 353 sq.—P. Ad. Innerkofler, C.SS.R., Lebensbild des hl. Kl. Hofbauer, 129 sq.—Heimbucher, Die Orden und Kongregationen, etc., III, 319 sq.—Catholic Encyclopedia, Vol. V, page 735.

[80]P. Jos. Schleinkofer, C.SS.R., Leben des Dieners Gottes Franz Xaver Seelos aus der Kongregation des allerheiligsten Erlösers—Acta Apostolicæ Sedis, 1912, 358—Beck, Die Redemptoristen in Pittsburg—History of the Redemptorists in Annapolis—Shea, History of the Catholic Church in the United States, Vol. I—Catholic Encyclopedia, Vol. XIII, p. 681.

[81]Acta Apost. Sedis 1910, 685 sqq.—Catholic Encyclopedia, Vol. V, p. 129.

[82]Acta Apost. Sedis., 1912, 374 sq.

[83]Die Katholischen Missionen, 1901-1902, 43, 70—Acta Apostolicæ Sedis, 1913, 252 sq.

[84]Der Sendbote des göttlichen Herzens Jesu, 1901, 12 sqq., 42 sqq., 80 sqq.

[85]"Maria Immaculata," 1893-94, 241 sqq., 269 sqq., 301 sqq.—Acta Apostolicæ Sedis, 1912, 358.

[86]Analecta Eccl. 1909, 12 sqq.—The Life of the Ven. Father Colin, translated from the French—Catholic Encyclopedia, Vol. IV, p. 101.

[87]Analecta Eccl. 1896, 399 sqq.—The Month, Vol. LX (1887), 139 sqq.—Life of Father Champagnat, Founder of the Society of the Little Brothers of Mary (1789-1840). By one of his first Disciples.

[88]Analecta Eccl. 1908, 386 sq.; 1909, 122 sqq.—Sacra Rituum Congr., Gratianopolitana seu Parisien., Beatif. et Canonis. Servi Dei Petri Juliani Eymard, etc.; Positio super Introductione Causæ—Leben und Tugenden des Dieners Gottes P. Petrus Julianus Eymard, veröffentlicht zu Rom vom Postulator des

Seligsprechungsprozesses—Herbert, The Priest of the Eucharist—
Catholic Encyclopedia, Vol. V, p. 735.

[89]Acta Sanctæ Sedis, XIX (1886), 356 sqq.—Leben und Wirken
des Ehrw. Diener Gottes Vincenz Pallotti, Stifters der Pallot-
tiner Missions-Kongregation, von Leonz Niderberger—Der Kath-
olik, 1867, II, 657 sqq.—Mellia, Vincent Pallotti—Catholic Encyclopedia, Vol. XI, p. 429—Lady Herbert, Venerable Vincent
Pallotti.

[90]Acta Sanctæ Sedis, 1899, 127—Leben des Ehrw. Vinc. Pallotti
von L. Niderberger, 161 sq.

[91]Acta Sanctæ Sedis, 1884, 399.

[92]Ibid., 1899, 59—Heimbucher, Die Orden, etc., III, 350 sq.—
Tyck, Notices Historiques, etc., 170 sq.

[93]Analecta Eccl. 1903, 214 sqq.

[94]Giulio Barberis, Memorie e Cenni Biografici del Sacerdote
Salesiano D. Andrea Beltrami, 2. ed.

[95]Kain-Rosati, Life of the Very Rev. Felix de Andreis, C.M.

[96]Une Fleur Canadienne dans l'Institut de St. Alphonse ou une
Notice biographique du serviteur de Dieu le R. P. Alfred
Pampalon, par son frère le P. Pierre Pampalon.

[97]Die selige Julie Billiart, Stifterin der Genossenschaft unserer
Lieben Frau, und ihr Werk. Dargestellt von Bernhard Arens,
S.J., 2 Aufl.—Sacra Rituum Congr., Namurcen., Beatif. et
Canonis. Ven. Servæ Dei Juliæ Billiart, Positio super Miraculis—
Sister of Notre Dame, Life of Blessed Julie Billiart—Catholic
Encyclopedia, Vol. VIII, p. 559.

[98]Analecta Eccl. 1898, 117 sqq., 163 sqq., 202 sqq.; 1908, 226 sq.—
Joh. Dröder, O.M.J., Die selige Maria Magdalena Postel—Der
Sendbote des göttlichen Herzens Jesu, 1908, 185, 200, 233 sqq.

[99]Analecta Eccl. 1908, 228 sqq.—Die sel. Magdalena Sophie
Barat und ihre Stiftung, die Gesellschaft der Ordensfrauen vom
hl. Herzen—Die selige Magdalena Sophie Barat—Leben der ehrw.
Dienerin Gottes Magd. Sophie Barat. Von Dr. L. P. J. Baunard.
2 Aufl.—Ward, Life of Venerable Madeleine Sophie Barat—
Catholic Encyclopedia, Vol. II, p. 283.

[100]Sacra Rituum Congr. Romana seu S. Ludovici, Beat. et
Canonis. Servæ Dei Philippinæ Duchesne, Positio super Intro-
ductione Causæ—Acta Apost. Sedis, 1910, 76 sqq.—Dr. L. P.
Baunard, Histoire de Mme. Duchesne—Abbé Baunard, Life of
Madame Duchesne—The Month, 1898, 468 sqq., 611 sqq.—
Baunard, Leben der ehrw. Mutter Barat, etc.—The Messenger,
1890—Catholic Encyclopedia, Vol. V, p. 182.

[101]Baunard, Leben der ehrw. M. Barat, l. c. XXXIX.

[102]Pascal Darbins, La vie et les œuvres de Marie Lataste,
Religieuse Coadjutrice du Sacré Cœur, 3 vols., 2 ed.—Kirchen-
lexicon, VII, 1433 sqq.—Baunard, Leben der ehrw. Mutter Barat
sup. cit. 488 sqq.—Catholic Encyclopedia, Vol. IX, p. 12—
Edward Healy Thompson M.A., The Letters and Writings of
Marie Lataste.

[103]Leben der verehrten Marie de Sales Chappuis aus dem Orden
der Heimsuchung Mariä. Von J. Deshairs—P. Al. Brisson, Leben

der ehrw. Mutter Maria Salesia Chappuis—Life of Ven. Mother Mary de Sales Chappuis—Analecta Eccl. 1898, 114 sq., 289 sqq.

[104]See Heimbucher, sup. cit., III, 354 sq.

[105]Anal. Eccl. 1903, 23 sqq.—Sacra Rituum Congr., Valentina, Beatif. et Canonis. Servæ Dei Michaelæ a SSmo Sacramento, etc., Positio super Introd. Causæ.

[106]Positio super Virtutibus Ven. Servæ Dei Magdalenæ Marchionissæ de Canossa—Heimbucher, Die Orden, etc., III, 556 sq.—Otto Braunsberger, S.J., Rückblick, etc., 91.

[107]Sacra Congr. Rituum, Neapolitana, Beatif. et Canonis. Servæ Dei Mariæ Rosæ Carafa e Dynastis Trajecti, Positio super Introductione Causæ—Anal. Eccl. 1907, 394 sq.

[108]Acta Apost. Sedis, 1911, 69.

[109]Acta Sanctæ Sedis, 1865, 641 sqq.—Anal. Eccl. 1902, 24 sqq.—S. Rit. Cong. Brixien. Beatif. et Canonis. Ven. Servæ Dei Barth. Capitanio, Nova Positio super Virtutibus—Luigi Ignazio Mazza, S.J., Della vita et dell' instituto della Ven. M. Bartolomea Capitanio, Vols. I-II—By same author, Scritti spirituali della venerabile Maria Bartolomea Capitanio, Vols. I-III.

[110]Sacra Cong. Rit., Brixien., Beatif. et Canonis. Servæ Dei Vincentiæ Gerosa, etc., Positio super Introductione Causæ—Anal. Eccl. 1906, 494—Luigi Ign. Mazza, S.J., Vita della ven. Suor M. Vincenza Gerosa.

[111]Anal. Eccl. 1901, 212 sqq.—Blanche Anderdon, Life of Ven. Mother Jeanne Thouret, Foundress of the Sisters of Charity.

[112]O. Braunsberger, Rückblick, etc., 111.

[113]Sacr. Rit. Cong., Parisien., Beatif. et Canonis. Servæ Dei Cath. Labouré, Positio super Introd. Causæ—Analecta Eccl. 1907, 422 sqq.; 1908, 20 sqq., 146 sqq.—Edmond Crapez, La Vénérable Cath. Labouré, 2 ed.—"The Miraculous Medal" in "The Month," LXI (1887), 1 sqq.—Catholic Encyclopedia, Vol. X, page 115—"Stimmen aus Maria Laach," LXXXI (1911), 465 sq.—Lady Georgiana Fullerton, Catherine Labouré, Life and Visions of a Sister of Charity.

[114]Breviarium Romanum. Pars Autumnalis, officia propria pro aliquibus locis, 27 Nov.

[115]Dr. Wilhelm Hohn, Barmherzige Schwestern vom hl. Karl Borromäus, 1652-1900. Bilder aus der Geschichte der Katholischen Charitas, 324 sqq.

[116]Acta Apost. Sedis 1913, 432 sqq.—Bernadette Soubirous, mit dem Klosternamen Schwester Marie-Bernard, ihre letzten Lebenstage und ihr Tod. Aus dem Französischen übersetzt von Frf. v. A. Einsiedeln, 1880—Heinrich Lasserre, Bernadette, Schwester Maria Bernarda. Autorisierte Übersetzung von Vera von Vogelsang—Bernadette of Lourdes. Entitled in French, "La Confidante de l'Immaculée Bernadette Soubirous. Translated by J. H. Gregory.

[117]Lourdes-Rosen, 1911, 170.

[118]Anal. Eccl. 1898, 113 sqq.—Heimbucher, Die Orden, etc., III, 384 sq.—H. Pasquier, Leben der ehrw. M. Maria v. d. hl. Euphr.

Pelletier, 2 Bde.—Julius Bernard, Das Liebeswerk der Frauen "Vom Guten Hirten"—Clarke, Life of Mother Mary of St. Euphrasia Pelletier.

[119]Julius Bernard, sup. cit., 37.

[120]Sacra Rit. Congr., Parisien., Beatif. et Canonis. Servæ Dei Annæ Mariæ Javouhey, etc., Positio super Introductione Causæ—V. Caillard. La Vénérable Anne-Marie Javouhey, 2 ed., 105—Stimmen aus Maria Laach, 77 (1909), 588—Analecta Eccl. 1908, 143 sq.—Heimbucher, Die Orden, etc., III. 382—Catholic Encyclopedia, Vol. VIII, p. 326.

[121]Maria Cherubina Clara, Ordensfrau im Kloster der hl. Klara zu Assisi.

[122]Report of the Postulator of the Process of Beatification, Father Arthur Fugazza, C.M.

[123]Analecta Eccl. 1904, 206 sq.

[124]Analecta Eccl. 1898, 198 sq.

[125]Ibid., 1896, 225.

[126]Ibid., 1898, 199.

[127]Heimbucher, Die Orden, etc., III, 526.

[128]Analecta Eccl. 1907, 24 sqq., 75 sqq.

[129]Analecta Eccl. 1897, 76 sqq.

[130]Théophile de Ville, Geschichte des Lebens und Wirkens der Mutter Maria Theresia, Stifterin der Genossenschaft der Töchter vom hl. Kreuz in Lüttich. Autorisierte Übersetzung—Acta Apostolicæ Sedis, 1912, 103 sq.

[131]Catholic Encyclopedia, Vol. VII, p. 59 sq.—Mother Theodore Guerin, Life and Life-Work of.

[132]Sadlier, Eliz. Seton. Foundress of the American Sisters of Charity—Robert Seton, Memoirs, Letters, and Journal of Eliz. Seton—"Charitas," Bd. 15 (1910), Männer und Frauen der Charitas, 109 sqq., 225 sqq. Von Auguste von Pechmann—Helene von Barberey, Eliz. Seton und das Entstehen der Kath. Kirche in den Vereinigten Staaten Nordamerikas—Barberey, Elizabeth Seton—White, Life of Mrs. Eliz. A. Seton—Catholic Encyclopedia, Vol. XIII, p. 739—Historical Records and Studies, Vol. XIII, p. 129.

[133]Lady Fullerton, Leben der Mutter Maria von der Vorsehung.

[134]Sœur Thérèse de l'Enfant Jésus et de la Sté Face, Histoire d'une âme écrite par elle-même—Schwester Theresia vom Kinde Jesu, Geschichte einer Seele. Bearbeitet und Übersetzt von Gabriele von Frentz-Gemmingen—Dr. Jos. Drammer, Schwester Theresia vom Kinde Jesu aus dem Karmeliterorden—Rev. T. N. Taylor, "As Little Children"—Thoughts of Sœur Thérèse of the Child Jesus—Mgr. R. de Teil, The Cause of Beatification of the Little Flower of Jesus—Very Rev. W. M. Cunningham, V.F., The Unfolding of the Little Flower—Sœur Thérèse of Lisieux, The Little Flower of Jesus, An Autobiography—Life of Sister Thérèse of the Child Jesus and of the Holy Face.

[135]Leben der ehrw. Mutter Maria von Jesus, Maria Deluil-Martigny, von L. Laplace. Übersetzung aus dem Französischen—

Briefe der Dienerin Gottes Maria von Jesus, Übersetzung aus dem Französischen—Heimbucher, Die Orden, etc., III, 400.

[136]Msgr. d'Hulst, Vie de la Mère Marie-Thérèse—The same in German by a member of the Capuchin Order—Acta Apost. Sedis, 1913, 162 sq.—Tyck, Notices Historiques, etc., 180 sqq.

[137]Msgr. d'Hulst, German Ed., 7.

[138]Msgr. d'Hulst, sup. cit., 23.

[139]Moulinen, Beatif. et Canonis. Servæ Dei Ludovicæ Theresiæ de Montaignac de Chauvance, Fundatricis Piæ Unionis Oblatarum a SS. Corde Jesu.

[140]K. E. Schmöger, C.SS.R., Das Leben der gottseligen Anna Katharina Emmerich. 2 Bde., 2 Aufl.—Dasselbe im Auszug bearbeitet von einem Priester derselben Kongregation, 3 Aufl.—Thomas a Villanova Wegener, O.S.A., Das Wunderbare innere und äussere Leben der Dienerin Gottes A. K. Emmerich, 2 Aufl.—Dr. C. F. Krabbe, Erinnerung an die selige A. K. Emmerich—Wegener-McGowan, Life of Sister Anne Katherine Emmerich—Cazales, Life of Anna Catherine Emmerich (prefixed to The Dolorous Passion of Our Lord, 2 ed.)—Catholic Encyclopedia, Vol. V, p. 406.

[141]Wegener, sup. cit., 115.

[142]On the bright prospects of a successful issue of the Process, consult "Pastor Bonus," XXIV (1911-12), 233.

[143]J. P. Barthel, Mutter Maria Dominika Clara Moes vom hl. Kreuz. Als Manuskript gedruckt.

[144]Barthel, sup. cit., 484 sq.

[145]Sacra Rituum Congr. Nucerina, Beatif. et Canonis. Servæ Dei Mariæ Agnetis Steiner a SS. Latere Jesu, etc., Positio super Introd. Causæ—Anal. Eccl., 1909, 191 sq.—Kurze Lebensgeschichte der Dienerin Gottes Maria Agnes Klara Steiner von der Seitenwunde Jesu, von P. F. von Reuss, O.F.M., aus dem Italienischen von Peter Paul Ausserer, O.F.M. 2 Aufl.

[146]P. Ign. Jeiler, O.S.F., Die gottselige Mutter Franciska Schervier—Rev. Ign. Jeiler, O.F.M., Venerable Mother Francis Schervier.

[147]Jeiler, sup. cit., 87 sqq.

[148]Louis Chasle, Mutter Maria von göttl. Herzen Droste zu Vischering. Nach dem Französischen frei bearbeitet von Leo Sattler, O.S.B., 3 Aufl.—Dr. Jos. Drammer, Mutter Maria v. göttl. Herzen—Stimmen aus Maria Laach, LXX (1906), 450 sqq.

[149]L. Raylet, La vénérable Mère Emilie de Rodat.

[150]F. Mourret, La vénérable Mère Marie Rivier.

[151]Heimbucher, Die Orden, etc., III, 562—Tyck, Notices Historiques, etc., 122.

[152]Salesian Bulletin, Nov., 1911, 311.

[153]Don Bosco, Leben des Knaben Domenico Savio. Herausgegeben vom Deutschen Don Bosco-Institut—The same in English, with a preface by the Bishop of Salford.

[154]Salesian Bulletin, Jan., 1910.

[155]Acta Sanctæ Sedis, V (1869-70), 487 sqq.—Dr. Franz Zorn v. Bulach, Der ehrw. Diener Gottes und jugendliche Arbeiter

Nunzio Sulprizio—Graf Eduard Le Camus, Nunzio Sulprizio, Ein Vorbild für Lehrlinge. Deutsch von J. Fuss.

[156]Dr. M. Scheeben, Die Heiligkeit der Kirche im 19. Jahrhundert. Frankfurter Broschüren, 1867, N. 6, S. 17, sq.

[157]Edward H. Thompson, The Life of Léon Papin-Dupont, second edition—Jos. Neumann, Leo Dupont, sein Leben und Wirken—J. M. Villefranche, Dix Grand Chrétiens du Siècle.

[158]Carlo Pellegrini, Contardo Ferrini, Appunti biografici—By the same, Contardo Ferrini, Scritti Religiosi—"Civiltà Cattolica," 1912, IV, 56 sqq.—Hist.-Folit. Blätter, 152 (1913), 207 sqq.

[159]Salv. Trama, Piccolo Cenno della vita del servo di Dio Francesco Maione.

[160]Raffaele Pica, Vita de Luigi Avellino.

[161]Kirchenlexicon, VIII, 751 sq. Artikel von Otto Pfülf, S.J.—Joh. Jak. Hansen, Lebensbilder hervorragender Katholiken des 19. Jahrhunderts, IV, 173 sqq.

[162]Der Sendbote des göttlichen Herzens Jesu, 1880, 343 sqq.; 1881, 28 sq.—Kirchenlexicon, VIII, 753, Artikel von Otto Pfülf, S.J.

[163]Leben der ehrw. Dienerin Gottes Anna Maria Taigi. Bearbeitet nach mehreren Französischen Schriften und den Akten des Seligsprechungsprozesses. Mit einem Vorwort von Prof. Dr. M. Scheeben, 3 Aufl.—Sacra Rituum Congr. Romana, Beatif. et Canonis. Ven. Servæ Dei Annæ Mariæ Taigi, etc., Positio super Virtutibus, Positio super Miraculis—Catholic Encyclopedia, Vol. XIV, p. 430—Life of the Venerable Anna Maria Taigi. Edited by Edward Healy Thompson, M.A.

[164]Abrégé de la Vie admirable de la Servante de Dieu Elizabeth Canori-Mora—"Civiltà Cattolica," 62 (1911), I, 485 sqq.—Life of Ven. Elizabeth Canori Mora, Lady Herbert.

[165]Leonz Niderberger, Vincenz Pallotti, sup. cit., 158 sq.

[166]Anal. Eccl., 1909, 431 sqq.—Sacra Rituum Congr. Meten., Positio super Introd. Causæ Servæ Dei Car. B. Colchen Carré de Malberg, 3 sqq.

[167]Acta Apost. Sedis, 1910, 320 sqq.

[168]Acta Apost. Sedis, 1910, 162 sqq.—Positio super Introd. Causæ Beatif. et Canonis. Servæ Dei Adelaidis Cini.

[169]Germano di S. Stanislao, Biografia de Gemma Galgani, Vergine Lucchese, Quarta Edizione abbreviata dall' autore—P. Leo Schlegel, O. Cist., Leben der Jungfrau und Dienerin Gottes Gemma Galgani. 2 Aufl.—Dr. A. F. Ludwig, Gemma Galgani, eine Stigmatisierte aus jüngster Zeit—Rev. Philip Coghlan, C.P., Gemma Galgani: A Child of the Passion.

[170]P. Pio da Mazzarino, O.Cap., Leben der jungfräulichen Dienerin Gottes Veronika Barone, Tertiarin von Vizzini, Sizilien. Autorisierte deutsche Ausgabe von P. Leo Schlegel, O.Cist.

[171]Da Mazzarino, Leben, etc., sup. cit., 37.

Christ. Pesch, S.J., Prælectiones Dogmaticæ I. N. 253-255—Wilmers-Hontheim, S.J., Lehrbuch der Religion, II, 182 sqq.

[173]Anton Huonder, S.J., Der selige Johann Gabriel Perboyre, Ein Märtyrerbild aus dem 19. Jahrhundert.

[174]I Martiri Annamitici e Cinesi (1796-1856) sollennemente beatificati dalla Santità di Papa Leone XIII il 27 Maggio dell' anno MDCCC, 391 sqq.—Hilarius Walter, O.S.B., Leben, Wirken, und Leiden der 77 seligen Märtyrer von Annam und China—Canon Shortland, Persecutions of Annam. A History of Christianity in Cochin China and Tonkin—See also Catholic Encyclopedia articles China, Annam, Martyrs, etc.

[175]Ant. du Lys, Leben und Martyrium des Minderbruders Johannes von Triora, Autorisierte Übersetzung aus dem Französischen von Schwester M. Paula.

[176]H. Wegener, S.V.D., Opferleben und Opfertod oder Kurzgefasste Lebensbilder berühmter Missionäre und Märtyrer der neueren Zeit, 115 sqq.

[177]I Martiri Annamitici, etc., 99 sqq.—Canon Shortland, Persecutions of Annam.

[178]E. Vindry, Vie du Vénérable Jean Louis Bonnard, 3 Aufl.

[179]H. Wegener, Opferleben und Opfertod, etc., sup. cit., 91 sqq.

[180]Anal. Eccl., 1902, 207 sqq.; 1906, 234 sqq.—Giuseppe Clementi, Gli otto Martiri Tonchinesi dell' Ordine di S. Domenico sollennemente beatificati da Pio Papa X—Alfonso Bianconi, O.P., Vita e Martirio dei Beati Dominicani decapitati per la Fede Cattolica nel Tonchino.

[181]Launay, Les Trente-Cinque Vénérables Serviteurs de Dieu Français—Annamites—Chinois—Positio super Martyrio, etc.—Venerabilium Servorum Dei Stephani Theodori Cuenot, Episcopi Metellopolitani, etc.

[182]A. Launay, sup. cit., 191 sqq.—Vie et Correspondance de J. Théoph. Venard, 3 ed.—Die Kath. Missionen, 1878, 6 sqq., 45 sqq.—Le Bienheureux Théoph. Vénard, d'apres les Témoinages du Procès Apostolique.

[183]P. Carl Dilgskron, C.SS.R., Leben des sel. Peter Alois Maria Chanel, aus dem Französischen des P. Claudius Nicoleti—A. Huonder, S.J., Bannerträger des Kreuzes, I, 193 sqq.— Catholic Encyclopedia, Vol. III, p. 572.

[184]Die Kath. Missionen, 1876, 34 sqq.

[185]Ibid., 1874, 113 sqq., 169 sqq., 205 sqq.—Karl Reiching, Neue Siegespalmen Katholischer Märtyrer.

[186]Sacra Rituum Congr. Tonquinen. seu Ord. Prædicatorum, Beatificationis et Canonisationis seu Declarationis Martyrii Servorum Dei Josephi Mariæ Diaz Sanjurjo, Episcopi Platearum, etc.

[187]Jos. Spillmann, S.J., Durch Asien, 2d part, 335.

[188]Die Kath. Missionen, 1874, 210.

[189]Ibid., 258.

[190]Die Kath. Missionen, 1883, 157 sqq.

[191]Die Kath. Missionen, 1874, 152 sq.

[192]Die Kath. Missionen, 1875, 127.

[193]Die Kath. Missionen, 1889, 42 sq.

[194]Die Kath. Missionen, 1884, 198.

[195]Die Kath. Missionen, 1899-1900, 210.

[196]Die Kath. Missionen, 1901-02, 1 sqq., 148 sqq.—A. Huonder, S.J., Bannerträger des Kreuzes, I, 76 sqq.

[197]Die Kath. Missionen, 1900-01, 238.

[198]Die Kath. Missionen, 1900-01, 238.

[199]Ibid., 18.

[200]Ibid., 108.

[201]Ibid., 31 sq.

[202]Ibid., 142 sqq.

[203]Die Kath. Missionen, 1900-01, 146.

[204]Msgr. Georg Monchamp, P. Victorin Delbrouck,, ein Blutzeuge des Franziskanerordens aus unseren Tagen. Übersetzt von P. Remb. Wegener, O.F.M.

[205]Die Kath. Missionen, 1885, 38.

[206]Die Kath. Missionen, 1885, 19.

[207]Ch. Dallet, Histoire de l'Eglise de Corée. 2 vols.—E. Fourer, La Corée, Martyrs et Missionaires—The same in German—La Corée, par un Missionnaire, Société de Saint Augustin—Die Kath. Missionen, 1875, 159 sqq.; 1896, 6 sqq.—K. Reiching, Neue Sieges-Palmen, etc.

[208]See Bannerträger, etc., I, 112 sqq., by A. Huonder, for an account of James Tsiu.

[209]Ch. Dallet, sup. cit. I, 276.

[210]Ch. Dallet, sup. cit. I, 282 sqq.

[211]Ch. Dallet, sup. cit. II, 182 sq.

[212]Ibid., II, 192 sqq.

[213]Ibid., II, 204.

[214]Ibid., II, 326 sqq.

[215]Ch. Dallet, II, 149 sq.

[216]Ibid., II, 198 sq.

[217]Ibid., II, 218.

[218]Ibid., II, 152 sq.

[219]Ibid., II, 187 sq.

[220]Ibid., II, 147 sqq., 173, 189.

[221]Ch. Dallet, sup. cit. II, 543 sqq.

[222]Arthur Placentini, Msgr. Ridel, Evêque de Philippopolis, 2 ed., 265.

[223]E. Fourer, sup. cit., Motto on the title page.

[224]Die Kath. Missionen, 1873, 25 sqq.; 1905-06, 65 sq.—Rev. Joseph Broeckeart, S.J., Japanese Martyrs—Catholic Encyclopedia, Vol. IX, p. 744.

[225]A. Nicq, Le Père Siméon Lourdel de la Société des Pères Blancs, 2 Aufl., 385 sqq.—Die Negermärtyrer von Uganda. Herausgegeben von der Missionsgesellschaft der Weissen Väter. 3 Aufl.

[226]A. Nicq, loc. cit., 448 sqq.

[227]Die Kath. Missionen, 1909-10, 6, 20.

[228]Die Kath. Missionen, 1889, 82, 99.

[229]Philib. Seeböck, O.F.M., Der ehrw. Diener Gottes P. Engelbert Kolland—Heimbucher, Die Orden, etc., II, 428.

[230]Die Kath. Missionen, 1886, 72 sqq., 142 sqq., 164 sqq., 187 sqq. —Hist.-Politische Blätter, 136 (1905), 397 sqq.

[231]Die Kath. Missionen, 1886, 103.

[232]Hist.-Politische Blätter (1905), 410 sq.

[233]P. A. de Ponlevoy, S.J., Die Opfer der Insurrektion zu Paris im Jahre 1871 aus der Gesellschaft Jesu—Catholic Encyclopedia, Vol. IV, p. 168.

[234]Mariano Aguilar, Vida del Siervo de Dios P. Francisco Crusats, Protomartyr de la Congregacion de Misioneros Hijos de Jdo Corazon de Maria.

[235]G. M. Schuler, Märtyrer des Beichtsiegels. 3 Aufl. Kamillus-blatt, 1899, 120 sqq.

ALPHABETICAL INDEX

403

PAGE

Lambruschini, Aloysius, Cardinal 181
Lamennais, J. M. Robert de 82
La Mure d'Isère......176, 179
Landeron 208
La Neylière............. 172
Lantrua, O.F.M., Giovanni, Bl. 305
Lanzo 186
Lapini, Anna Maria...... 220
Laplace, L................ 396
Larigaldie, Gabriel....... 390
La Rochelle..........67, 305
Laserre, Heinrich........ 395
La Servianne............. 226
La Seyne-sur-Mer........ 178
Lataste, Marie........... 197
Launay, A................ 399
Laurentius, S.J., Jos..... 389
Lauria 78
Laval, Jacques D....... 143
La Valetta.............84, 293
Lavalla 174
Lawrence of St. Francis Xavier 189
Le Camus, Comte Edouard 398
Lecce 53
Leipsic 269
Le Mazel................ 134
Le Monnier, M.......... 391
Lenkiewicz, S.J., Gabriel. 122
Lentini, Dominic........ 78
Leo XII.........48, 100, 286
Leo XIII...183, 210, 245, 248, 253, 255
Leroy-Beaulieu 374
Les Sables d-Olonne...... 66
Le Vavasseur, Frederic... 141
Levis 188
Libermann, Francis M.... 140
Libermann, Samson....... 140
Liége 126, 222
Lieou, Paul, Bl.......... 304
Lieou, Peter, Bl......304, 307
Lieou, Thaddeus, Bl...... 304
Limberg, Fr............. 235
Limburg 114
Limoges 185

PAGE

Linz 41
Lisiéux 225
Livinhac, Mgr........... 361
Livorno 224
Lô, John B., Bl.......... 321
Loisey, Damase de....... 391
Lokovitz 372
Lombardy 205
Lombroso, Cæsar........ 157
Longo, O.F.M., Michael Angelo 116
Lopez, O.F.M., Peter..... 116
Loretto 28
Lorry 293
Louis Philippe........200, 263
Louis XV................ 279
Louis XVI............... 279
Lourdel, Simeon......... 362
Lourdes...........212, 379
"Lourdes-Rosen" 395
Louvain.....107, 114, 146, 152
Lovere 204
Luanga, Charles......361, 366
Lucca 295
Luçon................65, 67
Ludwig, Dr. A. F....... 398
Lun, Peter, Bl........... 321
Luxemburg 239
Lyons............60, 79, 178
Lys, Antoine du......... 399

M

Macerata.............48, 103
Madrid..........53, 199, 251
Maillé 81
Maione, Francis........ 276
Mangano, O.F.M., Francis 111
Mangin, S.J., Ignatius.... 341
Marchand, Joseph, Bl.... 311
Maria Aloysia of Jesus.. 250
Maria Christina of Naples 280
Maria Clotilda of Sardinia 279
Maria Crucifixa......... 219
"Maria Immaculata" 393
Maria Josepha of Saxony. 279
Maria Juliana of the Blessed Sacrament... 219
Maria of the Mother of Sorrows 250
Marielux, O.S.Cam., Peter 375

PRINTED BY BENZIGER BROTHERS, NEW YORK

BOOKS OF DOCTRINE, INSTRUCTION, DEVOTION, MEDITATION, BIOGRAPHY, NOVELS, JUVENILES, ETC.

PUBLISHED BY

BENZIGER BROTHERS

CINCINNATI
343 MAIN ST.

NEW YORK
36-38 BARCLAY ST.

CHICAGO
205-207 W. WASHINGTON ST.

Books not marked *net* will be sent postpaid on receipt of the advertised price. Books marked *net* are such where ten per cent must be added for postage. Thus a book advertised at *net* $1.00 will be sent postpaid on receipt of $1.10.

I. INSTRUCTION, DOCTRINE, APOLOGETICS, CONTROVERSY, EDUCATIONAL

ANECDOTES AND EXAMPLES ILLUSTRATING THE CATHOLIC CATECHISM. SPIRAGO. *net*, $2.75.

ART OF PROFITING BY OUR FAULTS. TISSOT. *net*, $0.75.

BOY SAVERS' GUIDE. QUIN, S.J. *net*, $2.50.

CATECHISM EXPLAINED, THE. SPIRAGO-CLARKE. *net*, $3.75.

CATHOLIC AMERICAN, THE. SCHMIDT. *net*, $1.50.

CATHOLIC BELIEF. FAÀ DI BRUNO. Paper, *net*, $0.30; cloth, *net*, $0.90.

CATHOLIC CEREMONIES AND EXPLANATION OF THE ECCLESIASTICAL YEAR. DURAND. Paper, *$0.45; cloth, *net*, $0.90.

CATHOLIC HOME ANNUAL. $0.35.

CATHOLIC PRACTICE AT CHURCH AND AT HOME. KLAUDER. Paper, *$0.45; cloth, *net*, $0.90.

CATHOLIC'S READY ANSWER, THE. HILL, S.J. *net*, $2.50.

CATHOLIC'S WORK IN THE WORLD HUSSLEIN, S.J. *net*, $1.50.

CEREMONIAL FOR ALTAR BOYS. BRITT, O.S.B. *net*, $0.60.

CHARACTERISTICS AND RELIGION OF MODERN SOCIALISM. MING, S.J. 12mo. *net*, $2.50.

CHARITY, THE ORIGIN OF EVERY BLESSING. *net*, $1.00.

CHILD PREPARED FOR FIRST COMMUNION. DE ZULETA, S.J. Paper, *$0.08.

CHRISTIAN APOLOGETICS. DEVIVIER-MESSMER. *net*, $3.50.

CHRISTIAN EDUCATION. O'CONNELL. *net*, $1.00.

CHRISTIAN FATHER. CRAMER. *net*, $0.85.

CHRISTIAN MOTHER. CRAMER. *net*, $0.85.

CORRECT THING FOR CATHOLICS. BUGG. *net*, $1.25.

DIVINE GRACE. WIRTH. *net*, $1.25.

EDUCATION OF OUR GIRLS. SHIELDS. *net*, $1.50.

EXPLANATION OF BIBLE HISTORY. NASH. *net*, $2.50.

EXPLANATION OF CATHOLIC MORALS. STAPLETON. *net*, $1.25.

EXPLANATION OF THE BALTIMORE CATECHISM. KINKEAD. *net*, ¶$1.50.

EXPLANATION OF THE COMMANDMENTS. ROLFUS. *net*, $0.90.

EXPLANATION OF THE CREED. ROLFUS. *net*, $0.90.

EXPLANATION OF GOSPELS AND OF CATHOLIC WORSHIP. LAMBERT-BRENNAN. Paper, *$0.45; cloth, *net*, $0.90.

EXPLANATION OF THE MASS. COCHEM. *net*, $1.25.

EXPLANATION OF THE HOLY SACRAMENTS. ROLFUS. *net*, $0.90.

EXPLANATION OF THE PRAYERS AND CEREMONIES OF THE MASS. LANSLOTS, O.S.B. *net*, $1.25.

EXPLANATION OF THE SALVE REGINA. ST. ALPHONSUS. *net*, $1.25.

EXTREME UNCTION. Paper, *$0.12.

FOUNDATION OF TRUE MORALITY. SLATER, S.J. *net*, $1.25.

FUNDAMENTALS OF THE RELIGIOUS LIFE. SCHLEUTER, S.J. *net*, $0.75.

FUTURE LIFE, THE. SASIA, S.J. *net*, $3.00.

GENERAL CONFESSION MADE EASY. KONINGS, C.SS.R. Cloth, *$0.25.

GENTLEMAN, A. EGAN. *net*, $1.25.

GIFT OF THE KING. By a Religious. *net*, $0.75.

GLORIES AND TRIUMPHS OF THE CATHOLIC CHURCH. *net*, $3.50.

GOD, CHRIST, AND THE CHURCH. HAMMER, O.F.M. *net*, $3.50.

GOFFINE'S DEVOUT INSTRUCTIONS ON THE EPISTLES AND GOSPELS FOR THE SUNDAYS AND HOLY-DAYS. *net*, $1.75.

GREAT ENCYCLICAL LETTERS OF POPE LEO XIII. *net*, $3.50.

GUIDE FOR SACRISTANS. net, $1.50.
HANDBOOK OF THE CHRISTIAN RE-
LIGIONS. WILMERS, S.J. net, ¶$2.50.
HEAVEN OPEN TO SOULS. SEMPLE,
S.J. net, $2.75.
HOW TO COMFORT THE SICK,
KREBS, C.SS.R. net, $1.25.
HOW TO MAKE THE MISSION. By
a Dominican Father. Paper, *$0.12.
INSTRUCTIONS ON THE COM-
MANDMENTS OF GOD AND THE
SACRAMENTS OF THE CHURCH.
ST. ALPHONSUS LIGUORI. net, $0.85.
LADY, A. BUGG. net, $1.25.
LAWS OF THE KING. By a Religious.
net, $0.75.
LESSONS OF THE SAVIOUR. By a
Religious. net, $0.75.
LITTLE ALTAR BOY'S MANUAL.
$0.50.
MANUAL OF SELF-KNOWLEDGE
AND CHRISTIAN PERFECTION
A. HENRY, C.SS.R. net, $0.75.
MANUAL OF THEOLOGY FOR THE
LAITY. GEIERMANN, C.SS.R. Paper,
*$0.45; cloth, net, $0.90.
MASS AND VESTMENTS OF THE
CATHOLIC CHURCH. WALSH, net,
$3.00.
MASS-SERVER'S CARD. Per doz. net,
$0.50.
MORALITY OF MODERN SOCIAL-
ISM. MING, S.J. net, $2.50.
NARROW WAY, THE. GEIERMANN,
C.SS.R. net, $0.90.
OUT TO WIN. Straight Talks to Boys
on the Way to Manhood. CONROY,
S.J. net, $1.50.
PASTORAL LETTERS. McFAUL. net,
$2.50.
PRINCIPAL CATHOLIC PRACTICES.
SCHMIDT. net, $1.50.
QUEEN'S FESTIVALS, THE. By a
Religious. net, $0.75.
REASONABLENESS OF CATHOLIC
CEREMONIES AND PRACTICES.
BURKE. net, $0.75.
RELIGIOUS STATE, THE. ST. AL-
PHONSUS. net, $0.75.
SACRAMENTALS OF THE HOLY
CATHOLIC CHURCH. LAMBING.
Paper, *$0.45; cloth, net, $0.90.

SCAPULAR MEDAL, THE. GEIER-
MANN, C.SS.R. Paper, *$0.08.
SHORT CONFERENCES ON THE
SACRED HEART. BRINKMEYER. net,
$1.25.
SHORT COURSE IN CATHOLIC DOC-
TRINE. Paper, *$0.12.
SHORT STORIES ON CHRISTIAN
DOCTRINE. net, $1.75.
SOCIALISM: ITS THEORETICAL
BASIS AND PRACTICAL APPLI-
CATION. CATHREIN-GETTLEMAN. net,
$2.75.
SOCIALISM AND CHRISTIANITY.
STANG. net, $1.50.
SPIRITUAL PEPPER AND SALT.
STANG. Paper, *$0.45; cloth, net, $0.90.
STORIES OF THE MIRACLES OF
OUR LORD. By a Religious. net,
$0.75.
STORY OF THE FRIENDS OF JESUS.
By a Religious. net, $0.75.
SUNDAY-SCHOOL DIRECTOR'S
GUIDE. SLOAN. net, $1.50.
SUNDAY-SCHOOL TEACHER'S
GUIDE. SLOAN. net, $1.25.
SURE WAY TO A HAPPY MAR-
RIAGE. TAYLOR. net, $0.85.
TALKS TO NURSES. SPALDING, S.J.
net, $1.50.
TALKS TO PARENTS. CONROY, S.J.
net, $1.50.
TALKS WITH THE LITTLE ONES
ABOUT THE APOSTLES' CREED.
By a Religious. net, $0.75.
TRAINING OF CHILDREN AND OF
GIRLS IN THEIR TEENS. CECILIA.
net, $1.25.
TRUE POLITENESS. DEMORE. net,
$1.25.
VOCATION. VAN TRICHT-CONNIFF.
Paper, *$0.12.
VOCATIONS EXPLAINED. Cut flush,
*$0.12.
WAY OF INTERIOR PEACE. DE
LEHEN. S.J. net, $2.25.
WHAT THE CHURCH TEACHES.
DRURY. Paper, *$0.45; cloth, net,
$0.90.
WHAT TIMES! WHAT MORALS!
SEMPLE, S.J. Cloth, net, $0.75.

II. DEVOTION, MEDITATION, SPIRITUAL READING, PRAYER-BOOKS

ABANDONMENT; or Absolute Surrender
of Self to Divine Providence. CAUS-
SADE, S.J. net, $0.75.
ADORATION OF THE BLESSED
SACRAMENT. TESNIERE. net, $1.25.
BLESSED SACRAMENT BOOK.
Prayer-Book by FATHER LASANCE. Im.
leather. $2.50.
BLOSSOMS OF THE CROSS. GIEHRL.
net, $1.75.
BOOK OF THE PROFESSED. 3 vols.
Each, net, $1.25.
BREAD OF LIFE, THE. WILLIAM.
net, $1.35.
CATHOLIC GIRL'S GUIDE, THE.
Prayer-Book by FATHER LASANCE. Seal

grain cloth, stiff covers, red edges, $1.50.
Im. leather, limp, red edges, $1.90; gold
edges, $2.25. Real leather, limp, gold
edges, $3.25.
CHARACTERISTICS OF TRUE DE-
VOTION. GROU, S.J. net, $1.00.
COUNSELS OF ST. ANGELA. net,
$0.50.
DEVOTION TO THE SACRED HEART
OF JESUS. NOLDEN, S.J. net, $1.75.
DEVOTIONS AND PRAYERS BY
ST. ALPHONSUS. WARD. net, $1.50.
DEVOTIONS AND PRAYERS FOR
THE SICK ROOM. KREBS. net, $1.25.
DEVOTIONS TO THE SACRED
HEART FOR THE FIRST FRIDAY

OF EVERY MONTH. Huguet. *net*, $0.75.

DOMINICAN MISSION BOOK. By a Dominican Father. $1.00.

EUCHARISTIC SOUL ELEVATIONS. Stadelman, C.S.Sp. *net*, $0.60.

FIRST SPIRITUAL AID TO THE SICK. McGrath. *net*, $0.60.

FLOWERS OF THE CLOISTER. Poems. de La Motte. *net*, $1.75.

FOLLOWING OF CHRIST. Plain Edition, $0.65.

FOR FREQUENT COMMUNICANTS. Roche, S.J. Paper, *$0.12.

GLORIES OF MARY. St. Alphonsus. *net*, $1.75.

GLORIES OF THE SACRED HEART. Hausherr, S.J. *net*, $1.75.

GREETINGS TO THE CHRIST-CHILD. Poems. *net*, $1.00.

HELP FOR THE POOR SOULS. Ackermann. $0.90.

HELPS TO A SPIRITUAL LIFE. Schneider. *net*, $1.25.

HIDDEN TREASURE, THE. St. Leonard. *net*, $0.75.

HOLY HOUR, THE. Keiley. 16mo. *$0.12.

HOLY HOUR OF ADORATION. Stang. *net*, $0.90.

HOLY VIATICUM OF LIFE AS OF DEATH. Dever. *net*, $1.25.

IMITATION OF CHRIST, THE. See "Following of Christ."

IMITATION OF THE SACRED HEART. Arnoudt. *net*, $1.75.

IN HEAVEN WE KNOW OUR OWN. Blot, S.J. *net*, $0.75.

INTERIOR OF JESUS AND MARY. Grou, S.J. 2 vols. *net*, $3.00.

INTRODUCTION TO A DEVOUT LIFE. St. Francis de Sales. Cloth, *net*, $1.00.

LITTLE ALTAR BOYS' MANUAL. $0.50.

LITTLE COMMUNICANTS' PRAYER-BOOK. Sloan. $0.25.

LITTLE MANUAL OF ST. ANTHONY. Lasance. *net*, $0.25.

LITTLE MANUAL OF ST. JOSEPH. Lings. *net*, $0.25.

LITTLE MANUAL OF ST. RITA. McGrath. $0.90.

LITTLE MASS BOOK, THE. Lynch. Paper, *$0.08.

LITTLE MONTH OF MAY. *net*, $0.60

LITTLE MONTH OF THE SOULS IN PURGATORY. *net*, $0.60.

LITTLE OFFICE OF THE BLESSED VIRGIN MARY. In Latin and English, *net*, $1.75; in Latin only. *net*, $1.25.

LITTLE OFFICE OF THE IMMACULATE CONCEPTION. Paper, *$0.08.

MANNA OF THE SOUL. Prayer-Book by Father Lasance. Vest-pocket edition. Silk cloth, red edges, $0.60; imitation leather, limp, gold edges, $1.00; American seal, limp, gold edges, $1.50.

MANNA OF THE SOUL. Prayer-Book by Father Lasance. Extra large type edition. Im. leather, limp, red edges, $1.90; gold edges, $2.25; Am. seal, limp, gold edges, $3.25.

MANNA OF THE SOUL. Prayer-Book by Father Lasance. Thin edition. Im. leather, limp, red edges, $1.15; gold edges, $1.40; Am. seal, limp, gold edges, $2.00.

MANNA OF THE SOUL. Prayer-Book by Father Lasance. Thin edition with Epistles and Gospels, Im. leather, limp, red edges, $1.50; gold edges, $1.85; Am. seal, limp, gold edges, $2.50.

MANUAL OF THE HOLY EUCHARIST. Lasance. Imitation leather, limp, red edges, $1.25; Am. seal, limp, gold edges, $2.00.

MANUAL OF THE HOLY NAME. $0.75.

MANUAL OF THE SACRED HEART, NEW, $1.00.

MANUAL OF ST. ANTHONY, *net*, $0.90.

MARIÆ COROLLA. Poems. Hill, C.P. *net*, $1.75.

MARY, HELP OF CHRISTIANS. Hammer, O.F.M., *net*, $3.50.

MASS DEVOTIONS AND READINGS ON THE MASS. Lasance. Im. leather, limp, red edges, $1.25; Am. seal, limp, gold edges, $2.00.

MEANS OF GRACE. Brennan. *net*, $5.00.

MEDITATIONS FOR ALL THE DAYS OF THE YEAR. Hamon. S.S. 5 vols. *net*, $8.75.

MEDITATIONS FOR EVERY DAY IN THE MONTH. Nepveu, S.J. *net*, $1.25.

MEDITATIONS FOR EVERY DAY IN THE YEAR. Baxter, S.J. *net*, $2.00.

MEDITATIONS FOR EVERY DAY IN THE YEAR ON THE LIFE OF OUR LORD. Vercruysse, S.J. 2 vols. *net*, $4.50.

MEDITATIONS FOR MONTHLY RETREATS. Semple, S.J. *net*, $1.25.

MEDITATIONS FOR THE USE OF THE SECULAR CLERGY. Chaignon, S.J. 2 vols. *net*, $7.00.

MEDITATIONS ON THE LIFE, THE TEACHING AND THE PASSION OF JESUS CHRIST. Ilg-Clarke. 2 vols. *net*, $5.00.

MEDITATIONS ON THE MYSTERIES OF OUR HOLY FAITH, Barraud, S.J. 2 vols., *net*, $4.50.

MEDITATIONS ON THE PASSION OF OUR LORD. *net*, $0.85.

MEDITATIONS ON THE SUFFERINGS OF JESUS CHRIST. Perinaldo. *net*, $1.25.

MISSION-BOOK OF THE REDEMPTORIST FATHERS. $0.90.

MISSION BOOK FOR THE MARRIED. Girardey, C.SS.R. $0.90.

MISSION BOOK FOR THE SINGLE. Girardey, C.SS.R. $0.90.

MISSION REMEMBRANCE OF THE REDEMPTORIST FATHERS. Geiermann C.SS.R. $0.90.

3

MOMENTS BEFORE THE TABER-NACLE. Russell, S.J. *net*, $0.60.

MORE SHORT SPIRITUAL READINGS FOR MARY'S CHILDREN. Cecilia. *net*, $1.25.

MOST BELOVED WOMAN, THE. Garesché, S.J. *net*, $1.50.

MY PRAYER-BOOK. Happiness in Goodness. Reflections, Counsels, Prayers, and Devotions. By Rev. F. X. Lasance. 16mo. Seal grain cloth, stiff covers, red edges, $1.50; gold edges, $2.25. Im. leather, limp, red edges, $1.90; gold edges, $2.25. Real leather, limp, gold edges, $3.25.

NEW MISSAL FOR EVERY DAY. Lasance. Im. leather, limp, red edges, $2.50; gold edges $2.75; Am. seal, limp, gold edges, $3.75.

NEW TESTAMENT. 12 mo. edition. Large type. Cloth, *net*, $1.75; 32 mo. edition. Flexible cloth, *net*, $0.45.; Stiff cloth, *net*, $0.80., Amer. seal, gold edges. *net*, $1.35.

NEW TESTAMENT AND CATHOLIC PRAYER-BOOK COMBINED. *net*, $0.85.

OFFICE OF HOLY WEEK, COMPLETE. Latin and English. Cut flush, *net*, $0.40; silk cloth, *net*, $0.55; Am. seal, red edges, *net*, $1.35; Am. seal, gold edges, *net*, $1.50.

OUR FAVORITE DEVOTIONS. Lings. *net*, $1.00.

OUR FAVORITE NOVENAS. Lings. *net*, $1.00.

OUTLINE MEDITATIONS. Cecilia. *net*, $1.75.

PARADISE ON EARTH OPENED TO ALL. Natale, S.J. *net*, $0.75.

PATHS OF GOODNESS, THE. Garesché, S.J. *net*, $1.50.

POCKET PRAYER-BOOK. Cloth. *net*, $0.25.

POLICEMEN'S AND FIREMEN'S COMPANION. McGrath. $0.35.

PRAYER-BOOK FOR RELIGIOUS. Lasance. 16mo. Imitation leather, limp, red edges, *net*, $2.00; Am. seal limp, gold edges, *net*, $3.00.

PRAYERS FOR OUR DEAD. McGrath. Cloth, $0.35; im. leather, $0.75.

PRISONER OF LOVE. Prayer-Book by Father Lasance. Im. leather, limp, red edges, $1.90; gold edges, $2.25; Am. seal, limp, gold edges, $3.25.

PRIVATE RETREAT FOR RELIGIOUS. Geiermann, C.SS.R. *net*, $2.50.

REFLECTIONS FOR RELIGIOUS. Lasance. Im. leather, limp, red edges, *net*, $2.00; Am. seal, limp, gold edges. *net*, $3.00.

REJOICE IN THE LORD. Prayer-Book by Father Lasance. Im. leather, limp, red edges, $2.00; gold edges, $2.50; Am. seal, limp, gold edges, $3.50.

ROSARY, THE CROWN OF MARY. By a Dominican Father, 16mo., paper, *$0.12.

RULES OF LIFE FOR THE PASTOR OF SOULS. Slater-Rauch. *net*, $1.50.

SACRED HEART BOOK. Prayer-Book by Father Lasance. Im. leather, limp, red edges, $1.25; Am. seal, limp, gold edges, $2.00.

SACRED HEART STUDIED IN THE SACRED SCRIPTURES. Saintrain. *net*, $1.25.

SACRIFICE OF THE MASS WORTHILY CELEBRATED. Chaignon, S.J. *net*, $2.75.

SECRET OF SANCTITY. Crasset, S.J. *net*, $1.25.

SERAPHIC GUIDE, THE. $1.25.

SHORT MEDITATIONS FOR EVERY DAY. Lasausse. *net*, $1.25.

SHORT VISITS TO THE BLESSED SACRAMENT. Lasance. *net*, $0.25.

SODALIST'S VADE MECUM, *net*, $0.90.

SOLDIERS' AND SAILORS' COMPANION. McGrath. Vest-pocket shape, silk cloth or khaki. $0.35.

SOUVENIR OF THE NOVITIATE. Taylor. *net*, $0.85.

SPIRIT OF SACRIFICE, THE, AND THE LIFE OF SACRIFICE IN THE RELIGIOUS STATE. Giraud. *net*, $3.00.

SPIRITUAL CONSIDERATIONS. Buckler, O.P. *net*, $1.25.

SPIRITUAL DESPONDENCY AND TEMPTATIONS. Michel, S.J. *net*, $1.75.

SPOILING THE DIVINE FEAST. De Zulueta, S.J. Paper, *$0.08.

STORIES FOR FIRST COMMUNICANTS. Keller. *net*, $0.60.

SUNDAY MISSAL, THE. Lasance. Im. leather, limp, red edges, $1.90; gold edges, $2.25; Am. seal, limp, gold edges, $3.25.

THINGS IMMORTAL, THE. Garesché, S.J. *net*, $1.50.

THOUGHTS ON THE RELIGIOUS LIFE. Lasance. Im. leather, limp, red edges, *net*, $2.00; Am. seal, limp, gold edges, *net*, $3.00.

THOUGHTS AND AFFECTIONS ON THE PASSION OF JESUS CHRIST FOR EVERY DAY OF THE YEAR. Bergamo. *net*, $3.25.

TRUE SPOUSE OF CHRIST. Liguori. *net*, $1.75.

VENERATION OF THE BLESSED VIRGIN. Rohner-Brennan. *net*, $1.25.

VIGIL HOUR THE. Ryan. S.J. Paper, *$0.12.

VISITS TO JESUS IN THE TABERNACLE. Lasance. Im. leather, limp, red edges, $2.00; Am. seal, limp, gold edges, $3.50.

VISITS TO THE MOST HOLY SACRAMENT. Liguori. *net*, $0.90.

WAY OF THE CROSS. Paper, *$0.08.

WAY OF THE CROSS, THE. Very large-type edition. Method of St. Alphonsus Liguori. *$0.25.

WAY OF THE CROSS. Eucharistic method. *$0.25.

4

WAY OF THE CROSS. By a Jesuit Father. *$0.25.

WAY OF THE CROSS. Method of St. Francis of Assisi. *$0.25.

WAY OF THE CROSS. Method of St. Alphonsus Liguori. *$0.25.

WITH CHRIST, MY FRIEND. Sloan. net, $1.25.

WITH GOD. Prayer-Book by Father Lasance. Im. leather, limp, red edges, $2.00; gold edges, $2.50; Am. seal, limp, gold edges, $3.50.

YOUNG MAN'S GUIDE, THE. Prayer-Book by Father Lasance. Seal grain cloth, stiff covers, red edges, $1.50. Im. leather, limp, red edges, $1.90; gold edges, $2.25. Real leather, limp, gold edges, $3.25.

YOUR INTERESTS ETERNAL. Garesché S.J. net, $1.50.

YOUR NEIGHBOR AND YOU. Garesché, S.J. net, $1.50.

YOUR OWN HEART. Garesché, S.J. net, $1.50.

YOUR SOUL'S SALVATION. Garesché, S.J. net, $1.50.

III. THEOLOGY, LITURGY, HOLY SCRIPTURE, PHILOSOPHY, SCIENCE, CANON LAW

ALTAR PRAYERS. Edition A: English and Latin, net, $1.75. Edition B: German-English-Latin, net, $2.00.

AMERICAN PRIEST, THE. Schmidt. net, $1.50.

BAPTISMAL RITUAL. 12mo. net, $1.50.

BENEDICENDA. Schulte. net, $2.75.

BURIAL RITUAL. Cloth, net, $1.50; sheepskin, net, $2.50; black morocco, net, $3.50.

CASES OF CONSCIENCE. Slater, S.J. 2 vols. net, $6.00.

CHRIST'S TEACHING CONCERNING DIVORCE. Gigot. net, ¶$2.75.

CLERGYMAN'S HAND BOOK OF LAW. Scanlon. net, $2.25.

COMBINATION RECORD FOR SMALL PARISHES. net, $8.00.

COMMENTARY ON THE PSALMS. Berry. net, $3.50.

COMPENDIUM JURIS CANONICI AD USUM CLERI ET SEMINARIORUM HUJUS REGIONIS ACCOMMODATUM. Smith. net, ¶$2.50.

COMPENDIUM JURIS REGULARIUM. Bachofen. net, ¶$3.50.

COMPENDIUM SACRÆ LITURGIÆ. Wapelhorst, O.F.M. net, ¶$3.00.

CONSECRANDA. Schulte net, $2.75.

ECCLESIASTICAL DICTIONARY. Thein. 4to, half mor. net, $6.50.

GENERAL INTRODUCTION TO THE STUDY OF THE HOLY SCRIPTURES. Gigot. net, ¶$4.00.

GENERAL INTRODUCTION TO THE STUDY OF THE HOLY SCRIPTURES. Abridged edition. Gigot. net, ¶$2.75.

HOLY BIBLE, THE. Large type, handy size. Cloth, $2.25.

JESUS LIVING IN THE PRIEST. Millet, S.J.-Byrne. net, $3.25.

MANUAL OF HOMILETICS AND CATECHETICS. Schuech-Luebermann. net, $2.25.

MANUAL OF MORAL THEOLOGY. Slater, S.J. 2 vols. net, $8.00.

MARRIAGE LEGISLATION IN THE NEW CODE. Ayrinhac, S.S. net, $2.50.

MARRIAGE RITUAL. Cloth, gilt edges, net, $1.50; sheepskin, gilt edges, net, $2.50; real morocco, gilt edges, net, $3.50.

MESSAGE OF MOSES AND MODERN HIGHER CRITICISM Gigot. Paper. net, ¶$0.15.

MORAL PRINCIPLES AND MEDICAL PRACTICE. Coppens, S.J. net, $1.50.

OUTLINES OF DOGMATIC THEOLOGY. Hunter, S.J. 3 vols., net, $7.50.

OUTLINES OF JEWISH HISTORY, FROM ABRAHAM TO OUR LORD. Gigot. net, ¶$2.75.

OUTLINES OF NEW TESTAMENT HISTORY. Gigot. net, ¶$2.75.

PASTORAL THEOLOGY. Stang. net, ¶$2.25.

PENAL LEGISLATION IN THE NEW CODE OF CANON LAW. Ayrinhac, S.S. net, $3.00.

PHILOSOPHIA MORALI, DE. Russo, S.J. Half leather, net, $2.75.

PREPARATION FOR MARRIAGE. McHugh, O.P. net, $0.60.

PRAXIS SYNODALIS. Manuale Synodi Diocesanæ ac Provincialis Celebrandæ. net, $1.00.

QUESTIONS OF MORAL THEOLOGY. Slater, S.J. net, $3.00.

RITUALE COMPENDIOSUM. Cloth, net, $1.25; seal, net, $2.00.

SANCTUARY BOYS' ILLUSTRATED MANUAL. McCallen, S.S. net, ¶$1.00.

SHORT HISTORY OF MORAL THEOLOGY. Slater, S.J. net, $0.75.

SPECIAL INTRODUCTION TO THE STUDY OF THE OLD TESTAMENT. Gigot. Part I. net, ¶$2.75. Part II. net, ¶$3.25.

SPIRAGO'S METHOD OF CHRISTIAN DOCTRINE. Messmer. net, $2.50.

TEXTUAL CONCORDANCE OF THE HOLY SCRIPTURES. Williams. net, $5.75.

WHAT CATHOLICS HAVE DONE FOR SCIENCE. Brennan. net, $1.50

CHRISTIAN MYSTERIES. Bono-
MELLI, D.D.-Byrne. 4 vols., net, $9.00.
EIGHT-MINUTE SERMONS. De-
MOUY. 2 vols., net, $4.00.
HOMILIES ON THE COMMON OF
SAINTS. Bonomelli-Byrne. 2 vols.,
net, $4.50.
HOMILIES ON THE EPISTLES AND
GOSPELS. Bonomelli-Byrne. 4 vols.
net, $9.00.
MASTER'S WORD, THE, IN THE
EPISTLES AND GOSPELS. Flynn.
2 vols., net, $4.00.
OUTLINES OF SERMONS FOR
YOUNG MEN AND YOUNG
WOMEN. Schuen-Wirth. net, $3.50.
POPULAR SERMONS ON THE CAT-
ECHISM. Bamberg-Thurston, S.J.
3 vols., net, $8.50.
PULPIT SKETCHES. Lambert. net,
$2.25.
SERMONS. Canon Sheehan. net, $3.00.
SERMONS FOR CHILDREN'S MASSES.
Frassinetti-Lings. net, $2.50.

SERMONS FOR THE SUNDAYS
AND CHIEF FESTIVALS OF THE
ECCLESIASTICAL YEAR. Pott-
GEISSER, S.J. 2 vols., net, $5.00.
SERMONS ON OUR BLESSED LADY.
Flynn. net, $2.50.
SERMONS ON THE BLESSED SAC-
RAMENT. Scheurer-Lasance. net,
$2.50.
SERMONS ON THE CHIEF CHRIS-
TIAN VIRTUES. Hunolt-Wirth. net,
$2.75.
SERMONS ON THE DUTIES OF
CHRISTIANS. Hunolt-Wirth. net,
$2.75.
SERMONS ON THE FOUR LAST
THINGS. Hunolt-Wirth. net, $2.75.
SERMONS ON THE SEVEN DEADLY
SINS. Hunolt-Wirth. net, $2.75.
SERMONS ON THE VIRTUE AND
THE SACRAMENT OF PENANCE.
Hunolt-Wirth. net, $2.75.
SERMONS ON THE MASS, THE SAC-
RAMENTS AND THE SACRA-
MENTALS. Flynn. net, $2.75.
SHORT SERMONS FOR LOW MASSES.
Schouppe, S.J. net, $2.25.

V. HISTORY, BIOGRAPHY, HAGIOLOGY, TRAVEL

AUTOBIOGRAPHY OF ST. IGNA-
TIUS LOYOLA. O'Connor, S.J. net,
$1.75.
BEGINNINGS OF CHRISTIANITY.
Shahan. net, $3.00.
CAMILLUS DE LELLIS. By a Sister
of Mercy. net, $1.75.
CHILD'S LIFE OF ST. JOAN OF
ARC. Mannix. net, $1.50.
GROWTH AND DEVELOPMENT OF
THE CATHOLIC SCHOOL SYS-
TEM IN THE UNITED STATES.
Burns, C.S.C. net, $2.50.
HISTORY OF ECONOMICS Dewe.
net, $2.00.
HISTORY OF THE CATHOLIC
CHURCH. Brueck. 2 vols., net, $5.50.
HISTORY OF THE CATHOLIC
CHURCH. Businger-Brennan. net,
$3.50.
HISTORY OF THE CATHOLIC
CHURCH. Businger-Brennan. net,
¶$0.75.
HISTORY OF THE PROTESTANT
REFORMATION. Cobbett-Gas-
QUET. net, $1.25.
HISTORY OF THE MASS. O'Brien.
net, $2.00.
HOLINESS OF THE CHURCH IN THE
NINETEENTH CENTURY. Kempf,
S.J. net, $2.75.
LIFE OF ST. MARGARET MARY
ALACOQUE. Illustrated. Bougaud.
net, $2.75.
LIFE OF CHRIST. Businger-Brennan.
Illustrated. Half morocco, gilt edges,
net, $15.00.
LIFE OF CHRIST. Illustrated. Bus-
INGER-Mullett. net, $3.50.
LIFE OF CHRIST. Cochem. net, $1.25.

LIFE OF ST. IGNATIUS LOYOLA.
Genelli, S.J. net, $1.25.
LIFE OF MADEMOISELLE LE
GRAS. net, $1.25.
LIFE OF POPE PIUS X. Illustrated.
net, $3.50.
LIFE OF SISTER ANNE KATHARINE
EMMERICH. McGowan, O.S.A. net,
$2.50.
LIFE OF THE BLESSED VIRGIN.
Rohner. net, $1.25.
LITTLE LIVES OF THE SAINTS
FOR CHILDREN. Berthold. net,
$1.25.
LITTLE PICTORIAL LIVES OF THE
SAINTS. With 400 illustrations. net,
$2.00.
LIVES OF THE SAINTS. Butler
net, $1.25.
LOURDES. Clarke, S.J. net, $1.25.
MARY THE QUEEN. By a Religious.
net, $0.75.
MIDDLE AGES, THE. Shahan. net,
$3.00.
NAMES THAT LIVE IN CATHOLIC
HEARTS. Sadlier. net, $1.25.
OUR OWN ST. RITA. Corcoran,
O.S.A. net, $1.50.
PATRON SAINTS FOR CATHOLIC
YOUTH. Mannix. 3 vols. Each, net,
$1.25.
PICTORIAL LIVES OF THE SAINTS.
With nearly 400 illustrations and over
600 pages. net, $5.00.
POPULAR LIFE OF ST. TERESA.
L'Abbé Joseph. net, $1.25.
PRINCIPLES ORIGIN AND ESTAB-
LISHMENT OF THE CATHOLIC
SCHOOL SYSTEM IN THE UNITED
STATES. Burns, C.S.C. net, $2.50.

RAMBLES IN CATHOLIC LANDS. BARRETT, O.S.B. Illustrated. *net*, $3.50.

ROMA. Pagan Subterranean and Modern Rome in Word and Picture. By REV. ALBERT KUHN, O.S.B., D.D. Preface by CARDINAL GIBBONS. 617 pages. 744 illustrations. 48 full-page inserts, 3 plans of Rome in colors, 8½ X12 inches. Red im. leather, gold side. *net*, $15.00.

ROMAN CURIA AS IT NOW EXISTS. MARTIN, S.J. *net*, $2.50.

ST. ANTHONY. WARD. *net*, $1.25.

ST. FRANCIS OF ASSISI. DUBOIS, S.M. *net*, $1.25.

ST. JOAN OF ARC. LYNCH, S.J. Illustrated. *net*, $2.75.

SAINTS AND PLACES. By JOHN AYSCOUGH. Illustrated. *net*, $3.00.

SHORT LIVES OF THE SAINTS. DONNELLY. *net*, $0.90.

STORY OF JESUS SIMPLY TOLD FOR THE YOUNG, THE. MULHOLLAND. *net*, $1.00.

STORY OF THE DIVINE CHILD. Told for Children. LINGS. *net*, $0.75.

STORY OF THE ACTS OF THE APOSTLES. LYNCH, S.J. Illustrated. *net*, $2.75.

WOMEN OF CATHOLICITY. SADLIER. *net*, $1.25.

VI. JUVENILES

FATHER FINN'S BOOKS.
Each, *net*, $1.50.
FACING DANGER.
HIS LUCKIEST YEAR. A Sequel to "Lucky Bob."
LUCKY BOB.
PERCY WYNN; OR, MAKING A BOY OF HIM.
TOM PLAYFAIR; OR, MAKING A START.
CLAUDE LIGHTFOOT; OR, HOW THE PROBLEM WAS SOLVED.
HARRY DEE; OR, WORKING IT OUT.
ETHELRED PRESTON; OR, THE ADVENTURES OF A NEWCOMER.
THE BEST FOOT FORWARD; AND OTHER STORIES.
CUPID OF CAMPION.
THAT FOOTBALL GAME, AND WHAT CAME OF IT.
THE FAIRY OF THE SNOWS.
THAT OFFICE BOY.
HIS FIRST AND LAST APPEARANCE.
MOSTLY BOYS. SHORT STORIES.

FATHER SPALDING'S BOOKS.
Each, *net*, $1.50.
HELD IN THE EVERGLADES.
AT THE FOOT OF THE SANDHILLS.
THE CAVE BY THE BEECH FORK.
THE SHERIFF OF THE BEECH FORK.
THE CAMP BY COPPER RIVER.
THE RACE FOR COPPER ISLAND.
THE MARKS OF THE BEAR CLAWS.
THE OLD MILL ON THE WITHROSE.
THE SUGAR CAMP AND AFTER

ADVENTURE WITH THE APACHES. FERRY. *net*, $0.75.

ALTHEA. NIRDLINGER. *net*, $1.00.

AS GOLD IN THE FURNACE. COPUS, S.J. *net*, $1.50.

AS TRUE AS GOLD. MANNIX. *net*, $0.75.

AT THE FOOT OF THE SANDHILLS. SPALDING, S.J. *net*, $1.50.

BELL FOUNDRY. SCHACHING, *net*, $0.75.

BERKLEYS, THE. WIGHT. *net*, $0.75.

BEST FOOT FORWARD, THE. FINN, S.J. *net*, $1.50.

BETWEEN FRIENDS. AUMERLE. *net*, $1.00.

BISTOURI. MELANDRI. *net*, $0.75.

BLISSYLVANIA POST-OFFICE. TAGGART. *net*, $0.75.

BOB O'LINK. WAGGAMAN. *net*, $0.75.

BROWNIE AND I. AUMERLE. *net*, $1.00.

BUNT AND BILL. MULHOLLAND. *net*, $0.75.

BY BRANSCOME RIVER. TAGGART. *net*, $0.75.

CAMP BY COPPER RIVER. SPALDING, S.J. *net*, $1.50.

CAPTAIN TED. WAGGAMAN. *net*, $1.00.

CAVE BY THE BEECH FORK. SPALDING, S.J. *net*, $1.50.

CHARLIE CHITTYWICK. BEARNE, S.J. *net*, $1.50.

CHILDREN OF CUPA. MANNIX. *net*, $0.75.

CHILDREN OF THE LOG CABIN. DELAMARE. *net*, $1.00.

CLARE LORAINE. "LEE." *net*, $1.00.

CLAUDE LIGHTFOOT. FINN, S.J. *net*, $1.50.

CUPA REVISITED. MANNIX. *net*, $0.75.

CUPID OF CAMPION. FINN, S.J. *net*, $1.50.

DADDY DAN. WAGGAMAN. *net*, $0.75.

DEAR FRIENDS. NIRDLINGER. *net*, $1.00.

DIMPLING'S SUCCESS. MULHOLLAND. *net*, $0.75.

ETHELRED PRESTON. FINN, S.J. *net*, $1.50.

EVERY-DAY GIRL, AN. CROWLEY. *net*, $0.75.

FACING DANGER. FINN, S.J. *net*, $1.50.

FAIRY OF THE SNOWS. FINN, S.J. *net*, $1.50.

FINDING OF TONY. WAGGAMAN. *net*, $1.50.

FIVE BIRDS IN A NEST. DELAMARE. *net*, $1.00.

FIVE O'CLOCK STORIES. By a Religious. *net*, $1.00.

FLOWER OF THE FLOCK. EGAN. *net*, $1.50.

FOR THE WHITE ROSE. HINKSON *net*, $0.75.

FRED'S LITTLE DAUGHTER. SMITH *net*, $0.75.

FREDDY CARR'S ADVENTURES. GARROLD, S.J. *net*, $1.00.

FREDDY CARR AND HIS FRIENDS. GARROLD, S.J. *net*, $1.00.

GOLDEN LILY, THE. HINKSON. *net*, $0.75.

GREAT CAPTAIN, THE. HINKSON. *net*, $0.75.

HALDEMAN CHILDREN, THE. MANNIX. *net*, $0.75.

HARMONY FLATS. WHITMIRE. *net*, $1.00.

HARRY DEE. FINN, S.J. *net*, $1.50.

HARRY RUSSELL. COPUS, S.J. *net*, $1.50.

HEIR OF DREAMS, AN. O'MALLEY. *net*, $0.75.

HELD IN THE EVERGLADES. SPALDING, S.J. *net*, $1.50.

HIS FIRST AND LAST APPEARANCE. FINN, S.J. *net*, $1.50.

HIS LUCKIEST YEAR, FINN. S.J. *net*, $1.50.

HOSTAGE OF WAR, A. BONESTEEL. *net*, $0.75.

HOW THEY WORKED THEIR WAY. EGAN. *net*, $1.00.

IN QUEST OF ADVENTURE. MANNIX. *net*, $0.75.

IN QUEST OF THE GOLDEN CHEST. BARTON. *net*, $1.00.

JACK. By a Religious, H.C.J. *net*, $0.75.

JACK-O'LANTERN. WAGGAMAN. *net*, $0.75.

JACK HILDRETH ON THE NILE. TAGGART. *net*, $1.00.

JUNIORS' OF ST. BEDE'S. BRYSON. *net*, $1.00.

JUVENILE ROUND TABLE. First Series. *net*, $1.50.

JUVENILE ROUND TABLE. Second Series. *net*, $1.50.

KLONDIKE PICNIC, A. DONNELLY. *net*, $1.00.

LEGENDS AND STORIES OF THE HOLY CHILD JESUS, LUTZ, *net*, $1.00.

LITTLE APOSTLE ON CRUTCHES. DELAMARE. *net*, $0.75.

LITTLE GIRL FROM BACK EAST. ROBERTS. *net*, $0.75.

LITTLE LADY OF THE HALL. RYEMAN. *net*, $0.75.

LITTLE MARSHALLS AT THE LAKE. NIXON-ROULET. *net*, $1.00.

LITTLE MISSY. WAGGAMAN. *net*, $0.75.

LOYAL BLUE AND ROYAL SCARLET. TAGGART. *net*, $1.50.

LUCKY BOB. FINN, S.J. *net*, $1.50.

MADCAP SET AT ST. ANNE'S. BRUNOWE. *net*, $0.75.

MAD KNIGHT, THE. SCHACHING. *net*, $0.75.

MAKING OF MORTLAKE. COPUS, S.J. *net*, $1.50.

MAN FROM NOWHERE. SADLIER. *net*, $1.50.

MARKS OF THE BEAR CLAWS. SPALDING, S.J. *net*, $1.50.

MARY TRACY'S FORTUNE. SADLIER. *net*, $0.75.

MELOR OF THE SILVER HAND. BEARNE, S.J. *net*, $1.50.

MILLY AVELING. SMITH. *net*, $1.00.

MIRALDA. JOHNSON, *net*, $0.75.

MORE FIVE O'CLOCK STORIES. By a Religious. *net*, $1.00.

MOSTLY BOYS, FINN, S.J. *net*, $1.50.

MYSTERIOUS DOORWAY. SADLIER. *net*, $0.75.

MYSTERY OF HORNBY HALL. SADLIER. *net*, $1.00.

MYSTERY OF CLEVERLY. BARTON. *net*, $1.00.

NAN NOBODY. WAGGAMAN. *net*, $0.75.

NED RIEDER. WEHS. *net*, $1.00.

NEW SCHOLAR AT ST. ANNE'S. BRUNOWE. *net*, $1.00.

OLD CHARLMONT'S SEED-BED. SMITH. *net*, $0.75.

OLD MILL ON THE WITHROSE. SPALDING, S.J. *net*, $1.50.

ON THE OLD CAMPING GROUND. MANNIX. *net*, $1.50.

OUR LADY'S LUTENIST. BEARNE, S.J. *net*, $1.50.

PANCHO AND PANCHITA. MANNIX. *net*, $0.75.

PAULINE ARCHER SADLIER. *net*, $0.75.

PERCY WYNN. FINN, S.J. *net*, $1.50.

PERIL OF DIONYSIO. MANNIX, *net*, $0.75.

PETRONILLA. DONNELLY. *net*, $1.00.

PICKLE AND PEPPER. DORSEY. *net*, $1.50.

PILGRIM FROM IRELAND. CARNOT. *net*, $0.75.

PLAYWATER PLOT, THE. WAGGAMAN. *net*, $1.00.

POLLY DAY'S ISLAND. ROBERTS. *net*, $1.50.

POVERINA. BUCKENHAM. *net*, $1.00.

QUEEN'S PAGE, THE. HINKSON. *net*, $0.75.

QUEEN'S PROMISE, THE. WAGGAMAN. *net*, $1.00.

QUEST OF MARY SELWYN. CLEMENTIA. *net*, $1.50.

RACE FOR COPPER ISLAND. SPALDING, S.J. *net*, $1.50.

RECRUIT TOMMY COLLINS. BONESTEEL. *net*, $0.75.

RIDINGDALE FLOWER SHOW. BEARNE, S.J. *net*, $1.50.

ROMANCE OF THE SILVER SHOON. BEARNE, S.J. *net*, $1.50.

ST. CUTHBERT'S. COPUS, S.J. *net*, $1.50.

SANDY JOE. WAGGAMAN. *net*, $1.50.

SEA-GULL'S ROCK. SANDEAU. *net*, $0.75.

SEVEN LITTLE MARSHALLS. NIXON-ROULET. *net*, $0.75.

SHADOWS LIFTED. COPUS, S.J. *net*, $1.50.

SHEER PLUCK. BEARNE, S.J. *net*, $1.50.

SHERIFF OF THE BEECH FORK. SPALDING, S.J. *net*, $1.50.

SHIPMATES. WAGGAMAN. *net*, $1.00.

SUGAR CAMP AND AFTER. SPALDING, S.J. *net*, $1.50.

SUMMER AT WOODVILLE. SADLIER. *net*, $0.75.

8

TALES AND LEGENDS OF THE MIDDLE AGES. DE CAPELLA. net, $1.00.

TALISMAN, THE. SADLIER. net, $1.00.

TAMING OF POLLY. DORSEY. net, $1.50.

THAT FOOTBALL GAME. FINN, S.J. net, $1.50.

THAT OFFICE BOY. FINN, S.J. net, $1.50.

THREE LITTLE GIRLS AND ESPE-CIALLY ONE. TAGGART. net, $0.75.

TOLD IN THE TWILIGHT. SALOME. net, $1.00.

TOM LOSELY; BOY. COPUS, S.J. net, $1.50.

TOM PLAYFAIR. FINN. S.J. net, $1.50.

TOM'S LUCK-POT. WAGGAMAN. net, $0.75.

TOORALLADDY. WALSH. net, $0.75.

TRANSPLANTING OF TESSIE. WAG-GAMAN. net, $1.00.

TREASURE OF NUGGET MOUN-TAIN. TAGGART. net, $1.00.

TWO LITTLE GIRLS. MACK. net, $0.75.

UNCLE FRANK'S MARY. CLEMEN-TIA. net, $1.50.

UPS AND DOWNS OF MARJORIE. WAGGAMAN. net, $0.75.

VIOLIN MAKER. SMITH. net, $0.75.

WINNETOU, THE APACHE KNIGHT. TAGGART. net, $1.00.

YOUNG COLOR GUARD. BONESTEEL, net, $0.75.

VII. NOVELS

ISABEL C. CLARKE'S GREAT NOVELS. Each, net, $2.25.
URSULA FINCH.
THE ELSTONES.
EUNICE.
LADY TRENT'S DAUGHTER.
CHILDREN OF EVE.
THE DEEP HEART.
WHOSE NAME IS LEGION.
FINE CLAY.
PRISONERS' YEARS.
THE REST HOUSE.
ONLY ANNE.
THE SECRET CITADEL.
BY THE BLUE RIVER.

AGATHA'S HARD SAYING. MULHOL-LAND. net, $1.65.

ALBERTA: ADVENTURESS. L'ER-MITE. 8vo. net, $2.25.

BACK TO THE WORLD. CHAMPOL. net, $2.25.

BARRIER, THE. BAZIN. net, $1.65.

BALLADS OF CHILDHOOD. Poems. EARLS, S.J. net, $1.50.

BLACK BROTHERHOOD, THE. GAR-ROLD, S.J. net, $2.25.

BOND AND FREE. CONNOR. net, $1.00.

"BUT THY LOVE AND THY GRACE." FINN, S.J. net, $1.50.

BY THE BLUE RIVER. CLARKE. net, $2.25.

CARROLL DARE. WAGGAMAN. net, $1.25.

CIRCUS-RIDER'S DAUGHTER. BRACKEL. net, $1.25.

CHILDREN OF EVE. CLARKE. net, $2.25.

CONNOR D'ARCY'S STRUGGLES. BERTHOLDS. net, $1.25.

CORINNE'S VOW. WAGGAMAN. net, $1.25.

DAUGHTER OF KINGS, A. HINKSON. net, $2.25.

DEEP HEART, THE. CLARKE. net, $2.25.

DION AND THE SIBYLS. KEON. net, $1.25.

ELDER MISS AINSBOROUGH, THE. TAGGART. net, $1.25.

ELSTONES, THE. CLARKE. net, $2.25.

EUNICE. CLARKE. net, $2.25.

FABIOLA. WISEMAN. net, $1.00.

FABIOLA'S SISTERS. CLARKE. net, $1.25.

FATAL BEACON, THE. BRACKEL. net, $1.25.

FAUSTULA. AYSCOUGH. net, $2.25.

FINE CLAY. CLARKE. net, $2.25.

FORGIVE AND FORGET. LINGEN. net, $1.25.

GRAPES OF THORNS. WAGGAMAN. net, $1.25.

HEART OF A MAN. MAHER. net, $2.25.

HEARTS OF GOLD. EDHOR. net, $1.25.

HEIRESS OF CRONENSTEIN. HAHN. net, $1.00.

HER BLIND FOLLY. HOLT. net, $1.25.

HER FATHER'S DAUGHTER. HINK-SON. net, $2.25.

HER FATHER'S SHARE. POWER. net, $1.25.

HER JOURNEY'S END. COOKE. net, $1.25.

IDOLS; or THE SECRET OF THE RUE CHAUSSE D'ANTIN. DE NAV-ERY. net, $1.25.

IN GOD'S GOOD TIME. ROSS. net, $1.00.

IN SPITE OF ALL. STANIFORTH, net, $1.25.

IN THE DAYS OF KING HAL. TAG-GART. net, $1.25.

IVY HEDGE, THE. EGAN. net, $2.25.

KIND HEARTS AND CORONETS. HARRISON. net, $1.25.

LADY TRENT'S DAUGHTER. CLARKE. net, $2.25.

LIGHT OF HIS COUNTENANCE. HART. net, $1.00.

"LIKE UNTO A MERCHANT." GRAY. net, $2.25.

LINKED LIVES. DOUGLAS. net, $2.25.

LITTLE CARDINAL. PARR. net, $1.65.

LOVE OF BROTHERS. HINKSON. net, $2.25.

MARCELLA GRACE. MULHOLLAND. net, $1.25.

MARIE OF THE HOUSE D'ANTERS, EARLS, S.J. net, $2.25.

MELCHIOR OF BOSTON. Earls, S.J. *net*, $1.25.

MIGHTY FRIEND, THE. L'Ermite. *net*, $2.25.

MIRROR OF SHALOTT. Benson. *net*, $2.25.

MISS ERIN. Francis. *net*, $1.25.

MR. BILLY BUTTONS. Lecky. *net*, $1.65.

MONK'S PARDON, THE. de Navery. *net*, $1.25.

MY LADY BEATRICE. Cooke. *net*, $1.00.

NOT A JUDGMENT. Keon. *net*, $1.65.

ONLY ANNE. Clarke. *net*, $2.25.

OTHER MISS LISLE. Martin. *net*, $1.00.

OUT OF BONDAGE. Holt. *net*, $1.25.

OUTLAW OF CAMARGUE. de La-mothe. *net*, $1.25.

PASSING SHADOWS. Yorke. *net*, $1.65.

PERE MONNIER'S WARD. Lecky. *net*, $1.65.

PILKINGTON HEIR, THE. Sadlier, *net*, $1.25.

PRISONERS' YEARS. Clarke. *net*, $2.25.

PRODIGAL'S DAUGHTER, THE, AND OTHER STORIES. Bugg. *net*, $1.50.

PROPHET'S WIFE. Browne. *net*, $1.25.

RED INN OF ST. LYPHAR. Sadlier. *net*, $1.25.

REST HOUSE, THE. Clarke. *net*, $2.25.

ROSE OF THE WORLD. Martin. *net*, $1.25.

ROUND TABLE OF AMERICAN CATHOLIC NOVELISTS. *net*, $1.25.

ROUND TABLE OF FRENCH CATH-OLIC NOVELISTS. *net*, $1.25.

ROUND TABLE OF GERMAN CATH-OLIC NOVELISTS. *net*, $1.25.

ROUND TABLE OF IRISH AND ENG-LISH CATHOLIC NOVELISTS. *net*, $1.25.

RUBY CROSS, THE. Wallace. *net*, $1.25.

RULER OF THE KINGDOM. Keon. *net*, $1.65.

SECRET CITADEL, THE. Clarke. *net*, $2.25.

SECRET OF THE GREEN VASE. Cooke. *net*, $1.00.

SHADOW OF EVERSLEIGH. Lans-downe. *net*, $1.00.

SHIELD OF SILENCE. Henry-Ruf-fin. *net*, $2.25.

SO AS BY FIRE. Connor. *net*, $1.25.

SON OF SIRO, THE. Copus, S.J. *net*, $2.25.

STORY OF CECILIA, THE. Hinkson. *net*, $1.65.

STUORE. Earls, S.J. *net*, $1.50.

TEMPEST OF THE HEART. Gray. *net*, $1.25.

TEST OF COURAGE. Ross. *net*, $1.00.

THAT MAN'S DAUGHTER. Ross. *net*, $1.25.

THEIR CHOICE. Skinner. *net*, $1.00.

THROUGH THE DESERT. Sienkie-wicz. *net*, $2.25.

TIDEWAY, THE. Ayscough. *net*, $2.25.

TRAINING OF SILAS. Devine. *net*, $1.65.

TRUE STORY OF MASTER GERARD. Sadlier. *net*, $1.65.

TURN OF THE TIDE, THE. Gray. *net*, $1.25.

UNBIDDEN GUEST, THE. Cooke. *net*, $1.00.

UNDER THE CEDARS AND THE STARS. Canon Sheehan. *net*, $2.25.

UP IN ARDMUIRLAND. Barrett, O.S.B. *net*, $1.65.

URSULA FINCH. Clarke. *net*, $2.25.

VOCATION OF EDWARD CONWAY, THE. Egan. *net*, $1.65.

WARGRAVE TRUST, THE. Reid. *net*, $1.65.

WAR MOTHERS. Poems. Garesché, S.J. *net*, $0.60.

WAY THAT LED BEYOND, THE. Harrison. *net*, $1.25.

WEDDING BELLS OF GLENDA-LOUGH, THE. Earls, S.J. *net*, $2.25.

WHEN LOVE IS STRONG. Keon *net*, $1.65.

WHOSE NAME IS LEGION. Clarke. *net*, $2.25.

WOMAN OF FORTUNE, A. Reid. *net*, $1.65.